POLITICAL CAMPAIGN
CRAFTSMANSHIP

POLITICAL CAMPAIGN CRAFTSMANSHIP

A Professional's Guide to Campaigning for Public Office

EDWARD SCHWARTZMAN

With a new introduction by the author

Transaction Publishers
New Brunswick (U.S.A.) and Oxford (U.K.)

Library of Congress Catalog Number: 88-15998
ISBN: 0-88738-742-X
Printed in the United States of America

Library of Congress Cataloging-in-Publication Data

Schwartzman, Edward.
  Political campaign craftmanship.

  Reprint. Originally published: New York: Van Nostrand Reinhold, c1984.
  Bibliography: p.
  Includes index.
  1. Electioneering--United States--Handbooks, manuals, etc. 2. Campaign management--United States--Handbooks, manuals, etc. I. Title.
JK2283.S38 1988   134.7'0973
ISBN 0-88738-742-X   88-15998

In memory of my sister Martha and
my friend Walter Diamond

Introduction to the Transaction Edition

This is the third edition of *Political Campaign Craftsmanship*. The last edition was published in November 1984. This introduction, then, gives me the opportunity to describe some of the significant changes in political campaigning that have taken place in the last four years.

In a purely technical sense there really haven't been any significant innovations in campaigning. While the mix of ingredients has remained pretty much the same, it is extraordinary that the dominant media form–television–has become even more dominant and by itself accounts for the greatest proportion of the massive and somewhat frightening increase in campaign costs. The strategy of television commercials now almost completely controls campaigning for U.S. senate races, congressionals, and big city mayorals.

Costs have skyrocketed in the last four years and are continuing to grow like a child's monstrous and bizarre toy that expands almost obscenely when water is added. A parent watches in disbelief as the toy's expansion grows without its end in sight. In campaigning, it is the cash requirements for which there seems no end. The toy gives the child pleasure; television costs give pleasure to no one except perhaps media consultants and television stations–they add nothing to the democratic process and in fact may be detracting very considerably from it. The essence of the matter is that consultants are charging more and more for media emphasis which causes candidates to have to raise more and more from contributors, the majority of whom are not dominated by altruistic purposes. As a result special interest groups directly develop a significant measure of control in some legislative areas and an effective veto power in others. Consequently, public policy formulation and the ability of the Federal government to respond rapidly and appropriately to major problems is severely limited. Often the real questions can't even be addressed at the time they need to be addressed. The reasons for the exponential escalation of costs are several.

In the first place, television time costs have increased a great deal in cities nationwide.[1] Secondly, many candidates think television is magic, hearing stories (many quite true) of how a clever television campaign turned around a losing effort in the last two weeks from 35 points down. Thirdly, production costs, with union minima increasing for actors, technicians (I always liked occupational titles such as best boy, chief gaffer, master property man) and the extraordinary array of talents and specialists required for even the simplest shoot (take a meeting, do lunch, power breakfasts, revenue enhancements [taxes]– our rhetoric in campaigns and in life have become cryptic indeed) have also sharply increased.

Another important reason for increasing costs is that television, of all the media used in political campaigning, provides the biggest markup for media consultants for the time and talent invested; media people from all accounts obtain the biggest profit per man-hour worked from television commercials. Candidates seem to enjoy watching themselves and their campaigns on television; they can sit at home and watch where their money is going and satisfy their egos at the same time; for many candidates campaigning is the biggest ego trip they will ever experience. One seasoned consultant commented to me that campaigning seemed to provide some type of fix for many of the people he had worked for–a transcendent high. Henry Kissinger said that power is an aphrodisiacs–it is also a semipermanent high for some candidates.

The prevailing television emphasis and the concomitant increase in costs for campaigning have resulted in constant and severe pressures on candidates to concentrate on fund raising, almost to the exclusion of governing for periods of time. This in turn exacerbates the increasing power of PACs and special interest groups who are well funded (perhaps too well funded for the good of the nation). The public interest, so difficult to define and almost impossible to sensibly measure statistically (warranting a Nobel Prize in economics for anyone who even partially solves this puzzle) fades further and further from the mindset and preoccupations of even the most idealistic and caring of politicians.

Karen Diegmueller, writing in *Insight*,[2] commented that,

> The downside, of course, is that the full-time legislator's livelihood is tied up in winning reelection. "The people who are committed to political careers can't afford to lose," says

Rosenthal. Consequently, resources are channeled into campaigning, and legislative votes are calculated on the basis of constituent votes. "The nature of the campaign has changed the nature of the legislator more than anything else. The ones that win [when an incumbent vacates] are usually the ones that did nothing but campaign for the seat for six to ten months before the election," says Wisconsin Assembly Speaker Loftus.

Congressmen, for example, often complain that almost as soon as they are elected they already have to concentrate on raising money for the next campaign. Many claim resentment of this process but unfortunately the many congressional initiatives in the past four years to provide public financing of elections have not been successful primarily because most successful politicians do not want to be placed in the position of funding potential opponents–generally people don't like to pay for their own hit men.

In recent years some congressmen have left politics finding the fund raising game demeaning, distasteful, and in complete conflict with what they had wanted to accomplish in governance in the first place. For example, some congressmen resent the power of PACs and lobbyists. There are 5,000 registered lobbyists in Washington, many with staff, many with considerable PAC financing. They don't sit on the sidelines observing; they are not elected by anyone but they tend to be a major subset in developing the programs and policies that together are government. They can accomplish often what congressmen can't; they find it easy to kill threatening legislation. Major PAC groups seem to have something like a presidential veto in certain policy areas.

Another significant change is that negative campaigning has become extremely widespread in the last four years. Humor, thought, grace, and explicating ideas to the voting public have all but disappeared from professional-style campaigning. More and more campaigns are informed by a mean spirited and tawdry approach; consultants and candidates' staff sometimes take pride in how down and dirty they can get, and how quickly they can do it. Shamefully, these campaigns are sometimes effective. If one candidate does it, his opponent is often compelled to retaliate in kind. Minor and major indiscretions and flaws of early adulthood are hammered away in an orgy, a torrential frenzy of mindless innuendo and gossipy garbage. It is not surprising that many voters are disgusted with these graceless and nonproductive performances. These commercials don't offer substance to the problem solving that is urgently required in our cities and in our nation.

Voting and registration ratios are declining markedly throughout the country. In New York City and New York State, for example, the number of adults registered to vote has dropped to under 50 percent resulting in the announcement in September 1987 that the city and state were looking for ways that public funds could be employed to get people of all parties to register and vote.[3] If one-half of all registered voters went to the polls it means that only one in four actually voted.[4]

Many observers are becoming extremely concerned about whether the democratic process can be expected to continue to be effective when so many Americans clearly are not finding candidates worthwhile or responsive, or elections important enough to bother registering and voting. This trend is occurring despite the emergence of extraordinarily difficult and pervasive problems-housing inadequacies for the young, the old, and the poor; severe regional inequities in economic health and growth patterns; increasing inequities in income and asset distribution (the Federal Reserve Board reported that in 1986 one percent of American households controlled 50 percent of all wealth while another 25 percent was controlled by foreign institutions and investors,) the huge and growing trade and budget deficits that no one in power was prepared to deal with until the New York stock market collapsed by 508 points in one day in October 1987, on unprecedented volume.

It could be that many voters have been simply numbed by the phantasmagoric parade of venal and shabby characters, nonentities, and scandals. Voters are being told more and more about less and less (drug dependencies of spouses and children, venality of aides, problems with college grades, affairs of the moment, and operations major and minor). The Deavers, Nofzigers, and Meeses of today are always around it seems.[5]

Part of the problem is the changing lifestyles of so many American families. In the autumn–the election season–people will think nothing of spending eight hours on a Sunday to drive and enjoy the unbelievably beautiful colors of fall; they will watch professional football games for three hours in which particular talents and abilities for focused viciousness are cheered and rewarded with one million dollar a year contracts, but not many will spend thirty minutes in considered thought of the significance of their local and congressional elections. For many there seems little relevance of what they hear and read about the campaigns to their day-to-day concerns.

They are not altogether wrong of course. Concern with substance seems to have gone out of American campaigning. Honor, grace, informed and intelligent rhetoric have all but disappeared. A hint of nobility and passion would stun us all at this point. An example of the current impact of inspired rhetoric is provided by Governor Cuomo. Cuomo spoke for three hours to the Council on Foreign Relations on foreign policy in October 1987. The New York Times made it a major story. The Council members said that he said pretty much what experts have been saying for some time, but his candor, rhetoric, overall presentation, sincerity, and presence were very convincing. Add humor, which he has, and he will probably be the next president.

Communicating abilities are important in most media campaigns and not the substance of what is being communicated; too much is surface patina and not enough is solid and reasoned thought. Television and newspaper emphases are part of the problem but the nature of current candidacies and consulting business economics is the major cause of the problem.

The context for the public's perception of politics and campaigns is changing. Currently 60 percent of American households have two incomes. I once calculated that in these circumstances (which for many years I shared) the average couple has maybe a total often to fourteen of discretionary time a week. Our lives are dominated by jobs and the logistical minutiae that necessarily glut and control us daily (car and home maintenance, house improvement and repairs, lawns and gardening, going to church and one or two civic groups occasionally, paying bills, doing laundry, food shopping, taking care of children and aging parents and chauffeuring them). The Wall Street Journal in one of its recent daily statistical tables reported that the average working mother spends 14 minutes with her children in direct quality time.[6]

Candidates seldom stimulate or educate our minds or arouse our passions for public equity and sensibility, seldom make us stop and think seriously about the issues. The safest bet is to concentrate on likability (using voice overs if direct likability is too difficult) and avoiding controversy. The problem is that the great and long term structuring matters of the day are precisely the controversial ones, desperately requiring explication, discussion and our complete attention.[7]

It is certainly clear to most observers that current political commercials (thirty seconds) do not and probably cannot address themselves to the real issues but often only to those manufactured from polling results that suggest safer secondary foci. A decade ago two minute TV commercials for candidates were not uncommon. Then some years ago there was a gradual reduction to sixty seconds, then more recently to thirty seconds. Consultants now are being forced to fifteen second commercials because TV time and production costs are rising rapidly and secondly, to be able to rapidly respond to negative attacks–to neutralize them quickly and to counterattack. In these circumstances only a calculated impression becomes possible–a single tactile image of memory. since campaigns speak less and less to the great issues it would not be surprising if the voting ratios continue to decline so that laws would be required mandating a quorum (perhaps of 10 percent for elections to be valid).

Barbara Tuchman, the noted historian, writing in the New York Times Magazine in August 1987 concluded that our society had seen its peak in power some years ago and that the recent examples of massive incompetence and immorality on high policy levels were evidence of it (going into the hostile Gulf in 1987 without minesweepers was one example given.) Her view was that the country desperately needed an informed electorate. While she knew it wasn't a panacea, her only specific suggestion was that a minimum two minute political commercial schedule be required of all candidates for presidential or congressional offices.

Part of the problem is the costs themselves and by themselves. There seems to be almost a consensual consortium of greed among many consultants–like real estate agents in hot areas they can informally fix prices for periods of time if the demand is out there. It is, I'm afraid, a form of the "yennim money" syndrome which is to say it's easy to spend someone else's money. The cost has no reality of its own at its base like the stock market in the euphoria of 1982-1987.

A media consultant in a major U.S. Senate race recently earned a $75,000 creative fee plus 15 percent of the two million dollars spent on television buys of a total of $375,000 less perhaps the $50,000 it cost to cast, film and produce ten television spots. In addition, he was involved in at least four other major campaigns that season.

A radio specialist writing and producing four thirty second spots can charge and get $10,000. A fifteen minute interview with five open ends and an eighty five qualifying rate costs $14-18 an interview in the East; an interviewer paid perhaps $6.-8. an hour can complete two and one half interviews an hour. To provide a ten person focus group, a room for one and one half hours, and an operator for a video machine, consultants charge $1,000 plus another $1,000 for their time leading the group and analyzing the session results. TV time buyers can get $10,000 for doing the buy-matching stations and the demograhics of the target groups. Like jewelry and top of the line sports cars the markup has skyrocketed because there are so many people willing to pay the prices.

Another change, probably a fallout of the increasing use of consultants who cannot expect significant fees from them and the increasing use and costs of television, has been the discernible decline in the use of shopping bags, buttons, bumper stickers, banners, and balloons and the use of small giveaways such as nail files and key chains. These were remnants of another time in American campaigning, when candidates could provide scotch and a few dollar bills to workers leaving a factory to encourage a favorable vote. Perhaps in another form it might still be effective and it would certainly be considerably less expensive and more charming than today's methods as well.

A related development is the lack of emphasis in campaigning on personal visiblity and pressing the flesh. There's little time for this any more, and generally most political consultants don't regard it as critical. Campaigning in a professional-style media campaign has become extremely specialized. There are pollsters of course, TV men, radio specialists, specialists in campaigns where minority groups are important, print (brochure) specialists, negative TV specialists, focus group specialists, different advance functions, convention specialists, cable TV men, and policy and issues analysts. Psychologists are now political consultants (and one thinks psychiatrists will be needed very soon considering Biden, Hart, Dukakis, etc. in the 1987 Democratic presidential sweepstakes). The work of these specialists is regarded as being more effective than simply going out and meeting the voters.

Party organization importance has declined to its lowest point. Today, only people on the government payroll can be expected by candidates to work without salary in a campaign. (The Hatch Act excludes this activity on the Federal level.) Other organizational volunteers are now few and far between. Union volunteers are the last resource of volunteers in the big cities with the special interest groups-environmental, anti-tax, pro and con abortion, etc., providing volunteers from time to time.

Use of personal computers and laser printers is increasing significantly in campaigns. Lists are completed and controlled carefully. Letters look like originals and are sent to the right people and only one is sent to the same address. Financial accounts are precise and up-to-date.

The latter are efficient changes but the end product is less time and thought for dealing with the big problems–the more than current or expedient semi-manufactured issues.

Overall, the most important thing that has happened to campaigning is the exponential increase in costs and the dominance of consultants in all the major campaigns.[8] A congressional race costs $400,000-$800,000, a senate race averages $3-5 million and can go over ten million (Cranston in California). The rising and spending of money in a campaign takes a substantial part of the campaign's energy. The rest is spent avoiding controversy, responding to negative campaigning, getting endorsements, etc. Developing ideas and solutions to major problems, instead of a short term, dramatic fix up, explicating complex and concentrated social-economic problems, discussing foreign policy problems are beyond the ability of any series of thirty-second commercials and beyond the residual energy of most candidates.

Many voters now perceive that campaigns in their areas have become almost obscenely expensive. In 1984 the U.S. Senate race in North Carolina between Hunt and Helm spent a total of over twenty two million; nothing before in the state's history came even close. Mayor Ed Koch, running against weak and unmonied opponents in New York City, spent over seven million nonetheless in 1984. The money was raised largely from major real estate interests (who are the largest contributors in many local races and are also very significant political spenders through their national PAC groups).

This is not surprising; many elections in our cities and suburbs are ultimately about the price of land, just as the issue in Third World elections is the price of bread. Manhattan keeps building office buildings where space is the most expensive in the nation. A condominium in Manhattan in a decent location is $350-$550 a foot. Many observers said that the expanding costs may not be unrelated to the importance of real estate contributions to the campaigns of all New York City major candidates. Rezonings are very frequent in most cities and are not often examined in detail by civic watchdog groups or newspapers.

The large number of wealthy people and corporations, who are happy to contribute funds to provide access and possibly favorable review of their subsequent requests, fuels candidates who can then afford to pay for the most expensive and well-known of political consultants. Hiring a well-known consultant serves several functions. First, the work gets done. (Most candidates, in my experience, are not able to tell good creative work and excellent technical mastery in a campaign. They tend to believe the reactions of friends and observers who usually know even less than they do. In twenty six years of campaigning, a current client, a wealthy self-made industrialist, is the first to ask me to take him to the survey interviewing headquarters one hundred miles away to see for himself why the service was asking so much money for an interview; he decided to hire his own interviewers after looking into it). Secondly, hiring such consultants is almost a sure guarantee that the media will pay attention to his campaign–that by itself is worth money to many candidates. Also, such hirings interest significant contributors who want proof that their candidate is a serious contender–a probable winner. In addition, many top consultants on a personal level are part of the network of heavy hitter contributors and can themselves raise serious money.

Political newcomers are shocked at how high the campaign ante has become. Often, only the truly rich can have the luxury of a hot media race. It is not an accident that over one-half of members of the U.S. Senate are multi-millionaires. It has become almost like an elected English House of Lords.

Political campaigning has become an industry grossing over one billion dollars a year in a congressional year. An industry is how it is thought of by the practitioners and by the candidates who have to pay bills that can exceed the rates of senior partners in the best law firms, which is to say, over $500 an hour. In part, the media has helped matters along by describing some consultants as magicians, and therefore worth the high price. Some consultants have become multi-millionaires, branching off into corporations serving business on research, lobbying, and policy matters. Pat Caddell and Richard Wirthlin, two leading pollsters, were reported as earning huge fees for researching and recommending the new Coke, one of the most expensive and well publicized disasters in market research in the last decade, according to the Wall Street Journal.

Indicating the criticality of money and PACs in modern campaigning is the existence of a 1987 manual available for eighty dollars, designed for Republican candidates, advising them how to deal effectively with PACs. The manual was produced by a Washington consultant, Terry Cooper. (In Washington consultants are known as Beltway Bandits since they are located within the peripheral highway surrounding the district and because of the fees they charge.) His eighty seven page manual offers advice on the proper etiquette at PAC meetings, how much to ask for, how not to sound like a naive idealist (sure losers in PACs' judgement.) There is very little material on substantive issues. Cooper notes the candidates usually compete for funds against candidates from their own party. According to the New York Times,[9] he shows how to project winnability, picking and choosing carefully from polling data. He advises that most PACs are located outside of Washington and that candidates should develop local contacts with businessmen and companies that sponsor PACs, to become part of the political network.

I see two problems: 1) who is advising the potential candidates on solving the problems of the nation and 2) PACs like to give money to winners–congressional incumbents in 1986 won 95 percent of their elections. Must a newcomer have to wait for the death or retirement of a member of Congress before he or she can make a decent race?

An old friend of mine, a thoughtful politician with thirty years of political experience, has a simple, and in some ways quite accurate theory, of what has happened to campaigning. He believes that modern campaigning has resulted in the democratic process in most cities becoming notably less democratic because access to power (representation) now depends almost exclusively on money. Money always has been the critical mass in American political involvement, in some ways more so than power itself. However, years ago in my friend's experience, an average citizen who needed something was able to appeal to his district or ward captain who in turn could take him to the district and county leaders. The latter could get him to the state chairman if he had to who then could, if necessary, get to the national chairman, meaning the office of the President itself. The individuals might be expected to help out in elections and be there, as the current expression has it, when he was needed. But he was not expected to mortgage his house although if he was on the public payroll as the result of political intercession he might be expected to tithe his weekly or monthly salary.

But today the process is almost completely monetary, in my friend's view. So the average citizen is denied access unless the local newspaper or television takes an interest in him and makes a public relations issue out of it. Then and now the political leadership often felt firstly responsible for taking care of themselves, their families, and friends. Without money as an end many politicians would see no point to working in politics–for them it would become a senseless activity. This was so years ago and probably to a major extent remains so today.

For example, this year Mayor Koch of New York City, is having a birthday party fundraiser. His "present" is $2,000 a plate. While he has not announced for fourth term the money received by Koch, after paying the hotel and the food, could be used by him for any purpose, including personal ones, if he decided not to run. For people in business and politics in New York the reality is if they don't give the $2,000 (they don't have to attend to be noticed–politicians have long memories and keep longer lists) and then decide subsequently to ask the Mayor's office for a favor, the probability is that they would be politely denied access altogether, unless they had over the years built up a line of unused credits, or unless it was an errand of mercy (a "rachmonnis contract" is still often honored by politicians in New York).

This is not unique to New York–it goes on all over the country. This is one of the results of the expenses of campaigning. My own view is that public financing of campaigns within four years would effectively remove 90 percent of the waste in government expense and capital spending–by forcing controlled low bidding, by removing cronyism and minimizing the number of policies and programs designed exclusively for special interests.

A sad spectacle in late 1987 was the indictment of the former Miss America, Bess Myerson, a friend of Mayor Koch's for twenty years, but, announced Koch, a friend no more since the indictment. Miss Myerson, a millionairess, had been showered with furs and jewels by her friend, a contractor, twenty years younger, who was able to obtain one hundred million dollars in city contracts in the last few years, before being tried and convicted by federal courts for several crimes. New York voters had to ask themselves the value of political friendship and how it was that no one asked questions about the contractor and his relationships until the federal prosecutors became involved, and how much of their tax dollars went for this type of thing. Perhaps their view of building contractors now mirrors their view of the Mafia involvement in New York industry: that's the cost of doing business, and at least it has a stabilizing effect.

Another important development has been that targeting media appeals has become almost automatic in both professional and amateur style campaigns. Targeting politically is the direct offshoot of commercial market segmentation analysis. Very specific groups are now targeted for messages by radio, television, newspaper, and written appeals. For example, in areas with concentrations of Italian-Americans, Italian supporters of the candidate will sign letters addressed to voters with Italian names, similarly with Jewish, Mexican, Chinese or whatever segment is deemed important numerically and in voting patterns. (Generally, an ethnic group, all other things being equal, will vote 70 percent-30 percent or 80 percent-20 percent in an election for its own. It's not very much different than the vote a native son will get in an election).

Since the population over sixty is the fastest growing one, it is extremely common today for commercials and literature to trumpet the candidate's devotion to preserving the integrity of the social security system. Where waste disposal is a problem, the candidate will typically indicate that he has been devoted to environmental concerns since puberty. Where there are two income families with school age children continuous salvos can be expected resonating the candidate's concern with the quality of day care as well as with educational quality generally.

Since, from my viewpoint, our society is coming very close to a triage era I find the almost automatic avoidance of the discussion of essential and long range problems insulting to many voters. I've thought for some time that the voters of this country have much more sense than most candidates and consultants think they have. The voters see that the nation had overextended its credit, that while unemployment is down and inflation quiescent, basic industries have been having trouble for years, that takeovers benefitted only a few and hurt many workers, that we are not competitive in world markets. The parking lots of textile factories in the South are filled with many Japanese cars–they are perceived to be more reliable and of higher quality. Voters have common sense and believe our government is not responding to national needs.

By triage I mean, for example, how long can the nation afford medical care for an expanding AIDS population when the last year of a patient's life costs $100,000 for care and medicine, and it costs perhaps $25,000 a year to incarcerate a convicted person in jail. In the foreseeable future some leaders will have to start talking about it-and not wait for some enormous debacle like the crash of October 1987 to act on it-our budget and trade deficits in this case.

Another development is that in recent years there is a diminishing emphasis on newspaper advertisements in campaigns. In the smaller towns and cities they are still used with some frequency but rarely in big cities and then only for very special purposes. Print is not generally regarded by experts as a "hot" medium–it doesn't affect voters' emotions or thought processes as much as television and radio are generally considered to. (Lawn signs remain very popular in suburban and small city locations. They go back at least fifty years. The most that I can say for them is that they are cheaper and less unsightly than the use of billboards which seem to be disappearing rapidly). Partially these trends are the result of financial displacement by the other media which are rising so rapidly in costs. They are also small ticket items from a consultant's point of view.

Minority groups have increasing representation in city and state politics. There are many black mayors and some Hispanic mayors of big cities–Newark, Philadelphia, Los Angeles, San Antonio, and Miami. The role of women in elective office has been increasing as well. Diane Feinstein of San Francisco, Senator Barbara Mikuski of Maryland, and Representative Pat Schroeder of Colorado are examples of the many successful women politicians active today. However, their number seems to be increasing at a slower rate while their acceptance is at a much faster rate. There may be some concern among some observers that the proportion of truly distinguished minority and women elected officials does not seem to be exceeding that of mainstream white males.

The growing importance of fundamentalists–evangelicals in American politics is clear. The support of this group, estimated to number between twenty five million and forty million nationally, is very important in state-wide elections, although apparently still not dominating. The political credibility of Pat Robertson in the 1987 Republican presidential primary was an acknowledgement of the importance of the group. Robertson raised eleven million dollars very quickly and did well in the first debate.[10]

Finally, one of the basic trends in American political life has been the constantly increasing number of Americans for whom loyalty means little or nothing. The independent or moderate voters, now, according to some estimates, number about 35 percent to 40 percent nationally. In presidentials, however, there is some tendency for the increment of voters over the congressional year to be party loyalists, perhaps because ideology has a greater degree of broad scale differentiation in a presidential election. The number of voters who switch their vote from party to party has been very significant for many years–I don't see evidence that that has changed very much. Ticket splitting has been going on for over a generation now.

What Can Be Done?

When I review what has happened in the twenty eight years that I have been active in politics, a phrase that one hears in the South comes to mind, "I'm sad as I can be."

I have met hundreds of candidates and campaign professionals and volunteers. Many were decent, bright people and became excellent elected and appointed government officials. Some retired early from politics finding the context depressing and discouraging. Few remained idealistic for any length of time. And most importantly, they found that the great problems are becoming part of the scenery; many concerned politicians give up on solving societal problems of magnitude because of the huge obstacles-getting media and voters' attention, finding the funds, not insulting any important special interest, working within the shortness of the terms of office, and many others. The problems seem to be growing in number and depth just as our capacity to deal with them seems to be diminishing. The system works after 200 years but it is starting perhaps to creak somewhat.

After Black Monday on the New York Stock Exchange in October 1987, many commentators galked of the possibility of the world financial markets collapsing and the urgent compelling need for competent political leadership in America. Muddling through simply wasn't enough any longer. "It'll just have to do" wasn't satisfactory. Something seemed very wrong and no one seemed to know what to do about it.

Since the United States is the greatest consuming market on the planet, a major recession here could drive the world into a great depression; there seemed to be a paucity of thought on how to handle it, except that the budget and trade imbalances would have to be adjusted by increasing personal savings, raising taxes, and doing some long range thinking. But the political apparatus, very much including modern campaigning methods, doesn't encourage long range thinking, just the opposite. The problems of housing, the rapidly increasing population of the old–with fewer active workers to support the whole system, the problem of providing affordable housing, of educational quality, of jobs for minority youths, of caring for the homeless, of escalating medical costs, of controlling military expenditures, of nuclear disarmament, of protecting the environment, of Third World political and economic tragedies seem to be almost insoluble.

I thought in 1984, and still do to a degree, that changing campaign financing would almost assuredly provide us with more, better qualified candidates. Now I think that may not be nearly enough. Campaigning methods and successful campaigning skills may not be totally correlated with the skills necessary for governing and administering ably, and may in fact depend on skills in opposition with one another.

The table that follows compares the skills necessary to be a good campaigner with those required to govern well, which is to say to make thoughtful and effective policies for the short and long term, based as much as possible on facts and an objective contextual view. This is not so easy now, and never has been. In the last decade there have been many universities offering degrees in public policy, and for many more years in public administration. But somehow public policy formulation doesn't seem to be improving significantly in ways the public can perceive. To be sure computers are used by elected officials and by public administrators in large numbers. Social security checks go out; the mail service delivers billions of pieces of mail fairly promptly and many logistical functions are carried out very well for the huge society that we are.

But there seems to be a vague, general apprehension now that we are not well governed nationally–that we are drifting towards some insanely dangerous historic precipice and that there isn't much that we individually can do about it, except to continue to concern ourselves about the things we can do something about–our jobs, our children, our leisure time pursuits. We seem less involved politically as a people. How much of this is a result of the Reagan administration is impossible to say; but clearly there may be something more needed than the "sunrise years in America," reduced inflation, and a lower unemployment rate that people want and are concerned about.

Too much of public policy seems to have become how to take care of good old boys, contractors friendly to those in power, what seems expedient at the moment to quiet or neutralize intense media criticism (the 7:00 news), trying to establish one's income base after leaving federal government employment, doing favors, taking calls from connected people; one gets the sense sometimes that on the national level there is not a great deal of time left for thought and reading and discussion. It seems to be what deals can be struck in committee sometimes a deal may be struck that is incorrect–and it can take decades to get it out of the national system like some powerful virus that becomes part of the chemical makeup of a human body, that stays for half a lifetime. Professor Lindblum's theory of muddling through doesn't seem to be working as well as before; it may be like the story of the man in water waving at people on shore–by God, he's not waving, he's drowning.

There may be a graduate school somewhere in a desolate desert that gives degrees in vileness and venality for public officials. A moral basis for public policy seems too often to be absent. Every national administration offers a parade of semi-scoundrels and they don't have the style or humor of such politicians generations ago. For example, President Reagan's friend and advisor, Michael Deaver, went on trial in 1987 for lying to a grand jury and other crimes. He had gone into a public relations business after resigning from his White House position. On October 28, 1987 the New York Times reported that Deaver had gotten $250,000 for making *one* telephone call to Elizabeth Dole, Secretary of Transportation, for a corporate client interested in a policy change. He saw nothing inappropriate in doing this. Like many who come to Washington for the power, the glamour, and the excitement he also realized that he had to build a network so that he could make "serious" money afterwards.

There are 100 Senators and 535 congressmen with staffs of 7,000 assistants, many bright, young and ambitious. There are perhaps another 10,000 assistant secretaries, deputy assistant secretaries, bureau chiefs and GS 17s and above in the federal bureaucracy who run the country. Improving this group's continuity and long range interests is an important, perhaps critical, part of improving government quality nationally; improving their quality is related to improving the quality of candidates and the legislators they become.

Thoughts on How to Improve Campaigning/Government

When one thinks about the overall problems of achieving competent government in our society, public financing of elections

COMPARISON OF CAMPAIGNING AND GOVERNING SKILLS

Skills and Concerns

Campaigning	Governing
fund raising budgeting;	spending money;
	development of programs
reliance on consultants, experts, advisers	relying on small personal staff and a large bureaucratic resource, except reading and analysis more important, committee development of
policies	as programs
looking fit and fashionable	same
speaking well, projecting goodwill and sincerity	same
handling contributors and constituents	same
avoiding controversy/seeking problems;	studying long term
	establishing moral basis for policy; trying to establish the long term good of the district and the nation
doing what can be done to get elected and stay in office- public relations skills/hype- comfortable	getting reelected

becomes only a partial solution at best. The really critical issue becomes how to attract candidates who are intelligent, educated, capable of taking the long view, whose ideology and prior commitments do not make creative thought and common sense an impossibility, who are willing to spend at least ten years of their lives in public service, who would be acceptable to the public as human and attractive yet possessing integrity and substance and good humor, who can juggle special and overall interests, who can understand and have the patience to study line item budgets and ask the right questions of technicians, who can hire competent people and as importantly fire incompetents, who can say to operating agencies–"I don't know"–"explain it to me in detail,"–and who are not bound to the old boys; code of cronies and party loyalties at any price, who can explicate complex problems and the options in solving them in a way that the public can understand and remain interested.

How to get the public involved is also critical. Along with the Tocqueville, I believe it would be well that the majority of candidates not be lawyers. As the great Frenchman pointed out 150 years ago, too many lawyers can delay and subvert the democratic process.

The following are my suggestions to open up the number of such candidates and ways to replenish them as they burn out, phase out, wear out, and age out:

1. Public financing should be provided for all congressional races as well as for the Presidential race. A financial cap should be put into effect and public financing should account for at least one-half the total amount. However, each candidate should be required to provide both a certain number of signatures and at least one-tenth of the monetary cap limit.

2. To qualify, candidates would have to state all contributors, their relationships, how long they know each other, if they have business interests in common, provide tax returns for the last five years, etc.

3. Radio and television stations, licensed by the government should be directed to provide time to qualified candidates in prime time at 50 percent of commercial rates in the month before the election. In addition, in congressionals and gubernatorials each candidate should get 120 minutes of commercial time free of charge in the

six weeks before the election–in the hours before 6:00 p.m. and after 10:00 p.m. The criteria: minimum ad time–two minutes, no negative advertising, devoting to substance only. In addition, each candidate getting this time would be required to participate in three one-half hour debates.

4.   Salaries of elected officials should be raised significantly so that they are perceived as comparable with the salaries of businessmen and corporate executives. The view that public service should be part time and pay little doesn't make sense either in terms of the management ability required, the size of public budgets today, or the magnitude of the problems that have to be dealt with. As the comedian Jack Mason pointed out in his brilliant 1987 Broadway show, talking about elected officials, "How can they be efficient. Are they on commission?"

5.   It seems to me that it would be extremely cost-effective to institute a National Academy of Public Policy and Services similar to the U.S. Naval Academy, the Air Force Academy, and West Point to provide a curriculum of how the system works in detail and how it can be improved–to provide a degree in the details of managing government.[11] The Public Equity, Special Interest Calculus, The Public Interest, Whose Money Is It Anyway? would be mandatory courses. Those qualified by testing and referrals would be required to serve eight years after graduation either as a candidate, elected official, or staff to elected officials in states, major cities and the federal government. Scholarships would include a two year graduate school of their choice from a list of recommended universities.

Each major special interest group (farm, labor unions, fundamentalists, textiles, the arts and literature, coal, real estate, printers, etc.) would nominate ten people of which six would be selected, so too each of the 500 standard and poor large corporations would nominate three, as would Ralph Nader's groups and the city clubs of the 200 largest cities.

A student body of 1500 and 150 teachers would be optimal–the teachers would nominate persons for chairmanships that then would be selected with consultations with the student body. The faculty, I think, would have to be a revolving one to be effective and would consist of scholars and practitioners named by the Academy of Social Sciences and other appropriate bodies. Leading professors and experts in each of the subject matters covered by the University would select professors; each subject would have minority professional technical viewpoints represented. One-tenth of the faculty would have to be Japanese, German, and other nationalities. The instilling of long range planning instincts and sensitivities, the ability to balance many factors, to teach the appropriateness of a sense of morality and professionalism in the public arena would make any public cost acceptable.

6. Congress' occupational distribution is normally over 65 percent lawyers. Their expertise in writing legislation, cutting deals to get bills to the floor are necessary but the staff lawyers do most of this anyway. Somehow the number of lawyers, as well as multi-millionaires, should be capped at a reasonable limit.

7. The term of a member of congress would be increased to four years. I believe one term of six years for the presidency makes a great deal of sense.

8. National campaigns should adopt the British restriction on time; they should be limited to sixty days and not the year a congressional very commonly takes today–and the one and one-half years for a presidential.

9. One national party presidential primary in September should be instituted.

10. Campaign spending caps, based on historic data and per capita amounts, should be established for congressionals, gubernatorials, and big city mayorals.

11. School hours should be extended with one-fourth of the increment devoted to civic and public policy studies in high school and college.

12. It has been reported that only one in five of those 18 to 25 years old vote. Institutions like the Youth Policy Institute in Washington, D.C. should be funded by public or foundation money in each state. This group is run by recent college graduates. They conduct forums on public policy issues, and public special reports for young people on the major issues concerning the young. Youth Action, also in Washington, raises money for services such as work with the elderly and the homeless, voter registration drives and other services involving the young directly with community problems. Young people are thus encouraged to get involved in a way that gives them a sense of accomplishment.

13. Church leaders to some extent have always been involved in politics. They seem to be getting directly involved more and more. They recommend candidates. They field their own candidates. Perhaps church leaders can also get their congregations more involved in issues not directly concerning the church with candidates, invited specialists, forums onproblems, etc.

14. It was reported by the J.C. Penney Company that their national survey of 1000 adults showed that more than one-half in 1986 had been involved as volunteers in religious organizations (64 percent), education (44 percent), youth organizations (41 percent), health care (34 percent), and civil improvements (26 percent). Perhaps this structure of volunteer groups can become the basis of an educational program to establish quarterly meetings of volunteers to listen to and discuss presentations of the broader issues concerning their communities and the nation in a series of forums.

15. Large corporations should consider using big screen television at work to allow their employees one hour a week before the general elections to see a debate or listen to a discussion of campaign issues.

16. In some states only seven weeks elapse from the primary election to the first Tuesday in November. This of ourse is designed to favor the incumbent. Spring primaries should be made mandatory in each state.

17. High school and college students should get credit for working in campaigns.

18. Congressmen should make progress reports every three months to the student bodies of the local high schools on the issues of the day and to answer any questions the young people have.

19. A conflict of interest law should be put in place in large cities, state offices, and congressionals–minimum fines–$100,000 and one year in jail. To accompany this each legislature should have a Board of Ethics consisting of newspapermen, contractors, real estate developers, bankers, etc. who have been indicted for fraud. The chairman should be a member who was found guilty and served time.

20. Newspapers should be required to print issue statements in large print. The same size print should be used for contributors' names and the amount contributed.

21. Political media consultants of both parties should be asked to do pro bono work in their communities of residence or employment. They should be asked to prepare slide shows and ten minute videos on what urban problems are and how they can be solved.

22. AARP has 25,000,000 members. They should prepare booklets on major regional and national issues besides those of medical insurance and social security. People over fifty aren't quite as provincial and narrow-minded as the AARP leadership seem to think.

23. Movie-sports-musical celebrities should be asked to make their talents available not only for fund raisers but in dramatizing and exploring issues in a way that the voters would find interesting. The top ten fund raisers and the top ten contributors in the area should be asked to fund these prepsentations.

24. If all else fails we should return at once to back room moninations. This didn't work out so badly, Missouri State district leaders produced Truman, and Roosevelt, Wagner and Lehman came out of the Tammany backroom in New York, and Stevenson out of

Chicago. The top of the ticket was not left to clever or kindly incompetents in the old days. There was patronage and thievery, God knows, but there was substance maybe and some style. And the abyss didn't seem quite so near.

November 1987
Greensboro, N.C.

Notes

1. Television stations in Greensboro, North Carolina, where I live, a city of 180,000 which had never experienced a modern media campaign for mayor, in 1987, were charging $1000 for a thirty-second spot, shocking many local observers. At the same time monied candidates used ad agencies, not political media consultants, and relied on the most simplistic of polls, although media investments were significant. With six mayoral candidates, only 18 percent of registered voters went to the polls, possibly because the real issue was the price of undeveloped land (rezoning) and no candidate discussed it.

2. *Insight*, pp. 18-19, October 26, 1987.

3. In New York City in the 1960s when reform groups in the Democratic party were developing and campaigns were vigorous and idealism energized people, a *turnout* of 50 percent in a *primary* was regarded as not usual.

4. Stem, a small town in North Carolina, solved the problem of getting people involved in the political process very directly. There are 121 registered voters in the town. Board of Elections workers went door-to-door. As a result eleven candidates for the six public offices were found, or one in ten voters. A maximum turnout was expected. There's a lot to be said for small scale.

5. Such people are in both parties, in all parts of the country. A politician, an old friend, remarked that the working title for my first book should be, *A Multiplicity of Motherfuckers*, to describe the Democratic machine of the city we lived in during the late 1960s. Alternatively, he suggested *A Plenitude of Putzes*.

6. The nation is changing more rapidly than ever before. The fact that there are more single person households also no doubt explains why fewer people vote; on average, single people have fewer ties to the comunity than do families with kids. Note the following from the U.S. Bureau of the Census:

   Married-couple families in 1970--73 percent; 1985--58 percent;
   Non-family households in 1970--18 percent; 1985--28 percent;
   Female-headed families, no spouse present in 1970--2 percent; in 1985--12 percent;

Male-headed families, no spouse present in 1970--2 percent; in 1985--3 percent. (Percentage may not total 100 percent due to rounding)

7.   Ronald Reagan is often pointed to as the ideal modern media campaign candidate. (More recently he has been seen to represent the dangers of modern campaigning-a pleasant, decent man with great presence and a good speaking style-but not well-informed on issues, often dealing with problems anecdotally.) His campaign emphasized orchestrated likability, sunrise again in America, optimism triumphant and it worked well. At the same time his opponents ran bad campaigns and the economic climate favored Reagan both with Carter and Mondale. At the same time that polls showed Reagan's personal popularity, the majority of Americans disagreed with most of his major policies.

8.   There are, thank God, some pleasant aberrations. Senator Proxmire, in his last campaign, spent $78, largely for postage to return contributions.

9.   *New York Times*, October 18, 1987.

10.   A national poll in 1986 found that one-half of adult Americans believed in the literal Bible; they believed that mankind started ten thousand years ago and that the theory of evolution is a liberal fantasy. This is quite a big base for the religious right, and quite an indictment at the same time of the American educational system.

11.   Transition devices are already in place. The federal "Senior Seminar" offers courses for one year for bureaucratic officials of high rank. The National War College offers courses on East-West problems, etc. for senior and mid-level federal government employees. The government also sends some employees to Harvard's Kennedy School of government.

Preface to the Second Edition

It has been ten years since I started my research for the first version of this book. The book was designed, as this new edition has been designed, to help candidates without a great deal of money conduct a professional-style campaign and to help students understand the details of the process of campaigning. I was gratified that the original publisher was able to backlist the book for eight years. It came to be used as a text, although it was not designed as such: Thirty-eight colleges and universities adopted it. The book examined the ways that candidates could run respectable (and, it was hoped, successful) campaigns without having to mortgage their futures and their policy options. Since the publication of that first edition, I have worked in over forty campaigns doing survey research, telephone banks, and strategy consultation in New York and Connecticut.

In updating the book, I was genuinely surprised by how well the structure held up. The basic approaches to professional campaigning haven't really changed that much. What seems to have happened is that candidates are spending a great deal more money (one billion dollars in 1982) and that everyone seems to understand the critical need for targeting. The campaigning vocabulary is commonly understood; the thinking process which allows for creativity, originality, and the ability to recognize the critical opportunities, I'm afraid, is not that commonly understood. I have tried to distill the essence of that thinking process in this new edition.

In the last decade books on campaigning have substantially improved. When my book was originally published there were very few on the details, the "mechanics" of campaigning. Now, there are several, in addition to mine, that are very helpful on these details.

I have had to modify some of the advice I gave in 1973 and have had to add material on consultants, whose growing number and influence have affected not only the methods and costs of campaigning but also the style and substance of governance that follows a campaign success. As Jimmy Breslin wrote, "power is . . . mirrors and blue smoke." A good deal of campaigning is a charade, endlessly varied and endlessly interesting.

I'd like to thank a number of people for their thoughts and suggestions on the second edition. In Washington, D.C., I talked to Alan Baron,

Mike Fraoli, Susan Tolchin, Charles Cook, and Gene Miller; in New York City, Walter Diamond, Guy Velella, Mel Spain, Morris Sweet, Ken and Andrew Fisher, and Sheng-tao (Sam) Wang; and in Connecticut, Bob Baskin. All were most helpful. I also appreciate Stella Heiden's advice and her encouragement to update the book.

I'd especially like to thank several of my clients whom I think of as friends: Denise Scheinberg (New York), State Senator Richard Schneller (Connecticut), and Congressman San Gejdenson. I learned a great deal from them; I was very glad to have been involved in their campaigns.

Norman Adler, who directs the political action activities of a major union, very generously shared his thoughts about campaigning. Since his union had used over 1,000 copies of the book's first edition in training its members over a period of eight years, his suggestions for improvements were very valuable.

My wife, Robin, helped considerably in editing and reviewing drafts, and my sister, Martha Schwartzman, typed early drafts of new chapters.

EDWARD SCHWARTZMAN
Friendship Heights
Chevy Chase, Maryland
Greensboro, North Carolina

Preface to the First Edition

I have been involved professionally in more than thirty political campaigns, from district leader to presidential primary. I have never advised presidential candidates or written campaign strategies for president or determined the expenditures of millions of dollars in any one campaign. I have, however, been a professional political "mechanic" for more than a decade, having first become involved as an activist in reform Democratic politics in Bronx County in 1961. I have participated in campaigns at virtually every level of political life—for president, governor, senator, congressman, mayor, judge, city councilman, borough president, assemblyman, and district leader—as a technical consultant specializing in research and telephone work. I have worked on the East Coast, mainly in New York City and New York State, but the experience of colleagues in other parts of the country indicates that the problems and techniques of political campaigning are basically similar throughout the United States and Canada.

Political mechanics receive no press attention, nor do they require it for ego gratification. They are detail men; they do jobs the public is not aware of but that must be done for successful campaigns. Even experienced politicians sometimes are not too knowledgeable about these details—petition collecting, petition binding, which typeface to use in a brochure, how a sample survey is selected, to name only a few. This book is about these details, all of which I have done myself, except for the preparation of a television campaign.

Many books are available by advisers to presidents and senators, some of which are brilliantly written and some of which are inaccurate and even offer dangerous advice. But there is hardly anything on the day-to-day substance of campaigning, and as far as I know, there is no other book by a professional political detail man that covers all aspects of campaigning.

The book is intended for a number of audiences but primarily for the local candidate who faces a campaign for the first time in the 1970s, when many people are realizing that political campaigning is not a mystique accessible only to lawyers and public relations men, and when more and more citizens—notably women and minority group leaders—are bringing their talents, ambitions, and sense of community priorities to the political arena. At the same time, urban problems are becoming so massive that new types of governmental responses are clearly necessary, and new types of candidates are seeking and are needed to provide them.

Some books regard political campaigning as a sport or game and suggest ways to win. I don't see it that way. There is no magic way to win an election, and no honest technician or political mechanic in his right mind would say that there is or could be. I do not guarantee that using the ideas and approaches contained in this book will *win* elections. That would be extraordinarily presumptuous. But a candidate who uses the book will not waste his or her money and energy on the imbeciles and imbecilities that are common in many campaigns. Instead, the candidate should be able to provide and sustain an early sense of direction and get the greatest possible benefit from the effort and money he invests in the pursuit of elective office.

New or potential candidates will get a realistic appraisal of what a political campaign involves in time, money, and work. Candidates concerned about the many press reports on the expense and mechanization of campaigning will perhaps realize that professionalism and rationalization can produce more economical campaigns as well as more expensive ones. Experienced politicians whose backgrounds do not include systematic concern with political research may find the book particularly useful.

Another group of people who may be helped is that sizable body of citizens who, campaigning every year for local organizational offices, receive little public attention but contribute significantly to the responsible functioning of their communities. Many of the techniques described here can be adapted effectively for such campaigns.

Particularly in view of their growing role in local and national campaigns, I would be especially gratified if high school and college students gained insights into an important component of the American political process.

I hope that concerned citizens will gain additional understanding of why the much-heralded "New Politics" depends in considerable part on a new professionalism and on their own substantial contribution.

Finally, the tens of thousands of amateur campaign workers who do poll watching, carry petitions, and listen to speeches and pep talks may get an idea of total campaign strategy and of how critical their efforts are.

The basic thesis of this book is that the use of professional techniques can provide a real chance for winning public office for candidates who otherwise could not hope to compete successfully. The key to professional-style campaigning is sensitivity to *detailing*—the main subject of this book. The proverb associated with the architect Mies van der Rohe, "God is in the detail," describes the necessary emphasis for campaign work. Many campaigns—even those organized by experienced politicians—are conducted as if no precedent existed, as if one could not learn from the experiences of other campaigners. The staggering escalation of campaign costs makes "learning by doing" a luxury that few candidates can afford and makes emphasis on proper detailing absolutely essential. Saving money is important for even the wealthiest campaigners. It is critical for the first-time campaigner, whose resources are usually limited and, in most cases, no match for those of the incumbent. Well-planned detailing also spares the candidate considerable irritation—a surplus commodity in most campaigns, even in the best of circumstances.

Although there will never be an exact science of political campaigning, each good campaign, like any good work of art, is based on a sound technical structure and is characterized by a sensitivity to real and potential turning points. Sensitivity to such pivotal opportunities is a political instinct that probably cannot be acquired through reading or instruction. Building a good technical structure, however, can be learned, and it is accomplished by the most carefully planned and executed detailing. Proper detailing involves professional standards in research, petitioning, brochure design, and other campaign procedures and products, with constant concern for proper follow-through and implementation, whether what is at issue is something as exciting and dramatic as a public policy reversal or as prosaic as looking up telephone numbers for an opinion survey and copying them correctly.

Campaigns have been lost because campaign workers concerned themselves exclusively or primarily with presumably more important policy questions but forgot to check something so "simple" as whether the signatures on the candidate's nominating petitions were properly signed and witnessed. This book examines such not-so-prosaic and not-so-unimportant details and makes recommendations that my experience suggests are appropriate for every good political campaign.

Examples of research questionnaires, advertising messages, issue papers, survey cross-tabulations, and other campaign materials are included in the book, and a selected bibliography gives students and other interested readers an opportunity to pursue their special interests further.

If you're a candidate-to-be, I wish you luck and joy in a tough job. If you're a student, I envy you—there is no more fascinating field than political science, and good young politicians are as desperately needed now as they always have been. John F. Kennedy is said to have remarked, "Every American mother seems to want her son to be President, but none wants him to be a politician." However, there is no more responsible or exciting profession than politics; corruption and selfishness are only a small, if pervasive, part of the business. The positive side receives less public attention: You, as a candidate, can respond to community ideas, provide influence and a sense of direction, and use power and discretion with compassion, intelligence, and a sense of equity. You can try to do what needs to be done. No other profession provides so great an opportunity to benefit society.

This is my first book, and I've learned that even an unpretentious effort like this is quite complicated. I would particularly like to indicate my gratitude to Melvyn Spain and Dr. Susan Tolchin, who went over early drafts very carefully and provided many constructive suggestions. In addition, Arthur B. Levine and Morris Sweet read parts of the book and offered many valuable ideas. Beatrice Reinfeld first challenged me to write the book, which I had only talked about for the previous three years, and provided encouragement as the task went on. Lou Barron taught me a great deal about the English language; I hope I've taught him something about politics.

I appreciate the graciousness of Jeff Barrett, Walter Diamond, Ronnie Eldridge, Zane Klein, and Nat Sorkin, who allowed me to interview them. Doris Gelberg, Elizabeth Diamond, Ethel Bunin, and my sister Martha Schwartzman cheerfully gave their time and skills to translating my terrible handwriting and typing the manuscript. My wife helped immeasurably both in editing the manuscript and in recalling experiences from the campaigns on which we have worked together.

Finally, I wish to acknowledge the cumulative contributions of politicians and political mechanics I have worked with over the years. Some were brilliant and deeply involved, some were men of integrity with little political instinct for the jugular, and some were of such incompetence that it amounted to a positive flair. The book in part originates from them, for, one way or another, I learned from all of them—and some of them tell me that they have learned from me.

Contents

1
Setting Up Your Campaign

I wouldn't think of making a move nationally if I didn't have my state in good hands. The first lesson is don't sleep too long, don't trust too much, don't take anything for granted.
                                                                        —Hubert H. Humphrey

When you start to campaign, you will have to confront many troublesome details of housekeeping, from budget allocation to who gets a new desk and who gets the pretty secretary, as well as the very difficult questions of staff salaries and space assignments. Many candidates find these things boring, burdensome, and of little consequence, but cumulatively they can significantly influence the efficiency and success of campaign operations. To administer a campaign properly, you should personally work out all these details in advance of the active campaigning, in consultation with your key staff, your close advisors, and perhaps your principal contributors.

Although most campaign offices are managed inefficiently and a considerable waste of time and money is not only frequent but taken for granted as normal, this need not be the case.* It is both possible and essential for a candidate whose funds are limited to set up a campaign office in a businesslike way.

SPACE

The first problem is usually how much space to rent and where to look for it. Hotel suites are commonly used, but although their central locations have an obvious advantage, their convenience rarely justifies their high prices. Some politicians choose storefronts to give visibility to the campaign. In my experience, however, the value of such visibility (as well as that of large signs on the fronts of headquarters offices) is greatly overrated. You can get a short-term lease on an empty store for perhaps

---

*Campaigns too often operate on the O.P.M. (other people's money) principle which also pervades so many government operations. There are very notable differences between these campaigns and those where the candidate has limited means and has to pay for most campaign expenses himself.

six or eight dollars a square foot per year (prorated), but since empty stores are not always available in all sizes, you may have to take a much bigger one than you need, so that you not only spend too much but are also burdened with a large, half-empty headquarters, which gives the impression of a lackluster campaign. Often campaigners or their representatives rent thousands of square feet of prestige office space, realizing later that only a fraction of it was really necessary. Such a mistake has a cumulative impact: larger stores mean higher maintenance expenses, more staff, larger signs. Often the signs stay in place for years after the campaign is over as shabby testimonials to the nagging economics of American campaigning.

Neatly kept space, moderate in expense and expanse, is perfectly adequate. The candidate is seldom there, in any case, and the public relations impact of a modest but well-kept headquarters can be very positive. Twelve dollars a foot per year (prorated) is the most that should be spent for rent; in many circumstances, it is perfectly all right to campaign from your home or from the offices of a local club.

Few real estate salespeople bother to handle short-term space, and in many cities and towns, well-located and reasonably priced space is hard to come by for a short period. However, there is always some space available. In every city, there are offices that are empty between leases or scheduled for alteration in the near future. The only sure way to find appropriate accommodations is to start several months before campaign time. You may have to pay rent for an additional month or so when the space won't be fully used, but the certainty that you have the right space makes that a good investment, and the extra time allows you to plan the proper use of the space and to hire carpenters and install telephone wiring, air conditioners, and other necessities.

In a 1970 campaign, New York Congressman James H. Scheuer had difficulty finding appropriate short-term leases in a new district; he was one of the first urban-area candidates to rent trailers and move them throughout his area. This relatively inexpensive tactic undoubtedly helped him beat a strongly entrenched incumbent, and, indeed, this device is increasingly utilized by campaigners for reasons of mobility, visibility, and economy.

In another major campaign, a senatorial candidate in a close race had three separate offices in midtown New York that cost him between $50,000 and $100,000 for the campaign and deprived him of thousands of dollars he might have spent for other more important campaign needs. Presidential campaigns get similarly bogged down by high-rent space that often serves little useful purpose. Senator Edmund S. Muskie's presidential campaign, for example, was reported several times in 1971 and 1972 to be cutting back staff for lack of funds; yet more than a year before his first state primary, Muskie had already rented an entire floor in an expensive downtown Washington building. Unwise allocations of funds such as this undoubtedly contributed to Muskie's decision to drop out of active primary campaigning in April 1972.

Estimating space requirements with precision is difficult, but sensible planning can help. You should start by deciding exactly which people, performing which functions, you want at headquarters. Basically, you will want to include space for a receptionist-secretary, your personal secretary (to handle your schedule and appointments), the campaign manager, and two assistants to supervise petitioning, research, press relations, follow-through on special problems, and club liaison. In a professionally directed campaign, most of the technical work will be done by outside consultants and specialists, such as photographers, speech writers, and people for research, polling, brochure preparation, and TV setups, none of whom will occupy your headquarters space. Your headquarters should have some reserve space for small-scale conferences, storage of brochures, and other miscellaneous purposes. A reception area will be needed for visitors, as well as for press and possibly TV interviewers.

It may be necessary to reserve some space for volunteers, who will be involved in checking telephone numbers, running mimeograph machines, and getting out mailings. However, this aspect of the campaign should perhaps be housed separately. It is distracting to the regular headquarters staff to see volunteers come and sit around waiting for someone to assign them work.

Some thought and care should be given to how the office looks to visitors and the press. Many campaign headquarters are completely disorganized and look it; certainly this does not contribute beneficially to the candidate's appeal. Disarray is seldom attractive in any office.

It is usually advisable to rent headquarters furniture, typewriters, calculators, and other office equipment. The rental of refrigerators, air conditioners, and fans would also be a prudent investment. Cold drinks, beer, liquor, and some food should be available. There seems to be an unwritten law that much campaigning work is done late at night. I personally have found the availability of a folding army cot in a campaign office very useful. Three or four telephones will be necessary, and it may be worthwhile to engage an answering service for night calls.

Adding up all the items mentioned thus far indicates an expenditure of about $20,000 for office overhead to mount an urban congressional campaign. When you include cleaning, insurance, maintenance, and miscellaneous expenses, this estimate is probably conservative, and salaries for secretaries and full-time staff members may increase the operating costs for a twelve-week campaign by about another $25,000. Perhaps $50,000 would cover the basic needs and emergencies in a medium- to large-scale campaign. (The average congressional campaign in 1982 cost a total of $400,000 to $500,000, while several went over $1,000,000.)

STAFFING

The smaller the staff, the better, in almost every instance. An ideal full-time staff for most campaigns up to and including congressionals is five to eight workers; for most mayoral, senatorial, and gubernatorial campaigns, twenty key staff people should, in my judgment, be the absolute maximum. (Governor Nelson Rockefeller reportedly used more than 300 in his 1969 campaign; Senator George McGovern was reported to have 250 full-time paid staff members throughout the country when he made his presidential race in 1972.*)

The more people, the more infighting for position with the candidate, the more time wasted by turf wars, the more good ideas killed by bureaucratic compromises and accommodations, and the less chance for a creative, hard-hitting campaign.

A full-time staff chart, such as the one shown in Fig. 1-1, should provide for all the critical functions.

It is not always necessary to have one person handle only one function. Circumstances will dictate the size of the total staff among whom duties can be divided.

Campaigning involves relationships with contributors, legal advisors, and technical consultants. The campaign manager and the candidate should

---

The New York Times reported that on September 9, 1982 that Mario Cuomo ran for Governor of New York with nine paid staffers, while his unsuccessful opponent Edward Koch used 25. Headquarters staff generally are getting leaner, a trend surely not unrelated to the mushrooming corps of political consultancies.

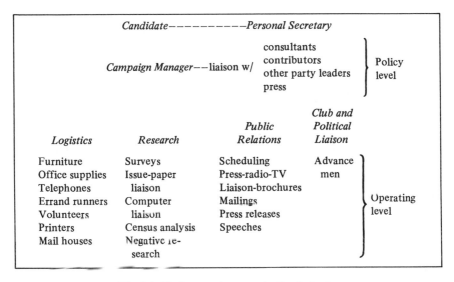

Fig. 1-1. Basic campaign organizational chart.

handle these personally in setting policy and priorities.* The manager should be completely in charge, naming a deputy in his or her absence. Other members of the headquarters staff should not be personally involved in the controversies that characterize most campaigns. Nor should the candidate intervene, except in unusual circumstances, in the daily operations of the staff. Violating the basic administrative rule—each worker should have only one boss—contributes significantly to waste and poor morale and is a common error in many campaigns.

AMATEURS OR PROFESSIONALS?

Jesse Unruh of California observed that in politics, as in everything else, you tend to get what you pay for. Most candidates like to have young volunteers at their headquarters, because they add to the appeal of a candidate and because many amateurs are energetic, devoted campaign-

*As a candidate, you should be involved in policy—in reviewing the substantive content of advertising, for example; you do not benefit the campaign if you involve yourself in the minutiae of every campaign process and problem. You'll only give yourself and your staff a series of bad headaches, and you'll simply reduce the time you have to "press the flesh," raise money, and take care of the meetings that no one else can handle for you.

ers. In the view of seasoned campaign managers, however, the use of experienced professionals is clearly advisable when judgment and efficiency are called for.

Amateurs can do many important things in a campaign, but they tend to require much supervision, and because they are unpaid, it is difficult to control them. They like to discuss their assignments in great detail, sometimes taking as much time with that as in actually doing the job. Many volunteer in the hope of being elevated to policy-making positions after two days' work on details and become disappointed when that doesn't happen. On balance, volunteers are useful, but you have to pick their spots carefully, delineate their roles sharply, and keep them out of procedures in which timing and the exact following of instructions are primary considerations. One regular staff member should be charged with supervising them and keeping them happy.

In some circumstances, notably the presidential primary campaigns of Eugene J. McCarthy in 1968 and George McGovern in 1972, the role of volunteer canvassers was absolutely critical.* They gathered petition signatures in large numbers (proselytizing very effectively in the process), distributed literature, manned sidewalk stands in areas of heavy pedestrian counts, hand-addressed envelopes, made telephone calls, "pulled" (got out the vote) on election day, and in general provided an enthusiasm that caught on. Since it meant so much to these nice young dedicated people, many voters began to feel that maybe the candidate was worth thinking about after all.

Throughout this book I emphasize the necessity for professionalism, for rationalization of campaign procedures. However, many more laypersons are participating in public affairs than ever before—perhaps 10 to 20 percent of the populace is now involved in public decision making in some manner, compared to 1 or 2 percent only a decade ago—and any candidate should encourage volunteers to join his or her campaign. They can be recruited by the candidate, by the campaign area chairmen, and by other campaign workers during the course of their petitioning and canvassing (see pp. 55-63) or at kaffeeklatches or other small gatherings

---

*College students were the mainstay of these volunteers. Today, politics seems to have turned many students off; they are more concerned with the problems of getting a job, which, in today's very competitive environment, requires good grades. There are still, however, exceptional candidates who can inspire young people and so can develop a spirited, energetic, and motivated group of volunteers.

(see p. 31). If you are interested in recruiting volunteers, lists of prospective workers can be borrowed from your political party headquarters,
from local political clubs with which you are associated, from the previous
campaign files of elected officials with whom you are friendly, from
women's and men's clubs, and from civic and religious organizations.
Many older women, in particular, seem to enjoy political campaigning.
Your canvassers and other possible recruiters should carry with them
3 x 5 cards on which they can enter the names, addresses, and telephone
numbers of people who are interested in working for you.* Figure 1-2
shows what the cards should look like.

In smaller campaigns, volunteers can be crucial, and even in major
campaigns they can play a critical role. But you should know exactly
how to use them— both for your sake and for theirs. I have seen volunteers
used in demeaning ways—doing "make-work," for example, so that the
campaign headquarters looks busy, or sitting around waiting for someone
to tell them what to do. Such activities cannot possibly benefit your
campaign and may actually harm it, either by taking the attention of your
regular staff away from more important work or by alienating the
volunteers.

```
Name: _____

Address: _____     Telephone: _____

                                     I'll have time to work
                                     on these days from _____
  I have                 I'd like         _____ to _____
  done                   to do

  ____ Bookkeeping       ____       Sunday      ____ to ____
  ____ Filing            ____       Monday      ____ to ____
  ____ Publicity         ____       Tuesday     ____ to ____
  ____ Reception work    ____       Wednesday   ____ to ____
  ____ Research          ____       Thursday    ____ to ____
  ____ Shorthand         ____       Friday      ____ to ____
  ____ Typing            ____       Saturday    ____ to ____
  ____ Canvassing        ____
  ____ Petitioning       ____
  ____ Telephoning       ____       Primary Day ____ to ____
  ____ Other             ____       Election Day ____ to ____
```

Fig. 1-2. Example of volunteers' recruiting card.

*When a campaign uses a phone bank operation, it is usual to ask enthusiastic supporters if they
would care to volunteer.

Volunteers can usefully serve many campaign functions, including:

- Distributing or "stuffing"* literature.
- Organizing kaffeeklatches or small money-raising events.
- Accompanying you on walking tours.
- Gathering petition signatures.
- Canvassing (proselytizing voters door to door).
- Checking and binding petitions.
- Challenging opponent's petitions (a time-consuming job that entails checking individual voters' registrations and signatures at the local board of elections).
- Telephoning voters to discuss you and your views.
- Researching census and related data covering the district.
- Researching past voting patterns in the district.
- Preparing voter cards and lists.
- Conducting personal or telephone research interviews.
- Setting up street stands for literature distribution.
- In primary elections, identifying persons who actually voted in previous primaries by checking the records of past elections at the board of elections.
- "Pulling" on election day by telephone and household canvass.
- Poll watching on election day.
- Providing transportation to the polls for the elderly and infirm.
- Manning loudspeaker trucks and bullhorns.
- Putting up posters (and often tearing the opponent's down).
- Typing correspondence.
- Filing.
- Bookkeeping.
- Manning the office to take calls and answer questions.
- Recruiting other volunteers.

Most of the functions are discussed in detail in the following chapters. It should be emphasized that for many of these functions the presence of experienced professionals is advisable, especially for the more sensitive and difficult tasks, which include conducting research interviews and

---

*"Stuffing" describes the activity of putting brochures under each door or in each mailbox in an area.

answering inquiries. But many candidates can't afford to retain paid consultants for every function. If you are in this situation and you have no option but to use volunteers, be sure to give them specific directions and careful supervision.

THE CAMPAIGN MANAGER

Your campaign manager will probably have to work full time—and more— and, unless you've promised him or her a job once you are elected, will expect to be paid professionally. Fees as high as $3,000 to 4,000 a week plus expenses have been reported. (When I started in politics in 1960, campaign managers in congressional campaigns were happy to get $100 a week plus expenses.) For smaller campaigns, managerial fees will often consist of expenses and the promise of a future job.

Some experienced politicians believe that a good manager can account for 10 percent of the total vote, depending, of course, on the competence of the opponent's campaign manager. In 1981, when Elizabeth Holtzman, a well-known Congresswoman (New York), who had run for the U.S. Senate and lost, announced that she would run for District Attorney of Kings County against the unknown Norman Rosen, many politicians offered 20 to 1 odds and even 50 to 1 odds that she would win. When it was later announced that Walter Diamond, a seasoned and creative manager, would do the Rosen campaign, the odds plummeted to 5 to 1. The message should be clear: get the best manager you can. This doesn't mean the most expensive; creativity and administrative ability are what you need. Honesty is also very nice.

But you can't go into the job market looking for a full-time campaign manager. Some successful ones are business or professional colleagues or relatives of their candidates. Mario Cuomo's successful race for Governor of New York in 1982 was managed in large part by his 24-year-old son. Managers can also be supplied by your party's political leadership, who assign one of their professional staff. Congressmen often use an A.A., an administrative assistant.

Ideally, you want someone who is politically experienced, loyal, and equipped to raise funds and to represent you in important and critical negotiations; who can work sixteen hours a day six or seven days a week and will charge you only expenses; who is brilliantly sensitive to the opportunities that present themselves in campaigns; who can analyze

10,000 pieces of election data and find exactly what you have to know; who can draw other good people to work for you; who is completely honest and beyond party or press criticism; who will make no demands on you after you win; who can handle problems rapidly and well without troubling you; who can write speeches, keep financial records, read all the papers, and see and hear all the TV and radio reports about the campaign; and whom your wife, family, and contributors will love. That is what you want and need, but you're not likely to find it.

As soon as you decide to run, start inquiring about prospective campaign managers in journalistic, academic, and political circles. City hall reporters may suggest people who could help you; professors of political science, law, or sociology may have competent colleagues or students. Other sources of leads are political leaders in your own party or even friends in the opposing party. (There is a surprising amount of camaraderie among political mechanics, regardless of their registration, and they do cross party lines from time to time to work for candidates of another party.)

The choice of a campaign manager is critical. He spends your money and allocates your time. There are many smooth, confident, and persuasive talkers around who know the ball game but are without imagination, courage, or intellectual honesty, let alone modesty. You won't get a good man for nothing. Politics is no different from any other profession, and competent altruism is a special taste—a minority predilection.

If you intend to provide the creative direction of the campaign yourself, you may want a campaign manager who is strong in administrative talents. If you expect to go heavily into television, you probably want someone who has a reputation and experience in that area. If you're planning a campaign geared to issues, you may want a professor or academically oriented man, although you'll find few politicians who will recommend this course, since the concepts of political theory have little in common with the specifics a campaign manager must contend with. Don't worry too much about what other politicians may think—you have to pick a manager whom you can trust to spend your money and represent your best interests. It has to be someone you're comfortable with both intellectually and emotionally. The "vibrations" had better be good, because you and your manager are going to be married to each other for several months, living through the genial and ugly terrors and the constant turmoil of campaigning, and your eccentricities had better be mutually compatible.

Most first-time candidates are best off with an intelligent personal friend as manager, if he has sufficient time for all that the job entails. There is a natural temptation in campaigns involving substantial investments of time and money to assume that only the most seasoned managers can do the job . This is not always the case. Some very good men are emotionally unstable, some are too demanding in the event of a victory, some take kickbacks, some feel they have to go the "safe" way—to do only what is expected and what had been done in the past. A politically sensitive friend or colleague, devoted to your interests, someone with whom you can discuss things honestly and openly, can often do the job better and may well be your best campaign manager.

In a recent statewide campaign, one candidate, an experienced politician with a brilliant and loyal personal staff, felt obliged to go outside for his top people because he felt that his own staff members weren't up to the job in such a major race. In retrospect, it is clear that his experienced assistants understood his needs better than the campaign manager he chose, although the manager was a practiced and highly regarded campaigner. Some mistakes were made during the campaign that probably cost him the election. (In fairness, there is no way of knowing whether the outcome would have been different had he used his own people.)

According to some politicians, campaign managers and candidates are natural enemies. On the one hand, candidates often feel that their managers presume too much and take prerogatives no one ever gave them. When they see money flow out for expenses no one bothered to mention in advance, many candidates think the manager is padding the bill or arranging kickbacks; and, as a matter of fact, both practices are probably as common in political campaigns as in business affairs generally. On the other hand, many managers consider their candidates unappreciative of the energy, initiative, and dedication they pour into the campaign. At times, both may be right in their condemnation of the other. This natural enmity may be based on considerations of ego or just people under very great pressure all the time getting in each other's way and second-guessing each other constantly.

Many candidates feel an overwhelming need to be their own managers. That is seldom wise. Usually the candidate is too busy literally running to become involved in the minutiae of the campaign. (In England, politicians "stand" for election. In the United States, politicians "run" for election—and that is exactly what they do.)

There is another important reason why the candidate should completely discount the idea of being his or her own campaign manager. If you are running for office, each campaign is of critical importance to you, and you cannot expect yourself to se the race clearly. Mario Procaccino, running against John Lindsay for Mayor of New York in 1969, couldn't conceive of the possibility of losing, since he received such a warm reception on the streets wherever he campaigned. Since the polls showed him way ahead for so long, he refused to believe advisors who told him voter sentiments were starting to change. The principals in a political campaign clearly can't be expected to have an objective overview of how the campaign is going and what still needs to be done. The basic policy direction of your campaign should come from you, perhaps in consultation with your family, contributors, and close friends and personal advisors, but implementation should be completely in the hands of your manager. If you really want to manage a campaign, your best course may well be to resign your own candidacy and find another candidate to manage.

In many campaigns, managers make basic policy decisions for candidates and initiate major public pronouncements. This should be avoided except in emergencies. The manager is not running for office (although some managers do use their candidates as surrogates for their private ambitions), and only the candidate must ultimately live with the policies enunciated in the course of the campaign.

Many managers can dazzle an inexperienced candidate with the arcane details of a campaign, so that the normal response is, "OK, you take care of it—but don't spend too much." It is much better for a candidate, before entering the race, to make a quiet, reasoned inquiry into what is involved, what can be expected to be obtained for the money spent, which expenditures are mandatory, and which expenditures are discretionary. *Before your campaign,* you should familiarize yourself with the costs of such things as advertisements in local newspapers, 30-second TV commercials, giveaways, mailing 25,000 pieces, preparing 10,000 brochures, so that you can plan at least an outline of campaign strategy and required disbursements.

Some candidates feel they must be involved in every aspect of the campaign. That is exhausting and largely unnecessary. Once you appoint your campaign manager and define the responsibilities of the job and their limits (indicating which decisions must be reserved for your approval), let him or her get on with the job. Make your appraisal of the manager's capacity within 3 to 4 weeks; if by that time you are not confident of his or her skills, or don't like the way things are being done, get a new manager. Many campaigns have been lost by the failure to do this. Frequently, when candidates lose confidence in a manager, instead of replacing him or her, they appoint a coordinator or executive assistant who gradually preempts the manager's prerogatives. This is bad for staff morale and leads to conflicts and subversion of decisions, none of which benefits the campaign. The basic rule is that only one man can be in charge.

OTHER PAID STAFF MEMBERS

One of your first staff appointments will be a secretary to cover the office in the early stages of the campaign, take calls, keep files, and handle appointments. Many candidates take secretaries from their professional or business practice or ask their spouses to do the job. In a smaller campaign, either one of these courses is acceptable, if your business or family life won't suffer. In a tough campaign, when fourteen hours a day, seven days a week of work may not be uncommon, someone conditioned to political campaigning may be a better choice—someone from a political club, perhaps, or a volunteer who seems competent and strong, or the friend of a friend in politics.

Recruiting other staff members involves personal recommendations of people whose abilities you value; referrals from political allies; and your own observation of club workers whose honesty and ability are known to you. Putting together a group that can work well with you is the first requirement, but almost as important is their ability to work well together. This takes some doing; if each of your personal staff is busy trying to make points with you, the overall interests of the campaign may be sacrificed in the process.

OUTSIDE CONSULTANTS

According to an experienced New York politician, every candidate in a major campaign ultimately panics in one way or another:

> If they have money, they try to buy security by hiring all the expert advice they can. They're faddish, like mutual fund managers: they buy whoever was

hot last year. Very few candidates know exactly what they want and who the best consultant is to do it. The consultants are in business, you know, and politics is very seasonal—they have to make their money, and some are really thieves. But the good ones are more than worth their money—you just have to make sure you pick the good ones, and for the services *you* really need, not those *they* think you need.

Both the amount of money involved and their potential impact on the outcome of the election render the selection of outside consultants in larger campaigns very important. The basic rule in choosing outside consultants is to determine right at the start precisely which services you need, and to do your shopping early. The candidate should make the time to interview possible consultants personally.

My advice is to select one good consultant in a field that you and your staff are familiar with and check him or her out thoroughly. Talk to the consultant's technicians about exactly what has to be done and how they intend to do it, and do not hesitate to ask for detailed explanations of technical terms even if you think you may sound naive. (Such questions are far from foolish and should be asked.) Professionals of quality are happy to discuss their work with potential clients, and, as in other fields, the good ones are usually enthusiastic about what they do. Questions about price and payment schedules should be discussed equally openly. Most consultants will require a good deal of upfront money.

Once you've invested your time in searching for and hiring one specialist, ask him or her to recommend a number of specialists in other aspects of campaigning. Ask for client lists and a brief work proposal. After talking to previous clients and reviewing proposals, make your selection; keep in mind that price doesn't always correlate with quality.

Consultants may include the following:

An *advertising agency* can write copy, develop themes, work up radio and television commercials, buy space and time, etc. To choose an advertising agency, check those in your community first. Which have had political experience and are well-regarded by other politicians? Which agencies specialize in the media you wish to emphasize—television, newspapers, or radio? The agency that is best for you will not necessarily be one that has a lot of political campaign experience. An innovative agency that is willing to assign a creative team to your campaign may be better for you than a more conventional agency that may invest only a minimum of creative energy on your behalf. The agency must have an advertising style with which you can feel at home. For example, a famous television advertisement for an oral antiseptic hit the product's weakest point, its bad taste, and made that its selling focus. You may like this approach, but you may not.

The approach of the agency should be consonant with the rest of your campaign. If you are running for a judicial post, you will not want an advertising agency that specializes in psychedelic graphics. If an appropriate agency is not available in your locality, you may hear of someone in the area who does this sort of work on a freelance basis. If not, you may have to shop for an agency in a larger city. Agencies throughout the United States are listed (with their personnel and clients) in the *Standard Directory of Advertising Agencies,* available at many public libraries or by mail from the publisher, National Register Publishing Company, 5201 Orchard Road, Skokie, Illinois 60076. Another useful publication is a booklet, "Political Campaign Advertising and Advertising Agencies," available from the American Association of Advertising Agencies, 200 Park Avenue, New York, N.Y. 10017.

In all but the smallest neighborhood campaigns, you will surely need a *printer,* who should be selected with the assistance of your staff. There are differences among printers, not only in prices but also in quality of work and—most important in tightly timed elections—in reliability.* Missing a deadline by a week or ten days can destroy a brochure's effectiveness and negate the energies and monies invested in preparing and distributing it. Finally, in choosing a printer, in order to avoid arousing the antagonism of organized labor, you will want to use only a union printer and include the printer's union "bug," or stamp, somewhere on each piece of literature.

Your advertising agency, if you have one, may have an established relationship with a printer. Whether or not this is the case, you should interview a number of printers, inspecting samples of their work and asking for the names of local clients. Check with their clients to learn whether they were satisfied with both the quality of the work and the printer's ability to meet deadlines. Political clients of prospective printers may be particularly helpful to you in this regard.

---

*Some campaigns use "jobbers" who work with a number of printers and who can offer lower prices; often relationships with jobbers can be less than satisfactory in meeting tight deadlines. My advice is to get a quality printer and stick with it; it's well worth the additional cost, in my experience.

If you decide to use the printer recommended by your advertising agency—and sometimes you may feel you have no choice but to do so—they agency will probably receive a percentage of your printing bill from the printer, a common business practice called the "finder's fee." If you are able to deal directly with the printer, you may be able to get the price reduced by the amount—probably 5 to 10 percent of your total bill—which the printer would otherwise give to the agency that referred you.

For a *radio-television consultant* you may want one of the well-publicized hotshots, or you may get a local person. If you have a personal contact with an advertising agency, you may not need a separate radio-TV specialist. If not, and you see something on television that you especially like, call the station, find out which agency did the ad, try to trace the person who did it, and get in touch with him or her. This person may be willing to take a three-week leave of absence to do a job for you. (Some agencies stay out of campaign work and prefer to have any political work in which their staff members are involved done on a freelance basis.)

Novelty specialists are agencies or companies that handle giveaway items such as balloons, matchbooks, rulers, and ballpoint pens. You might try premium houses that work with advertisers; but I feel that you really shouldn't spend much time or money on such items. Except for shopping bags, which serve as walking posters, giveaways are generally nonproductive unless you can come up with something genuinely new and useful that will attract favorable public attention. Buttons are expensive and largely ineffective in producing new votes. In local campaigns, I would recommend your buying perhaps 200 or 300 buttons for your children, friends, and workers. Anything more would be wasteful. On election day, special buttons are sometimes given to staff to gain access to campaign headquarters and to identify those who are newcomers to the regular staff.

Other politicians will usually tell you who supplied their buttons and shopping bags; these suppliers will be able to lead you to other novelty merchants if they themselves cannot provide the products you desire. As in the case of printers, it is best to deal with novelty specialists directly rather than through your advertising agency, since the agency may expect to receive, as an additional fee, a percentage of the price you pay, and that may result in your paying a higher price for the novelties. The overall problem of giveaways is treated more fully on pp. 229-231.

In a smaller campaign, you probably won't need a professional *speech writer* at all. In that case, write a basic speech and try it out on your friends and colleagues. Then use it in kaffeeklatches and smaller gatherings before attempting it in front of a larger audience. Try not to sound pompous, and use a style you're comfortable with—don't mouth phrases you don't believe or care about, or that aren't natural to you. Keep your speeches short—ten minutes or so.

Senator Hubert H. Humphrey, in his presidential campaigns, was constantly criticized for speaking twice as long as the audience's attention span lasted. The joy of having a captive audience is great, but don't talk longer than you need to. Any time you speak in public, extemporize as much as possible, or at least appear to do so.

In larger campaigns, however, you may need a professional speech writer. Ask local political reporters whose political speeches they think highly of, and who wrote them. Interview the speech writers and consider whether your political sympathies and concerns are close enough so that they can understand your views and help communicate them effectively to the electorate. You might meet potential speech writers in the academic community by asking a supporter with connections at a local university to arrange to introduce you to politically oriented faculty members and graduate students whose ideas are compatible with yours. When you talk with them, you can judge which people may be interested in working for you and which have a style and philosophy consistent with your own. Unless you have previously heard or read speeches written by someone whom you are interested in hiring, start out by commissioning one relatively minor speech for him or her. If you are comfortable delivering that speech and it is well-received by the audience, you will feel confident entrusting more important speeches to that writer. Other potential sources for speech writers are the public relations departments of large corporations.

Survey specialists, whose services are discussed in detail in the advertising and research sections of this book, may surprise you with the magnitude of their price per interview, but keep in mind that good sampling can be done with no more than a few hundred interviews for a large area. Among the nationally famous pollsters are: Hugh Schwartz, National Opinion Research Center, William Hamilton, Peter Hart, Robert Teeter, Richard Wirthlin, and Arthur Finkelstein. Small firms that are somewhat less prestigious and probably less expensive may be as good or better for local candidates than more widely known ones, since your account is more likely to be personally handled by a principal in a smaller firm.

Many survey firms are reliable, but some are not, some are incompetent, and some are simply thieves. In considering any survey firm, you should interview both the principals and the technicians who would actually do the job, examine their work, and talk to a number of their earlier clients—not so much because of the amount of money involved as because their performance will contribute significantly to campaign strategy and will influence every critical decision you'll make.

In medium- to large-scale campaigns, your choice of a *computer firm* can be extremely important because a good computer service company can greatly increase your campaign's effectiveness or can significantly waste your money and time. Most of these firms—conventionally referred to as "houses"—are small service bureaus. Your computer house's integrity and sensitivity to your research requirements (in the event that you do your own surveys) will provide the context for much of your thinking in relation to the electorate and for many of your specific decisions on allocating your resources. Good houses will allow the political logic of your campaign to guide them in what they do for you, while lesser quality firms may simply manipulate data, often in ways that achieve only minimal results. Sending out thousands of computer letters generates a lot of activity and income for them. Many houses will simply be happy to send out letters to whomever you want. Good computer technicians, on the other hand, will question you closely on which groups should get which letters.

There are advantages to dealing with a computer firm that has a political mechanic on its staff. Only a few do. Even the best computer people know very little about campaigning, although they can talk knowingly. The best bet is a political technician who knows computer capabilities.

Many computer firms handling political advertising accounts are merely "list brokers"—they buy or develop lists and send out mailings for candidates as a purely mechanical process. The mailings are usually of limited utility, possibly because they are sent to the wrong people and run the danger of creating neutral or even negative impacts. (In 1972, for example, in a classic case, it was rumored that hundreds of thousands of computer letters intended for voters in Oregon were sent instead to Illinois residents because the firm used the wrong tape and no one bothered to check.) On the other hand, a creative house can contribute very substantially to campaigns.

In retaining computer service consultants, you should look for these characteristics:

1. *Reliability.* Do they deliver exactly what is required on time? Mistakes require reruns, whose cost is passed on to the candidate, since most firms charge their clients per hour of computer use. Since timing is so critical in campaigns, a computer mistake or delays that cause a mailing to go out late can seriously limit its impact.

2. *Political experience.* The firm's principals should have been involved in campaigns conceptually as well as mechanically. They should know how strategy is formed, the limits of mailing effectiveness, how to determine which client groups are crucial, how to develop ethnic-select lists, and how to find the raw data and make it useful for you.* Unless they've been through a campaign from beginning to end, they won't be able to contribute creatively to yours.

3. *Innovational capacity.* There should be some evidence that the firm can handle each situation on an individual basis, and not simply repeat what they or someone else did in a previous campaign. You must make this judgment on your impression of the principals of the firm and the professional assigned to your campaign, as well as on past performance. Much of their value will depend on the rapport you establish with them. If you have doubts, the probabilities are that the doubts will be a self-fulfilling prophecy.

4. *Technical capacity.* In a fair-sized campaign, the firm should have an IBM 370 or similar equipment. It should have access to another computer in the event of breakdown or super, massive rush jobs.

5. *Competitive pricing.* Prices should be established with precision—whether costs for computer mailings will include envelope stuffing and labeling and bagging for delivery to the post office, whether a printout will be provided in addition to cards, labels, and/or letters, and so on.

In many smaller areas, only one competent, reliable firm is usually available to perform a given service, and that firm may already have

---

*The concept of client groups is discussed on p. 39-41. Ethnic-select lists—voter lists broken down by ethnic or other basic characteristics—are discussed on p. 224.

agreed to handle your opponent by the time you approach it. That happened in a major congressional race in New York City, when a highly specialized computer firm informed each candidate that it was handling both accounts. One executive handled one candidate, while another handled his opponent. You should agree to such an arrangement only if you have full confidence in the firm's professional integrity.*

A *telephone specialist* is almost a necessity if you intend to make over 10,000 calls. Check the charges and list of past clients, as well as the principals' operating philosophy and technical background, for each firm you consider. There are local telephone advertising firms in most parts of the country, but there may or may not be one in your area that is experienced in political work, a factor to be considered. If no politician you know can recommend a good firm, look for telephone research and marketing specialists under "Market Research" in your classified telephone book. Or, since major advertising agencies hire these firms, you can get recommendations by talking with friends in the advertising business. You are likely to get the best results, however, by asking other candidates and politicians about the consultants and processes they have used: Did they make much difference in the campaigns in which they were involved? Was there a higher turnout than expected? Was the vote in the areas called significantly higher than that anticipated by the polls or than that in areas not called? Did they actually make all the calls they contracted for? Did they permit validation of calls? Did they make "I.D." (identifying favorables) or issue or pseudo research calls? The answers to these questions should enable you to pick a consultant that justifies its costs.

As in any professional relationship, once you decide to hire a consultant, you should be certain that the contract stipulates exactly what is to be provided and when. Have an experienced political attorney review proposed contract specifications carefully. Most telephone consultants will charge you a flat fee per call, which includes an unspecified profit for them. Some may also be willing to accept an arrangement whereby you pay all costs directly, paying them either a percentage of the costs or a consulting fee. Few consultants will be willing to advance you credit.

---

*Situations like this are practicable for data processing, but usually impossible for research survey and advertising firms, since their functions require a more partisan involvement by the firm's principals. In such cases, you may have to go outside your own locality to shop for a consultant.

That is not unreasonable, since political finance committees disband instantly at the end of the campaign, and often no one is available to take fiscal responsibility after election day. Because of the poor payment record of many politicians, most consultants require 50 percent of the contract total on signing, 25 percent during the campaign, and the final 25 percent shortly before the election.

CONCLUDING NOTE ON CONSULTANT SELECTION.   Choosing consultants in the last decade has become perhaps the most troublesome problem for new campaigners, and indeed even for experienced ones. Consulting charges and the relatively exotic techniques used are offputting to many candidates. Many are afraid of not sounding knowledgeable or politically sophisticated; others don't really see the relevance of consultants but feel they have to retain them for the sake of face. Today, even relatively small-scale campaigns use consultants in order to be competitive and to buy a certain credibility with the press, fellow politicians, and, very importantly, contributors. Very basic questions are where do you look for them, and how do you know when you're getting fair value? Lists of reliable consultants are generally not easy to come by in smaller areas; there exists no consumers' guide to help select political consultants in each area of the country.

In addition to the sources that I've described earlier, the most complete lists are those available from the Republican and Democratic National Committees in Washington, D.C. The address of the RNC is 310 First St., S.E., 20003; the DNC is located at 1625 Massachusetts Ave., N.W., 20036. These lists contain the names of consultants by specialty and by state. Some past clients are listed, as are the percents of their work by political party. (Today many consultants work both parties. There is nothing particularly immoral about this as long as there is some compatibility on ideology. Some consultants specialize in conservative candidates of both parties, some like myself prefer to work with candidates representing the two major parties' progressive elements.) These lists have an important limitation. The inclusion of a firm does not mean that the Committee is recommending its quality, reliability, and competitive pricing, or suitability for your specific campaign needs. But if you obtain these lists early and combine them with the names you have gathered from the sources I've described earlier (political reporters, colleagues, major contributors, sympathetic PACs, and special interest groups), you should have a very good beginning.

In larger states it is usual for the parties to employ full-time political mechanics, under varying titles, to assist members of the state legislature in their campaigns and with their public relations problems. The offices of the state party chairmen should be able to put you in touch with these professionals who can in turn make recommendations to you. Party leaders in the large cities in your state will also be able to make recommendations. But you should be cautious with those officials who may tell you that they themselves are available at the usual professional fees to do consulting. Similarly, just because party officials recommend someone does not mean that you should suspend the same objective and practical evaluating criteria that you would apply to any other consulting service. Sometimes these recommendations are forms of political contracts, and once committed you will find it very difficult to remedy errors and pull out of the situation gracefully.

Write or call the consultants that interest you. Tell them as precisely as you can what services you are interested in and when you will need them. Ask them to send you their brochures describing their services, their clients, their prices, and the experience and education of the key staff members. You should request a work proposal specifying what they recommend doing and the cost of each service and the turnaround time for each work component. Keep in mind that consultants frequently will give potential clients a full package price assuming that you will negotiate from that base. In a recent campaign, for example, I was startled by the chutzpah of a local consultant specializing in mail (it later developed that he actually jobbed his work to other suppliers and simply added on a whopping fee) suggesting a mail budget of $50,000 when his information was that the entire campaign was scaled at $55,000.

Invite the firms and freelancers whose proposals, prices, backgrounds, and recommendations suggest a decent professional quality, appropriate experience and the absence of an unseemly greed to come in for an interview. Ask to see the principals and staff members who would actually be doing your campaign if selected. If they are located a good distance away it is probably preferable to offer to pay expenses so that your sense of obligation is limited. Alternatively, and the course I would recommend, offer that you and your manager will meet them in their offices, giving you the chance at first hand to evaluate their business and to talk to their specialists and subcontractors. Today, consultants commonly use subcontractors whose quality and reliability are as important as the consultants'. Establish during the interview which candidates they are representing now and how many additional candidates they expect to be handling during the election period. (Many consultants sell first and then staff when a cash flow is assured; you want to make sure that experienced staff is available for the work you're paying for and ready for you when you need it and not when the consultant's schedule permits.) Find out what happened in their previous campaigns, which approaches were used, why they think some worked and some didn't. Always ask to see samples of their work. In these interviews be aware that political consultants in one way or the other are in the business of hype; they are not above using the same skills in selling potential clients.

When you get home you may want to review your reactions with local consultants or political mechanics whom you can retain for a modest fee. This type of second review requires consultants not linked in directly with the major network of consultancies so that an objective independence is possible.

Start the selection process early and make enough time available so that you can consider alternatives realistically.

CAMPAIGN VOYEURS

Try to minimize the time you spend with the campaign buffs who hand around headquarters. If you win, they may think that they helped and expect you to feel a sense of obligation to them. If you lose, they can always say, "Well, he didn't want to listen to me when I warned him that . . . "

Many of these "sometime mavens" have participated in so many political discussions that at times they sound quite profound.* Use any of their ideas that seem to you to be sensible, but bear in mind that most of them have never invested anything in a campaign except talk. These campaign voyeurs are harmless, except that they will take as much of your and your campaign workers' time as you will allow them. One tactic is simply to make a policy of allowing only those with business to transact into campaign headquarters.

---

*"Maven," a Yiddish word meaning an informed or expert person, is often applied sarcastically, as in this case. Almost everyone in a campaign thinks of himself as a maven; this can cause a lot of problems in campaigning.

Unfortunately, your friends and relatives may be among those who enjoy this role. If you make an exception for your intimates at campaign headquarters, you will find it hard to deny the others.

BUDGETING

That additional money is often regarded as the only solution to problems in government programs may in considerable part originate from campaign practices, where "more" is the usual operative strategy. Many candidates and their managers regard more money and more workers as the only solution for campaign problems. Although sufficient monies are indeed critical for basic expenses—overhead, salaries, mailings, and promotion—large additional expenditures that fall outside the overall campaign strategy may simply deceive the candidate into believing that everything that can be done is being done, while, in truth, the results of this additional spending may be all but negligible.

You must remember throughout every campaign that many voters make up their minds quite early and that their voting decisions are controlled largely by their predispositions rather than by anything said or done in the campaign. Perhaps only 10 percent of this relatively large group will ever change their minds—and as many as change to you will probably change from you. The best you can really expect is a split. It is to the undecided vote of 20 to 30 percent, then, that you must direct a major portion of your energies and your funds. For this reason, expenditures for saturation mailings, billboards, and posters are not sensible investments, since they are directed at everyone, including the 70 or 80 percent who have already made up their minds. Marginal increment analysis—the practice of evaluating the probable practical effects of any proposed additional expenditure—is as important in campaigning as in business. This technique cannot always be practiced in campaigns with precision, but even roughly applied, it may save you significant sums of money that might better be used elsewhere. For example, mailing only to areas where the outlook is promising is a much more efficient use of funds than a saturation mailing to every voter in a district.

For another illustration, take the question of deciding among various types of visual material. The choices may be:

- Five painted outdoor signs for clubhouses: $2,500.
- Ten billboards throughout the district: $10,000 (including preparation, space rental, etc.).
- One thousand posters: $1,000 (design, putting up).
- Ten thousand car stickers: $2,000 (design, printing, distribution).
- Ten thousand general-purpose stickers: $1,000 (design, printing, putting up).

Separately, none of these may seem particularly expensive, but combined they add up to $16,500, a significant amount.

In most campaigns, what happens is that the policy group and/or the manager decides at first that the billboards at key locations are important, since they've heard via the grapevine that these locations are already being considered by the opponents. (Information on strategy and tactics—much of it erroneous—generally flows from one candidate's group to another and is a main topic of conversation over drinks during most campaigns.) No one is likely to ask how effective the billboards are, how many people will be reached, and how many votes will be changed. If these questions do come up, the response usually is that billboards have been put up in every campaign for as long as anyone in the district can remember and that therefore they must be effective. That may have been true in the past, but the expenses of campaigning are much higher today and the technological alternatives are altogether different. Because there is no scientific evidence for evaluating the impact of each of the campaign media, it is natural to rely on mechanisms that apparently have worked in the past. *You must learn to avoid this habit.* If you think the choices through, you will probably change your emphasis and save money, since the impact per $1,000 invested clearly will be greater from one or two thoughtfully planned visual promotions than from indiscriminate saturation. The following table illustrates this point.

ITEM	COST	ESTIMATED NUMBER REACHED	COST PER VOTER REACHED
Clubhouse signs (5)	$ 2,500	5,000	$0.50
Billboards (10)	$10,000	10,000	$1.00
Posters (1,000)	$ 1,000	10,000	$ .10
Car Stickers (10,000)	$ 2,000	10,000	$ .20
General Stickers (10,000)	$ 1,000	15,000	$ .07
Shopping bags (1,750)	$ 1,750	5,000	$ .35

(The figures in this table arc rough estimates, and costs will vary from place to place. Traffic and pedestrian counts for various street corners, often available from city traffic departments, will assist you in judging the number of people who may be reached by signs, billboards, or posters. There is no scientific way to judge the number of people reached by stickers, but you or your manager should be able to come up with a reasoned estimate based on your knowledge of the community.)*

In an area containing 50,000 registered voters, the distribution may approximate that shown in the table above. All of the types of visual media listed in the table are probably effective with the same segment of the voting public, so to buy all of them, as is common in many campaigns, does not make good fiscal sense. If you feel you must buy any, keep in mind that car stickers advertise the campaign quite cheaply and are not offensive. They will not change many votes, but they will give the people who like your candidacy a chance to feel they are contributing to it, thereby reinforcing their vote at little cost. With conspicuous billboards or multitudinous posters, however, as with loudspeaker trucks, mass mailings, and stickers posted indiscriminately on mail boxes and telephone poles, you run the risk of irritating citizens and losing votes, including those of the important undecided bloc.

This approach to decisions on expenditures for visual media has wide application; for every significant expenditure you should consider alternatives and try to evaluate the impact of the various options. In many campaigns the temptation is very strong, after investing in billboards, for example, to respond to a campaign worker's plea for stickers for his district and then accede to a club's demand for a sign so that its candidates may be advertised at your expense. You cannot altogether dismiss the goodwill that these expenditures probably buy, but the object is to win, and the goodwill of club officials alone will not produce all the votes necessary. Generally, you are better off focusing your expenditures on potentially receptive voters.

I am often struck by the fact that many major budget decisions are made without the benefit of any objective research. Polls are common in

---

*Bumper stickers and buttons are much beloved by candidates who often believe that they are the most effective, almost magical mechanisms in smaller campaigns to get "name recognition." My experience suggests that this is one of the many myths of campaigning that originated in another era of campaigning and is believed because no one bothers to think about it, and because there are visible "results" for the money spent.

campaigning, but few candidates and managers seem to base their advertising commitments on research showing the impact of different media. If you are having a sample poll conducted by professionals, it may repay you to try to establish which investments in media seem to be most effective. (For sample polls, see Chapter 3.) Advertising agencies do this kind of research for commercial clients, but it is rarely done in political campaigns, partly because everything in most campaigns is conducted in a frenzy and partly because managers, intent on protecting their ignorance of how to weigh the options sensibly, tell their candidates it is unnecessary. The time for the careful analysis of options is at least six months before the campaign starts in earnest. Opportunities for quiet reflection are nonexistent once the campaign is under way. Good decisions and policies cannot be made in the confusion, panic, anger, or resentment that often prevail during the heat of the campaign. Chapter 5 offers practical suggestions.

CONTROL OF EXPENDITURES

Who authorizes expenditures is always the key question. In well-funded campaigns, my experience is that the candidate prefers to disburse everything through his personal accountant. This procedure makes for control of the money but often involves costly delays. If the budget is mapped out carefully in advance, it is preferable for the candidate to tell the manager exactly how much can be spent on a certain item and how much is available for emergencies, and then to instruct his accountant to release funds in each category as requested by the manager. To have to clear with an accountant, however, who in turn may have to clear with the candidate and contributors, does not make for a smooth operation. But since most campaign managers are not intimates of their candidates, and since substantial sums of money do change hands and kickbacks are not unheard of, a candidate should protect himself by requiring the manager to account for expenditures. A detailed weekly accounting is frequently required of those campaign managers with a large degree of control over expenditures.

Major items such as advertising, mailings, computer printouts, polls, and television and radio spots should be contracted for *in writing* early in the campaign, and the candidate's attorney and accountant should carefully check *all* contract stipulations in advance. In some campaigns, for example, media consultants receive a fee from the candidate plus a 16 percent rebate from the newspapers or radio and television stations. This can add up to a great deal of money, some of which may be saved if the consultants' contracts are written carefully.

How To Raise Money

A basic premise of this book is that the candidate who uses accurate research and devotes some time and thought to his campaign while it is still in its early stages can conduct an effective, sophisticated campaign relatively economically. Money counts, of course, but spending money is, by itself, no guarantee of victory. From my own experience, I know that a well-financed campaign can lose to a well-directed, less-well-financed one. This occurs often enough to make it worthwhile for those who are so minded to consider campaigning even if they know in advance that they cannot match their opponents' financial resources. There is ample evidence to argue that almost anyone can win and that almost any candidate, no matter how well-entrenched, can be beaten.

Incumbents have a considerable advantage over new candidates, if for no other reason than that they may have done favors for individuals and business firms. In the natural course of events, they may also have extended themselves for certain individuals, arranging introductions, helping to obtain zoning variances, getting a job for this or that one, or recommending new business loans. (The topic of patronage—of which this one aspect—is the subject of Martin and Susan Tolchin's book *To the Victor* [New York: Random House, 1971].) Often these favors are arranged "contracts," with the proviso that the recipient of the favor will buy a seat or a table at the annual testimonial dinner at $100 a plate, provide campaign workers or campaign services, pay for printing costs, or make an appropriate campaign contribution when requested.

Basically, a new candidate is selling "futures" when he or she raises funds—and a new candidate can't do anything else until an office and some discretion are obtained. The incumbent, however, is selling "nows"—things that can be done right away for his or her constituents. As long as campaigns cost what they do, these problems will exist. Not every such political contract is necessarily a personal favor against the public interest. A firm may have been waiting six months to be paid for goods the city purchased from it. If an official in the city government can see that the bill is paid relatively promptly, the public interest is not substantially harmed, yet the firm is likely to be grateful. But many political contracts do result in "favoritism" and pork barrelling involving large amounts of money, that ultimately the consumer/taxpayer pays for.

Since raising money for new candidates is difficult, a candidate should name an experienced finance (or fund-raising) chairman who has extensive contacts in the business community and among civic groups.* In larger campaigns, friends and colleagues may volunteer their services, since, if you win, you may be able to recommend them for appointments to judicial posts or to prestigious jobs (such as chairman of a commission). Many wealthy people do not desire public office but want to be involved in public affairs to satisfy their need to express themselves on public matters that they are concerned about. In smaller campaigns, you're best off asking political colleagues for the names of effective finance chairmen in past campaigns. Bankers, builders, and attorneys with contacts in the business community and with civic groups are probably your best bet. Unless they are close friends or family, you'll probably have to offer some concrete incentive—for example, your support for a judgeship or for mayor or your support for a public issue of concern to them. In an ideal situation, this chairman should organize all fund-raising events.

If a contributor wants specific assurances of "favors," the candidate, not the finance chairman, should judge the propriety of the request. Many people contribute without asking a specific favor, expecting simply to be able to speak to the candidate, if he wins the election, on matters affecting them. They expect a sympathetic ear without specific assurances.

Senator Birch Bayh (Democrat, Indiana) spoke frankly about this matter in an interview on CBS's "Face the Nation," April 20, 1972:

> Every contribution we take, I think we ask ourselves, all right, now what does this obligate you to? And in my judgment, the most it should obligate us to is to provide a forum to listen to the problems of anyone who makes a contribution. In the final analysis, I as a senator have a responsibility to listen to the problems and listen to the case of those who don't make contributions, even those who support my opponent.

---

*The critical importance of a finance chairman is exemplified in Fred L. Zimmerman's description of the activities of Eugene Wyman, who was associated with Hubert Humphrey's presidential bid in 1972. ("The Money Man," *Wall Street Journal*, New York edition, March 8, 1972, pp. 1, 13.) (The *Journal* consistently provides some of the best political reporting in the nation.)

Many candidates prefer not to beg, which fund-raising often seems to involve, and many will not trade elements of their official discretion in order to raise funds. Once New York politician I know refuses contributions in excess of $100 from any individual, on the theory that although he owes a contributor a hearing on any given problem, he does not want to incur any specific obligation beyond that. Unfortunately, this view is usually possible only in relatively small districts.

Campaign budgeting can't be done with precision. (The appendix contains a full listing of expense items that you may find helpful.) The unexpected expense can easily play havoc with your estimates. Even so, you can certainly anticipate the major expenditures: office overhead, paid staff, research, printing, mailing, radio and television time, newspaper advertisements, novelty giveaways, etc. Prepare your budget for the basic necessities and worry about the refinements later. If you find that you need $40,000 to make the race and that you can afford only $10,000, while the finance chairman thinks only another $10,000 can be raised, you may decide not to run. But if making the race means a great deal to you, you may decide to go into debt, a course many campaigners are forced to follow.

If you are a new candidate, your best sources of funds or services will include the following:

1. *Your own money.* Ask yourself some fundamental questions. How much of your family's savings are you willing to commit? Most financial advisors believe a prudent family should have one year's income in the bank for emergencies. Do you want to mortgage your home or borrow funds?

2. *Relatives.* It may be unpleasant for you to ask them for money, but close relatives will often find the idea of your running for office exciting and will want to help; they may be willing to contribute money *and* volunteer to work in your campaign. They also can interest their friends and colleagues in helping you.

3. *Friends.* The people you work with and old family friends can be surprisingly generous with their time and money. Young attorneys, with an eye perhaps on a judgeship or referrals, will often contribute, hoping for a friend in the party. People you know in civic groups may sympathize with your stands on the issues and be willing to help.

4. *Previous contributors.* An important source will be found in the list of contributors filed with the local or State Commission on Elections. If you're running for Congress, previous and current candidates' contributors are on file in the offices of the Federal Election Commission. Former contributors should be canvassed, preferably by phone and surely by mail.

5. *Cocktail parties, teas, and kaffeeklatches.* Your friends and neighbors may be willing to sponsor small gatherings (20 to 25 people) for you, with each guest contributing perhaps $10 to $25 to your campaign. You will not make a great deal of money, since you should pay for the food and liquor, but each such party can raise $100 or more, and, in addition, you will be able to discuss your views in a relaxed setting. You may gain additional workers and contributions from those voters whom you impress as a good candidate. These parties should be arranged with careful attention to such details as how much, if anything, should be charged, how many and which people should be invited, the form of the invitation, and the type of food and entertainment.*

6. *Newspaper and radio advertisements* soliciting contributions are sometimes effective if your stands on controversial issues attract certain groups. In addition to bringing in small donations, such appeals may attract rich people you might not otherwise know how to approach. (In New York City, for example, the press has reported that two millionaires, Carter Burden and Stewart Mott, have contributed hundreds of thousands of dollars to various candidates whom they did not know personally.) Advertisements of this sort tend to be costly and usually do not produce a great outpouring of money. They may, however, have beneficial side effects: Volunteers may offer their services, your campaign will be dramatized and publicized, and the idea that you have to appeal to the public for funds may be effective in getting across your honesty and independence. George McGovern used this device to great advantage during his primary campaigns in 1972. Such appeals are now common; every candidate for national office sets up a committee early and does mass mailings. (The 1983 Mondale letter is shown in Fig. 1-3.)

7. *Testimonial dinners* are a most important source of funds for both incumbents and new candidates. Your political club or a civic group in

---

*For a detailed account of how to organize kaffeeklatches on the local level and how to maximize the results, see Dick Simpson's *Winning Elections: A Handbook in Participatory Politics* (Chicago: Swallow, 1972), pp. 41-47.

Walter F. Mondale

My dear friend:

On February 21st I formally announced my decision to seek the Presidency.

I did so against a backdrop of a very troubled America and a dangerous world. The pain and suffering around us is enormous. The threat to world peace looms large. Our nation is on a reckless course which assaults both the people and the spirit of America.

That is why you and I must not delay a single moment in getting to work to alter that course.

Today, I want to do more than tell you of my commitment, I want to ask for yours. Your commitment to work with me in preventing greater suffering and in bringing a spirit of resurgence and renewal to America.

This is not just talk. It can be done. You and I know it.

We need not repeat the mistakes of the past. Our future lies not in the stars -- it lies with us. No problem this nation faces is beyond the imagination and hard work of the American people.

I learned this lesson in the most personal of ways. While growing up in the throes of the Great Depression in a small town in Minnesota. My father, a man of tough Norwegian descent lost his farm -- but not his confidence in himself or his hope for the future.

Struggling in Minnesota during the 30's and 40's I learned two principles of life which remain with me . . .

. . . With clarity of purpose, hard work and determination nothing is beyond our reach; and,

. . . In times of great hardship you don't abandon your struggling neighbor, you reach out with compassion and together survive and prosper.

These are the lessons I learned from my father and mother. And they are the lessons that came alive for me in the politics of populist Minnesota Governor Floyd Olson and my dear friend and mentor Hubert H. Humphrey.

Hubert Humphrey, Floyd Olson and my parents all spoke of the politics of hope, courage and compassion. Of being bold enough to try new ideas, even at the risk of failure. Of individual excellence in all that we do. Of fierce honesty and independence. And of compassion and fairness for those struggling alongside.

(over, please)

730 East 38th Street   Minneapolis, Minnesota 55407

Paid for by The Mondale for President Committee

Fig. 1-3. Example of a fund-raising letter (one of eight pages), Walter Mondale, 1983.

which you are an active member can sponsor such events. Dinner tickets can be $25, $50, or even $100 or more, depending on the precedent in the area. Usually a prominent politician appears as a speaker. It is advisable to supplement the speeches with entertainment (preferably entertainment that is donated)—music for dancing, a comedian, a singer, or whatever else is customary or might be well-received in your locality. In a large city, if you use a good hotel banquet room with quality food, liquor, and service, the cost may be from $25 to $35 per person, but you may raise several thousand dollars if you sell enough tickets. In a smaller community, costs, as well as proceeds, will of course be smaller. You may be able to gain additional money from a testimonial dinner by publishing a program (sometimes called a journal) in which contributors buy ads wishing you well. These devices are the chief moneymaking techniques of most experienced politicians.

In organizing a testimonial dinner or any other fund-raising affair, attention to detail is important. Many political functions literally leave a bad taste in people's mouths—the food is served cold and the wine may be bitter or the waiters indifferent or insulting. The prices normally charged for tickets to these affairs should justify a choice of quality entrees, and, since some people don't eat meat, fish should be available. The temperature of the room should be comfortable and the seating uncrowded. The microphones should be tested for the speakers and the band. The seating list should be sensitive to who is not speaking to whom, and care should be given in general to a sensible placement of guests at the tables. You may or may not want to have a published seating list, since such lists have been used by reporters to ask why a certain contributor was there and what favor was requested in return for the contribution. (The seating lists of most political dinners are filled with the names of architects, planners, attorneys, builders, union officials, and others whose work and income involve dealing with the government. Recently, such lists have been harder to come by, since they make some political relationships clearer than ticket-buyers and office-holders may wish.)

8. *Political club and/or party.* The political organization you belong to may provide some campaign funds, but generally it is still paying off debts from previous campaigns. Increasingly, the individual candidate must rely on his or her own financial resources, while the local political club may even ask the candidate for funds. The club and the county or city organization can often "contribute" experienced campaign workers,

which is a considerable help and sometimes even more important than cash. (In New York City, a political club with only ten reliable, experienced workers is generally regarded as a strong club.) The organization can also be helpful in providing expertise on when and how to file petitions, the best and most reliable printer, and other practical, important campaign matters.

9. *"Piggybacking"* is an often-used technique that involves sharing mailing and printing costs with another candidate—perhaps a better-financed one—on the party ticket. If you're running for the state legislature, for example, the party's congressional candidate can include your brochure in his or her mailing, and your only cost will be the printing of the brochure. Generally, you will be asked to provide workers or other campaign services in return for your colleague's help.*

10. *Direct-mail solicitation.* Letters soliciting contributions from voters registered in your political party are a common fund-raising device that I regard as most promising for candidates in medium- to large-scale races. Preparation, paper, copywriting, design, and postage (at the bulk rate of 9.3 cents a letter) bring the average cost of such appeals to about 20 cents a letter—and to that must be added about $35 per thousand for the commercial mailing lists that are used in most cases. To be economical and worth while, thousands of these letters must be sent out at once. In small campaigns, this method is not economical; but the principle of establishing lists of possible contributors who are likely to be receptive to your candidacy and then appealing to them for funds is a good one. Businesses and individuals who are potential contributors might be identified by going through local newspapers to see which local groups have taken positions on which issues, or by having a member of your staff check through the city commercial directory and chamber of commerce and professional association membership lists.

The financial returns from large-scale direct-mail solicitations may not always be great enough to justify the investments of time and money that they require, but since the process has the added virtue of advertising your candidacy, you may wish to make use of it anyway. The technique

---

*The term "piggybacking" is also used to describe an unethical practice in campaigning or in business generally. Some consultants, for example, set up a computer program or a telephone or other research study for one client, who pays the full rate, and then sell the same operation to other clients at reduced rates without the permission of the first client, who is not informed of the questions that are added to his research.

was used by Senator George McGovern in the winter of 1971 to raise funds for his presidential bid, and there were reports that the effort was notably successful, raising some $1.25 million.

Most commercial concerns that specialize in direct-mail fund raising charge a percentage of the total amount collected, but others charge a flat fee of 16 to 25 cents a letter, or a few cents more per letter than the cost of doing the mailing directly from the candidate's own headquarters. The additional expense may or may not be justified by increased rates of contributions. This is how the *New York Times* described the situation:

The direct-mail professionals are devoting increasing attention to writing more skillful letters for their clients and to the application of numerous technical advances that make the overall package more attractive.

Computers can scatter the individual prospect's name throughout a typed letter, and now there is even a way to produce an appeal that is faintly smudged so as to look even more like the work of a secretary.

But all these elaborate touches depend entirely on the quality of the mailing list, according to the direct-mail experts. . . .

The direct-mail experts borrow the names of contributors from some friendly politicians, or they rent the subscription lists of liberal or conservative publications at rates that average three or four cents a name. . . .

But the professional carefully records the names of those who respond to his own appeal because these he can legitimately add to his own stock and, after a suitable interval, approach again. . . .

By working in campaigns around the country and renting lists of one kind or another, he slowly begins to identify the people who are most forthcoming and, equally important, those who are least generous.*

11. *Professional fund raisers.* There are people who make their living as professional fund raisers, but their charges are generally too high—30 percent or more of the total contributions received—to be of practical value to a new campaigner.

12. *Do-gooders.* There are people in most urban communities who are truly devoted to the public interest. Very effective national campaigns on ecological problems have recently been led by private groups of such concerned citizens. Nuclear freeze and disarmament groups are springing

---

*Walter Rugaber, "Politicians Turn to Direct Mail to Bring in Campaign Funds," *The New York Times,* September 8, 1970, p. 29. See the discussion of direct mail on pp. 00-00.

up throughout the nation. They and others like them may be willing to support your candidacy, providing funds and campaign workers, if you have taken a favorable stand on their positions. Reviewing local newspapers and discussions with city hall reporters can usually provide you with a list of organizations and people with whom you should get in touch.

13. *Anti-incumbent groups.* Any incumbent is bound to incur the disapproval of some voters and some special interest groups. Reviewing the incumbent's record should give you a good idea of which people he or she is likely to have alienated. Many of these people or groups may wish to contribute to your campaign simply to get even with the incumbent. Vendettas fuel many campaigns.

14. *Local religious organizations.* In cities and in suburban areas, churches and other religious organizations that own large properties are interested in assuring that proper public services remain or become available, and they are often willing to purchase blocks of tickets for political functions or provide other support to candidates in their area.

15. *Local business organizations.* There are groups, usually business-oriented, who contribute to both sides in order to have a sure winner and therefore, they hope, a sure friend in government. It takes some research and questioning of reporters and other politicians to find out which groups make a practice of contributing to all candidates in your area, but the financial return may well make it worth the effort.

16. *Contributions in services.* Finally, you should be able to think of numerous sources for contributions in services rather than cash. The printers' union, for example, may not be willing or able to give you a cash contribution, but it may agree to provide free printing of your brochures if you provide the paper. Other unions might be willing to provide workers to distribute your material or even to mail some campaign material for you or to provide you with a phone bank and callers (a fairly common practice in large cities). If you live in a university town, you may be able to get capable graduate students to write position papers for you without charge. Your specific needs and your ingenuity will dictate other possible sources of contributions of necessary services.

A major, and sometimes controlling, source of contributions are the PACs, or Political Action Committees, which represent and lobby heavily for special interest groups. Their contributions, however, are seldom to the smaller campaigns but rather to congressional and statewide campaigns. I had occasion to see new congressional candidates from all over the country convene in Washington under the auspices of the Democratic party to meet potential PAC contributors.

PACs generally like to contribute to incumbents; newcomers have a much tougher time getting money. In this instance all the candidates had prepared handsome folders containing their resumes, accomplishments, campaign themes, and other material designed to attain credibility with the "money people." I felt the dismay these people were feeling when they realized that money would not be likely from these sources, although they had spent considerable time and trouble arranging to come in from all over the country.

For local campaigners, PACs are potential contributors if they are involved in a very special issue or when it is believed that the candidate has a very big future in politics. Washington, New York City, and Los Angeles are the centers for major contributors, both individuals and the "institutional" PACs (trade associations, single-issue groups, etc.). Local campaigners seldom have access to this critical political linkage. Newspapers in Washington frequently report the activities of newcomers who come to Washington, "hat in hand," and go from one to another, selling themselves, their issues, their personalities, their future importance. There is something very basically wrong about this. (A listing of every PAC in the country is to be found in *PAC Directory*, Cambridge, Mass.: Ballinger, 1982.)

As soon as possible after receiving a campaign contribution, make certain to acknowledge its receipt and your gratitude to the contributor in the form of a personally signed letter. This is not only common courtesy but also an inducement for the contributor to help you again later in the campaign or in a future campaign.

No one owes you a contribution just because you have decided you want to run. Many potential contributors will be discouraged if they see evidence of waste and misuse of funds in your campaign. Don't commit funds you don't have, and don't spend money on discretionary items before the basic expenses of the campaign are met. Careful spending of money is also a habit worthwhile in your term of office, should you win. Taxpayers around the country have voted down many bond issues because they have seen evidence of government waste around them. Additional money is not the solution to every problem, in political campaigns or in government. Better planning and management can go a long way in dealing with problems in campaigning *and* government.

It must be emphasized that campaign fund-raising activities and commitments made to obtain contributions may "contract" or obligate you to such an extent that your discretion in office may be severely limited. If you have too many "contracts" outstanding you may not be able to serve your own political needs or the needs of your constituency effectively. Sometimes it may be wise to turn money down, hard as that course always is, so that you retain some maneuverability as an official and as a human being.

2
Detailing

Nova's law is simple: Do it yourself, and believe no one. If you have
a commercial to send from Washington to Minneapolis, carry it to the
airport, hand it to Bill and tell him what flight to take. Run back to the
office, call Harry in Minneapolis, tell him to meet the flight, then take
a cab to the TV station, ask for Charley, and stand over Charley while
he puts the commercial on the film chain. It's the only way.

— *Barry Nova*

This chapter discusses specific campaigning details, as distinguished from
the structuring elements described in the previous chapter. Usually there
is nothing glamorous about these specifics—although advance men, for
example, may encounter hectic, tense conditions—but in many campaigns
the quality of the detailing described here makes the difference between
winning and losing.

CLIENT-GROUP ANALYSIS (TARGETING)

The most important detail is the identification and analysis of voter client
groups, for this determination will key the campaign in numerous ways
by providing the focus through which you see all options in a campaign.
These are commonly referred to as target groups, or campaign
constituencies.

Client-group analysis identifies groups of voters who are united by
feeling, attitudes on given issues, racial or religious identity, or other
relationships or opinions. The members of one client group are likely to
react to events and issues in roughly the same manner and intensity. An
ethnic minority, the elderly, welfare recipients, and parents of school-
children are examples of client groups. Nothing can save more money
and more campaigns than competently applied specific targeting analysis.
Nonetheless, it receives cursory attention in most campaigns, and only
the most brilliant, experienced, intuitive campaigners seem to use it properly. This problem is part of a considerably more general issue, the role
of research in a campaign, which is examined in detail in Chapter 3.

Here, one principle must be emphasized: No campaigner should try to make everyone a convert. Although only a completely inept or overly optimistic candidate would ever think it possible, too many primary and general election campaigns have proceeded on the singularly absurd assumption that everyone is a potential convert. Shutouts take place in baseball, not in political contests.

Once this fact is acknowledged, the critical question becomes, "Whom can you reach?" or, to put it another way, "Who is potentially sympathetic to your programs, priorities, and personality?" These are your particular client groups. Identifying these people should provide the cornerstone for your campaign, for once they are established, your allocations of time and money investments can be more effectively focused.*

Client-group analysis is used in market research, in urban planning, and in other professional fields. In political campaigns, it can determine where your potential strength is and help maximize the potential there. The data can come from two sources: past voting records (usually by geographic district) and sample surveys (showing voter attitudes by age, sex, ethnic background, party, income, and other demographic characteristics). The required research procedures and their potentials are described in Chapters 3 and 4.

At this point, a simple example may demonstrate the utility of client-group analysis. In a primary campaign involving 50,000 registered voters, perhaps 15,000 people will vote. Analysis of past primaries would suggest the likely geographic and demographic distribution of these 15,000, enabling you to tell your local workers or election district captains where they can most profitably invest their time. Instead of touring the streets of the entire area indiscriminately, you can spend most of your time in locations where the actual voters are—canvassing buildings, meeting voters at subways, bus stops, and train stations, and anticipating the issues that interest the client groups in these areas. Rather than saturating all registered voters, mailings can be selective, and telephone campaigns, focusing on areas containing most of the probable voters, can include appeals to which these groups can relate.

---

*A leading consultant, Joe Napolitan, states, "So far as I am concerned, there are only three steps to winning any election. . . . First, define the message the candidate is to communicate to the voters. Select the vehicles of communication. Third, implement the communication process." (*The Election Game*, New York: Doubleday, 1972, p. 2.) To this I would add: Decide which are your key groups of voters and design your media for them.

If your research polls are carefully designed, they will establish the characteristics and attitudes of voters in the prime areas (those with particularly heavy votes in previous elections), as differentiated from the voters in secondary areas. In some cases, your major appeals may be to women (who generally make up the majority of voters), or to certain ethnic groups, or to the young or the old.*

It is prudent to set up the client-group or targeting analysis considerably in advance of the actual campaigning, since the necessary coordination of surveys with information from experienced local workers is extremely difficult during the tense period of day-to-day campaigning.

As a practical matter, all candidates must concern themselves particularly with one client group: the undecided. Although there can be no assurance that one or two characteristics unite the members of this group, any information from surveys regarding the undecided is extremely worthwhile, for this group is worth at least one-third of your campaign funds and time.

DECISION MAKING

Important policy decisions should be made rapidly and sensibly, with provisions for good implementation and follow-through. In too many campaigns, there is never a clear definition of who makes the decisions, and the process is thereby delayed. Sometimes the decision-making group may consist of the candidate, the manager, and technical consultants. Too frequently, however, the group making the decisions may vary from day to day, based on who is around campaign headquarters, or which contributor or party representative has an interest in the matter, or who last met the candidate in the men's room. In a well-managed campaign, a policy guidance group, established early and held constant, provides continuity in overall direction as well as proper coordination of each sector of the campaign.**

---

*President Reagan's administration was considerably less popular with women than with men; published polls in 1983 started referring to the "gender gap" among voters. There was also a single-married gap. Pollsters have been aware of these differentiations for a long time, but analysis in magazines and newspapers had previously focused only on differences in voting patterns that were rural-urban, or by race and ethnic groups.

**Murray B. Levin describes this aspect of Edward M. Kennedy's senatorial campaign in Massachusetts in 1962 in *Kennedy Campaigning* (Boston: Beacon, 1966).

The composition of the policy guidance group varies from candidate to candidate and from situation to situation. Normally, however, it includes representatives of major contributors and the party in addition to the campaign manager, close friends of the candidate, and sometimes the candidate's spouse. The policy guidance group should met once a week for a general review of the campaign. In addition, it should be summoned whenever a major problem occurs. When you bring the group together to deal with a specific problem, you may wish also to include whichever consultant is involved in the problem. Today, the policy group almost automatically includes the pollster and the media consultant.

In dealing with your policy guidance group, remember that only one person can be in charge, and that person must be the candidate. Listen to everyone, but if there is disagreement, you are the one who must make the decision. The policy guidance group has an advisory function only; you must have the final say.

Robert F. Kennedy, an experienced and effective campaigner, used to say that all the big campaign decisions are made quickly, synthesizing experience and insight in a way that is not fully explainable. In politics as in personal life, the most profoundly important decisions may be made from essentially unconscious sources. An inexperienced campaigner tends to defer to his advisors who have been through this before. In part, there is absolutely no way to avoid this. But you must develop your own instincts as soon as possible; you will not always have time to think about the proper action, phrase, or strategy. Sometimes, a misguided phrase to a reporter can destroy six months of work.* It is, after all, your career, your money and energies that are at stake. If you can't develop your political instincts, you will have to go the most careful route in every situation, and your campaign staff will have to learn to guard you in a structured way, to screen you from dangerous questions and issues until a thoughtful strategy has been developed. They will have to anticipate such things as the questions that are likely to come up in a press conference, so that answers can be prepared and you won't have to extemporize. Similarly, you will always have to screen speeches with your staff and avoid speaking off the cuff unless it is absolutely necessary.

---

*For example, Senator Ted Kennedy's hesitation in a CBS interview in 1980 finished his presidential campaign hopes in the judgment of many. The question asked was the most basic: Why do you want to be President?

SCHEDULING

Scheduling is a problem in every political campaign. In many campaign offices, as the campaign gets under way, speaking engagements, meetings, and other events are entered on a giant calendar. As time passes, however, advance scheduling, while obviously sensible, becomes difficult to guarantee. Conflicts about time and place become complex; fundraising and party problems sometimes arise that must take precedence; late-breaking issues demand an immediate response. For these reasons, flexibility is necessary in scheduling.

Underlying most campaign strategies is the assumption that the more often the candidate speaks, the better, since TV news spots and the press may feature the candidate if he is making news or being interviewed. Also, many candidates believe that unless they're actually doing something or in constant motion, they're losing ground. The focus should be exposure but in a strategic way—making news and reinforcing campaign themes. The object of making campaign appearances is to get votes. In every campaign I have seen, at least 10 to 20 percent of the candidate's time has been wasted with protocol appearances at political functions, wedding receptions, or honorary dinners. These activities keep the candidate moving but can hardly be expected to produce new votes in significant numbers. There is such a thing as running too hard and in the wrong direction.

In some situations, candidates seem to think that speaking engagements with specific client groups assure the support of those groups. In a recent campaign in a predominantly Jewish area of the Bronx, one of the candidates, who later became a New York Supreme Court judge, felt that he could not lose, since his calendar showed he had an appointment to speak before each important synagogue group. He lost, and to this day he probably doesn't understand how or why.

Mario Procaccino, in his 1969 New York mayoralty campaign, provided another example of mistaken scheduling commitments. Since at the beginning of the campaign he was far ahead of John V. Lindsay, some of his advisers told Procaccino to hold his public appearances to a minimum, so that he would avoid losing votes. One commentator, perhaps facetiously, went so far as to suggest that Procaccino get sick and leave the country during the campaign. Procaccino disregarded this advice, campaigned actively, and lost the election to Lindsay. You can't always assume that more street campaigning and more speeches are more effective than selective campaigning.

Whenever possible, coordinate your scheduling with your research on probable voting patterns, the distribution of the undecided vote, and other aspects of the campaign. Similarly, if you have scheduled a speaking engagement at a community center weeks in advance, your walking tours should include that neighborhood the day before the speech. If you have a telephone campaign going, the ''message'' should go into the area in which you're speaking, with the information, if interest develops, that you'll be there at a certain time and place.

The scheduling function should rank priorities in a specific way. For example, the following list might apply to some candidates: (1) presentation of major positions in speeches and at press conferences; (2) interviews with press, radio, and television; (3) addresses to local political clubs; (4) addresses to local religious and ethnic organizations; and (5) street campaigning and door-to-door canvassing.

The proper coordination of your schedule requires both administrative talent and thorough knowledge of your research. It can come only from the campaign manager and the staff person assigned to scheduling and should never be a function of the loudest screamers or most active arm twisters on the staff or in an allied political club. Your manager should see to it that your time and energies are invested as efficiently as possible in making voters conscious of your candidacy and in motivating them to vote for you. A campaign seems like a very long time to most campaigners—it's important that your schedule allow you some rest and a day off once in a while.

ADVANCE MEN

When a circus or carnival comes to town, it is preceded by ballyhoo men who drum up interest and encourage ticket sales. In campaigning, the ballyhoo men are called advance men. Their responsibilities are many and important, but the basic purpose of their work is to stimulate public interest as well as press and television attention for the candidate. They arrange interviews with journalists, make hotel reservations, rent halls for speeches, get police permits for street rallies, try to insure turnouts for public appearances, coordinate with local party officials on such matters as who is to be invited to a function and who is not and which important contributors and potential contributors should be contacted when the candidate is in the area, and attend to myriad other details.

Advance men must see to it that all aspects of the candidate's public appearances go smoothly. Are there major events scheduled at the same time that may take away from the candidate's press and television coverage? Are public functions scheduled at hours when people are on the streets?* Are hecklers expected? If so, what type of police security is needed, and with whom must arrangements be made? What size audience can reasonably be expected? A good advance man knows that it is far better to book a small hall and fill it than to fill a large hall only half way. Will the guest list of a rally offend anyone who is important to the campaign effort? Local workers should be given the opportunity to check such lists in advance so that no such unintentional offense is committed.

Being an advance man is a full-time job in state and national races.** In local campaigns, the functions of advance men are often performed by the staff member who is responsible for the candidate's schedule or by another experienced person working under his direaction. Whoever functions as your advance man must be familiar with your overall campaign strategy, so that he has a good idea of where and with whom the candidate should be spending his time. In large-scale campaigns an advance man has to concentrate on getting television and newspaper coverage, since that is now generally regarded as having more impact than paid ads.*** In smaller campaigns, the scheduler-advance man must work closely with the campaign manager (who sometimes performs this function himself) to keep the candidate in areas where he can meet different voters, since there is little to be gained by his repeatedly meeting the same voters. In New York, for example, shopping centers, parks, and subway entrances are prized locations, because their constant streams of

---

*Observers noted that during Senator Edmund S. Muskie's presidential bid in 1971, his staff sometimes scheduled parades for the dinner hour, when no one was on the street.

**The Advance Man, by Jerry Bruno and Jeff Greenfield (New York: Morrow, 1971), describes the experiences of an advance man in a major campaign. Bruno was an advance man in Robert F. Kennedy's senatorial campaign and Arthur Goldberg's gubernatorial campaign. Allen L. Otten wrote an excellent article describing the work of advance men (whom he referred to as "schedulers") in the Democratic presidential primaries in the Wall Street Journal (New York edition), March 1, 1972, p. 1. In presidential campaigns, schedulers and advance men may do separate jobs.

***More and more politicians are becoming convinced that making news—breaking into television news shots—is more important than television advertising (TV Guide, June 1, 1972). In smaller campaigns, the focus is on developing controversies and sustaining the interest of local newspapers.

passers-by maximize the candidate's investment of time and energy. Since there are limited numbers of such locations in most districts, advance men who recommend appearances there must consider strategies to be followed should the opponent choose the same location at the same time.

In these details of campaigning, as in all others, coordination with research findings is very important. Which areas and groups have doubts about the candidate and the issues that concern them should be uppermost in the minds of staff members involved in scheduling and advance work.

The tasks of advance men sometimes seem trivial, petty, or insignificant, but they make the difference between a successful campaign trip, walking tour, or speech, and an unsuccessful one. Don't assign these tasks to anyone unless he is an experienced administrative detailer and has some political instincts. Advance men represent you, and they can cause real harm to your campaign if they are incompetent. It can be a major error to yield to the temptation, common to many candidates, to assign a volunteer or a young staff person to handle advance details. Inexperienced people should not be allowed to serve as advance men until they have spent time accompanying someone who is competent and experienced in advance work.

STREET RALLIES

Street rallies are used to drum up interest and excitement. The important decisions are when and where the rallies should take place and which speakers should appear with the candidate. The campaign should be off the ground before street rallies are scheduled; a street rally that falls flat is far worse than no street rally at all. Saturdays, Sundays, and early evenings when good weather is anticipated are the best times. Pick a corner with high pedestrian counts: a location in or near a shopping center or near a theater where a popular movie is playing is likely to be a good one. Be sure to obtain the proper permit from the local police.

Leaflets announcing the rally should be distributed to pedestrians and residents of the neighborhood a few days before the rally, and an ad should be taken in the local paper. If you have a telephone campaign, coordinate it with your street rally and have your callers remind people in the neighborhood that they can see the candidate at the rally and form their own impressions. Sound trucks can also be used to advertise the meeting. Some candidates like to use live or taped music to create a stir.

An outside speaker—a leader of the party, a celebrity, or a well-known neighborhood leader—adds appeal to the program.

Use your research to anticipate the questions that people in the neighborhood are likely to throw at you, and be ready with specific answers or proposals. Pronounce people's names properly, and make sure you acknowledge every local leader in the audience. Above all, don't forget what neighborhood you're in, as many politicians have. In the 1980 presidential campaign, Ronald Reagan repeatedly mentioned the wrong city in a major speech. Be sure to have appropriate literature and campaign workers to distribute it. Finally, see to it that the litter is cleaned up. Don't antagonize residents of the neighborhood by abandoning the massive amounts of paper that pile up after a rally. Some campaigners use large barrels where voters can throw literature away if they choose to.

SPEAKERS' BUREAUS AND SPEAKERS' GUIDES

In some larger (city-, state-, or nationwide) campaigns, a formal speakers' bureau is established, and when a candidate cannot meet all demands for his or her presence as a speaker, substitute speakers cover the appearances of lesser importance. The speakers may be friends, staff members, members of the candidate's family, or teachers from a local university. A senior staff member should be present when an untested speaker makes his first presentation, and obviously, ungifted speakers should not be permitted to represent the candidate.

It is prudent to prepare a speakers' guide—a collection of statements on important issues—which makes it possible for the speeches of substitutes to be authoritative as well as lively, informative, and to the point. It also enables the candidate's surrogate to respond to audience questions accurately, without running the risk of misrepresenting the candidate.

Some compilers of speakers' guides try to avoid sensitive issues. That, in my judgment, is a serious mistake, since most voters come to public meetings precisely to hear a candidate's stand on controversial matters. You will lose votes if your representatives are unable to state positions on these issues lucidly. Some issues are dynamite in their potential to damage your campaign: If they come up when you are not present, your spokesmen must be prepared to meet them as you wish them met.

Figure 2-1 shows part of a typical speakers' guide—this one compiled for the spokesmen for citywide candidates. These are simply lists of talking points; speeches should not be read if at all possible.

AIR POLLUTION

Summary

1. Equip buses and other city vehicles with after burner devices.
2. Take the lead in regional and interstate control projects.
3. Enlarge Department of Air Pollution Control.
4. Strict enforcement and stiffer penalties.
5. Mandate up-grading of sub-standard incinerators.
6. Launch public education program.

1. Seven point air pollution program.
   a. Title "To Clear the Sewer in the Sky."

2. The City must take the initiative.
   a. Seek out and correct defective city owned installations and equipment.

3. Telegram sent to Mayor Wagner, by Mr. Beame.
   a. Require all "future" city owned buses and vehicles to be equipped with after burner devices.
   b. Require all city vehicles, owned by city to be equipped immediately, if possible.

4. Seven point program is as follows:
   1. City leadership in regional and interstate Air Pollution projects.
   2. Enlarge the City Department of Air Pollution Control.
   3. Strict enforcement of rules with stiffer penalties for violations.
   4. Up-grading of sub-standard incinerators.
   5. Correction of defective city equipment.
   6. Creation of advisory citizens committee.
   7. Intensive public education program.

Factual Information

1. 60 tons of soot per square mile fall, every day, on New York City.

2. Pollution is from:
   1. Burning of fuel oils for power and heating.
   2. Burning of waste from cars, buses and trucks.
   3. Demolition and construction.
   4. Littered and dirty streets.
   5. Dry cleaning operations.
   6. Surface coating operations.

NEIGHBORHOOD CITY HALLS

1. Set up in councilmanic districts.
2. "Open door" policy to all Departments and Mayor's office.
3. Greater personal involvement of citizens.

Fig. 2-1. Example of speakers' guide using "talking points".

JOBS

1. Strong City action for immediate increased job opportunities for all.
2. Press for trade union membership for minorities.
3. Hold back payments and cancel contracts for city work where job discrimination is practiced.

ANTI-POVERTY

1. More federal aid on a continuing basis.
2. Separate city agency with full-time head responsible to Mayor.
3. Active role for the poor in local areas.

REAPPORTIONMENT

1. Immediate special session of Legislature to set up non-partisan group to devise fair plan and take subject out of partisan politics. In keeping with Supreme Court one-man-one-vote principle.

CIVIL SERVICE

1. Review and update Career & Salary Plan.
2. Make pay and fringe benefits comparable to federal–state jobs and private industry.
3. Cross-promotions by competitive exams, on a service-wide basis.

Fig. 2-1. (Continued)

ELECTION LAW

Knowledge of the technicalities of local election law is absolutely crucial to any campaign. Some candidates have been literally knocked off the ballot because their petitions were invalid; no one had bothered to read the laws governing elections. Most states have a political calendar advising candidates of filing dates and other important legal deadlines. In some states, a board of elections publishes the calendar; in others, it is the secretary of state. Part of a sample political calendar appears in Fig. 2-2.

State law generally regulates not only when but how election petitions are filed—for example, on what form, how many signatures are required, and who can witness signatures. The form usually calls for a committee on vacancies—that is, a group of people you name who are on the ballot so that, in the event of your illness or death, they can name a replacement. Ironically, although campaign headquarters tend to attract many young lawyers, few seem to enjoy examining the election law or checking petitions. It is extremely important to have a lawyer on your staff who

SUPERVISORS OF ELECTIONS FOR MONTGOMERY COUNTY, MARYLAND

ELECTION DATES AND DEADLINES - 1982

Deadline for CHANGE OF PARTY AFFILIATION . . . . May 14, 1982
(Any time prior to four months before primary)   3-8(b)

Deadline for FILING CANDIDACY - candidates running in   9 PM . .   July 6, 1982
party primaries   4A-3
(Monday which is 10 weeks or 70 days before primary)   7-1(b)(1)

Deadline for filing declaration of intent to seek   9 PM   July 6, 1982
nomination by petition candidate   4A-3,7-1(b)(1)

Deadline for WITHDRAWAL OF CANDIDACY before PRIMARY   Friday . . . . July 16, 1982
election (Within 10 days after filing deadline)   5 PM   9-1(a)

Deadline for petition candidates to file certificate   5 PM   August 2
of candidacy and petitions   7-1(b)(1),(2),
(Not later than 5 PM on first Monday in August)   (c)(1)

Deadline for certification of candidates to local boards . . . .   August 15, 1982
(Not less than 30 days before primary)   8-4, 5-3(a)

LAST DAY TO REGISTER before Primary Election, Monday   9 PM . .   August 16, 1982
(5th Monday prior to any election)   2-9(e), 3-8(a)

Deadline for 4th TUESDAY PRECEDING PRIMARY Campaign   5 PM . .   August 17, 1982
Fund Report by all candidates and political committees   26-11(a) (1)

Deadline for local boards to submit nominating . . . . August 23, 1982
petitions to State Board   7-1(j)(1)
(Within 3 weeks or 21 days after first Monday in August)

Deadline for 2nd FRIDAY PRECEDING PRIMARY Campaign Fund   5 PM . . September 3, 1982
Report by all candidates and political committees   26-11(a) (2)

Deadline for receipt of APPLICATIONS FOR ABSENTEE VOTING in . . . . . September 7, 1982
Primary Election, except for specified emergencies, Tuesday   27-2(a)
(Not later than the Tuesday preceding an election)

          (Elections office will be open 9 AM - 5 PM the previous
          Saturday, September 4, to accommodate absentee voters).

PRIMARY ELECTION (second Tuesday after 1st Monday in September). . . . September 14, 1982
Polls open 7 AM - 8 PM continuously   5-2(a)

Reporting of official primary election results by . . . . September 23, 1982
local boards of canvassers (2nd Thursday after primary)   17-5(a)

Deadline for WITHDRAWAL OF CANDIDACY before general   5 PM . . September 24, 1982
(Within 10 days after primary)   9-1(b)

REGISTRATION REOPENS for voter registration and   Monday . . . . September 27, 1982
other transactions (Not during 10 days following a primary)   3-8(a)

Deadline for certification of nominees to local boards . . . .   October 3, 1982
(Not less than 30 days before general)   8-4

LAST DAY TO REGISTER before General Election, Monday   9 PM . .   October 4, 1982
(5th Monday before election)   2-9(e), 3-8(a)

Deadline for 3rd TUESDAY POST-PRIMARY Campaign Fund   5 PM . .   October 5, 1982
Report by all candidates and political committees   26-11(a) (3)

Deadline for filing candidacy - write-in candidates   12 NOON   October 19, 1982
(Not later than 2nd Tuesday preceding day of election)   4D-1(c)

Deadline for 2nd FRIDAY PRECEDING GENERAL Campaign Fund   5 PM   October 22, 1982
Report by all candidates and political committees on   26-11(a) (2)
General Election ballot   Tuesday

Fig. 2-2. Example of a political calendar.

has been through petitioning and knows the laws regarding elections, including how to challenge opponents' petitions, how to file petitions, and the results of previous court challenges. (Petitioning requirements are discussed more fully later.) Your lawyer should also be on call on election day for advice about action to be taken if your poll watchers report voting irregularities.

An example of how crucial legal technicalities can be was provided by Richard L. Ottinger's campaign for the U.S. Senate from New York in 1970. Ottinger's staff believed it important to have two lines on the ballot, the Democratic Party and one other, since each of his two opponents was running on two separate lines. Since Ottinger was well known for his strong stand on issues involving the conservation of natural resources, someone decided to use the name Conservation Party. A great deal of effort and expense was exended to get the required thousands of signatures throughout the state in each county for the Conservation Party.

Political journalists and experienced political attorneys warned Ottinger's campaign staff that Conservation was too close to the already-existing Conservative Party name (probably one of the reasons the name was chosen) and that a court case might deprive them of the second line. In fact, Ottinger's Conservative Party opponent, James L. Buckley, did take the matter to court, and the Conservation Party line—which was thought to be worth 25,000 to 50,000 votes—was voided.

CAMPAIGN LAWYERS

One of the skills sometimes overlooked as too mundane to be very important in smaller campaigns is that of election lawyers. Often, it will be difficult to find an experienced election lawyer in a campaign that does not have high visibility and that cannot pay the fairly high professional fees that lawyers generally expect. The lawyer's role can be critical, and it is advisable to assign an able young lawyer to be responsible for the tasks and procedures described below. The assigned lawyer may have to ask a lot of questions and do some library research, but generally the job will get done.

Since de Tocqueville, many observers have commented on the proliferation of lawyers in American political campaigns and in administrative jobs in federal and state governments. Many lawyers, seeking a judgeship, major clients, or an important post in government, will be disdainful of the minutiae involved in campaign law; they are not in keeping with the image of senior policy responsibilities they wish to project. Politics is a business for many in which perceptions are thought of as more important than the actual substance. Professional election lawyers, if they charge at their normal billing rate of $75 to $100 an hour, can cause problems for the candidate. And often, besides reimbursement, they expect automatically to have a place in the senior campaign policy council. It may then actually be very much better to employ a younger, less well-established lawyer with the added advantage that he or she may be a real enthusiast of the candidate.

PETITION FILING REQUIREMENTS

There are a number of basic tasks for which the campaign attorney should be responsible. Perhaps the most basic and the most important is to be sure to meet the legal filing requirements for the petitions to get on the ballot. To do this the lawyer should obtain copies of the state and local election laws. The most critical part of this are the specific filing requirements: how many signatures are required on the petition to place the candidate on the ballot, which list of registered voters can be used to determine valid voters, who can be legal witnesses on each petition sheet, whether the signature has to be exactly the same name as it appears on the voter rolls or slight variations are acceptable, whether signatures have to be obtained in the individual's home or can be gotten on the street (so-called boardwalk petitions), when and where and in what form the petitions are due, how you knock out opponent's petitions in a challenge and at the same time protect your own from a successful challenge, and whether petitions that are gathered at a set price (fifty cents to one dollar a signature is not unheard of in large cities) are legal. After immersing himself with this material and calling the local election commission with any questions, the lawyer should be placed in charge of training the petition gatherers; he should also check each person's work for the first week of petitioning.

These are not trivial matters. Even experienced attorneys can make grievous and sometimes terminal errors for the campaign. For example, in 1982, in one of the most politically sophisticated counties in the country, the New York County Democratic Party forgot to file its judicial nominating petitions on time, with the result that four judicial candidates were found ineligible. The resulting ballot was anomalous, with four vacant spaces on the vertical Democratic line; this had the additional chilling effect of negatively affecting every Democratic candidate below the judicial lines.

Strange things indeed can happen in the petitioning process. Years ago in a large eastern city all the nominating petitions, consisting of tens of thousands of signatures, were placed in the trunk of the law chairman's car and driven to the Board of Elections for filing a few hours before the deadline for filing. Upon arrival, minutes before the deadline, the car having broken down, the trunk lock was found jammed and nothing could be done to open it. There was not time to try to get a locksmith. Inspired by the nightmarish qualities of the situation, the law chairman, realizing that the building contained warehouses and had heavy-duty elevators for freight, bribed or bullied the building personnel into allowing time to drive the car and the petitions into the elevator. He took the car to the Board of Elections floor and had the car locked in officially by the city personnel, using delivery time as the legal time for filing. The car was opened the next morning.*

It is not uncommon for candidates to challenge each other's petitions, and to conclusively prevent the opponent from even campaigning. It takes some doing, but it can be done and sometimes to even experienced politicians. In one situation, a candidate noted the names and addresses of all his opponent's subscribing witnesses (a witness is generally required for each page of petitions) and had his staff check that each was actually a legal witness—properly enrolled and living in the jurisdiction. They discovered a number of illegal witnesses; since each illegal witness was responsible for a number of pages of petitions, they were able to knock out the opponent. The procedure was very time-consuming and expensive; the actual buff or enrollment card for each witness had to be obtained and checked.

On the other hand, the most extraordinary petitioning errors can be made and the candidate can get away with it. Some years after the race riots in New York City, a well-known minority civil rights leader ran for Mayor. His opponents, the Democratic organization, reviewed his petitions and found that the signatures were in exact alphabetical order, and

*I am indebted to Ken and Andrew Fisher, election lawyers of Brooklyn, New York, for the anecdotes and for advice on this section.

moreover that the names on the petitions were signed, last name first, first name last as printed in the Board of Elections petition. It seemed clear that these were "kitchen petitions"; the names had been simply copied from the enrollment books. However, because the racial tensions still had raw scars the party leadership decided not to challenge.

In some situations it may be important for the lawyer to check the election rules concerning ballot position. Experienced campaigners believe that physical position on the ballot can be worth one to five points. For example, if the names are listed vertically, the candidates on the first line is significantly advantaged. In some states, position by party is rotated district by district to provide an equity that no one can question. In some states the position is by the sequence the candidates file; the first one to file gets the preferred position.

REVIEW OF CONTRACTS

A lot of money changes hands even in modest campaigns, and many services are contracted for. While most vendors providing services to campaigns are reasonably businesslike, there are a substantial number who may not be above reproach, in fact who often may be plain hustlers. It is extremely important for the campaign attorney to protect the candidate by making certain that any service costing more than a thousand dollars be covered by a written contract even if only a brief one. Because of the constant time constraints that are the common nightmares of all campaigns, it is essential that the contracts specify delivery dates, and perhaps financial penalties be stated for nonperformance. This precaution is absolutely critical for printing, labeling, and mail house services.

Campaign suppliers may be doing 25 to 50 campaigns at the same time and often will cheerfully promise each candidate timely service and preferred treatment. However, machines do break down, staff gets sick, married or drunk, or more lucrative contracts come along and the supplier's priorities undergo a remarkable change. In part, good early planning can solve some of these problems by simply allowing you to get your orders in earlier than other campaigners. But campaigns have an ever-expanding number of urgencies. For example, with the best planning, it still happens that a week before election day a completely new piece of literature has to be developed, designed, printed, and mailed. To do this you have to have reliable and quality suppliers.

FINANCIAL FILINGS

In congressional campaigns, the Federal Election Commission financial forms have to be filed. The lawyer should obtain copies of the procedures and forms and ask to be placed on the mailing list for commission rulings. The forms themselves require the campaign's accountant to prepare. Essentially, contributors' names, addresses, and amounts donated are needed, as are the details of expenditures. (For those having the time, it is an experience to read the expenditure patterns of the larger campaigns: They are available in the Washington headquarters of the Commission). These forms have to be filed periodically during the campaign. State and legal laws vary but should be checked to ascertain what financial reports are required, if any.

CANVASSING

The basic strategy in conducting a campaign is to get on the ballot, develop reasons for voters to vote for you, construct a list of favorable voters, and, finally, to get them to the polls—or "pull" them—on election day.

Canvassing—visiting households in a district in person ("hand canvassing") or by telephone ("telephone canvassing")—has traditionally played an important role in these jobs. It is done in the early stages of a campaign to gather signatures for nominating petitions and to proselytize on a candidate's behalf, and in the final stages of the campaign to pull favorable voters to the polls. Although hand canvassing used to be regarded as the key to successful campaigning, the rising importance of the mass media and the concomitant destruction of many city political machines have recently diminished the reliance on local captains that hand canvassing entails. (Radio and television bring the candidate himself into the voters' living rooms, so canvassers, while serving other necessary functions, no longer need to introduce the candidate to the voters.) In smaller assembly or council races or in suburban or rural districts, however, hand canvassing is important. In some cities, the regular organization has access to election district captains, some of whom are paid $35 to $60 for a day's work.* This is no longer a great deal of money,

---

*Some candidates pay petition canvassers as much as $0.50 to $1.00 a signature. I would advise against this course except, where it is legal, in emergencies; in many places it is illegal, and where it is legal, it is likely to result in forgeries.

but it provides some motivation for people to show up and do their jobs.* In a recent judicial delegate race in New York, a district leader whose funds were limited did not spend anything at all on loudspeakers, mailings, or other such traditional campaign devices. Instead, he relied entirely on canvassers, asking his 115 captains to bring in 15 votes apiece. The resulting 1,725 votes were decisive in electing his ticket.

In the New Hampshire presidential primary in March 1972, Senator George McGovern received 37 percent of the vote after public opinion polls had predicted only 25 percent as his likely share of the vote. It seemed clear to me as a professional involved in the early stages of McGovern's campaign in New Hampshire that the efforts of an estimated 2,000 volunteer canvassers during the campaign and on primary election day were a significant, and possibly decisive, factor in his excellent showing. (An effective professional telephone campaign and McGovern's public disclosure of the names of all his contributors also played major roles in the outcome.) Although it is impossible to say exactly how much any one thing contributed to his extra 12 percent, it would be difficult to dispute that the saturation canvassing by enthusiastic volunteers was an important factor.

PETITIONING

State election laws specify the form in which petitions are to appear and the number of signatures required to place a candidate's name on the ballot. (Part of a sample petition is reproduced in Fig. 2-3.) Before your workers begin canvassing for petition signatures, someone on your staff—preferably an attorney, but otherwise someone who is experienced in petitioning and who knows something about local election law—must read your state's election law very carefully. This staff member should also examine the review procedures used by the local board of elections, whose members may be political appointees who can express their political biases in their rulings. After the signatures have been collected, he should take personal charge of "binding" the petitions—checking to make sure that they are legally signed and witnessed and then literally putting them into binders and presenting them to the board of elections.

---

*Similarly, running a slate of county committeemen (party posts) provides motivation for people to work for the candidate, since their names are on the ballot as well.

SAMPLE PETITION (For nomination of Council member, Friendship Heights Village Council, election of May 9, 1983)

    As registered voters and residents of Friendship Heights Village, we would like to nominate _____ for a position on the Friendship Heights Village Council in the election of May 9, 1983.

PRINT NAME	SIGNATURE	ADDRESS
1		
2		
3		
4		
5		
6		
7		
8		
9		
10		

More than ten names may be on petition. Each person must be a registered voter residing in the Village.

Name of Treasurer:_____(Required)

Address of Treasurer:_____(Required)

Signature of Candidate, agreeing to have name placed in nomination.

    I agree to have my name placed in nomination:_____

                                              (Signature of candidate)

                                              (Address of candidate)

ANY QUESTIONS: CALL THE VILLAGE COUNCIL OFFICE AT 656 2797

Fig. 2-3. Example of a nominating petition.

Among the things that should be carefully checked under his supervision are the following: Signatures should be collected in homes and not on the street or in parks. Signatures collected in public places—so-called boardwalk petitions—are invalid in many localities. The petitions must be properly witnessed, usually by an adult who resides in the election district in which the signatures are being collected. Petitions have been set aside and candidates knocked off the ballot because of seemingly minor irregularities in witnessing.* It is imperative that each voter sign the petition exactly as he is listed on the voting rolls, that the address be noted properly, and that the signatures be in black or blue ink. In many localities, if a voter's middle initial is listed in the election books, the voter's signature on the petition must have his middle initial or it will be disqualified. Married women should be particularly careful to sign their names exactly as they appear in the registration book.

Another common cause for petition signatures to be thrown out is that the signer signed more than one petition for the same office. A surprisingly large number of people are apparently willing to sign almost anything that is thrust at them, including the petitions of several different candidates for the same office. Your workers should impress potential petition signers with the fact that they may legally sign only one candidate's petition per office. This problem becomes even more acute when candidates running for several different offices share petitions, a practice that is common in some localities. Generally, the first petition a person signs for any given office is determined to be his only legal signature for that office.

Usually, each canvasser is given ten petitions with spaces for ten signatures per sheet. This should be the canvasser's quota. If he can do more, fine; but in my experience, after twice the number of valid signatures required by law has been obtained, the canvasser can probably be more useful in other functions. Some local political leaders seek large numbers of petition signatures which they use to gain a trading advantage in their dealings with candidates for such higher offices as congressman, mayor, senator, or governor. In these cases, the petitions are used as evidence of potential support, which is presumably influential in gaining endorsements (or at least preventing endorsements of opponents) and/or

---

*Many courts will review petition challenges only if a substantial number of irregularities can be demonstrated. However, I have seen candidates removed from the ballot because one or two canvassers, providing many signatures, had made only minor errors.

financial assistance. Unless you have a reason of this sort, however, I believe that you should simply come in with enough "good" signatures to prevent a challenge, and certainly twice as many signatures as are required is usually a safe number. Some technicians believe a candidate should get as many signatures as he can, to impress the voting public; but in my judgment, not too many voters know or care how many signatures any candidate obtains.

Politicians who are interested in testing a candidate's strength on the basis of his petitions sometimes look more closely at the number of petition witnesses than at the number of signatures. Since the person who carries a petition normally witnesses it, the number of witnesses a candidate has provides a fair indication of how many workers he has. People who carry petitions presumably also are willing to lend their efforts to other campaign activities which one can hope will result in additional votes for the candidate on election day.

The petitioning procedure should start as early as you can manage. As a first step, the current registration lists for your party should be purchased from the appropriate source—board of elections, department of commerce, or other body, depending on the locality. Any citizen may purchase or have access to these records, and you will probably be correct in suspecting a political motive if anyone tells you that they are not available, even if you are given some excuse such as that the election rolls are stored on computer tape or that mechanical problems make it impossible to make them available to you. However the rolls are stored, you are entitled to access to them, even if in a rare case you have to go to court to get them.

Using the roll books, the campaign manager selects the areas where canvassing can best be done—that is, the areas with the largest concentrations of voters (in a primary campaign, voters in your party) who can reasonably be hoped to be sympathetic to your candidacy. It is usually unwise and practically impossible to cover each election district fully, and much time can be wasted in even attempting to do so. Some areas simply have to be written off as "no contest," or at best made the target of a minimal mail campaign emphasizing whatever issue or ethnic identification might salvage 10 to 20 percent of the vote in the area. Your research should determine the selection of the potentially favorable areas and groups the canvassers must reach.

Each voter in your target area should be listed on a 3 x 5 card containing items similar to the following:

SMITH, JOHN (Dem.)   29 A.D.
                                        32 E.D.
        0000 Main Street, ZIP
Canvass: Date_____   Worker_____
        Signed petition_____
        Thank-you sent_____   Other family voters:
        Literature_____   Jane (Rep.)
        Kaffeeklatch sponsor_____
        Volunteer for_____
Comments: _____
          _____

The cards prepared for this purpose can also be used later as the basis of mailings. They are most useful for this purpose if members of a family are combined on a single card, to avoid duplication of mailings to a single household. The cards can be prepared by computer (somewhat expensive, but a massive saving of time) or by hand (less expensive, but very tedious work with a probable loss of quality).

If you can afford it and if there is a good, reliable computer house near you, it will probably be well worth your while in a medium- or large-scale campaign to have the cards prepared by computer. Creatively used, computers can aid your petitioning effort in other ways besides preparing the cards. For example, in 1982 a New York computer firm developed a "finder's book" that provided the election district and assembly district numbers for any street address. Since New York had just been extensively redistricted, there was no other quick way to identify the election and assembly districts of each petition signer—information that was required alongside each petition signature. Checking them by hand would have been a laborious—and probably error-ridden—project.

Once they are completed, the 3 x 5 cards should be arranged according to street addresses; in the case of large apartment buildings, the canvassers' working decks of cards should normally be grouped by floor and apartment number unless some special situation makes it preferable to divide them by ethnic group or other such criterion.

Areas (blocks or buildings in the city) are assigned to a team of your canvassers, preferably a man and woman. There are security problems at night in many large cities, so women should not canvass alone. The teams should be supervised by the campaign manager after an orientation that gives them a good understanding of your background as well as your stands on major issues and your criticisms of your opponent(s). (A typical set of instructions for primary petition carriers appears in Fig. 2-4.) You should make yourself available to answer questions from the canvassers.

Since you cannot get around to seeing or being seen by all the potential voters in your district, your canvassers are, in effect, your personal representatives. Their primary purposes in visiting households are to get your petitions signed, if possible; to identify issues that may affect their vote; and, in any case, to find out if the voters plan to cast their ballots for you on primary and election day. Canvassers should be able to tell voters where and when to register and where to vote. Depending on the type or amount of interest shown, they can let voters know in a few sentences what you are thinking or planning to do about issues and problems of local and national concern. They should understand, however, that they cannot commit you to new positions on issues. Voters who have further questions about you or who express interest in volunteering should be given the address and telephone number of campaign headquarters. The names of potential campaign workers should be turned in that evening so that someone in your campaign office will follow up their expression of interest and try to enlist their active support. After thanking the voter, and after putting down pertinent information, the canvassers should go on to the next household or individual on their list.

Literature should be available to give out during the interviews. This is often neglected since petitioning is the first step in the campaign and literature is generally not prepared until later. Such an omission is an enormous waste of potential strength, since literature given out in a personal canvass is much more apt to be read than literature received in the mail.

Some voters will ask for favors: "Do something for me and I'll probably vote for you." Your canvassers should not promise anything! However, they should know the name and telephone number of the police precinct captain; where the local hospital is; whom to call for public housing; where to obtain services for the aged; and similar details about other public services. This type of helpful information can be listed on

INSTRUCTIONS FOR PRIMARY PETITION CARRIERS

1. *Who May Circulate the Petition.* In order to circulate the petition and witness signatures, you must be a registered voter, enrolled in the party and living in the district where you carry petitions. All signatures witnessed by you will be invalid if these conditions are not met.

2. *Who May Sign.* Petition signers must also be registered voters, enrolled in the party and residing in the district.

3. Signatures must be in black or blue ink. Carriers should have pens.

4. The voter must sign his own name in the presence of the witness.

5. The witness must see the petition being signed by each signer.

6. No carrier may witness his own signature.

7. Do not fill in Election District and Assembly District numbers. These will be filled in later at headquarters from the enrollment lists. Leave the "Sheet No." blank also.

8. The date and address should be filled in carefully by the carrier before the signer signs his name. If an error is made, strike out the entire line and start over on the next line. Write dates out in full, without abbreviations. Dates should be consecutive on any one sheet.

9. Never use ditto marks—for dates, addresses, or anything else.

10. Each person's name should be signed in full or in the same manner as they appear in the voter registry. Women should sign their full first names (Elizabeth Scotto, not Mrs. Donald Scotto).

11. On a separate piece of paper list each signer's name, together with your name. This will be used for checking the voter list and defending challenges.

12. Return petitions and lists to headquarters as soon as possible. It is better to turn in a sheet with only a few signatures on it than to risk losing or damaging it.

13. *Statement of Witness.* Print your name carefully in the first blank and print the address at which you are registered in the second blank. Leave all other items blank. Sign your name at the bottom. Put your initials at the edge of any line containing erasures, strike-overs, or other changes (which, however, should be avoided if at all possible).

14. If your address at the time of the 1981 general election was the same as it is now, on the back of the petition write in pencil "1981-same." If your address has changed, write the old address lightly in pencil on the back of the petition with the notation "1981 address."

Fig. 2-4. Example of written directions for canvassing for petition signatures.

a small card that the canvasser can carry. Although canvassers must not make any commitments in response to requests for such things as public housing assistance, a new street light, or more police protection, they should note them on the 3 x 5 cards and/or report them to the campaign manager, for two reasons: (1) you may be able to do something abut them; and (2) they may prove to be important campaign issues.

As in every other aspect of campaigning, details are important. Canvassers should take care to use the correct spelling and pronunciation of voters' names. People get annoyed if these particulars are in error. Evenings are best for canvassing — after the dinner hour until perhaps 9:30 or 10:00 is ideal. Some of your canvassers may want to interview neighbors as they arrive home from work, but it is better to interview strangers in their homes after dinner.

Personalized thank-you notes should be sent to all the people who sign your petitions.

PETITION CHALLENGES

In a three-way race, if your research determines that the presence of a third candidate will hurt you (see p. 95), it is usually wise to examine the weakest candidate's petitions to determine whether to try to knock him off the ballot by legal procedures.

Challenging an opponent's petitions is a laborious, expensive, time-consuming task which involves court action and will take your workers' time away from other necessary work. To shortcut the procedure, start by checking the legal address of your opponent's witnesses. Usually, the campaign worker who carries a petition serves as the petition's witness, and legally, he is often called the petition's "subscribing witness." Generally, he must be a legal resident of the area in which he ostensibly carried the petitions. Since one man usually carries and witnesses ten to fifty petition sheets, each containing ten or more individual signatures, invalidating one witness can invalidate hundreds of petition signatures.

Although they are illegal in most places, "boardwalk petitions" (defined on p. 58) are quite commonly used and, if that is so, they are sometimes "witnessed" *ex post facto*. If it can be proven that this had been done, the witnessing procedure can be declared invalid and the petitions can be set aside.

An example, which almost cost a man his professional reputation, concerned a lawyer who, although he was known to live in Westchester County, used someone else's address to witness petitions in New York City. As an attorney, he should have been aware that his act was a breach of election law. The witness was known personally to the opponent's staff, who, having discovered what he had done, confronted him with the evidence and offered to let him withdraw the petitions, or they would sue to invalidate them. Naturally, he withdrew all his petitions.

Unless you can challenge a witness privately, as in the foregoing case, a legal petition challenge will require that someone photocopy all your opponent's petitions—which may run to hundreds of pages—and check each signature against the registration cards at the local board of elections for validity of signature, accuracy of address, and any other features that are required by local law. Checking whether anyone signed more than one petition is particularly bothersome, since the signatures do not appear in any particular order on the petitions. If anyone did sign more than one, a check must be made to see whose petition he signed first, since the first signature will probably be declared the valid one.

Before doing a full-scale petition challenge, make a spot check to determine whether the opponent's petitions are so weak as to make the effort worthwhile. If you are sure you can eliminate your opponent on the basis of his invalid petitions, the challenge is certainly worth any effort it requires, but if you doubt that you can knock out enough signatures to do that, you will have to decide whether the advantage to be gained by finding even a large number of invalid signatures merits the diversion of your workers' time and energies from other campaign activities.

THE NEED TO COUNT

The district leader referred to earlier was an experienced politician; he understood the need for counting. He estimated fairly closely how many voters would come out in a primary and how many of those he needed to win. Anyone who has ever had to pull for a close club election when one vote can be decisive knows how important counting can be. This leader reviewed previous campaigns for judicial delegates in an off-year and realized that asking for a saturation campaign was impossible—he didn't have the money or the workers such a campaign would require.

Asking for fifteen votes per worker was realizable, and past voting records in his district indicated that would be enough to win.

Counting is also a vital and too-frequently-forgotten factor in allocating basic resources. You know the voter registration in your district. However, you must count how many households are represented, so that you can make appropriate contractual commitments for direct mail and telephone campaigns, allowing a single piece of mail or telephone call for each household. Similarly, you must count the number of available telephone numbers for these households, subtracting an estimated percentage for those with unlisted telephone numbers (up to 20 percent in some areas) and for those who have moved or died recently, to know how many telephone calls to contract for. The importance of counting in petitioning is discussed elsewhere in this chapter. Before ordering thousands of flyers or extra shopping bags, count the number of voters in the district. One candidate I know ordered 50,000 flyers to be printed for distribution the day before the election. Had he counted first, he could have saved part of his printing expenses, for his twenty volunteers could reasonably deliver only 500 flyers each, or a total of 10,000. Clearly, some of his money was spent unproductively. A basic rule of politics is "when in doubt, count."

FIRST POSITION

In horse racing, the horse in the first position—the one next to the rail—usually is regarded as having a slight edge. In political campaigning, where the first position is the top line of the ballot or the first column on the left, the design of the ballot and your position on it can be important.

In many states, each party's candidates used to be listed on the ballot in a single column or slate, and people tended to vote the whole party slate. In such a situation, the location of your name wouldn't mean much. But the design of the ballot has changed in many localities, and today many more people vote independently, crossing party lines and voting for the individual rather than the party. (Walter De Vries and Lance Tarrance examine the importance of such selective voters in *The Ticket Splitter: A New Force in American Politics* [Grand Rapids, Mich.: Eerdmans, 1972].) Experienced political mechanics are convinced that in a primary fight the first slot on the ballot is worth 5 to 8 percent of the entire vote, and in a three-way race such an edge can be decisive. In some states, first position in a primary election is drawn by lot, and in the general election the party that received the largest vote in the last statewide election gets the first spot. Different states have different formulas for determining the order of candidates on the ballot. New York City has solved the problem by changing the order in which candidates are listed from district to district. If you don't live in an area where the first position advantage is neutralized by some such method and if you are not assigned the first slot, you'll have to work harder in your campaign to make the voter want to seek your name out on the ballot.

ELECTION DAY PROCEDURES

The first thing to do is to vote yourself and make sure your family and staff take the time to vote. If you're having a final canvassers' meeting, you should be there with the campaign manager. You should also make appearances at the telephone canvassing operating both to motivate the workers and out of courtesy to them. Campaigns are hard for everyone involved, but you'll be amazed at how effective such simple acts of courtesy and thoughtfulness can be.

Election day procedures should be set up so that your campaign manager knows where everyone will be working. On the previous day, meetings will have been held with your field supervisors, canvassers, telephoners, poll watchers, messengers, literature distributors, troubleshooters, and other campaign workers to make certain that they know what they will be doing at all times during the course of election day, how they are to solve whatever problems they encounter, and when they are to call campaign headquarters.

To coordinate the election day pull, a copy of the master list of favorables, organized alphabetically within election districts, should be made available to each area's team captain. (A list of favorables for each voting district within the larger area should be provided for each of your poll watchers.) The campaign manager should indicate which districts are to be covered by a hand pull, and which by a telephone pull. Arrangements should also be made for the distribution of palm cards (small replicas of the ballot with your slot clearly marked, designed to be carried into the voting booth) and campaign literature near voting places. In complicated elections, a sample ballot should be used instead of a palm card. (Examples of the two appear in Figs. 7-16 and Fig. 7-17.)

If your pull is being done mainly by telephone, your telephone consultant or research person should have identified the order in which districts should be called, but this may have to be altered during the day, since even with the best planning, the pressures of election day usually break down the organizational plan for canvassing. Therefore, it is particularly important to have a coordination committee that can communicate rapidly with people in the field to make changes when required. For example, if poll watchers report a light turnout in districts that are known to be favorable to you, the coordinator may wish to transfer some canvassers from other areas to these, where the numbers and probabilities are more advantageous. At the same time, the telephone operation can also easily be diverted into problem areas. The logistical problem is that many individual canvassers or area captains will have to call in to headquarters every hour to report results and to receive instructions. Walkie-talkies, if they can be rented, are useful on election days in large districts in which perhaps fifty teams of canvassers may be out at the same time.

Most of the principles of petition canvassing described earlier in this chapter apply equally to the election day pull, with one important difference: On election day, your canvassers call or visit only those voters who are known to be sympathetic to your candidacy. The election day pull in fact is frequently done by telephone rather than in person or "by hand," but if more than one technique is used, there should be some reasonable measure of coordination and communication so that duplication is avoided and the objective—to pull the favorables—is accomplished. The focus, of course, is on areas that you think are mostly favorable to you but that are identified by your poll watchers as having light turnouts.

It is not unusual for a hand canvass and a telephone canvass to take place in the same election district, or for one election district to be telephoned twice by different teams working for the same candidate. Voters who are saturated in this manner may become so irritated they won't vote for the candidate. Similar negative results are likely to occur when candidates for several different offices all seek to pull the same voters.

The election day pull uses the same basic method whether done by telephone or in person—and, if possible, is done by the same canvasser who made the original contact. A telephone canvass should be short, since it need only remind people to go to the polls. The canvasser identifies herself as calling on your behalf and asks whether the voter has voted. If he has voted, she thanks him and moves on. If he has not voted, she seeks to impress him with the importance of his vote for you and reminds him of where the polling place is and the hours when it is open. In every campaign, a surprisingly large number of voters indicate that they don't know if they are registered or where they can vote. Canvassers should be familiar with the rules of the board of elections and should have a list of voting places. They should be able to provide babysitters for mothers with small children as well as transportation to the polls for elderly or infirm persons. Weeks earlier, someone on your staff will have compiled a list of volunteers, some of whom have cars at their disposal, and organized them to be available for these services. There should also be a crew of troubleshooters with cars at their disposal to put out fires—or example, emergencies requiring poll watchers to go home, arguments between poll watchers of different parties, and opponents' people electioneering at the polls. Staff members or volunteers should also see to it that poll watchers and other workers are relieved from time to time and that they are provided with food and drink.

Your poll watchers, who have probably been selected because of their previous experience in doing that kind of work or because of their demonstrated good judgment, represent your interests at all the polling places in your district. Since each of them should have attended orientation and training sessions at your headquarters, they should know the election law for your state and district and whom to call to report irregularities. Elections do get "stolen," even today when machines are widely used. In some areas, for example, machines have an oddly fortuitous habit of breaking down when the challenger is expected to have a heavy vote in a district. Poll watchers should have some basic understanding of how the machine works. They should arrive at the polling places fifteen minutes or half an hour before the polls open so that they can read the counters on the side and back of the voting machines to make certain that they register zero. Where paper ballots are used, your poll watchers must see to it that the ballots are complete, bound, and unopened. As each voter signs the affidavit and his name is called out, the poll watcher checks it in the precinct poll list to make certain that he has the right to vote at that voting place. Whenever possible, the poll watcher compares the poll list with a list of your "favorables" and, from time to time, sends back to your campaign headquarters a list of your favorables who have not yet voted, so that your canvassers will know who should still be called and reminded to vote. After the voting is completed and the voting machines are opened at the back, your poll watchers (1) check the side and back counters to make certain their totals match and (2) record the number of votes you and your opponents have received, for transmittal to your headquarters. (Later on, if the announced vote differs from that recorded by your poll watcher, you can take legal action, if necessary.) One of your poll watchers should go with the election judges and clerks to the board of elections to see to it that no changes are made before the votes are handed in to the board.

You yourself probably should take some of the day off until the voting is almost over. Your campaign committee and manager can do what is needed. One thing, your congratulatory speech—for yourself or your opponent—must be prepared, but in most cases, only a brief statement is called for.

Many campaigners hire a hotel ballroom for a victory celebration. This can be embarrassingly morbid and depressing, even if there is eventually a victory to celebrate (and all the more so if there isn't), since people mill about waiting while results trickle in, looking for famous and/or important people. In major elections, the press and television newsmen interview the same people over and over again at these "parties" trying to build suspense as long as the election remains undecided. A party given to thank your staff a week after the election may be a much better idea. Then, they will not be exhausted and dirty after working hard since early election morning, and you will not have to maintain the candidate's artifice that seems obligatory at election night parties.

Many candidates maintain their own spot-polling operation on election nights, using representative precincts to get early results and predict the probable outcome of the election. This seems a needless waste. You'll know the outcome soon enough.

At the end of the evening, send telegrams of congratulations to victorious friends and respected political enemies. There is no law that says you have to go much further than that, and hypocrisy is not seemly.

POST-ELECTION CHORES

Whether you win or lose, certain things you've paid for belong to you and may be helpful to you in future elections or to political friends if you don't intend to campaign again.

You should keep:

- The canvass cards, by election district
- Names, addresses, and telephone numbers of canvassers
- Lists of favorables, unfavorables, and undecideds
- Telephone canvass records (3 x 5 cards)
- Campaign scrapbook (newspaper clippings, etc.)
- Samples of literature
- Samples of giveaways used
- Copies of transcripts of speeches
- Lists of contributors
- Lists of debts and liabilities you've incurred.

The final chore—if you've won a primary—is to start to prepare for the general election. Take a real vacation—you may be in good shape physically, but from primary day to the first Tuesday in November is a long time, and even if you really love campaigning, it is exhausting and seldom exhilarating. If you've won a general election, your problems will include staff selection and analysis of the legislative and service needs of all your constituents—as a beginning. But that is another book.

3
Political Research:
How To Do It And
How To Use It

Nothing is more dangerous than to live in the temperamental atmosphere of a Gallup poll, always taking one's pulse and taking one's temperature. . . . There is only one duty, only one safe course, and that is to try to be right and not to fear to do or say what you believe to be right.
—*Winston Churchill*

Recently I was asked by an experienced district leader for professional advice on a primary campaign for judicial office. The candidate had been involved in politics for twenty years and was prepared to spend whatever he had to on a fully professional campaign. Only after several long discussions, however, was I able to convince both the district leader and the candidate that an initial budget allocation for basic research was critical before active campaigning began. These were my specific research recommendations:

1. Record and analyze the results of the two previous primary elections by individual election district to delineate reform-regular party-faction votes for various offices, and to show the level of "drop-off" from the top line on the ballot to the judicial line—that is, to determine the proportion of voters who vote for the top (and normally most important) office on the ballot but do not bother to vote for the lesser offices (in this case, judgeships), which are listed lower on the ballot.
2. Obtain U.S. census data by tract for the area showing distribution by age, sex, income, race, ethnic group, and nationality (country of origin).
3. Obtain the names of the voters in the previous two primaries from the original buff-colored signature cards filed at the board of elections. This is often called the "prime list."
4. Obtain the election district maps for the area from the board of elections and mount them together onto a single map showing the entire judicial district.

5. Obtain the names and addresses of new registrants.*

6. Do a probability sample survey of all recorded primary voters and new registrants to ascertain their characteristics generally and their attitudes about the candidates and their views.

This chapter discusses the reasons for such recommendations, and the ways in which they are carried out by consultants. The following chapter describes how your staff can perform such services directly, if necessary.

Political research can be defined as the scientific search for those aspects of campaign reality that can help concretely in making both immediate decisions and longer-range policy, using objective data that are amenable to detailed, precise analysis and evaluation.** As in business and in government programs, the existence of good research cannot by itself guarantee intelligent decision making. It is nothing more or less than a tool; to be effective, it must be used skillfully. This is why experienced consultants call it an art form as well as a scientific process. Data are subject to analysis and judgments can very, sometimes considerably, using the same data.***

Good research can be employed in making bad decisions, and good decisions are sometimes made based on poorly done research or on no research at all. Sometimes intuition, guts, and the synoptic capacity of a politically skilled candidate and campaign manager can be as important as all the research in the world. Nonetheless, political research of profes-

---

*Recent surprise victories in 1982 and in 1983 of black candidates in Baltimore and Chicago were to a large extent attributable to very massive and successful registration drives of blacks. Surveys may or may not have picked up attitudes of these new registrants since some pollsters often use board of election registration tapes that may be last year's to pull samples in primaries. Other pollsters, using random digit select programs to sample, might have trouble in selecting the proper weights to reflect these registration drives. In any case, a lot of important and expensive pollsters have been caught with their weights wrong. In addition, in the last few years shifts of 20 to 30 percent of the voters' attitudes in the last few weeks of a campaign have occurred with startling frequency. To be able to capture such enormous shifts in voters' attitudes requires constant polling, which few candidates can afford.

**Abraham Kaplan, *The Conduct of Inquiry: Methodology for Behavioral Science* (Scranton, Pa.: Chandler, 1964), a college text, contains a brilliant general discussion of research.

***Peter Hart, a leading survey specialist, was quoted as saying, "A poll is not a substitute for brains or insight. . . . As with any invention in our society, it is a more efficient way of planning campaigns and making the most of one's resources. It still goes back to a candidate's ability to make judgments, deal with issues." (*Washington Post*, October 8, 1982, p. A4.) While there are many responsible pollsters, such as Hart, too many charge for magic, and if they lose, blame the candidate, staff, and circumstances.

sional quality should be regarded as mandatory in any reasonably well-financed campaign and should be a factor in all major campaign decisions. Most professionals agree on the necessity for research, but considerable controversy exists on how best to do it and how much to spend on it.

TYPES OF POLITICAL RESEARCH

There are four basic types of political research: polling or probability sample surveys, voting behavior analysis, supporting demographic analysis, and issue or policy studies.

1. *Polls*—more properly referred to as *probability sample surveys*—are the best-known basic type of research work required in political campaigns.* Published polls often show little more than where one candidate stands vis-à-vis his opponent at given intervals during the campaign, the so-called horse race data. More important, however, is the fact that polls can also be designed to provide specific indications of why you stand where you do. Surveys provide information on which issues are of concern to which groups of voters and on the adequacy of your appeals to the groups you wish to focus on; and a major goal of surveys is to establish as objectively as possible which groups you should try to appeal to. They can also indicate how voters respond to you as a personality. Surveys are critical in laying out campaign strategy and testing and revising tactics during the course of a campaign.

---

*The use of the word "polling" dates from the time when surveys consisted almost exclusively of polls asking whom the respondent expected to vote for. Surveys include much more than this now, but the word "poll" remains in wide use. A probability sample of voters is one in which each voter in the area or "universe" has an equal chance of being interviewed. The first political poll in the United States was done by George Gallup for a relative in 1932 without charge. The first paid political surveys were done in the early 1940s, mostly in presidential campaigns. By the late 1950s polls were relatively common in state and congressional campaigns. It has been estimated that in 1980 $20 million was spent on 2,000 polls, or an average of $10,000 a poll. (Charles Roll and Albert Cantril, *Polls: Their Use and Misuse in Politics,* Cabin John, Md.: Seven Locks Press, 1980, p. xxxix.) In 1982, over one billion dollars were spent on campaigning; I would estimate that over $35 million was spent on polling. As to the number of polls, I would estimate the number including presidentials (many states), gubernatorials (primaries and general elections), congressionals (primaries and general elections), city mayoralties, state, county, and town elections to easily exceed 3,000 polls, keeping in mind that in many campaigns it is common to do more than one poll. It is no wonder that a number of pollsters are reported to be millionaires. It is estimated that there are over 250 firms and freelancers doing polling; if the number of college professors of sociology and political science doing occasional polling is added, the total exceeds 500.

Many candidates pay only lip service to political surveys. They prefer to make basic campaign decisions on "gut response" or on the advice of trusted political intimates, even though they may make an investment, sometimes a sizable one, in research, simply because it is expected for credibility or to keep a contributor happy. If, for any reason, you don't expect to use survey results, don't go to the trouble and expense of commissioning these studies. If, however, you want and know how to use survey data, get the very best work that you can afford or that your staff can provide.

Some politicians still cannot believe that a survey of a few hundred voters can provide a sensitive, accurate reflection of the total electorate. Yet many studies demonstrate the reliability and accuracy of most professional surveys. Based on extrapolations from only a few election district returns, the major radio and television networks for many years have fairly accurately predicted the outcomes of elections early on election evenings.

2. *Voting behavior analysis* consists of recording the results of previous elections by the smallest geographic units available (usually election districts, which are also called wards or precincts in various parts of the country). In primary campaigns, you would use data from previous primary elections, while in general elections you would naturally study previous general elections. These data should be used in conjunction with an election district map of the area in which you are campaigning, so that supplemented by the results of the attitudinal surveys, decisions on geographical emphasis in your campaign strategy can be made. These maps can be of enormous help in scheduling the candidate's appearances.

3. *Supporting demographic analysis* consists of recording decennial U.S. census data and then mapping the census tract data as an overlay on a map of your election district, making separate maps to show the distribution of older people, young people, families with young children, nationalities, races, and any other variables that are important in determining your allocations of time, energy, and money in the campaign.

4. *Issue or policy studies* are written to aid a candidate and his staff in developing explicit positions on matters of interest to the electorate. These studies are issued to the press and the public in many campaigns. Positions on foreign policy, police protection, budget priorities, tax measures, and other issues of concern to local voters are prepared to indicate the candidate's views of what has to be done and how to do it. I find it

extraordinary that candidates almost never feel public pressure to make a similar announcement of the appointments they intend to make if elected; in many ways, this would indicate a great deal more about how they intend to govern than do general policy statements. As has been noted, the skills necessary for successful campaigning have less and less to do with the skills needed to govern well; media advertising emphasizes the "communicator" skills much more than the substance of what has to be communicated in a campaign. Similarly, many political consultants have stronger skills in selling new candidates than in doing first-rate economical campaigns.

INFORMAL RESEARCH AND ITS LIMITS

In addition to the formal types of research described above, all candidates, whether consciously or not, do informal research—they reach conclusions based on what they see around them, and they act on those conclusions by saying or not saying something, by emphasizing one issue over another, or in various other ways. The difficulty with informal research of this sort is that it is impossible to estimate its accuracy in advance. A common problem of even some experienced candidates is that they trust conclusions based on their subjective impressions from street campaigning more than those based on their objective research. Because he had received enthusiastic responses in his street campaigning for the New york mayoralty in 1977, Mayor Abraham Beame, in his disastrous campaign against Ed Koch and others, was said to have ignored a number of polls that showed him losing voter support. The Mayor was always greeted warmly on the streets. He and his manager believed incumbency had to be worth more than the polls indicated. Had he heeded the surveys, he might have been able to alter his campaigning style in time to regain the lost votes and win the election.

Some politicians greatly emphasize what they hear from cab drivers. Others read and are influenced by political columns in local newspapers, often despite their knowledge that the columnist is merely pulling together a series of guesses to make a deadline. Some like to talk with people in bars or candy stores or shopping centers. The supposition that these conversations may be significant assumes that the people being interviewed in this way constitute a probability sample in which all voters have an equal chance of being chosen—which of course they do not.

Such conversations may give you an idea of what's on people's minds, but you should not treat them as representative or use them to make any far-reaching decisions.

Many candidates have friends or acquaintances who turn up at headquarters two or three times a week to provide moral support or to suggest new perceptions, criticisms, or matters to be concerned about. Some are sincerely concerned; others trade on the doubts and worries most campaigners face daily. The advice of these "ego-support advisors" should almost always be completely disregarded. Usually, their opinions are about as useful and constructive as that of the sidewalk superintendent who reports to you that there is a crack in the foundation of your house—after the house has been built over the foundation. If they make you feel good, keep a few around, but don't take their information or advice seriously.

Other secondary information usually originates from campaign mavens. In most cases, the time you spend with them is apt to yield little reliable information while weakening the morale of the staff and volunteers who are really extending themselves for you. It would be better to allow an hour a week for your headquarters staff and full-time volunteers to air their gripes and tell you how they think things are going. That way, you'll benefit not only from keeping lines of staff communication open and from background information they are bound to have gained through working full-time on the campaign, but also because their effectiveness would be weakened if they couldn't get to you at least in this way. There's no satisfaction in working hard for someone who doesn't seem to know you're there. If you do choose to have such regular staff "bull sessions," remember the classic administrative principle: Compliment publicly when you feel it is appropriate, but criticize quietly and in private.

Minority problems and the growing political importance of blacks, Mexicans, Puerto Ricans, and other minority groups in the big cities of the United States have led to the emergence of a relatively new phenomenon. Most large-scale campaigns now have a "professional black" (or Jew, Puerto Rican, Chicano, etc.) to advise the candidate on how best to reach his or her group. In my experience, however, many of these advisors are openly opportunistic and don't represent their ethnic groups as much as their own personal ambitions. Their advice and liaison with community organizations may be useful, but I would emphasize the necessity of using sample surveys as the controlling data for any of your decisions about ethnic-group politics, rather than the views of individual, self-proclaimed "spokesmen" for these groups.

TYPES OF POLITICAL SURVEYS

Only three basic types of surveys should be considered in your political research: household surveys, telephone surveys, and mail surveys.

1. *Household interviews* of respondents in their own homes constitute the best research source, but they are also the most expensive. Prestigious firms charge over $50 per household interview, and larger campaigns (major congressionals and city- and statewide races) often require at least 500 interviews. In the 1980 presidential primary in New Hampshire, for example, three candidates used samples of about 600 respondents each. (It would make sense if candidates hard pressed for funds pooled their survey expenditures, since professional-quality research should not vary according to who commissions it, and each candidate would interpret the data for him- or herself in any case. I know of no example of this commonsense way of saving money, although campaign staffs often exchange polls.) These surveys are usually conducted from three to five times during a campaign to provide a picture of the direction in which public opinion is moving. If subsamples of quality are required, making it possible to obtain reliable data for given subgroups as well as for the group as a whole, such research can cost from $400,000 to $750,000 in a presidential campaign.* If a key decision has to be made and the whole campaign depends on it, a household sample in a large-scale campaign is probably cheap even at a high price, for without question, household interviews of respondents selected by a probability sample provide the highest quality of information available to any candidate. (To repeat an important definition, a probability sample—also called a random sample—of voters is one in which each voter in a given locale or "universe"

---

*President Carter's second campaign spent close to $750,000 for Pat Caddell's polling. Because survey costs have escalated sharply in recent years, some survey specialists have reduced sample size. I regard this as a dangerous trend. While the sampling reliability of totals and large subgroups in the sample is not threatened, campaign decisions often depend on the reliability of smaller subcells, e.g., women with children, or unemployed minority workers. The reliability of these cells is considerably affected by the reduction of overall sample size.

has the same chance of being interviewed as any other. Sampling specialists are able to estimate the reliability of such well-designed probability sample surveys with great accuracy.)

2. *Telephone surveys.* Although household interviews generally are best in providing detailed attitudinal information based on face-to-face discussions, telephone surveys are increasingly used when funds are more limited or informational requirements are of a lesser order of sensitivity. Telephone surveying has two advantages over household interviewing: it is considerably cheaper, and it can be done relatively quickly. If you need and can afford detailed answers to open-ended questions, household surveys are recommended. (Open-ended questions are those for which responses cannot be fully anticipated. Structured questions are essentially multiple-choice questions whose range of response is predictable to a large degree.) Otherwise, telephone surveys using centralized locations with professional supervision offer a more reasonably priced alternative. (Professional telephone surveys cost $15 to $35 an interview.)

In 1983, the consensus of political campaign professionals was that, if funds were available, polling generally should utilize telephones and consist of a comprehensive benchmark survey followed by at least two monitoring polls. The benchmark or full sample survey provides data on issues, problems, and reactions to the candidate's personality, information that is required to intelligently plan and organize a campaign.

The monitoring studies are usually only a partial sample focusing on certain demographic groups of voters (older people, younger women, Italians, etc.) that become critical as the campaign issues and the differences between candidates come into sharper focus as the campaign comes closer to election day. Other follow-up studies may focus on certain geographical areas or election districts.

Another type of tracking survey in wide use in the more lavishly financed gubernatorial, congressional, and presidential campaigns are daily or flash surveys, perhaps 50 to 100 interviews a night, in the last two weeks of a campaign. These data are not probability sample data and take a very experienced analyst to make them useful; these surveys, in my judgment, should *never* be used by inexperienced campaigners. They are designed to pick up changes, nuances of opinion that can reshape advertising, usually TV, and provide direction for new emphasis in theme or in geographical area and/or target groups.

My experience suggests that a less expensive tracking-type device would be the use of *focus group panels,* which only some of the major campaigns use. These panels have been found useful by advertising agencies in selling consumer goods for over thirty years. A group of people, varying in age, sex, ethnic background, education, etc. are asked to participate, perhaps once a week for two hours, in reviewing literature and TV and radio copy, and are asked to talk candidly about their reactions. The group may consist of 10 to 14 people.

It must be emphasized that these panels are not surrogates for a probability sample survey. But it is remarkable, if properly implemented, how much a candidate's staff can get from such panels. Panels should be run by campaign workers who can put people at ease and make the discussions enjoyable and interesting. The participants should not be paid; refreshments, however, should be served and campaign premiums or giveaways distributed.

3. *Mail surveys* sacrifice so much in quality and quantity of response that they have only limited utility as a last resort when nothing else is possible financially but any information is regarded as better than none. Despite this, even experienced politicians sometimes use postcard surveys, often for their public relations impact more than for their research value. In early 1972, for example, a county leader in New York sent out 20,000 postcards asking voters' preferences for presidential candidates. A professional survey could have been undertaken for the same expenditure of money but without the public relations benefit. (An example of a mail survey appears in Fig. 3-1.)

Bastardized or eclectic techniques include "scientific" postcard surveys in which a given number of cards is sent to each election district, and comparisons of total newspaper linage given to your campaign with that given to your opponent. The press often picks these up and gives them a credibility they do not deserve. Although the public is sometimes influenced by such surveys, the candidate shouldn't take them seriously.

A notable example of the dangers of such pseudo-surveys occurred in the U.S. senatorial campaign of 1970 in New York. It was rumored (such things are difficult to prove, as the people involved are rarely willing to discuss them on the record) that *The New York Times* was prepared to endorse the incumbent Republican Senator Charles E. Goodell in a three-way race, but was afraid that Goodell could not win and that to endorse him would take votes away from his Democratic opponent, Richard L.

ISSUES QUESTIONNAIRE

Please take the time to answer this questionnaire on issues that effect us all. After you are finished, please separate this page, fold on dotted line and stamp. Your answers are greatly appreciated.

1. Do you support or oppose giving public employees the right to strike?   SUPPORT ☐   OPPOSE ☐

2. Do you support State funding for legislative campaigns to replace the present system of private contributions?   SUPPORT ☐   OPPOSE ☐

3. Some people say that the California Supreme Court is doing a good job in protecting our constitutional rights. Others say that it has gone beyond its authority and makes law rather than interpreting it. Do you believe that the California Supreme Court is performing well?   YES ☐   NO ☐

4. Do you favor or oppose charging a fee of approximately $75.00 per semester to attend community colleges full-time?   YES ☐   NO ☐

5. Do you favor or oppose an increase in the tax on liquor and tobacco to provide additional funding for education?   FAVOR ☐   OPPOSE ☐

Comments _____

_____
_____
_____
_____
_____

Fig. 3-1. Example of a pseudo-survey (mail).

Ottinger, and thereby give the senate seat to the Conservative candidate, James L. Buckley. Goodell's manager was said to have assured the *Times* that his research demonstrated that Goodell could win, even though no other available research confirmed such a conclusion. The *Times* allegedly checked with Goodell's polling company, which swore that the results of the survey were reliable; meanwhile, some leading Republicans were said to have told the firm to give the *Times* any assurances that were sought. Staff men close to Ottinger believed that what probably happened was that the *Times* was considering not making any endorsement at all and that Goodell supporters put pressure on the paper to back up its previous praise of the candidate. It was later reported that the surveys cited in Goodell's behalf were hardly professional, apparently consisting merely of comparisons of the linage given to each candidate in New York City newspaper coverage of the campaigns. The *Times* endorsed Goodell, who did not come close to winning but did split the liberal vote with Ottinger. The *Times* endorsement probably was the *coup de grâce* for Ottinger, and Buckley won the election.

RETAINING A SURVEY CONSULTANT

All other things being equal, half of the quality of a probability sample depends on the precision and care exercised in choosing the people to be interviewed. The concept of picking samples is simple; proper implementation of the process, however, is a laborious task that requires a considerable degree of experience and skill. (In a 1972 congressional campaign in New York, for example, it took me four days to pull a sample of 500 voters for a telephone survey. This included the preparation of two additional substitution lists or ''decks'' of 3 x 5 cards for voters who had moved, refused to answer, were ill, or did not respond for other reasons. A single substitution deck is usually sufficient in most cities.)

Since most political research contracts involve relatively small amounts of money for the research firm, which must pay top sampling design men fees as high as $500 a day plus expenses, some firms are forced to compromise on sampling quality. Sometimes, for example, a prospective survey consultant may want to economize by using a sample for you that has already been selected for another use and that may not be perfectly appropriate to the new situation, or by permitting shortcuts in the sample selection process. Such a sample may or may not be adequate for your needs. If it is not, do not permit its use, for such a compromise can seriously decrease the reliability of the results. Professional advice on this point is absolutely critical—but you must make the decision. However, if you can't afford to hire a professional to check the sample design, there are a few simple rules that may help you judge for yourself the representativeness and randomness of a sample:

1. Check the sampling proportions of men and women against the universe (the entire voting group that interests you).

2. If the sample is for a large district, say a state senatorial or a congressional, check the sample by comparing its distribution by assembly districts against the distribution by assembly districts within the actual universe.

3. If the proportions of one or two ethnic groups in your district are known to you—for example, 35 percent of the population is Italian and 18 percent is black—the sampling proportions should approximate this (adjusting for differences in the age distribution and registration habits of each group).*

4. The sampling process should use the universe in which you're interested. If you're concerned only about one group of voters or one area in your district, the sample should not be drawn from the entire district.

5. Acceptable reliability limits, expressed as 95 percent probability (meaning that there are 95 chances in 100 that the sampling results are within 2 or 3 percent of the actual universe), should be stated.

6. The substitution process, absolutely critical in controlled sampling, should be spelled out explicitly for you.**

---

*Often, problems of this type are solved by using computer programs to reweight the new data, but it is important to know the original number of respondents in the cell. Many survey consultants simply show the reweighted tabulations. For example, in one campaign in which I was involved in 1981, the cell of Italian voters became critical in developing campaign strategy. The original cell contained 34 Italian respondents. The computer reweighting program blew up the cell and it then appeared reasonable; in reality the cell was underweighted and caused an early major distortion in campaign strategy.

**Substitution is a "pure" sampling procedure. Often political survey consultants will use modifications to reduce costs and to speed up the process. Whichever process is used, it should be clearly spelled out for you. Don't be embarrassed to ask basic questions; once the survey is completed the questions you can ask will be limited to what's on the computer tabulation printouts and to the analysis itself.

If these questions are answered satisfactorily, you are probably in good hands.

Because of the critical nature of the sampling process, your research specialist and campaign manager should make a detailed inquiry of prospective consultants, including the following questions:

- What will be the nature of the sample and the universe?
- Who will design the sample?
- How will the sample size be determined?
- Which statistical reliability limits will be used?
- Who will pick (or "pull") the sample?
- How will the interviewers be trained, and by whom?
- Which quality-control routines will be used during polling?
- How will substitutions for non-respondents be done?

The best time to ask these questions is when you are considering retaining a consultant, before a contract is signed. Many candidates and their managers base their hiring decisions exclusively on the amount of the bid (choosing the lowest) or the prestige of the firm (choosing the highest). Neither way is correct. A low bid may mean that quality procedures and quality supervisors and interviewers will not be provided; prestigious names and high prices do not always guarantee top quality. Any professional should be happy to discuss procedures in detail with you or your staff before expecting you to sign a contract.

Like all contracts signed in the course of your campaign, your research contracts should always be checked by a lawyer before you sign them. In addition to any recommendations your lawyer may make, you should insist that all tabulations of the survey results be made available to you, as well as the original questionnaires used by the interviewers.

If you do obtain the original questionnaires, you should take the time to read the comments of respondents as recorded on the questionnaires. Professional questionnaires usually include open-ended questions, which must be edited and coded before they can be fed into the computer. Reading respondents' actual answers to such questions may provide you with interesting insights that are lost when the answers are processed for computer use. Most will be of value only as parts of the whole sample, but a few may provide you with ideas that are of importance in planning the rest of your campaign.

An illustration of the technique that was used by the staff of Senator Edmund S. Muskie to choose a survey consultant in his 1972 presidential primary campaigns may be useful here. Twenty-five nationally known firms were invited to bid for a research contract expected to fall in the $250,000 to $500,000 price range, involving both national and regional samples. Each bidder was sent a list of possible research alternatives including alternative sample sizes. Quotes were invited for household as well as telephone interviews, central or localized supervision of the telephone interviews, and various numbers and types of questions to be asked.

After receiving the bids, Muskie's research director narrowed the field to five consultants, each of whom was invited to Washington to discuss his proposal in even more detail with the campaign staff. Each bidder was interviewed in depth about his sampling technique (developing a national sample is a very expensive and painstaking job), who his samplers and interviewers were, how they were to be trained and supervised, how the coding and editing were to be done, and other similar details. The consultant who was originally selected as a result of this process was not the most prestigious of those who had been considered, and since he guaranteed top quality he probably was not the lowest bidder. Unfortunately—but demonstrative of a not uncommon fact of political life—the completely professional and ambitious research that was contemplated was reportedly never carried out, because the campaign staff was unable to raise the money to pay for it. Instead, a lower-cost compromise was worked out and another consultant was retained.

COSTS OF POLITICAL RESEARCH

Budgeting for research studies is difficult. Spending money on radio advertisements and brochures seems to result in something tangible, visible, or measurable, but many campaigners don't see direct productive results from research. Examples throughout this book should clarify and concretize the value of political research and demonstrate its importance in the budget of any well-run campaign.

In any large-scale, professionally conducted campaign, 5 to 10 percent of the total amount available can reasonably be budgeted for research.*

---

*A large-scale campaign would be defined for this purpose as one costing in excess of $50,000. In smaller campaigns, the decision on the amount to spend on research would have to depend on how tight the race is and on whether adequate information is available from a political ally; it is impossible to establish even general guidelines for research expenditures in these instances. I would strongly recommend that even in smaller campaigns the requirements of objective research not be overlooked.

Costs of thorough professional research surveys are approximately $35 to $50 per household interview and $15 to $35 per telephone interview, with several hundred interviews usually required in a sample.** These fees include the following: (1) overhead, (2) profit, (3) training, (4) supervision, (5) interviews, (6) questionnaire design, (7) sample design, (8) sample selection, (9) coding schedules, (10) key punching (with 100 percent verification of the process), (12) cross-tabulation design, (13) computer program development and testing, (14) computer running time, (15) preparation of final tables, (16) analysis and presentation of final results, and (17) consultation with candidate and campaign staff.

This is the full job without shortcuts. You can pay less and get less, but you would also run the risk of defeating the purpose of performing the research in the first instance: getting the best information in order to make the most informed and thoughtful campaign policies and decisions. Research is not inexpensive, but it more than pays its way if done correctly: It increases the return on all media expenditures and structures the campaign sensibly.

WHICH DECISIONS SHOULD BE SUBJECTED TO RESEARCH

In designing political surveys, you should know in advance the questions you need answered. Too often, the right questions are not asked, so the results of the survey contribute very little to guiding decisions rationally, although that is the main purpose of any useful research survey. Every other purpose, such as public relations impact, should be secondary. This section describes certain major questions that every campaign has to answer in some fashion and that are susceptible to research.

Many professional politicians still think that modern campaigning depends too much on outside consultants and computer printouts; they maintain that the big "gut" decisions still have to be made intuitively

---

*Costs vary considerably. Often candidates are willing to pay very high fees to get the credibility of a "name" pollster; the fact that a candidate retains Richard Wirthlin (Reagan's polling consultant) or Pat Caddell (Carter's pollster) makes it easier for him or her to be taken seriously by major contributors. There are hundreds of polling firms and freelancers in the nation. The smaller firms take longer to turn a survey around but often do good work, since their number of clients is often fewer and the principals themselves can devote time to even a small campaign.

or by the seat of the pants.* They are probably partly right: Many candidates don't understand the import of the data and don't trust their advisors' interpretation of data; in addition, some of the larger decisions simply aren't susceptible to statistical analysis.** In some instances, research only identifies the larger problems without necessarily providing the answers, but at least the research enables the candidate to isolate, and concentrate on, the issues to which he or she must respond. Often, campaigners and their managers simply don't know how to use the data that may be made available to them. Nonetheless, nowadays, more than ever before, many more decisions in campaigns are made objectively on the basis of survey data. The decisions that research should influence include the following.

WHICH GROUPS TO APPEAL TO AND WHICH THEMES TO USE.   These are perhaps the most basic questions that campaign research has to answer for the organization of a successful campaign. There are several ways of using research to help answer them, all of which require the identification of relevant client groups. (The term "client group" is defined on p. 39.)

In congressional and city- and statewide campaigns, specific appeals usually are developed for specific client groups. In one area of your district, for example, the unreliability of garbage collection may be a hot issue. People will want to hear your ideas on improving garbage collection, and not on open space planning. For another client group in your district, narcotics may be the priority issue. You can speak in general

---

*Former Governor Edmund ("Pat") Brown of California was one of these. He believed in paying some attention to polls, but "I give at least equal weight to my own sensing of how things are going, developed primarily from conversations with people I meet during the day's campaigning." (Quoted in James M. Cannon (Ed.), *Politics U.S.A.: A Practical Guide to the Winning of Public Office,* Garden City, N.Y.: Doubleday, 1960, p. 45.)

**In 1982, reputable polls showed Mayor Tom Bradley, a black, with an 8 to 10 percent lead over his opponent George Deukmejian for Governor of California. Most political consultants seemed to think Bradley had it "locked." Bradley lost by a narrow margin, and in the outpouring of post mortems, it was clear that 3 percent of the white voters had been affected by racial prejudice which hadn't surfaced in the polls. Campaign variables are very fluid and changeable; Congressman Harold Washington, a black, was thought to be out of it in a three-way race for Mayor of Chicago in 1983. The polls showed him a weak third. However, Washington had a successful registration drive for blacks which the sampling process may not have reflected. In addition, an extraordinary 69 percent of all registered blacks voted, and 90 percent for Washington. He picked up six percent of the whites in the higher income liberal districts, and his two white opponents split the rest of the white vote. These variables weren't reflected in polling. Three- and four-way races in themselves are tough sampling problems; most candidates can't afford the expanded samples required to get decent reliability for the cells, and some pollsters forget to recommend the need for the expansion.

terms to all groups, but that is rarely the most effective thing to do. The voters want specific answers to their own problems, not platitudes and polite commiseration. If you don't have an answer, say so and ask for their ideas. Political research, supplemented by information provided by your experienced election district workers, should provide you with the themes that would appeal to the various groups in your district.

In a small sample for a minority candidate in New York, the analysis of the questionnaires suggested that Democratic women voters preferred the candidate in larger proportions than did Democratic men. However, a significant number of men appeared to be prejudiced against him. The poll suggested a very close race in the primary (the candidate finally won by less than 200 votes), so an additional mailing was sent to middle-income Jewish areas, mentioning that the candidate had worked his way through college, was graduated magna cum laude, and was both a certified public accountant and an attorney. This information —chosen to maximize the candidate's credentials among the undecided male voters—probably contributed to his victory.

Client groups in many areas are concerned about crime. The Manhattan congressional district represented by then Congressman Edward I. Koch includes Greenwich Village, and a neighborhood inhabited by large numbers of people who live alone. In recent years, the increasing crime rate in Greenwich Village has alarmed many of its single-woman residents. In the winter of 1971, Congressman Koch made the news by proposing that everyone who lived in the area carry a whistle. In the past, when someone screamed in the street, people hid in their apartments; Koch suggested that if anyone was heard screaming, everyone should come out and blow whistles. Community groups picked up the idea and began giving whistles to local residents; people began to feel safer walking in the streets; and Koch, in addition to doing a genuine service for his district, undoubtedly gained new supporters among his sizable client group of fearful women.

Sometimes your appeal is a counter-appeal. For example, should your research indicate that many voters resent the incumbent's having voted for tax increases after he had promised no tax increases, you may want to focus deliberately on the groups who are most concerned. It is probably unwise to promise no tax increases. Urban problems have shown voters that some increases are necessary to provide the services they want. You may therefore want to focus on the unfulfilled promise and on how, specifically, you will work to eliminate wastage and duplication in government spending and meet the real priority needs.

It is common in political attitudinal surveying to learn that many voters feel an incumbent has been in office too long. The theme, "It's time for a change," has considerable merit in these instances. A number of other possible "anti-themes" can become apparent from survey data. Each one must be evaluated. Whichever themes you choose must be tested by your research during the campaign. Sometimes such a theme is a natural, and your campaign may catch fire from it, but such positive results are rare from anti-themes. It is more likely that your positive positions will catch on; the one that does will undoubtedly be one that your client groups can relate to personally. Ideally, it will be a phrase or an idea—like Roosevelt's New Deal or Truman's Fair Deal—that focuses on what you are like as a person, as a politician, and as a leader. Attitudinal survey research can contribute greatly to the development of themes by showing you which subjects are most important to your voters and what type of leaders they most admire.

WHOSE ENDORSEMENT IS HELPFUL. The importance of endorsements was well illustrated in a Democratic primary election in New York City. In a light voter turnout in Queens in 1983, the Democratic candidate, State Senator Gerry Ackerman, ran away with the election although reportedly outspent five to one by the independent, Doug Schoen. It was commonly reported that although Schoen spent $350,000 in a four-way race, his opponent was endorsed by Governor Cuomo and Mayor Koch and these imprimaturs were too much to overcome.

Endorsements work both ways. They will attract some voters but they will repel others. It is important to do research on whose endorsements are valuable before asking for or accepting endorsements. The research should ascertain something that is quite basic but that is nevertheless lost sight of in many campaigns: whether, on balance, a given endorsement will help your cause or whether it will be the kiss of death, particularly among the groups of voters you wish to attract.

The impact of endorsements can be absurd but effective, like a famous ballplayer endorsing breakfast cereals for children: The endorsement itself isn't really relevant, but sales of the endorsed cereal increase markedly. In Manhattan, Leonard Farbstein, a regular Democrat, a steady if unglamorous congressman of some years, lost the 1970 primary election to

Bella Abzug, an active and vocal partisan of Women's Strike for Peace and other causes. Having been personally subjected to the campaigns of both candidates, I believe that Ms. Abzug won for several reasons: (1) Farbstein, who was in his early seventies, did not campaign hard and did not get a great deal of active support from the Democratic clubs; (2) Women's Liberation sympathizers and some non-Jewish groups in the primarily Jewish district found Ms. Abzug's opposition to the establishment attractive; and (3) most effective of all, in my judgment, and what actually made the difference in a tight race, was the booming endorsement of Barbra Streisand, who made appearances and rode on the sound trucks with Ms. Abzug. Ms. Streisand's appearances gave a touch of romantic show business and excitement to the campaign. She had as much (or as little) relevance in the campaign as Marlon Brando or Jane Fonda would have had, but that strictly logical judgment was beside the point. Had Jane Fonda endorsed Ms. Abzug, the results might have been negative, but Barbra Streisand was Jewish and originally from Brooklyn, and her strident voice and down-to-earth manner were effective with Jewish women particularly, and probably with Jewish men as well.

To research endorsement potentials, include a direct query in your questionnaire: "Whose endorsement among the following names would be most important to you in deciding your vote?" or "Whom among the following names do you most respect?" You may also wish to find out what newspaper's endorsement would be most advantageous to your candidacy. Another device is to ask with which segment of the party the respondent is aligned. The exact wording of the question should be decided only after intensive pre-testing, or interviewing respondents to test the relative effectiveness of the various versions of the question in obtaining meaningful responses.

Associative questioning—using adjectives to describe an ideal candidate or an ideal party spokesman—sometimes suggests the traits the voter values most highly. The descriptive words are then applied to individual politicians, and the respondent is asked which word or words best describe the candidate or the potential endorser.

Not all decisions about endorsements are based on research. Some perhaps including the decision to use Barbra Streisand in the Abzug campaign, may be based entirely on intuition or on intuition fortified by research. Always keep in mind, however, that such critical decisions should be based on the best information you can obtain within the short time available, so that the degree of risk can be established—and perhaps minimized as well.

Primary fights present a special endorsement problem. There, your problem normally won't be in associating with famous show business people, but rather in dealing with bitter intra-party rivalries. It's hard to know without some research who in the party may actually help you by lending you his name at any given time. In some cases, nobody the public is familiar with may offer any assurance of help; in such a situation, you may have to build up your endorsers as part of your campaign.

WHERE TO SPEND TIME.   Research can help enormously in deciding this essential question by keeping you advised about where and with what voters you are doing well and where that is not the case. To emphasize a point that has been made earlier in this book, most campaigns are decided by margins of less than 10 percent of the total vote. As the campaign progresses, you should be able to ascertain fairly closely the characteristics of the undecided voters and the reasons why they remain undecided. You'll have to examine your own conscience to determine how much you want to emphasize an issue that interests the uncommitted; it makes sense, however, to stay in the character and political form you've developed during the campaign. Too much switching around may make some voters uneasy about you; too little response may bother others.*

Using research should help you to decide how to spend your time by showing you where the undecided are, what concerns them most, and to what appeals they are most receptive. For example, although enthusiastic receptions may seduce you into wanting to spend a large proportion of your time campaigning in the streets, research may show you that radio and television interviews have a greater impact on the undecided voters in your district. In such a case, quietly preparing for interviews by studying the major issues very carefully may be a better investment of your time than street campaigning.

MODULATING CAMPAIGN THEMES.   Research is helpful in determining how the voters feel about developing controversies. Some of this research may come from a clipping file, from talking to people in shopping centers

---

*The 1972 McGovern presidential campaign is the best example of this in the last generation.

and on walking trips, from watching local television and listening to local radio programs, from talking to taxi drivers, or from other informal sources. The most reliable information, however, will come from telephone or household interviews with people chosen in a scientifically planned sample. Such a survey has two principal advantages over the informal sources of information: Its reliability is known, and it is relatively inexpensive—possibly even cheaper than feeding and caring for the hangers-on who often haunt campaign headquarters and are always ready to provide opinions and advice on policy.

A sequential "panel" or "continuity" approach is important in objectively establishing how the voting public is reacting to developing issues as well as in providing data indicating what bothers voters about you and/or your opponent. This technique consists of interviewing the same group of respondents a number of times during a campaign to see how their attitudes change in response to changes in the campaign. The virtue of the panel approach is simple: By interviewing the same sample at intervals during the campaign, you're able to develop a sense of which groups are responding to each appeal and which groups are not.

The U.S. Census Bureau Current Population Survey uses a modified panel approach in which a given percentage of the panel is carried over into each succeeding survey and the remainder of the panel is replaced by new respondents. Theoretically, any series of perfectly chosen probability samples should provide accurate comparisons. The panel approach is useful, however, because in practice it is almost impossible to draw a series of samples that is absolutely without some bias.

Although it is unwise to change campaign strategies and tactics frequently, some modulation of campaign themes is generally necessary. Often these changes will reflect opportunities that may pop up: an opponent's friend is accused of taking a bribe; the opponent has people call voters on their religious holidays and represent themselves as your workers (this reportedly happened to Richard L. Ottinger in his New York senatorial campaign in 1970) and you learn of the ruse and take it to the press, etc. Research can help you modulate your campaign appeals in a more sophisticated manner by showing you which appeals are getting through and which aspects of your program are ambiguous. The panel approach discussed above is probably most helpful in this regard. The results are of great value in adapting campaign literature to current needs and deciding on content and emphasis for television and radio commercials; the research should provide very useful data on advertising effectiveness.

ESTABLISHING AN OPPONENT'S VULNERABILITY.   Survey data can indicate with some specificity the content of the most effective attacks on your opponent. For example, research analysis may sometimes indicate the advisability of attacking the opponent's leader or party rather than the opponent himself. Many Republican politicians used this tactic with great success against local Democratic opponents when Jimmy Carter was heading the Democratic ticket in 1980. In 1972, local Democratic candidates were reported to be disassociating themselves from George McGovern out of fear that an overwhelming Nixon victory would lead to their defeat, just as many local Republican candidates had been defeated as a consequence of Goldwater's disastrous loss in 1964. In some instances, particularly in primaries, survey analysis may indicate that the public really likes your opponent but doesn't think he or she has a real chance of winning. Your move then may be simply to compliment your opponent whenever possible but keep indicating that this person can't win.

WHICH RADIO AND TELEVISION STATIONS AND TIMES TO BUY.   Information from polling is now often used to determine which radio and television stations voters prefer, which hours of the day or night and which particular shows. Since in major campaigns expenditures on TV can be perhaps 50 to 60 percent of the entire campaign budget, accurate information on viewing patterns and preferences can be quite critical. These data on the preferences of voters is cross-tabulated against those voters who are undecided, voters for whom a single issue may be controlling, or voters who have indicated a preference for your opponent but not a very strong one, etc.

Radio and television time buying is an important skill, and there are specialists in every major city. Some consultants recommend saturation buys, this ostensibly to make certain that every voter is reached.* This strategy is not always affordable and not cost-effective in any case. A

---

*It should be remembered that time buyers and media consultants are often paid based on a percentage of the buy. Recently a journalist explained that New Yorker articles may run long because the magazine pays its writers one dollar a word. Essentially, some political media consultants may have an incentive to commit monies especially to television, which are big-ticket buys.

recent example, discussed above, was the March 1983 off-year election for congress in Queens. An independent candidate spent a reported $350,000 in a four-week race, using TV very liberally, supported by mail, radio, and phone banks. The candidate bought the New York region to reach a congressional district. The Democratic candidate made the lavish expenditure part of his campaign. The issue was to make the independent credible as a superior Democrat to the organization's candidate, who had the endorsements of Governor Cuomo and Mayor Koch. The TV saturation by itself could not accomplish this. It is also possible that television is not automatically the best mechanism in every campaign. The general rule is that selective buys matched to what your surveys show is happening to your various "target" groups is much preferable.

In addition, I believe that it can be very helpful to campaigners in large urban areas to determine cable television station preferences in the research surveys. They are relatively inexpensive yet allow you to reach many voters, particularly in primaries.

WHEN, WHERE, AND TO WHOM TO MAIL POLITICAL LITERATURE.
These are important decisions that can be made rationally on the basis of sample surveys and demographic analysis. The content of brochures is also a proper subject for research. An average congressional district may require as many as 100,000 letters and perhaps three separate mailings to have impact. Mailing 300,000 letters, including the cost of design, preparation, computerized addressing, sealing, and bulk rate postage, amounts to about $50,000.* That is a lot of money even for wealthy campaigners. It makes no sense not to use it as effectively as possible by researching to establish the subjects to which voters will respond.

Voting behavior analysis and supporting demographic analysis (discussed on pp. 74-75) can also be used to great advantage in targeting mailings of political iterature for maximum economy and effectiveness. One campaigner did an analysis of past voting patterns by election district. He then mapped the results of his analysis on translucent paper and made a postal zip code map of the same election district on the same scale, also on translucent paper. When he put one map on top of the other on

---

*Congressional incumbents have an advantage in this regard; they often manage to use their franking privilege—which may not be legally used for purely political literature—for semi-political mailings to their constituents. Hundreds of thousands of congressional "newsletters" flood the county a few months before election time, all paid for by public funds.

a light table (that is, a table with a frosted glass top and lights inside), he was able to see at a glance which zip code areas were likely to be sympathetic to his candidacy and which were highly unlikely to be receptive to his appeals. Since mailings into the latter zip code areas were clearly not a good investment, he directed that the computer addressing the mailings "suppress" or discard all addresses having those zip codes. As a result, mailings were sent only into districts where optimal impact was probable, and money was saved that would in effect have gone down the drain by mailings into hostile areas. Supporting demographic analysis might have been used in a similar way, to identify the zip code areas having a high concentration of certain client groups—for example, young voters or Spanish-speaking voters. Specially prepared brochures could then have been sent into those zip code areas.

Survey research in some areas may reveal that 90 percent of the people of a certain ethnic ancestry really hate you. In such a situation, you certainly don't want to remind them to come out and vote—in effect, you would be pulling for your opponent. It is possible to design computer programs to suppress surnames suggesting a certain ethnic background. such programs cost money to write, but they produce substantial savings in large-scale operations. (This is a variation of what is known as "ethnication," which is treated more fully in the section on computer mailings.)

POSITION PAPERS

Almost every campaign includes substantive research papers, which are usually called position papers, white papers, or issue statements. (The term "white paper" comes from the nomenclature and cover paper used by the British Government for its evaluations of policies and programs.) In some campaigns, I have seen much staff time and money go into preparation of these papers for no other reason than that the opponents were doing it. Don't do position papers merely to do what your opponent is doing. Use them to dramatize your priorities and your feelings about problems.

If you're running in a small area, you probably won't need or even wish to ask professional help for preparing position papers, but you will probably be generally familiar with local issues and will want to bring yourself up to date in great detail for participating in public debates or providing sensible answers to questions you may be asked about problems that confront the community. On highly critical issues, or in larger areas, you will need background papers by specialists to give you an overview of problems with which you may not be as familiar. Your political survey research will be supplying you with ideas of what's on people's minds. This information should indicate which topics require position papers. Before the papers are typed for distribution, go over them critically with your principal advisors and associates to make certain they reflect your views accurately. Have copies made for distribution to persons who will be speaking on your behalf as well as interested voters, civic groups, editorial writers, and the press generally.

RECONCILING RESEARCH WITH YOUR INSTINCTS

Although research is critical for a sensibly run race, sometimes the data can't be totally conclusive.* Ambiguities in survey data often reflect honest confusion or voter disinterest. sometimes in a three-way race, for example, the data will show that Candidate B, say, is the one whose challenge is strongest. If you therefore put Candidate C in the background and don't attack him, you may find that, near the end of the campaign, your final panel survey shows that C has gained considerable strength. It is then too late to recoup.** This kind of problem is occurring more frequently as multi-candidate elections have become common. Research is necessary as a basis for informed decision making, but intuition is sometimes absolutely necessary to anticipate trends before research data can fully document them. Professional-quality research is critical—but it cannot control everything. The creative campaigner and campaign manager use research, but they integrate it with their own well-developed political instincts. Sometimes you must take a chance before you have conclusive research results; if you are afraid of taking risks in a campaign, how can you expect to react promptly to rapidly changing problems if you are elected?

---

*In recent years it has not been unusual for 20 to 30 percent of the voters to switch as the campaign closes. It has made life for pollsters difficult. These experiences probably occasion such stories as this: "How do you define a consultant? Someone who can talk to you intelligently about 83 positions for making love, but doesn't know any women."

**This is precisely what happened in the Ottinger-Goodell-Buckley New York senatorial race in 1970. Ottinger made Goodell his main target and only at the very end turned his attack toward Buckley. The change came too late; Buckley emerged the winner. Because of this race and others, the New York State legislature passed a bill in its 1972 session providing for a run-off election if no single city- or statewide candidate received 40 percent of the vote.

On other occasions, you may find it difficult to balance research results with your own view of what is right or prudent. About twenty years ago, I set up a write-in survey for the challenger in a congressional campaign in the South Bronx, a formerly nearly all-white area into which large numbers of blacks and Puerto Ricans were beginning to move. We received 2,000 responses which revealed that the middle-income white voters feared blacks and increasing crime—each respondent seemed to want a private moat and a personal policeman. The candidate sincerely wished to minimize racial tensions and was therefore reluctant to issue a position paper on the subject, despite the research finding that race was a major issue. By now, he has been a congressman for many years and has sponsored bills to do crime control research. A generation ago, however, he didn't feel the issue could be talked about from the campaign platform. Most politicians then shared his view.*

There are times when you have to stop looking over your shoulder. Doing what you really believe may lose some votes, but people's respect for your honesty may also earn you votes that you might not have gotten otherwise. Senator Muskie's frankness in 1972 in indicating he would prefer not to have a black vice presidential running mate irritated many blacks and liberals. But some black organizations, noting that he was simply stating openly a fact of political life, supported him by admitting that, nationally, a black vice presidential candidate would hurt the chances of the Democratic party for victory. In 1983, Democratic presidential candidates face the problem again because of the great successes Democratic black mayoral candidates have had in major cities.

---

*It's possible that the nuclear freeze issue is undergoing a similar transformation. For years politicians have discussed it as a marginal issue despite the warnings of polls years ago. But by 1983, because of the enormous budget deficits of the federal government and the need to cut spending, it has become a respectable position for many politicians, and one causing them relatively little risk.

4
Doing Survey Research Yourself

In many campaigns, the candidate simply can't afford to pay a professional research consultant to do a sample survey. Often, when this occurs, campaign staffs attempt to do their own surveys. These surrogate "surveys" sometimes include postcard surveys, interviews with taxi drivers, a few telephone interviews, or reliance on press reports on the candidate's position in the race. These are not true probability surveys, and they have no reliability whatsoever.

Furthermore, strange things happen in campaigns when "bad" data are produced: Other people hear of the "study"— or are even told about it by members of the campaign staff—and comments are made to reporters. The data take on a life of their own, and staff people start believing them even when they are aware of their serious limitations. These surveys (and some professional ones as well) lend a magical cast to a campaign, much like the effect of magicians and astrologers in the courts of medieval kings. Good surveys are not magical, and inferior ones are magical only in their acceptance by unsuspecting politicians and in the great damage they can do. Good, professional-quality surveys depend on detailing, intensive training, and using quality-control routines from beginning to end.

Using inferior surveys in an attempt to manipulate public opinion is dangerous. After all, a full "survey" will be available on election day, and that is what campaigning must influence. Using unreliable data is not a good way to go about this job.

If you can possibly afford to have your surveys done professionally, by all means do so. If you must use campaign staff for surveying, at least try to obtain the advisory services of a professional statistician. If you cannot afford a professional statistician, try to have the job done as close to professional standards as possible, as described in the course of this chapter, retaining consultants only for sample design and for computer tabulations, which require skills and experience that amateurs simply can't replicate.

The steps in doing a probability attitudinal survey were enumerated earlier. The remainder of this chapter explains in detail how to take each step.

Sample designing is extremely difficult to do well without specialized training and experience. To approximate professional standards, the following rough guide is recommended when detailed information is needed on specific issues:

UNIVERSE	SAMPLE SIZE
Under 10,000 voters	150
10,000–24,999 voters	250
25,000–49,999 voters	400
50,000–99,999 voters	500
100,000–249,999 voters	600
250,000–499,999 voters	750
500,000 and more voters	1,000

Technically, the correct sample size is a function of the smallest "cell" for which your information must be reliable. A cell is a unit of information—for example, all the black families in the election district whose annual income is under $10,000. The sample size needed to provide adequate information if this were the critical cell would vary considerably from the sample size necessary to provide reliable data for a cell composed of all women in the area who are 35 to 55 years old and have been married at least once. To give another example, if for a citywide sample you need reliable information on the views of divorced women 18 to 45 years of age who have children under 6 years old (which may make sense if you think day care might be a significant issue), your overall sample size would have to be considerably larger than if the smallest single group for which you needed reliable information was all women 18 to 45 years old (which might be adequate if you were interested in views on abortion reform). This example illustrates the basic principle that the smaller the critical cell, the larger the necessary sample. (The critical cell is the smallest group for which you need reliable information.)

Developing exact sampling routines is a highly technical process, and if you cannot afford to hire a professional, you should attempt it only after consulting, first, the U.S. Bureau of the Budget's *Household Survey Manual 1969* (available from the Superintendent of Documents, Washington, D.C. 20402), the U.S. Bureau of the Census' *Current Population Survey* methodologies, and, for specific statistical procedures, other texts that are listed in the bibliography in the back of this book.

In many political surveys, the sample should be picked from the voter registration books that are usually available from the local board of elections. State laws generally require that these books be published, and frequently they are available in local libraries. In a primary contest, of course, the sample is picked only from among those voters who are registered in a single political party. Names of voters in voter registration books are usually alphabetized by election district, with each registrant's party enrollment listed. If you have staff time available, it is preferable to select samples for primaries from a list of actual primary voters— usually 20 to 30 percent of all registrants. Since this requires checking each enrollment card in the district to see who has actually voted in a primary, it is thus usually a major piece of work and so expensive that it is not done as frequently as it should be. However, this single step can save more campaign monies than any other in primary contests; such a list allows you to save money on direct mail, phone banks, door-to-door canvassing, and other campaign operations.

If your district includes 8,000 registrants for your party, your sample control total from the universe/sample size table above is 150. An additional sample deck of 150 3 x 5 cards should be prepared for substitution purposes, since some voters move, die, get sick, or refuse to answer questions—and since, in some cities, as many as 20 percent of the telephones may have unlisted numbers.* The usual routine is to attempt to interview the respondent (either by telephone or by household interview) at least three times during the course of the survey. If this fails for any reason, make a substitution. The new respondent should match the characteristics of the original sample respondent as closely as possible: woman for woman, election district for election district, and even street for street if at all possible. The smallest sample you should ever use is 100 interviews. The largest you'll ever need is 1,500, for statewide or complicated city races. The Gallup and Harris surveys use national samples of 1,500 respondents. The U.S. Bureau of the Census household survey uses a base of 50,000 interviews, but it is designed to provide an enormous

---

*In some cities, particularly with a large low-income population where many households have no telephone, three or four decks may be required. In one poll in New York City, I had to develop 10 decks to get an adequate sample of the Puerto Rican voters. In some situations the refusal rate can run as high as 50 percent, causing sampling problems. When the refusal rate is this high, you may end up getting an oversample of older retired people who enjoy the interview process and have the time for it. This is why the substitution process done properly provides a better sample.

mass of detailed information for the nation as a whole as well as for individual regions.

The proper way to select a probability sample employs tables of random numbers which are available in basic mathematical statistics texts. Since many registration books are arranged in columns, the variables requiring random number selection are page numbers, line numbers, and column numbers. Ideally, each of these variables should be separately selected. To do this, for a sample of 150 voters, you need 300 3 x 5 cards. The first 150 cards comprise your basic sample; the second 150 cards are a substitute deck. Since, as noted above, you have three variables, you go through 300 units of random number series three separate times, so that when you finish, each of your cards has three separate numbers on it. The first of these will denote the page number, the second the line number, and the third the column number of the name of the respondent associated with that card. If you are running in a primary election and the name designated by the random numbers is not of your party, you take the first appropriate name following that one. This process is tedious and time-consuming even for experienced people; it takes up to three days for two professionals to do it properly for a custom sample of 500 to 700 (including a substitute deck).*

With inexperienced people you may be better off sacrificing absolute professional accuracy and picking your sample in the following way: Take the number of pages in the registration book and divide by the total size of the necessary sample. For example, if you require a sample of 100 and the registration book contains 300 pages, your sampling guide would be one name for every three pages. Decide to start on one of the first three pages. If you choose to start at page 2, then one name should be selected on every following third page, that is, pages 5, 8, 11, etc. The book may be divided into pages of three columns containing thirty names each. Make an arbitrary decision that your sample line will be the twentieth name in each second column. The substitute deck sample can start on page 1 and use the tenth name in the first column of pages 4, 7, 10, etc. For technical reasons, this sampling method is not as reliable as using random numbers, but it will still produce useful results, and you may consider it a sacrifice of some quality which is made worthwhile by the saving of a professional consultant's fee.

---

*In practice most pollsters use computer generated random numbers or use the services of firms that specialize in developing samples for market research purposes.

There are other procedures for sampling beside the pure probability method just described. The "quota-sampling" method of sample selection allows the interviewers some discretion in choosing respondents. For example, the interviewer is instructed to interview any ten respondents residing in a specific block. When these ten have been interviewed, that part of the sample is complete. This method is cheaper and faster but considerably less reliable than probability sampling. Most interviewers are paid by the hour, and some may try to make their quota as fast as possible, sacrificing some quality in the process. It is more expensive, but far better, if you specify an address for each respondent. Sometimes, consultants pick an original probability sample and allow interviewers discretion for substitutions as needed in the field. In practice, this can be dangerous, since substitution must be exact if reliability is to be assured.

Household sampling usually involves the selection of sampling points; these define where clusters of personal interviews are required. The number and identification of these points require some skill and judgment, because the specialist has to balance economies of scale (it is cheaper to do ten interviews in one neighborhood than in five) against the need to distribute the points throughout the area to obtain adequate representation.

"Stratified sampling" involves selecting a sub-universe, perhaps males between 21 and 35 years of age, and selecting a sample from this group. Stratified samples are used when a candidate is interested in learning the opinions of only a given client group or client groups—for example, women or members of minority groups residing in his district. Stratified samples can be selected by either pure probability or quota sampling; the pure probability method is of course much more accurate.

After any sample is selected, it should be checked for consistency: proportions of men and women, geographic distribution, racial-ethnic distribution, etc. If there is a particular interest in one cell, you may wish to add to that portion of the sample to guarantee the reliability of data on that group's attitudes. For example, if one geographic area is important indeveloping your campaign strategy, that sample sector should be added to. This procedure really amounts to adjusting your sample for the critical cells necessary for making informed judgments and sensitive policy decisions. At the end of the process, you have a stratified probability sample that can be enormously useful to the campaign staff.

Political sampling is filled with problems. In most metropolitan area and city samples especially, there are enormous sampling difficulties.

The following technical remarks indicating the scope of the problem will be of interest only to those who are willing to do the background research and painstaking work that picking a quality sample requires. In some situations—particularly in urban areas, where unlisted telephone numbers can damage the reliability of a sample—sampling specialists use "random digit select" programs based on tables of random numbers taken from statistical textbooks or developed by computer software. In this technique, a random series of seven-digit numbers is chosen, with the choices limited to those beginning with three digits that represent local telephone exchanges and the chosen numbers representing local telephones. Although this procedure eliminates looking up telephone numbers for respondents whose names have been selected from the election rolls, it has its own complications: You may have to call each number to find out whether the resident is a registered voter and, if so, in the case of a primary election, what his party is. (If your local telephone company makes available a directory of telephones arranged by number or by street address, you can check the names in the voter registration book—but you are stuck with the problem of unlisted numbers.) In my view, although more tedious, it is preferable to sample from registration lists or actual primary voter lists.

In general elections many consultants will use computer generated random numbers and screen for party registration. (Screening is the process of asking preliminary questions to identify the appropriate respondent.) Many calls will be placed to non-residential numbers in this procedure. A modification is to obtain the first three digit codes for residential areas and develop your own sample by choosing random numbers—this will give you access to unlisted residential numbers or you can select residential numbers from the phone book and add or subtract a specified number from 1 to 9 from the last digit.

Shortcuts can sometimes be discovered. In many cities and towns, for example, as well as in many rural counties, each registered voter is assigned a number. The numbers are sequenced in the order in which the people register. It is possible to work out a reasonably good probability sample based on these numbers. The only bias here is that older voters who have not moved are concentrated in the lower numbers and may therefore be under-represented unless the sample is adjusted to allow for them. These problems are mentioned to indicate how much care has to be exercised in sample selection if the results are to be worthwhile.

Names chosen for the survey should be entered on 3 x 5 cards with election districts, assembly districts, and other details entered. The interviewers should be instructed to interview *only* the respondent listed and no other person in the family, or the sampling reliability of the work will be completely destroyed. The cards should look like the following example.

SAMPLING CONTROL CARD

Assembly District_____   Interviewer_____
Election District_____   Date of interview 1)_____ _____
Party registration_____   2)_____
Voted 1982 primary_____ _____   3)_____ _____
Voted 1984 primary_____   Substitution_____ _

Name_____ ____ _____ .
Address___ ____ _____
Telephone_____
Comments _____ _____
         _____ _____
         _____

Questionnaire designing is best done by starting with a list of questions that you have to answer in order to make sensible judgments on campaign strategy and tactics—questions such as:

- How do voters react to your personality vis-a-vis that of your opponent, and why?
- Whom would they vote for if the election took place at the time of the survey? If undecided, whom are they leaning to?
- Which issues are most important to them?
- How important are specific endorsements?
- Which politicians' names do they recognize and with what degree of approval?

Other questions that research is frequently called upon to answer were discussed earlier in this chapter, and others that are specific to your campaign should occur to you as well.

Figure 4-1 is an example of a telephone interview questionnaire.* This should be taken as a guide only, since it was developed for specific reasons having to do with a specific campaign at a specific time in a specific locality.

As much as possible, the questionnaires you develop should be pre-coded in order to facilitate subsequent coding, editing, and tabulation.** This is particularly important when inexperienced interviewers and editors are involved. The answers to open-ended questions such as "What do you think about . . . ?" must be looked at individually, are susceptible to misinterpretation, and are difficult for amateurs to code and edit. Generally the procedure is to review 25 percent of the questionnaires and prepare codes for open-end responses that will be appropriate for the entire sample.

Questionnaire design depends a great deal on whether you are using household or telephone interviews. You can do intensive probes in household interviews using both open-ended and associative questions, but this is much more difficult in telephone surveys.***

A good questionnaire is characterized by language so precise that each respondent clearly understands what is being asked and each understands the same way. Each interview must be conducted the same way, with exactly the same questions. To emphasize: The questions must be asked substantially as written in each case. In practice, many interviewers change the wording slightly to fit their usual habits of speech. This is not particularly dangerous as long as each interviewer is consistent about the focus and basic wording of the questions. Some interviewers say, "May I also ask you about . . . " as a transition from question to question.

---

*The Connecticut survey was done for now Congressman Sam Gejdenson. Mr. Gejdenson was regarded as a certain loser in a three-way race since one of his opponents was the son of a previous governor and well-financed. Gejdenson, a naturally gifted campaigner, worked hard, was creative, and scored a stunning upset. The survey data were found very useful in guiding the campaign. The questionnaire was designed so that volunteers could do it.

**Pre-coding is a process of structuring the probable responses into multi-choice questions. Such responses can be matched to "fields" (vertical columns) on IBM cards. Basically, an IBM card consists of 80 fields or columns, each of which can record up to twelve responses. Designing a questionnaire in such a way that it can be kept to one IBM card can save significant amounts of time and money in editing and data processing operations.

***"Probe" is an instruction to interviewers allowing them discretion to rephrase the question and explore a respondent's first answer to a question. An example of an associative question is: Which of these would you say best describes Congressman Jones? Energetic_____ Personable_____ Honest_____ Opportunistic_____ Incompetent_____ Represents us well_____ Means well but doesn't seem sure of what to do_____ Other_____

Edward Schwartzman   June 1980
Political Survey Consultant   (- - -) 1-3

Second Congressional District

Hello. Is this (or: May I speak with)_____?
My name is _____. I'm calling for E.S. Research
Associates. We're doing a survey of the attitudes of registered Democrats in the second
congressional district. I'd appreciate a few moments of your time. Thank you.

1. To begin with, did you vote in the Carter-Kennedy primary in March?

(Do not	1. _____ Yes	(4)
read)	2. _____ No	
	9. _____ DK Skip to 3	
	0. _____ Ref	

2. For whom did you vote in that election?

(Do not	1. _____ Carter	(5)
read)	2. _____ Kennedy	
	3. _____ Brown	
	9. _____ DK	
	0. _____ Ref	

3. How would you rate the Carter administration? Would you say it is . . .

(Read)	1. _____ Excellent	(6)
	2. _____ Good	
	3. _____ Fair	
	4. _____ Poor	
(Do not	9. _____ DK	
read)	0. _____ Ref	

4. If the election for President were held today, for whom would you vote?

(Read;	1. _____ Carter	(7)
rotate)	2. _____ Reagen	
	3. _____ Anderson	
	8. _____ (Other)	
	9. _____ Undecided	
	0. _____ Ref	

5. Now, turning to Connecticut, may I ask how you think Governor Grasso has
done her job? Would you say . . .

(Read)	1. _____ Excellent	(8)
	2. _____ Good	
	3. _____ Fair	
	4. _____ Poor	
(Do not	9. _____ DK	
read)	0. _____ Ref	

Fig. 4-1. An example of a telephone questionnaire used in a congressional campaign.

6. Now, the following are names of people involved in Connecticut politics. Would you tell me if you have a very favorable, favorable, unfavorable, or very unfavorable impression of each person? If you have no opinion, or haven't heard of the person, please just tell me that.

(Read; rotate)	Very Fav.	Fav.	Unfav.	Very Unfav.	Never Heard	DK	
1. Chris Dodd	___	___	___	___	___	___	(9)
2. Dempsey, Jr.	___	___	___	___	___	___	(10)
3. Richard Schneller	___	___	___	___	___	___	(11)
4. Toby Moffet	___	___	___	___	___	___	(12)
5. Patricia Handel	___	___	___	___	___	___	(13)
6. Jerry Murphy	___	___	___	___	___	___	(14)
7. Sam Gejdenson	___	___	___	___	___	___	(15)
8. Dempsey, Sr.	___	___	___	___	___	___	(16)

7. (For all rating responses for 6-2, 6-5, and 6-6) ask:
a) You say that you have a _____ impression of _____ Dempsey, Jr., can you tell me why you feel that way?

_____   (17 ___)

_____ (Probe) Any other reason? _____   (18 ___)

b) And for Patricia Handel, can you tell me why you have that impression?

_____   (19 ___)

_____ (Probe) _____   (20 ___)

c) For Sam Gejdenson, you indicated that your impression was _____, can you tell me why you feel that way?

_____   (21 ___)

_____ (Probe) _____   (22 ___)

8. What in your judgment are the two most important problems in your community?
(Do not read; check first two mentioned)

(23) 1. _____ Unemployment (24) 1. _____ Facilities for aged
    2. _____ Inflation   2. _____ Quality of life
    3. _____ Crime   3. _____ Lack of community
    4. _____ High taxes   4. _____ High-sulfur industrial
    5. _____ Trust and confidence   fuel
            in government   5. _____ Hazardous wastes
    6. _____ Gasoline prices/energy   dumping
    7. _____ Housing   6. _____ Drinking water quality
    8. _____ Racial tensions   7. _____ Middle-income educa-
    9. _____ Narcotics   tion problems
    0. _____ Education   8. _____ Environmental prob-
    X. _____ Recreation   lems
    Y. _____ Welfare/government   9. _____ (Other; specify)
            waste

Fig. 4-1. (Continued)

9. Which do you think are the two most important problems facing the   (25)
country today?   (26___)
    (Do not read; check first two mentioned)

     1. _____ Foreign policy
     2. _____ Inflation
     3. _____ Recession
     4. _____ Unemployment
     5. _____ Energy
     6. _____ Lack of national direction
     7. _____ Lack of competent leadership
     8. _____ Crime
     9. _____ High taxes
     0. _____ (Other; specify)

10. If you were the Congressman representing your district, what would you make
your top concern?

_____   _____ (27 ___)

_____   _____

11. (Rotate) Dempsey, Gejdenson, and Handel are running for Congress in the
Democratic primary this September. If the election were being held today, for whom
would you vote?

   a) 1. _____ Dempsey   (28)
     2. _____ Gejdenson
     3. _____ Hendel
     9. _____ Undecided

  b) If the race were between:

     1. _____ Hendel   (29)
     2. _____ Gejdenson
     9. _____ Undecided

  c) And between:

     1. _____ Dempsey   (30)
     2. _____ Gejdenson
     9. _____ Undecided

12. In your opinion, of the following which are the two most important qualities a
Congressman should have to represent your district?
    (Read; rotate. Check only first two mentioned)

     1. _____ Honest and competent   (31)
     2. _____ Legal background
     3. _____ Lived in the area for many years
     4. _____ Previous legislative experience
     5. _____ Hard working
     6. _____ Good working relations with other political leaders
     7. _____ Private business experience
     8. _____ (Other; specify)

Fig. 4-1. (Continued)

13. Whose endorsement, either political or community leaders, is most important to you in deciding which candidate to vote for?

(32 ____)

_____ (33 ____)

14. The issue of energy is very sensitive and important to all of us. Do you think . . .

a) That gasoline rationing should be established?

1. ____ Yes   (34)
2. ____ No
9. ____ Undecided
0. ____ Ref

b) That large oil companies should be broken up into smaller units?

1. ____ Yes   (35)
2. ____ No
9. ____ Undecided
0. ____ Ref

c) That new public investment in energy should emphasize nuclear generating plants?

1. ____ Yes   (36)
2. ____ No
9. ____ Undecided
0. ____ Ref

d) That new public investment in energy should emphasize solar and other renewable resources?

1. ____ Yes   (37)
2. ____ No
3. ____ Undecided
0. ____ Ref

(Comments on 14)

_____

_____

15. Are you in favor of wage and price controls as a means of dealing with inflation?

1. ____ Yes   (38)
2. ____ No
9. ____ Undecided
0. ____ Ref

16. Do you think gun control laws would help control crime?

1. ____ Yes   (39)
2. ____ No
3. ____ Undecided
0. ____ Ref

Fig. 4-1. (Continued)

17. a) Are you and your family generally optimistic or pessimistic about the future?

      1. _____ Optimistic   (40)
      2. _____ Pessimistic
      9. _____ DK
      0. _____ Ref

   b) Can you tell me why you feel that way?

   _____ (41)

   _____

18. Could you tell me whether you consider yourself . . .
   (Read; rotate)

      1. _____ Conservative   (42)
      2. _____ Middle of the road
      3. _____ Liberal
      4. _____ Independent
      5. _____ (Other; specify)
      9. _____ DK
      0. _____ Ref

19. What is your favorite radio station? _____   (43 ____)
                                               (44 ____)

20. Which TV station do you and your family enjoy watching the most?
   _____   (45 ____)

21. Are you:

   (Read) 1. _____ Under 21   (46)
         2. _____ 21–35
         3. _____ 36–55
         4. _____ 56–65
         5. _____ Over 65
         0. _____ Ref.

22. What is your occupation? _____   (47)
   (Do not read)

   1. _____ Professional/technical   5. _____ Housewife
   2. _____ Clerical/secretarial   6. _____ Sales
   3. _____ Farming   7. _____ Service workers
   4. _____ Production/factory   8. _____ (Other; specify)

23. Is your annual family income?

   (Read) 1. _____ Under $15,000   (48)
        2. _____ $15,000–$25,000
        3. _____ $25,000–$50,000
        4. _____ Over $50,000

Fig. 4-1. (Continued)

---

24. Recently, there has been a lot of talk around the country about ethnic group concerns. Could you tell me which national background most of your ancestors came from?
(Do not read)

         1. _____ Italian   (49)
         2. _____ French/Canadian
         3. _____ Oriental
         4. _____ Russian
         5. _____ Jewish
         6. _____ Hispanic
         7. _____ WASP (Scotch-English)
         8. _____ Irish
         9. _____ Black/Afro
         0. _____ Other (Specify) _____

Thank you very much for your help. Good-night.

Fill in from card:

25. Sex   1. _____ Male   (50)
               2. _____ Female

26. Town (key code): _____   (51)

Fig. 4-1. (Continued)

Each interviewer must be trained so that only such minor changes in language occur. The wording should be as colloquial and as comfortable as is both possible and consistent with the need for precision. A successful interview is really a structured conversation, and it should not sound artificial. Proper, natural sequencing of questions is as important as the proper wording.

Sequencing of questions can bias results. The *New York Times* found that its survey of the 1982 Connecticut Senatorial race between Lowell Weicker and Toby Moffet significantly varied in results from another reputable published poll. The *Times* poll was taken again, changing the sequence of questions, and the results of both polls this time showed Weicker leading.*

A questionnaire is most effective if it is designed around the appropriate focal question to which all other questions contribute. Too often candidates feel the focal question is simply "How well am I doing right now?"

New York Times, October 27, 1982, p. B1.

With thought and pre-testing, you can usually find a better focal question, which should then determine the logic of the questionnaire. Often, such a question does not involve the relative standings of the candidates but, rather, why one issue is predominant among the voters and what they expect the candidates to do about it. In other instances, you may be able to establish that some aspect of the candidate's personality or television presence is disturbing to voters. On the positive side, you may be able to establish the basis for favorable reactions and try to maximize these in the campaign.

A number of basic components should be structured into every questionnaire. It is common, for example, to lead the questionnaire by establishing who the most probable voters are. This is done by asking whether they voted in the last two or three elections, and sometimes by complex weighting systems based on asking the respondent's familiarity with certain politicians and specific issues. If the respondent doesn't meet the requirements of the screen, the interview is not continued. In campaigns in smaller communities, it may not be necessary to screen. First, you can readily determine the universe of most likely voters by examining the records of the Board of Elections. This list, as previously noted, will be enormously helpful for all aspects of campaigning. Secondly, in smaller communities there is less chance that the attitudes of the most likely voters will be completely different than those of the less likely ones.

Another component often included is a worst case scenario. Questions are asked how the respondent would react if he or she heard the worst things your opponent could say about you, and their reaction to the worst things you could say about him. These questions are being used more frequently in the negative campaign styles that have become so popular. If you're expecting a particularly nasty campaign, it may be wise to be prepared, although I prefer to avid this approach if I am able.

It is critically important to include the demographic questions (generally at the end). These are questions such as sex, age, ethnicity, race, income, party membership, viewing preferences, geographic location, etc. These data, when cross-tabulated with the answers to the subject-matter questions, allow you to target certain groups. In recent years it has been established that there is a gender gap in voting. For example, proportionately more women than men oppose President Reagan's policies.* Similarly, a 1983 poll shows that married people vote differently

---

*New York Times, October 27, 1982, p. A20.

than single people.* The demographic questions allow you to make specific mailing decisions and help you modify the campaign style and redistribute your resources thoughtfully.

The design of good questionnaires is a technical skill requiring experience, judgment, and adequate pre-testing. This brief discussion cannot possibly cover all the particulars. For those, I recommend the U.S. Bureau of the Budget's *Household Survey Manual 1969* and Robert Payne's *The Art of Asking Questions* (Princeton, N.J.: Princeton University Press, 1951). Studying these works will help you design an adequate questionnaire. This is one more area in which an early start and wise pre-campaign investments of time can be critical in helping you to mount a professional-style campaign.**

Some general rules about questionnaire design:

1. Always be conversational.
2. Be explicit.
3. Define terms if there is any chance respondents may misinterpret.
4. Generally open-ended questions should be placed before closed-end questions on the same subject matter.
5. Don't raise questions that make the respondent think it's a test; in polling, *any* answer given by the respondent is correct.
6. Don't ask people questions that may embarrass them or make them feel stupid.
7. Use the simplest words and the shortest sentences possible.
8. Lead in with questions that people can easily relate to; build to the more difficult or sensitive questions.
9. Break complex questions down to their components.
10. Always close with the demographic questions, but be aware that questions on income, or age, or ethnic background arouse some people's suspicions.
11. Always pre-test and revise.

Pre-testing the questionnaire, which should be the prelude to any survey, enables you to "shake out" the questionnaire and to anticipate

---

New York Times, January 6, 1983, p. A12.

**Another book I strongly recommend is Charles Roll and Albert Cantril's *Polls: Their Use and Misuse in Politics* (Cabin John, MD: Seven Locks Press, 1980).

most of the problems of completing and processing it. Your people must be instructed to use the exact language of each question without modifications, to follow the sequence of questions as given, and, in the case of open-ended questions, to write down the respondents' answers in the respondents' own phrases as accurately as possible; these are called "verbatims."

A minimum of twenty interviews by trained workers (or, lacking those, by your best available workers) should be carried out in the pre-testing process. A senior member of the campaign staff should be involved. New questions and revisions of others will probably occur as this staff member sees and hears the results of the pre-test calls. Any significant changes that he wishes to make in the questionnaire should be subjected to a new round of pre-testing. Generally, in pre-testing, questions can be profitably dropped as well as added or modified. Questions may be resequenced, and probing directives may be added. ("Probing" is defined in a footnote on p. 104).

After pre-testing has been completed and a final questionnaire decided upon, reproduce a sufficient number of questionnaires for the entire sample, plus about 20 percent to allow for mistakes and to provide copies for the records.

TRAINING INTERVIEWERS.   Impress upon your interviewers that they are to seek objective responses and that a sample survey is not an appropriate opportunity to proselytize for your cause. Remind them that they are not to say they are doing the survey for you (your questionnaire will include a statement to the effect that they are doing it for the party or for a research bureau, a political committee, or some other such body), and be sure that they understand that "no response," "don't know," and even refusals to discuss an issue are legitimate responses which should be duly entered on the questionnaire.

The best way to train interviewers is to go through the entire questionnaire word by word and not leave anything to the interviewers' interpretation. Then give each interviewer the opportunity to play the role of interviewer and the role of respondent, and allow the interviewers who participated in the pre-test to discuss their experiences. Interviewers should also be drilled in entering responses on the questionnaire forms with particular emphasis on writing down open-ended responses in the respondents' own words, being careful to register at least the key phrases of the responses. Inexperienced persons should be allowed to interview only after a minimum of three hours of training.

INTERVIEWING.   The supervisor should check the results of each day's interviews to assure that responses are entered properly and that each interviewer understands the assignment. One interviewer may be found to be "prompting" answers while another one may be discovered to be omitting "don't know" responses from the form. Constant supervision must be provided to anticipate or at least stem these errors in order to assure something approaching professional quality.

Each interviewer should be reminded to write down any important information volunteered by the respondent, whether or not it relates to the questionnaire. Such information should be entered in the spaces left for comments. It may be something detrimental to the candidate that the respondent has heard in the neighborhood (whether or not the information reported has any basis in fact), or it may be a comment about something that happened during a walking tour. Bits of information gathered in this way are sometimes very important.

CODING, EDITING, AND CROSS-TABULATING.   Coding consists of re-cording responses by category. Multi-choice questions are essentially self-coded—each question on the questionnaire has a blank space after each choice; when the interviewer checks the appropriate one, the response is coded—but at times new codes are needed for "other" responses. Ed-iting, necessary for open-ended questions and sometimes for other types of questions as well, involves checking responses for obvious mistakes (for example, answers filled in on the wrong line of the questionnaire) and then putting similar answers into a single category for coding. Cross-tabulating is drawing up final tables that summarize the data, for example, "crossing" income by candidate preferred.

Just as your interviewing should be done by no more than eight to ten persons, only two or at most three should do the coding and editing. A member of your staff whom you trust to perform detailed work properly should set up the codes for the open-ended questions and should personally review at least 25 percent of the completed questionnaires. The codes that he sets up at this stage are extremely important. They will determine the quality and style of the cross-tabulations, and it will be from the cross-tabulations that you will make some of the most important decisions of the campaign. If at this late stage, your representative discovers that the questionnaires have not been prepared properly, it makes more sense to abandon the project than to make cross-tabulations on the basis of the possibly misleading data of the questionnaires.

Questionnaires generally include demographic data so that political client-group information can be obtained from the completed survey. For example, it is usual to ask the respondent's age ("Are you under or over 65 years of age?"), race, sex, and any other such identification question that might be locally important ("Are you a member of a union?"). The respondent's name itself can often provide an indication of his or her ethnic or religious group, questions that can be asked directly but are often troublesome for amateurs. These characteristics are usually important in the design of the cross-tabulations, which are cumulations of questionnaire responses compared with demographic data (for example, what percentage of people over 65 plan to vote for you) or of questionnaire answers cross-classified with other questionnaire answers (for example, what percentage of people who intend to vote for your opponent would be impressed by an endorsement from a certain local politician).

As a practical example, a question that is usually asked is surveys is: "If you had to vote today in the primary, whom would you vote for? Candidate A_____, Candidate B_____, Candidate C_____, Undecided_____." Demographic cross-tabulations of the replies to this question might take the following form.

INCOME	CANDIDATE A	CANDIDATE B	CANDIDATE C	UNDECIDED	REFUSED
Under $10,000	%	%	%	%	%
Over $10,000	%	%	%	%	%
Totals	%	%	%	%	%
AGE					
Under 65	%	%	%	%	%
Over 65	%	%	%	%	%
Totals	%	%	%	%	%
GEOGRAPHIC					
Assembly District #1	%	%	%	%	%
Assembly District #2	%	%	%	%	%
Assembly District #3	%	%	%	%	%
Totals	%	%	%	%	%

Figure 4-2 is an example of cross-tabulations from computer printouts from a survey prepared for the 1980 primary congressional campaign of

ED SCHWARTZMAN
POLITICAL RESEARCH CONSULTANT
CHEVY CHASE, MARYLAND

2ND CONGRESSIONAL DISTRICT, CONNECTICUT

JULY, 1960

TABLE 14C QUESTION 14C

WHETHER THINK THAT NEW PUBLIC INVESTMENT IN ENERGY SHOULD EMPHASIZE NUCLEAR GENERATING PLANTS

	TOTAL	NOW PRI-MARY VO-TER	PRI-MARY VA-TER	IDEOLOGY CON-SER-VA-TIVE	MODE-RATE	LIBE-RAL	AGE UN-DER 30	30-55	56-65	OVER 65	OCCUPATION PROF	CLER ICAL	CR PROD	SA	SER-VICE	OTHER	FEELINGS ABOUT FUTURE OPTI-MISTIC	PES-SI-MIS-TIC	UNION MEM-BER	NON-MEM-BER
BASE-TOTAL RESPONDENTS	474	182	292	118	228	70	120	105	72	87	130	56	40	16	38	180	328	106	143	324
	100.	38.	62.	25.	48.	15.	25.	22.	15.	18.	27.	12.	8.	3.	8.	38.	69.	24.	30.	68.
YES	185	62	123	45	93	25	33	86	32	32	53	18	14	7	18	71	138	37	53	130
	39.	34.	42.	38.	41.	36.	27.	46.	44.	37.	41.	32.	34.	40.	45.	39.	42.	35.	37.	40.
NO	181	82	99	46	65	36	70	60	22	23	64	18	17	6	13	58	123	44	58	122
	38.	45.	34.	39.	37.	51.	58.	35.	31.	27.	49.	33.	41.	47.	34.	32.	37.	42.	40.	38.
UNDECIDED	102	37	66	27	50	8	17	36	18	31	13	20	10	2	10	49	66	25	32	70
	22.	20.	23.	23.	22.	12.	15.	19.	25.	35.	10.	35.	25.	13.	27.	27.	20.	23.	23.	22.
REFUSED	2	1	1	1												2	2			4
	1.	1.	*	*												1.	1.			*
NO ANSWER	4	4														1	1			1
	1.	1.														*	*			*

Fig. 4-2. Example of professional market research cross-tabulations.

Sam Gejdenson. Since the candidate was perceived as a severe underdog, one of the purposes of the survey was to establish just how strong his opponents were, among which groups, and why? In particular, since one of the opponents was the son of a very popular and powerful former governor and previous party chairman, it was critical to find out how much of the father's popularity was transferable to his son.

The questionnaire was developed with the candidate and his staff in a number of meetings and was lengthier (20 to 25 minutes for some interviews) than I like when volunteers are doing the interviewing, as was the case. Everyone involved, including the candidate, realized that in the early poll the "horse race" data wasn't likely to show the candidate doing well. Often, when candidates are unknown, journalists' evaluations of who is doing well and who is not tend to be self-fulfilling prophecies.

In this instance, the splits were:

Dempsey	36%
Gejdenson	11%
Hendel	20%
Undecided	32%

While these results could have been disheartening to many candidates, Gejdenson realized that it was early, that the issues hadn't been fully defined in the voters' minds, that Mrs. Hendel might drop out (which she did after the party convention), and that based on ideological compatibility a significant proportion of her vote should naturally go to him. (I have seen distinguished and experienced politicians drop out of races based solely on survey consultants' recommendations from early polls. Polling consultants have taken over strategy and policy roles in many campaigns; they are often good, but they are not gods, and they work with a sizable error margin.) The Gejdenson staff realized that the purpose of early polls is to examine objectively, removing ego and ambition from the analysis, the conditions of the contest, and not to take "bad" horse race figures as guaranteed portents of a marginal martyrdom.

Campaigning is a trial by a singularly large jury, and a good campaign is like a capital case; the members of the jury really think about their choices and often change their minds. Gejdenson is a very gifted natural campaigner and was not discouraged. He campaigned seven days a week and won a smashing upset. The data showed he had a shot; he and his staff and the voters did the rest. (Research is advisory, not controlling or conclusive. Market research showed the producers of *Star Wars* that "war" should not be in the title and the public would be turned off by robots in important parts; they made the picture anyway, and so far it has grossed $525 million.)

Note that my cross-tabs provide raw (actual) figures on respondents and vertical and horizontal percents. These cross-tabs were reviewed with the candidate and his staff; a written analysis was provided, including a review of major findings and recommendations based on the more than one hundred cross-tabulations that were prepared.

The following six tables are from a survey I did several years ago. Using a sample of 600 voters and the procedures recommended in this book, I was able to predict with considerable precision the outcome of each assembly race in Manhattan. The survey was costly, since the sampling took five days of work—it included two substitute decks because of unique difficulties in Manhattan involving unlisted telephone numbers, single persons not at home, and high move rates—but the results were extremely worthwhile. The possible cross-tabulations were in the hundreds, but I chose 25—of which 6 are shown here—as being most useful for the purposes of the survey. Some professionals actually run hundreds of cross-tabulations—sometimes because the campaign staff people are not certain what they are looking for—but it is unlikely that each of these tables can be especially critical.

Table 4-1 provides information in actual numbers useful in developing a profile of potential client groups that would react favorably to attacks on the administration currently in office.

Table 4-2 is a basic tool in political research—a measure of the endorsement strengths of various leaders at the time of the survey. The former governor's endorsement was clearly the most important.

Table 4-3 relates party-faction adherence to ethnic group and sex, giving the candidate a way of learning which groups of voters are likely to be sympathetic to his faction.

At the time of this study, New York City's fiscal problems were a critical political issue. Table 4-4 provides a sense of which solution was favored by voters in which geographic areas. Such information would be particularly useful in street campaigning and in preparing brochures for distribution on the street.

Table 4-1. Degree of Satisfaction with Current Afministration, by Ethnic Group and Sex.

ETHNIC GROUP	TOTALS	VERY SATISFIED	SATISFIED	HALF-SATISFIED	NOT SATISFIED
Irish	149	10	63	32	40
Italian	85	13	40	14	13
Jewish	262	6	91	57	81
Negro	178	11	91	32	30
Puerto Rican	54	7	35	1	6
Other	272	18	92	63	85
SEX					
Female	562	35	216	110	148
Male	438	30	196	89	106
Totals	1,000	65	412	199	255

Table 4-2. Endorsement Value of Specified Politicians, by Ethnic Group and Sex.

ETHNIC GROUPS	ATTORNEY GENERAL	FORMER GOVERNOR	CONGRESSMAN	MAYOR	TOTALS
Irish	6	38	23	44	149
Italian	–	23	7	43	85
Jewish	16	128	28	34	262
Negro	–	68	7	78	178
Puerto Rican	–	7	–	33	54
Other	2	98	25	72	272
SEX					
Female	8	191	43	177	562
Male	16	171	47	127	438
Totals	24	362	90	304	1,000

Table 4-5 provides information similar to that in Table 4-4, except that it registers favored solutions by ethnic group and sex. This information would be useful in targeting mailings.

Table 4-6 illustrates the frustrating but quite typical inconsistency of American voters. Many who expressed dissatisfaction with conditions in their neighborhoods liked the administration. The focus of the campaign would be to tie the voters' environmental dissatisfaction to the incumbent city administration.

Table 4-3. Party Segment Preference, by Ethnic Group and Sex.

ETHNIC GROUP	REGULAR	REFORM	INDEPENDENT	TOTALS
Irish	68	28	32	149
Italian	46	11	10	85
Jewish	101	59	60	262
Negro	85	33	28	178
Puerto Rican	35	7	6	54
Other	108	41	58	272
SEX				
Female	258	88	96	562
Male	185	91	98	438
Totals	443	179	194	1,000

Table 4-4. Preferred Solutions to Fiscal Problems, by Geographic Area.

	OFF-TRACK BETTING	INCOME TAX	STATE AID	FEDERAL AID	SALES TAX	CIGARETTE TAX	TOTALS
Greenwich Village	27	2	10	1	1	11	63
Lower Manhattan	58	6	10	5	–	10	106
West Side	113	5	26	12	5	23	212
Middle East Side	109	3	22	15	5	28	209
Harlem	184	16	22	23	3	12	280
Washington Heights	78	2	10	10	2	9	130
Totals	569	34	100	66	16	93	1,000

Even if you have only limited amounts of money to spend on research, completed questionnaires of good quality would justify hiring a professional computer house for the tabulation process. It is possible to do tabulations by hand, but only with the probable loss of accuracy and only for a limited number of cross-tabulations. Since, as can be seen even from the single example given above, cross-tabulations can extract a great deal of potentially useful information from a questionnaire, it is clearly in your interest to have as many of them available as seem relevant and

Table 4-5. Preferred Solutions to Fiscal Problems, by Ethnic Group and Sex.

ETHNIC GROUP	OFF-TRACK BETTING	INCOME TAX	STATE AID	FEDERAL AID	STATE TAX	CIGARETTE TAX	TOTALS
Irish	90	2	14	14	2	10	149
Italian	44	8	11	2	3	9	85
Jewish	135	9	46	15	2	32	262
Negro	118	4	7	18	2	9	178
Puerto Rican	37	6	–	2	1	2	54
Other	145	5	22	15	7	31	272
SEX							
Female	286	16	60	39	6	64	562
Male	283	18	40	27	10	29	438
Totals	569	34	100	66	16	93	1,000

Table 4-6. Degree of Satisfaction with Administration, by Degree of Environmental Satisfaction.

DEGREE OF SATISFACTION WITH ADMINISTRATION	ENVIRONMENTAL SATISFACTION		
	SATISFIED	DISSATISFIED	TOTALS
Very satisfied	20	43	65
Satisfied	176	233	412
Half satisfied	76	121	199
Not satisfied	81	165	255
Don't know or no response	35	28	69
Totals	307	591	1,000

useful. Doing sizable numbers of cross-tabulations by hand is so arduous and time-consuming as to be practically impossible. This is probably the research investment that many candidates may find most advantageous for focusing any small amount of money they may have for outside consultants.

Key punching on IBM cards (with 100 percent verification—that is, checking each punched card for accuracy) and computing 50 basic tables should not cost more than $1,000 for most smaller sample sizes. If you can afford it, this is an extremely sensible investment.

ANALYZING RESULTS.   All the work you've done on a survey is worth nothing unless it is analyzed intelligently. In many instances, a candidate concludes from survey data that he is gaining on his opponent, and this may comfort him. The data, however, are really only a beginning and not a conclusion. The whole purpose of campaigning is to act intelligently to change the conclusion. Governor Hugh Carey's victory over State Senator Duryea (N.Y.) in 1978 and Mario Cuomo's victory over Ed Koch in 1982 are only two of many examples in recent memory in which candidates have won elections after initial polls showed them to be certain losers. Many facts and perceptions can be gained from or confirmed by cross-tabulations. For example, a candidate who finds he is gaining on his opponent may discover which groups still are not responding to his appeals and why they are not. Areas and groups in which undecided voters are concentrated and demographic characteristics of the undecided voters are other critical types of information that can be obtained by doing the correct cross-tabulations.

Professional research reports analyzing survey results run at times over 100 pages and include perhaps 40 to 50 tables. Often you have to be a professional yourself to know how it all relates to specific decisions. Many times the candidate depends on the analyst to make recommendations without really having time to examine the results. Some professional statisticians are only infrequently in campaign work and cannot be depended on for major decisions, since, in order to cover themselves, they will often qualify findings even if a major political crisis is staring them in the face.

Analyzing the results of surveys usefully will depend very much on the political and statistical experience of your advisors. As has already been pointed out, each survey should be designed to answer specific, practical questions and not academic considerations. The cross-tabulations should help you decide at least these basics:

- Which are the important issues? Is there a single issue that dominates?
- How should you deal with the really hot issues? Which solutions are favored by voting groups?
- What are the characteristics of the undecided voters?
- Whose endorsement would be helpful?
- How are the firmly committed votes divided?

The techniques of statistical analysis cannot be summarized in a few pages. Professional-level analysis requires experience in both statistics and politics; few professional statisticians are really talented campaigners. sophisticated mathematical analysis is usually not required.* Cross-tabulating responses about issues with race, ethnic characteristics, income, age, sex, and residence of the respondents is usually sufficient to isolate the problems of greatest concern to the voters. (For example, in Table 4-7, note that crime and drugs concern groups in almost every county.) Percent change and percent distributions are usually the only statistical devices used in professional analyses; the critical skill required is not so much statistical as it is talent for combining the various tables to find the essential meaning of the voters' moods and opinions. Survey research in the hands of a talented, experienced person is a great blessing to a candidate; but the candidate still has to spend time to discuss results and devote some study to the data.

I would recommend not depending only on the most obvious data for decisions—for example, the percentage split between you and your opponent(s). Sometimes an issue comes up early in the campaign that at that time is statistically insignificant. Maybe, for example, 5 percent of the respondents don't like your "appearance."** This would show up in associative questions; as a result, you may be advised to wear different ties and a more (or less) modern cut of clothing. A second poll may show that 8 percent are not pleased by your appearance. Since sampling reliability generally declines as the sample size decreases, the difference of 3 percent is statistically insignificant, but the matter may be worth looking into anyway. It may be that you sound too intransigent or talk too fast or don't look at the camera, or that something is bothering the voters that they can't articulate. "It's only 5 percent" (or 8 percent), advisors may say. Keep in mind, however, that most elections are decided by less than a 10 percent difference between the candidates. What you must consider

---

*Larry J. Sabato, in *The Rise of Political Consultants* (Basic Books: N.Y., 1981), has an interesting discussion of a technique not often used. Called MDS (multi-dimensional scaling), it uses regression techniques to analyze various dimensions of response. Each factor is analyzed in relation to others. It is unlikely that this can be used in smaller campaigns.

**In one survey I discovered that male voters favored the candidate much more than women did. The candidate suggested that on his day-to-day campaigning he often referred to women as "honey" and that this might be thought sexist. He stopped with improved results.

Table 4-7. Perceptions of Major Problems, by County.

	DETAILED FINDINGS							
	County A	County B	County C	County D	County E	County F	County G	County H
Question 2:								
What do you think are the most important problems in your community (town)?								
Economic Issues (Inflation and Recession)	35	31	16	4	4	9	29	18
Youth	31	21	19	17	12	10	28	15
Drugs	22	39	40	49	31	16	34	53
Sanitation	6	1	3	6	8	7	1	1
Pollution	5	4	6	5	5	10	1	3
Transportation	3	6	6	8	4	3	3	–
Integration	3	6	6	1	–	3	8	3
Poverty – Welfare	3	4	5	1	2	9	4	1
Housing (Rents)	3	7	4	10	6	18	12	8
Crime	2	2	18	31	36	37	13	1
Other	3	1	3	–	2	4	–	3
Total (Including Duplication)	116	122	126	132	110	126	133	106

is how much of the other 92 to 95 percent may tacitly share the criticism of the vocal 5 percent.

In smaller campaigns, my recommendation is to have your survey consultant prepare the cross-tabulations on the questions most concerning you and then have the consultant's technician sit down with you and your advisors and discuss what the data mean. Often consultants will prepare handsome presentations, including tables, graphs, and charts and many pages of text in which people with limited political experience rehash the obvious. Top-quality consultants may charge $15,000 to $20,000 for doing 250 to 300 household interviews in depth and supplying a written report. Polling is competitive. Shop around, but check with previous clients before you decide.*

---

*See my article, *Picking a Pollster*, Empire State Journal, July-August 1979.

5
Campaign Problems

In campaigns people don't develop a reasoned approach, and the trouble with most analyses of political behavior by political scientists is that they attribute a reasoned working out of things which are not worked out reasonably.

—An advisor to Governor Volpe of Massachusetts*

Designing a campaign properly is a creative process that involves intuition, experience, and some luck in personnel and consultant selection.** There does not exist, and cannot exist, a computer software program to tell you that given certain conditions, there is only one way guaranteed to win your campaign; campaigning is an art form, a peculiar one and an expensive one, but very inherently an art, and not a science. Spending more money on media and paraphernalia can never be an assurance of victory. Some observers of the process, however, come away disenchanted and appalled at what they think is a deliberate, mechanistic effort, using artifice and sophisticated technology, to manipulate the emotions and predispositions of the electorate. Such a reaction is not always entirely rational: Some of the people who were favorably impressed by Robert F. Kennedy's use of the media found Richard M. Nixon's use of similar techniques somehow immoral and threatening.

The workings of the democratic process, in the final analysis, depend on the common sense and intelligence of the voting constituency. Although many political scientists are disturbed by the small and declining percentage of primary voters and by the inferior information voters respond to, the American political process has nonetheless worked for the past two centuries, and the American form of government has lasted longer than any other in the modern era.

---

*Quoted in Murray B. Levin and George Blackwood's *The Compleat Politician: Political Strategy in Massachusetts* (Indianapolis, Ind.: Bobbs-Merrill, 1962).

**Every campaign needs a few breaks. The brilliant campaigner can force some breaks, but no one can force them all. The Slavic maxim, "If you're lucky, even your broom will shoot," has relevance in some campaigns. Yet the role of "luck" in drawing the first position, in getting press and television coverage at just the right time, for example, has never been scientifically explored.

The process, often irrational and wasteful, can offer no assurance that the best man will win. Too often, it appears to guarantee merely that the shrewdest campaigner wins; it has been noted that the skills (communication and fund raising) necessary to win campaigns have little relation to the skills necessary to govern well (long-range conceptual power, integrity, courage, defining the public interest instead of currying to special interests). Indeed, many of the nation's best people have been denied elective office by their refusal to accommodate party leaders or by defeat at the polls.

Over a period of time, however, the basic intelligence and sensibility of the voters have made the process work. The continued effectiveness of the democratic process depends to some degree on attracting able, independent men and women to public office. Such candidates will not allow themselves to be completely encumbered by campaign promises, so they will be able to respond freely and intelligently to the massive, seemingly insoluble problems facing our cities and the nation. For such people, the use of sophisticated campaign techniques may make more economical campaigns possible and therefore limit the necessity for making political contracts in order to raise sufficient funds.*

This is not very different from the normal routines of American business. The process fails when taking care of friends and personal contracts results in the public's getting 70 cents on a dollar although they are entitled to, say, 95 cents (allowing for normal wastage), and when societal priorities are disturbed by the precedence given personal or political priorities.

In my experience, political contracts much inhibit the policy formulation aspects of government; there is such an abundance of aggressive incompetents in campaigns that a certain number are guaranteed to rise to the top in government. Venality is not the worst thing about political contracts; the assurance of highly place office-holders of limited competence is by far the greater danger.

---

*The law of political contract is as binding as the law of business contract, although it generally is not based on written or signed documents. "Carrying a contract" is an important part of political life; it means delivering a job to a party regular or delivering construction awards to a major campaign contributor. It means trading endorsements or judgeships for jobs, future unspecified favors, and policy discretion. For example, a contributor may ask to name the commissioner of urban development or ask for the right to veto certain nominees for the job. The press naturally emphasizes the shady aspects of such tradeoffs, but that is how the business of government gets carried out.

In order to compete while retaining most of their policy discretion, such men and women will need to use the techniques described in this book—techniques that are by no means Machiavellian and that have been used, in various forms, for decades. Television has changed the campaign context to some extent, but not as radically as some people apparently believe. A candidate can dissimulate on television, but not for very long without the charade becoming obvious. In this regard, the public is becoming increasingly sophisticated and sensitized to the uses of campaigning artifice. One of the "slickest" campaigns was the effort to get voter approval for the New York State transportation bond issue in 1971. The campaign, costing $2.5 million, used computer letter endorsements, TV, newspaper ads, and virtually everything else in the advertising arsenal—but the bond issue was overwhelmingly defeated.*

An example of a heavy media campaign not necessarily being effective occurred in the 1983 mayoral primary in which Chicago Democratic voters nominated Congressman Harold Washington, a black, who beat incumbent Mayor Jane Byrne and ex-Mayor Richard Daley's son although Byrne outspent him $10,000,000 to his $1,000,000. Washington's campaign features a strong pulling operation (69 percent of all registered blacks voted), posters and buttons, black radio, and near the end TV spots to refute opponents' negative campaigns. Blacks were canvassed and motivated to vote. About 90 percent of the black voters voted for Washington, while only an estimated 8 percent of whites voting embraced his candidacy. On the losing side, Byrne's much more expensive campaign, using media man David Sawyer, relied heavily on TV throughout the campaign in addition to phone banks and mailings, but managed only to split the white vote with the third candidate, Richard Daley, Jr.

Although each campaign has unique elements, almost all have similar characteristics as well. Fund raising, logistics, and certain other problems that candidates face are almost universally shared. Others are common but do not characterize all campaigns. These problems are the subject of this chapter.

---

*The major part of the answer to the question of why the bill lost "may be in the nature of politics which is supposed to be divisive. . . . In the American system . . . politicians are supposed to compete and dispute, and when two men [who are political enemies] . . . urge the public to vote 'Heck, yes,' the public's answer is more likely than not to be 'Heck, no!'" ("Talk of the Town," *The New Yorker,* November 13, 1971.)

COMPETITIVE FUND-RAISING

The growing incidence of multi-candidate party primaries has caused considerable difficulty for candidates who share philosophical and political positions with their colleagues. They inevitably share the same fund-raising base as well. In the winter of 1971, for example, there were many press reports that some of the potential financial contributors to Senator Edmund S. Muskie's drive for the presidential nomination were waiting to see whether Senator Hubert H. Humphrey intended to make the race. Mayor John V. Lindsay and Senator George McGovern had similar problems until Lindsay dropped out of the competition.

Similarly, in 1969, Herman Badillo encountered financial difficulties in his primary race for the new York City mayoralty. He was said to have received former Mayor Robert F. Wagner's blessing and encouragement regarding the probable generosity of past contributors to Wagner's campaigns. Then Wagner decided he might make the race himself, and Badillo's sources dried up. It was rumored that Badillo finally spent $500,000 in his primary bid in a five-way race. His campaign manager, Steve Berger, was quoted in press reports as saying that, since Badillo lost by a very small margin to Judge Mario Procaccino, the availability of additional money for television might have made the difference.

There is no easy way out of this problem. You have to make potential contributors believe you have a better chance of winning, or offer more than your opponents in the way of "contractual" obligations. (See footnote, p. 127.) Otherwise, you may have to recognize that you'll raise less money than you hoped for and plan your expenditures accordingly from the start. In the first instance, when it comes to money, a candidate should never count "possibles" as "probables." This is particularly important in budgeting. The budget should be as tight and as realistic as possible. For example, both Muskie and Badillo were reported to have maintained elaborate suites of offices, large staffs—25 to 40 full-time paid people in Badillo's case and hundreds in Muskie's national campaign—as well as other expensive appurtenances that may or may not have been absolutely necessary. Some commentators suggested that Badillo would have had the money for television if his overhead (including payroll) had been less costly. Running for city comptroller on the ticket headed by Badillo, State Senator Harrison J. Goldin leased a very small office (at the same hotel that housed the more extensive Badillo headquarters) and reportedly staffed it with an unpaid campaign manager and four or five unpaid workers. He was said to have spent three-fourths of his budget on television, and, although he lost, he still made an impressive showing.

POOLING RESOURCES WITH OTHER CANDIDATES

This problem is one aspect of the financial difficulties that characterize many campaigns. If you're running with a ticket in a primary against another segment of the party or in a general election, you can pool your resources with other candidates on your ticket to reduce costs. For example, a shared mailing can be done so the 9.3 cents postage per envelope is shared two or three ways. Or you can get together and share the cost of developing the computer tape of primary voters, including the expensive process of taking the names from the election rolls and putting them on IBM cards.

The ethnication process—machine sorting of voter lists by ethnic or other characteristics—is expensive. There is no reason for each candidate on a slate to do this separately, but many do.

Costs of "finders' books" can also be shared. These books listing the election district and assembly district for any street address have been developed by various computer firms. In New York in 1982, for example, since the state had been extensively redistricted, new finders' books were especially useful in assigning the election and assembly districts to the addresses given by voters in signing candidates' petitions. Filling them in by hand would have been a laborious—and probably error-ridden—project. A computer house compiled finders' books, which it sold to various candidates for $500 to $750 per district. The firm would have been delighted to run all addresses in the entire city through a computer for a single sales order that could have been shared by many candidates on one party slate. It would undoubtedly have given a quantity discount for so large an order, and candidates for many offices would have saved money, effort, and time. Yet it was not done. Such sensible sharing of basic overhead expenses is rare and, in my judgment, is an important reason why many campaigns are needlessly expensive.

If two or three candidates share one telephone location, they can save significantly in supervision and rent for telephone campaigns. In smaller campaigns, using a service bureau to look up telephone numbers will probably cost 9 or 10 cents a name, yet I have repeatedly seen candidates, supposedly allied, duplicate efforts and expenses in looking up telephone numbers.

Surveys conducted for several candidates on the same ticket who share the expenses can also save each candidate money. It is even likely that combining research budgets may result in better research for all participating candidates. Unfortunately, in many campaigns, every candidate appears to be in business for himself. Many politicians jealously guard their prerogatives even at the risk of incurring considerably increased costs. Some candidates wish to have exclusive control over design of brochures and to whom they should be mailed. Some candidates running together as a slate may disagree about placement of their names on shopping bags or on a billboard. Sometimes these concerns are legitimate, but more often they reflect the insecurities and incompetencies brought about by campaign anxieties and the fact that everyone involved seems to regard himself as at least as qualified to make decisions on every aspect of campaigning as anyone else. These are very expensive conceits, indeed. If you are running for the first time, you'll have your hands full without spending money that could be saved by working with the other people who are on your ticket. Of course, there are times when there is no chance to come to any reasonable agreement with your fellow candidates. Arguing and discussing are a waste of time in such cases, and any concessions will cost you money anyway. In such situations, you are simply forced to go it alone.

CONTROL OF THEME DEVELOPMENT

In many campaigns, media people or advertising people assume control of theme development, often without using sophisticated research even if that research happens to be available. Their concern is to put something on film or paper that has impact on the voter.

In some instances, you may be told by an advertising agency, after a few discussions lasting several hours, that such-and-such is the only logical theme. You and your campaign advisors are likely to be overwhelmed, since advertising is an area of expertise in which you may not consider yourselves competent. And once you commit the media theme, you'll find you'll have to live with it for good or bad and that it will directly affect other aspects of the campaign. It is much better to lay out the overall campaign strategy first, with or without media people, and then have them adjust their specific work to fit your strategy rather than let them decide on a theme perhaps quite arbitrarily and then design a campaign around this possibly peripheral theme. The agency's key decisions should include: specific media content illustrating the campaign theme, how many spots or ads to produce, their length, which stations to use, and how often to show the film or newspaper advertisements. There are specialists in this kind of planning and decision making, but since each is interested in maximizing the use of the medium or media he or she (or the firm) is involved in, you should bear this in mind and not rely exclusively on this person's judgment in setting up your campaign theme.

The advertising agency generally receives a commission or rebate based on volume. You may therefore decide to retain a specialist to purchase air time and let local advertising agencies produce the copy and/or films, paying them a consulting fee for this service. Some agencies may, in fact, prefer such an arrangement.*

TAKING THE FIRST LOSS

The stock market saying that the first loss is the best loss applies to campaigning as well. You may, for example, plan to distribute a brochure that your staff regards as brilliant and that involved much staff preparation but that has drawn a measure of negative public reaction. Despite the fact that preparation of the brochure was costly and that 10,000 copies were printed, you probably should destroy all the remaining copies. Don't assume anything categorically or automatically. Listen to the voters' reactions to media. If they are negative, you may save yourself future grief by taking the first loss.**

---

*Some advertising agencies have a policy of not participating in political campaigns. For example, Doyle, Dane, Bernbach, a leading firm, instructed its staff several years ago to take leaves of absence if they wished to work in campaigns. Candidates may be able to hire individual advertising technicians rather than an agency. Consultants who specialize in radio-TV time buying charge either a flat fee or 5 to 7 percent of the total buy. For these fees they are supposed to choose the right stations, times, and programs for your advertising matched to the demographic groups your research shows you should reach. It is a very important skill often overlooked in campaign planning. Don't assume it will get done properly just because you're paying a lot for it; indeed, this is a good rule to apply to all consultants involved in your campaign—their monetary price doesn't always automatically equate with their actual value.

**The use of focus groups to test copy and themes is often forgotten in the constant time pressures of campaigns. Focus groups can save you a lot of money and aggravation; they should be built into the campaign. But they do not and cannot replace research surveys.

In a recent campaign, a candidate widely distributed a palm card with his photograph on one side and a list of convenient telephone numbers (fire, ambulance, hospital, pollution control center, etc.) on the other. His photographer had suggested that he looked handsome without his glasses, but since his strategy depended heavily on street campaigning, and since he always wore his glasses out of doors, the palm card did not contribute effectively to increasing his voter recognition. Nevertheless, he refused to have another card printed showing him with glasses, even though it would have accomplished what he intended. He should have suppressed the first card, written off his investment, and replaced it with one that showed him as he normally looked.

Some candidates automatically assume that loudspeakers on cars and trucks can drum up interest, but many voters find them quite annoying. In some areas, a significant portion of the electorate may complain. Although you may have spent $1,000 or more to rent the equipment and the cars, it may be better to withdraw the equipment as soon as complaints begin to come in. Decisions such as these have to be made in every campaign; too often, the choice is made to gamble on an investment already made and to hope for the best. Such a course is neither good business nor good politics. Refusing to acknowledge a mistake and throwing good money after bad are common weaknesses in campaigning. You should face up to your mistakes, and sometimes you may simply have to write off a substantial investment. By making staff changes or developing better staff coordination, you may possibly insure against a recurrence. If, however, you are the one who made the mistake, and you choose to repeat it, it is of course your option, but you deserve to lose, and you probably will.

"IMPROPER" QUOTATIONS AND "DIRTY" TACTICS

Sometimes your opponent will attack you with one of your statements taken out of context. It is an effective tactic and often employed. If you defend yourself, your defense may be interpreted as a confession of guilt. For that reason, some candidates ignore such incidents altogether, preferring not to give the statement any more publicity. A better response may well be to attack your opponent for unfair campaign practices, make a formal complaint to the fair campaign practices committee in your city or state, and publicly attack his (or her) lack of integrity and call attention to that candidate's use of gutter tactics.* (See also the discussion of negative campaigning in Chapter 6.)

To adopt a defensive stance in such a situation generally accomplishes little. As a number of campaign professionals have observed, the American public likes a good fight and becomes really interested in a campaign only if it senses one. However, many politicians today are advised to be cool, not to display emotion. It is pretty hard to put up a good fight and not display emotion. The trick is to use your emotions without affecting your judgment, allowing the voters to sense your dimensions as a human being, not only as a political party representative who wants their votes. Senator Muskie's public tears because of a newspaper's attacks on his wife were widely believed to have contributed to his relatively poor showing in the New Hampshire Democratic primary in 1972. On the other hand, Richard Nixon's emotional "Checkers" speech in his vice presidential campaign of 1952 put sentiment to his advantage. The lesson seems to be to avoid unreasonable or excessive emotion and to control your feelings, carefully picking the spots when and where you let your emotions show. Campaigns conducted on a completely even emotional level can be deadly boring to the voter.

Fairly often the press may quote you out of context or make harmful and inaccurate statements about you, but it is difficult to attack the local newspapers in the course of a campaign. Sometimes you may have to— as Mario Procaccino attacked the New York *Daily News* in 1969 for its public opinion polling procedures—but only as a last resort. It's wise to have a good working relationship with the people who cover your campaign. They tend to appreciate candor and some personal attention— informal meetings over a drink are probably good supplements to the usual formal press conferences in a campaign. Like everybody else, they would probably appreciate any interest you show in them as human beings.

Some campaigns are "dirty," and they can be unpleasant. In vendetta campaigns, for example, a candidate runs not to win but to kill off the

---

*In 1982, low style campaigns were so common that I believe a significant proportion of voters was disgusted by the constant display of dirt, particularly when few candidates were responding directly to the great problems most Americans perceived weren't being dealt with: nuclear disarmament, government mismanagement, social security, etc. My advice to my consultant colleagues in 1983 was to answer the questions and inject humor into media; in the unlikely event that this were done, it would be a revolution in campaigning style.

chances of someone he or she doesn't like. In one such congressional primary in New York in the early 1960s, completely unfounded malicious personal rumors were started in local churches and synagogues, and boys giving out campaign literature were beaten by adults apparently paid by the opponent. It is hard to cope with such tactics dispassionately. When laws are broken, as they were in this instance, the responsible parties should be charged. Contacting the unfair practices committee won't help. You should bring civil and criminal charges where appropriate and get publicity for the reasons that compel you to make the charges.*

Whispering campaigns are in questionable taste. The New York congressional primary race in 1972 between Bella Abzug and William Fitts Ryan was tragic for many reasons, not the least of which was that both were outstanding congressmen of the reform faction and one had to lose. Ms. Abzug's supporters were alleged to have used the slogan, "The district needs a strong voice," making a clear although unspoken reference to the fact that Congressman Ryan, who had recently had a throat operation, was not physically strong. Ryan replied by issuing a brochure with the theme, "My work speaks louder."

Fighting back with equally dirty tactics is a natural and satisfying response, but it doesn't work and the public is apt to be sickened by the spectacle. There are no automatic solutions to this problem. In some cases, a brochure or a press conference counterattacking is effective. In others, when opponents claim endorsements they have not received, you must get the "endorser" publicly to disown your opponent. When campaign literature is really malicious—for example, a 1972 Democratic primary handbill implying an opponent was supported by President Nixon, your only recourse is to try to get press and television attention to the incident; the public usually will be sympathetic.

In many theaters where the award-winning motion picture "The Godfather" was shown, the audience applauded when someone was murdered to avenge the murder of a member of the hero's family. Revenge is a satisfying emotion, shared universally. Nonetheless, it has not yet become broadly accepted by voters as a reason to vote for or against candidates.

---

*In 1982, in a bitter New York State assembly race, the Democrat, John Dearie, accused the Republican, Guy Velella, of distributing a piece of literature, ostensibly from Dearie, showing how much Dearie had accomplished for blacks. The piece went to white households. Dearie was so incensed that he went to the press and the Bronx District Attorney for formal charges, which were later dismissed.

Vendetta races may sometimes be impossible to avoid, but they are sense-less and—perhaps more important—unattractive to most voters.

NEWSPAPER POLLS

These polls vary considerably in quality depending on who does them and how they are done. The *New York Times*-CBS poll is done to very high professional standards. Other newspapers also retain independent consultants, while many, in addition to subscribing to the Gallup and Harris national surveys and other syndicated polls, use write-in surveys, street sampling, and other non-probability surveys of doubtful profes-sionalism and accuracy. Most voters are not statisticians, and an improper poll that newspaper readers assume is reliable can cost you votes. All other things being equal, voters don't like to vote for a sure loser. In the event a newspaper poll shows you losing by a large margin, you are well advised to criticize the paper's survey and challenge the procedures and the results. In no event should your campaign strategy be based on the results of a newspaper poll of demonstrated non-professionalism; the newspaper's methodology, interviewing techniques, and sampling design should be checked out thoroughly before using its results as substitutes for polls you can't afford to conduct. If you can't afford professional consultants to make this appraisal, someone on your staff who has market research or statistical experience should be assigned to do the checking.

In Canada, the danger of newspaper polls is generally recognized, and they are not permitted by law, although private (that is, unpublished) polls are, of course, allowed.

DISASSOCIATION FROM THE TICKET

Many election ballots still consist of party slates; that is, all candidates of one party or one segment of a party are listed on one vertical line. In situations like this, a strong candidate on top of the ticket can carry his or her colleagues. But the opposite happens as well—a weak candidate at the top of the ticket can neutralize much work and expenditure. The defeat of many local Democrats in 1980 on tickets headed by presidential candidate Jimmy Carter is an example of this.

When your research shows that you're running stronger than the top of the ticket, you may have to disassociate yourself as well as you can.

Some candidates exclude the party name from their advertisements and emphasize their own name, giving the voters a reason to look for the name, not the party, on the ballot. In recent New York primary elections, reform candidates ran as independents, regular candidates avoided identifying themselves with this faction, and many voters were completely confused.

On the other hand, as a new candidate, you may have trouble getting yourself identified in a way that strengthens your candidacy. Some national movements have local followings with which you can identify. Current or recent examples of such groups are Ralph Nader's consumer advocates, John Gardner's Common Cause, the John Anderson presidential campaign, and ecology-oriented private groups such as the Sierra Club and Friends of the Earth.

REVERSING THE FIELD

If you use basic research to make decisions, there are usually occasions when the results of that research force you to consider changing your strategy, assuming that the campaign is not so advanced that all options are precluded. Reversals of field, sometimes involving changes in media emphasis, sometimes changes of themes, campaign managers, or endorsements, all have an element of danger.

In his race for the Senate in 1964, Robert F. Kennedy refused to participate in a public debate with the incumbent, Kenneth B. Keating, because the polls showed that he was ahead. But Keating gained strength as the race proceeded, and Kennedy decided to change his strategy and debate Keating about three weeks before the election, reportedly against the advice of his staff. Kennedy, however, was a consummate politician and sensed the necessity for this decision.

You'll have to balance the risk of introducing something new against the damage resulting from your present strategy. There is usually time for only one major reversal. Such a decision, therefore, deserves careful consideration. Research is helpful, but in my experience, this one case when research must defer to emotion and political instinct.

THIRD CANDIDATES

Sometimes one of the major candidates deliberately plants a third candidate to pull the votes of ethnic, racial, or religious minorities from his opponent. In 1971, for example, Queens County Democratic Leader Matthew J. Troy candidly admitted having done that in a New York City Council race. Troy's attitude was, "Well, doesn't everyone do it?" This tactic (so common that *The New York Times* gave the Troy story only a few paragraphs) is usually adopted to split the opponent's voter base. The ploy is based on the political reality that, all other things being equal, a given percentage of voters will vote for a name suggesting a religious, ethnic, or racial affinity. The only possible defense is to appeal directly and forthrightly to the group the third candidate hopes to split, indicating that a deliberate manipulation of ethnic or religious or racial ties is being attempted and that a vote for the third candidate cannot serve the group but only the politician trying to manipulate the group for his own purposes.

NAME IDENTIFICATION PROBLEMS

Deliberate splitting, as described above, relies on voters' recognizing a candidate's faith, ethnic group, or race from his name. such identification is probably worth 10 to 15 percent of the total ethnic vote, depending, of course, on the ethnic makeup of the district. A candidate may have difficulty if his name is not easily identifiable as belonging to the politically dominant group. Such a situation may be agonizing—you can't go out and advertise that, although your name is Brown, you're really Italian. In one case, a candidate, pushing the matter to excess, wore a Star of David medallion on his street tours in a Jewish area to identify himself as Jewish. One way to handle this is to use civic group associations, indicating your background in your literature, and taking "ethnic" sides of issues *if* your research and your convictions make this seem to be the proper thing to do. In his race for a judgeship in the Bronx, a Jew whose name did not sound Jewish considered using the slogan, "Put a *mensch* on the bench," to establish his religious ties in the voters' minds.*

JUDICIAL RACES

In special political races, such as those for judgeships, you can't really hit hard: Dignity and dispassionate discussion are expected prerequisites for judicial candidates. Many judicial races are arranged by a consensus

---

Mensch, a Yiddish word meaning a decent man.

of all the political parties beforehand, and judgeships may be parceled out, in agreed-upon quotas, to Italians, Jews, Democrats, Republicans, and others. Judicial races of this kind may be empty formalities and can hardly be described as open. Candidates who render substantial services to party leaders make their wishes known years in advance, eventually being given a judicial post as a reward for long service in carrying contracts, raising money, and other critical party tasks. The outright purchase of judgeships is not unknown.

Nonetheless, there are judicial contests for which prior arrangements have not been made. In recent years, judgeship campaigners have used direct mail, posters, and newspaper ads, but without the complete hoopla spirit of personal criticism of opponents that characterize elections for other posts. The necessary strategy is to bring some philosophy and/or emotion to the race and still appear credible. Judicial candidates can discuss the law as it operates to respond to or to thwart societal or community needs. For example, in a judicial campaign in which I was involved, the candidate developed a program that related to neighborhood problems. He wanted jurors' fees raised from $12 to $20 a day, since working men lost a day's pay when forced to accept jury duty; he asked that small claims courts try cases up to $1,000 instead of $500; and he advocated the trying of landlord-tenant cases at night so that tenants would not have to sacrifice their salaries to gain their day in court.

REAPPORTIONMENT: THE SALAMI AND THE KNIFE

Redistricting or reapportionment of election districts takes place at various intervals—usually after the results of a decennial census are announced, and sometimes more frequently than that. The need for redistricting arises from population increases and decreases.

State and federal laws require that districts be balanced in a reasonably equitable manner. As people move away from some areas into other areas, redistricting is required to assure equitable representation. For example, each congressional district is now supposed to contain a population of about 500,000. In practice, the party that controls the state legislature, which is responsible for drawing election districts, is likely to enact a redistricting plan with lines drawn in such a way as to be favorable to the interests of its own members, while technically including approximately equal members of citizens in each district.*

In a process known as gerrymandering, districts are drawn—sometimes in preposterous shapes—to suit not public equity but the needs of the party in power.** Tradeoffs are sometimes arranged between political parties so that leaders and other senior people of both parties are assured "safe" districts.*** Many election district maps look distinctly artificial because natural boundaries and existing neighborhood lines are completely ignored.

What does reapportionment mean for a new candidate? In the first instance, an examination of past voting behavior is particularly important if redistricted lines have just been drawn. The party in power assigns technicians to assure as many "safe" districts as possible for loyal party men. They occasionally make mistakes, but they are paid to know their business. If you are considering a race in a newly drawn district, examine the area's voting data very carefully. In some instances, you will find that it is better not to make the race there, and it may be wiser to try to find a district in which you have a better chance or simply not to run at all.

As a consequence of reapportionment in 1972, two congressional seats were eliminated in New York City, with tragic consequences for the reform wing of the Democratic Party. Incumbent Congressmen James H. Scheuer and Jonathan B. Bingham challenged each other in the primary

---

*"In New York, a legislative employee long noted for his artistry at drawing district lines greeted with joy the U.S. Supreme Court decision requiring the smallest possible deviation from district to district. He noted that from then on it depended on how you 'slice the salami,' and that his party had control of both the salami and the knife. In Ohio a leading political figure openly acknowledged that political party registration and past voting habits had been fed into a computer to assure that the majority party could get the maximum benefit from the forthcoming congressional redistricting.
. . . It is not too surprising that the legislature invariably 'sees fit' to give maximum protection to incumbents and to assure that the majority party continues and, if at all possible, expands control. New York has a new district which slices two sections out of Bronx County and fits them together. The state claims they are 'contiguous by water,' which a minority leader has likened to the contiguity of East and West Pakistan." (Editorial, *National Civic Review*, January 1972, pp. 4-5.)

**"Gerrymandering" is named for Elbridge Gerry (1744–1814), a Massachusetts governor who redistricted the state to give his party a number of state senators in excess of their voting strength,and for salamander, the animal whose shape Essex County, Massachusetts, resembled after Gerry redistricted it.

***Tradeoffs are a type of political contract. For example, in 1971, the Bronx borough president wanted New York City to rehabilitate Yankee Stadium at a cost of $24 million. According to rumor, the true cost to the city was probably much higher, since tradeoffs to other borough presidents for voting for the Yankee Stadium project would involve other major capital facilities for their boroughs.

election in one new district in the Bronx, and Bella Abzug, whose district in Manhattan had been eliminated by the reapportionment, chose to run in the district represented by William Fitts Ryan. All four were reform Democrats. Ms. Abzug was criticized in some reform circles for challenging Ryan, since many people felt that he had earned his seat and that she should have run against a conservative congressman elsewhere in the city. The district in which Scheuer and Bingham opposed each other included areas that both had represented previously. A convention of local reformers was called to decide which of the two men should run so that the party would not be further fragmented, but when Bingham lost the convention vote, he decided to campaign anyway rather than run outside his home district (which is legal in New York in a redistricting year) or step aside for two years. Bingham and Ryan won the primaries, but Ryan died soon thereafter, and Ms. Abzug was named to replace him on the Democratic ticket. In the November election, Congressman Ryan's widow ran on the Liberal party ticket and lost to Ms. Abzug.

If you have the misfortune of having to face such a situation, consider both the short-term and long-term political consequences of running in someone else's district or of not running at all. If you're redistricted out of office, you might more wisely pull out of the election but quietly and actively maintain your good will in the area. If you look only at the short term, you may decide to make the fight, as did Ms. Abzug and Bingham, and you may even win the election as Bingham did in the primary, but you will inevitably also make enemies. Political enmities are notoriously strong and long remembered, and most politicians can't afford many of them and still last over the long term. If you sit out one term but continue to make your presence felt, you are likely to earn good will, and the party will probably sense its obligation to you for maintaining unity and see to it that you are able to run in the next election.

SCANDALS

Political life is not the moral quagmire that many critics think it is, but the temptations—money and power—are very enticing. some men are tempted by the opportunity to make what appears to be easy money— sometimes thousands of dollars in cash for a simple telephone call arranging an important introduction, particularly when they see that so many others seem to be doing it.* Selling favors, as press reports constantly remind us, is not uncommon in American political life. Favors given for a small price are almost universally deplored as a form of whoredom. It seems, though, that as the price for favors increases—often astronomically—the transaction gains not only acceptability but even respect and self-esteem on the part of the participants. Nonetheless, the selling of favors at any price is a type of public prostitution and a personal betrayal of those who believe in and work for you as well. It is also illegal. There is not defense for a candidate or official caught participating in such acts.

If one of your staff or advisors gets involved in a public or private scandal, you will have a difficult decision to make. When, for example, Herman Badillo's executive assistant, who managed his campaign for Bronx borough president in 1966, was accused of improperly accepting hotel accommodations from a firm that did business with the city, Badillo forced him to resign. Various observers thought this was too severe. In some cases, you may find that you have no other way to go. In others, if there are extenuating circumstances, the public may respect you for being loyal to a friend. Badillo could have stood by his assistant until the charges against him had been proven in court or requested that he take a leave of absence until the case was decided. Such a stand would have had two positive effects: Badillo would have displayed loyalty, a trait highly valued by his largely Spanish-speaking constituency, where the assistant was known and probably well-regarded, and he would not have appeared to prejudge the case before it came to trial.

If, without your knowledge, one of your people splits fees or takes cash for a promise f a job, you may have to make charges before an outsider does. Generally, the best course is to face the problem squarely. It will not go away just because you pretend it is not there.

STAFF INCOMPETENTS

Incompetent staff members not only exist in every campaign; in some cases, they actually control the campaign.** New campaigners sometimes

---

*The F.B.I. Abscam sting in 1980 involved a number of Congressmen and one U.S. Senator. Many Americans were shocked to learn how much money was available to public officials on the take and how easily and cheaply they could be bought. Others wondered how many other officials were also finding the temptation too enticing to resist.

**In some campaigns, dedicated volunteers take things over solely by their intensity of commitment, because candidates tend to equate dedication with competence, a correlation not always justified.

allow their ignorance and inexperience to excuse incompetence. Generally, such inadequacies become clear only in the course of the campaign. Often, the candidate's response is to change the incompetent person's title and gradually reduce his responsibilities and the nature and amounts of his discretion. The situation becomes particularly complicated if the incompetent was sponsored by a party leader, a major contributor, or a family friend. The best thing to do is to fire him but to allow him to cite poor health, business pressures, or any other reasonable public excuse, as the cause of his leaving. To keep him is to guarantee staff resentment, because in any office, competent staff members have a fairly shrewd idea of who is goofing off or who has no real idea of what he is doing. There is no surer way to destroy staff morale and efficiency than by having competent people constantly picking up after the incompetents.

You don't benefit either yourself or the person involved by retaining him after he has established an incompetent behavior pattern that cannot be corrected. In one congressional campaign, for example, 10,000 shopping bags were delivered to the person in charge of liaison for the assembly district. Two hours later, when he was called with instructions on what to do with them, he said he had "given" them to the local butcher. Possibly he had sold them. In either case, he should have been fired immediately.

RUNNING OUT OF MONEY

In the spring of 1983, having spent a considerable amount of money and seeing no major contributors coming forth, Senator Dale Bumpers of Arkansas made a sensible decision to drop out of the Democratic presidential race.

In some smaller campaigns, although publicly your chances appear to be almost nil, your research may show that you have a good start and a small but genuine chance to win if you can get only several thousand dollars more. Some people of wealth are attracted by such a situation, for they feel that their money can have a significant impact and that, if you win, you will remember the contribution they made when you were in a desperate situation. If you do not obtain such contributions, you may have to make commitments about jobs or votes on specific measures to get the cash. Only you can evaluate the net benefits of such a tradeoff. It's your decision, and it's a hard one. Some candidates, in such a situation, prefer to go into debt. They hope that, if they win, testimonial dinners and other fund-raising functions will help pay off the debt. But if they lose, they may have to repay it from their personal funds over an extended period of time.

CAMPAIGNING IN AREAS WHERE RACE IS AN ISSUE

If racial feelings run high in your area, you shouldn't even attempt to run unless you have an extremely strong physical and emotional constitution. Campaigning in a race-conscious area is easier for racists of any color than for moderates or liberals. Racists are essentially single-issue candidates whose appeals are therefore simple, direct, and easily communicated. A liberal or independent has a more difficult and painful time, since his position is much more complex, reflecting an ideology that necessarily involves many issues.

My recommendation in these contests is to rely on household interviews-in-depth to establish exactly what the voters are thinking. You can then either trade on their fears, as the extreme candidates do, or advocate compassionate, understanding, concrete solutions to the community's problems. Both black and white voters will generally appreciate your candor in defining the issues and making specific recommendations on priorities in building capital facilities such as schools or roads. Truth is usually sensed and respected, if not universally appreciated and rewarded.

OUTSIDE "CAMPAIGN DOCTORS"

In the theater, if a play or musical show encounters difficulties during its preview period, the producer may bring in an outside consultant or "show doctor." However, when a political campaign seems to be going badly, the usual procedure is to call together the consultants, the "kitchen cabinet," the campaign manager, and the candidate's family to define what's going wrong and to develop remedies. Sometimes this works, but more often the result is confusion or reinforcement of the original problem.

If you are in such a situation, you may have to ask for advice from a political leader of your party or a political consultant from outside your area—one who has had no direct involvement in your campaign and who can be more objective about the options that remain open to you. Do this, however, before the campaign is half over, since after that point almost all major resources are usually committed. Check with local politicians and local political reporters for the names of possible campaign doctors. Such local campaign mechanics are not usually well-known, and people with national reputations may be unavailable or too expensive. The Democratic and Republican National Committees in Washington, D.C. can provide lists of consultants by geographic location. My advice would be to review these lists with local newspaper reporters, party leaders, and consultants you may know who are not involved in your campaign. Many consultants work by cross-referrals with colleagues; they recommend colleagues who may or may not be appropriate for your work. It is best to judge consultants separately and retain them separately, not by sets. (See the section on selecting consultants, pp. 21-23.)

DEBATES

Since the Richard M. Nixon-John F. Kennedy televised debates, which were widely regarded as a turning point in the 1960 presidential campaign, interest in the debate as a campaign device has been high. As television has assumed a major role in the campaigning process, political debates (and refusals to debate) have become particularly important. As a candidate, you have three options: debate as much as possible; debate only under stated conditions; or avoid debates altogether.

In some situations, such as the Gore Vidal-Jerry Brown California gubernatorial primary in 1982, one candidate considers himself so far ahead that he believes debate can only help the challenger. In this event, many stalling devices may be used, such as disputes over the format of the debate, who answers the first question, who is the moderator, whether the debate will be live or filmed, and which reporters should be present. Such tactics can delay the debate either indefinitely or so long as to permit only one or at the most two debates to take place. (An example of this, in another arena, was the behavior of the delegates to the organizing meetings for the Vietnam peace talks in Paris. They spent months arguing over the shape of the table and delayed substantive talks while the fighting and bombing went on in Indochina.) The challenger, however, may, in turn, buy television time and debate an empty chair.

Your strategy should be guided by what the voters want as expressed in probability sample surveys, tempered by your judgment of how well you can handle yourself in public debates. By and large, most voters do want to see the candidates in a personal confrontation.

In the debate itself, the usual technique is to talk to the audience and avoid answering your opponent's charges, while sounding confident and well informed.* But voters like a fight and have become somewhat turned off by the obvious artifice and sweeping generalities that have come to characterize most political debates. Try to turn the debate toward the questions that your research shows are of interest to the voters. Talk about them with conviction and in the most concrete terms possible. Address your opponent directly and with as much emotion as is appropriate. Viewers will respect you if you act like a concerned human being, not an emotionless marionette—but no matter how strongly you feel, stop short of name-calling or displaying open contempt.

RELATIONSHIPS TO POLITICAL CLUBS

Most candidates start their campaigns on the basis of their membership in or endorsement from a local political club. Such a base is important to provide a semblance of party blessing, as well as campaign workers and occasionally funds. Often, however, the club leadership will expect the candidate to pay for some club mailings, furniture rentals, signs, or other club expenses. If such costs and other club demands seem excessive in relation to what the club offers you in the way of workers or facilities, you may be better off campaigning independently.

Club sponsorship is less critical than it used to be. Efficient mechanical and electronic means—computerized direct mail, radio, television, news-paper advertising, and professionally manned telephones—can effectively replace large numbers of workers. Also, a candidate can usually attract campaign workers from other sources. Relatives, friends, business associates, and fellow members of civic groups often are willing to volunteer their services.

In some situations, you may get your club's endorsement simply because you have waited your turn in the club; and then you cannot turn your back on your sponsors. In other situations—for example, if the club needs a candidate to run for a given office and you consent to fill the

---

*Murray B. Levin describes this tactic in *Kennedy Campaigning: The System and the Style as Practiced by Senator Edward Kennedy* (Boston: Beacon Press, 1966).

void—you may be able to run the campaign with only token consultation with the club.

WHEN TO ANNOUNCE YOUR CANDIDACY

There are many views on the question of when to announce one's candidacy. Some candidates, particularly those who aspire to high office, prefer to "play it coy," to develop momentum and then announce—or accept a "draft"—at a suitable time and place. I am personally convinced, however, that once you've decided to make the race and are assured adequate funds, your best course is to announce as soon as possible. If you delay, there is a strong possibility of leaks to the press that you're looking for campaign funds or otherwise preparing to become a candidate. If you are confronted with a situation like this and still wish to delay your announcement, your best course is to state that you are considering making the race and will announce your candidacy when you have made a final decision.

For a June primary, you will probably wish to have an announcement ready by Easter or shortly thereafter. If you're going into a September primary, you may want to be ready to announce before people leave for their summer vacations. Examine local precedents by checking newspaper coverage of previous campaigns. (Back issues of local newspapers are normally available at the public library as well as at each newspaper's offices.) Ask previous candidates why they announced when they did, and see whether you agree with their thinking.

Try not to make your announcement on a holiday when people are not home to read the local paper. If there is an influential weekly newspaper in your area, make your announcement on a day when it can report the news.

When the time comes, simply find a convenient meeting place—a local press club, or your campaign office if you already have one. If you anticipate television coverage, be sure to choose a place which has adequate electrical wiring and outlets for television equipment. The television station will tell you what is necessary. Then telephone the radio and/or television stations and the local newspapers to inform them that you are having a press conference. At the conference, make the announcement in a businesslike way, stating the theme of your campaign, explaining why you have decided to make the race, and mentioning any major supporters and endorsements that you have. You can also announce that you welcome contributions and volunteers, giving an address and telephone number where they will be welcomed. have copies of your statement available for the reporters who cover the meeting, and be prepared to answer any questions they may have.

THE CARPETBAGGER ISSUE

In many campaigns the fact that a candidate doesn't really live in a district (whether or not he has an official residence there) is made much of by his opponent. The public usually disregards the residency issue unless other more emotional and solidly negative factors are related to it.

In lower Manhattan, carpetbagging was made the cardinal issue in a district leadership race in 1971. The front-runner's opponents had the facts clearly on their side: They circulated photographs of his suburban home with his listing in the suburban telephone directory superimposed on the picture. Additionally, while he still maintained an official address in the Manhattan district, they reported that his children went to school in the suburb in which the house was located. The evidence appeared to be irrefutable and was made known throughout the district. Nonetheless, the carpetbagger won the election by a large margin. (After he won the election, the new district leader, who held a responsible city job, was publicly accused of seriously mismanaging hundreds of thousands of dollars in connection with his job. It is interesting to speculate how the election might have turned out if, rather than spending all their time belaboring the carpetbagging issue, his opponents had made an effort to investigate his performance as a city employee with discretion over large amounts of money.)

My advice would be never to key an attack on the carpetbagger issue alone—the voters don't always buy this approach. However, the residency issue can be used effectively if it is made part of a larger theme with emotional impacts that the individual voter can feel and relate to. An effective way to use the carpetbagger issue against an opponent is *not* to start with it. Instead, start with something like "Last year Assemblyman Jones voted against Propositions A, B, and C—all of which would have benefited our district. Apparently he doesn't have our needs in mind. Maybe it's because he doesn't live here; he doesn't know what it's like here every day."

If an opponent uses the carpetbagger issue against you, your wisest course is probably to let your record speak for you and not to address the issue directly at all. If you need moral support in this position, simply remember how far the incumbent Senator Kenneth B. Keating got using the carpetbagging issue against Robert F. Kennedy in New York in 1964.

WHEN YOUR TACTICS ARE ADOPTED BY YOUR OPPONENT

Often problems occur in the most unlikely ways. Since everything in a campaign is in the public domain, no one thinks twice about stealing ideas or new campaign approaches. Political literature, for example, is often copied. With thousands of campaigns going on every year it is pretty difficult to think of new ideas, so people in campaigns commonly steal what they think worked so well for the other guy. The problem is that the theft is often without thought or concern as to whether the flow and logic of the campaign makes the theft appropriate.

For example, in a recent campaign I prepared a procedure for a professional telephone bank. Since the area had been redistricted, I recommended that the calls concentrate on the opponent's base, which was largely lower middle class Irish families with concentrations of blacks and Puerto Ricans. The message was designed to follow up on my client's door-to-door canvassing in the opponent's original district. Our reports and research indicated that our candidate made a fine impression—he was youthful, energetic, and responsive to the voters. The key to the campaign was the candidate's inherent personal likability contrasted to his opponent's standoffishness. The message pointed out that in his home district crime was lower and city services better. The calls got a significant measure of enthusiastic response.

A week after the calls started a staff aide learned that the opponent's campaign staff were using the same message directed to my candidate's old district, which was largely Italian. The reverse campaign assumed that the contexts for the calls were exactly the same while they actually varied in housing types as well as demographic characteristics.

In a campaign when the opponent imitates your strategy or tactics, the first instinct will be to switch to something else as soon as you can. Instead I would recommend that you reevaluate why you're doing what you're doing; if the approach is effective continue to use it. Don't change simply because the opposition has embraced your thought; it doesn't automatically mean that they've also embraced your vote.

CONTRACTS WITH CONSULTANTS

Most of the larger-scale elections such as mayorals, congressionals, gubernatorials, and other state offices use consultants for polling, phone banks, mail, media, public relations, and radio-TV time buying. Even smaller campaigns will usually retain consultants for one or two specialties. While a professional code of ethics is supposed to apply, unfortunately as in the legal and medical professions, some political consultants may not strictly adhere to responsible standards of professional conduct. Political consulting is a very competitive, and sometimes cutthroat, business with the shortest of seasons and with substantial annual overheads.

In the last few years I have heard of consultants whose staff have represented *both* the Democratic and Republican candidates for the same office. There are consultants who will threaten candidates with particularly vicious opposing campaigns unless they are retained. There are consultants who, once retained, will insist that certain other consultants be hired by the candidate. Strange things are forever happening in campaigns. In Washington, D.C. in 1982 a concern retained by the incumbent mayor had a disagreement with their client and went to the leading opponent and sold their services to that camp. There was considerable outcry in the press by the mayor as to the impropriety of the action, but he could do nothing about it.

It is very important that your contracts with consultants be reviewed carefully by your attorney. There are generally considerable amounts of money involved. There should be a condition, for example, that if for stated reasons you wish to dispense with the consultant's services a specific payment schedule will be followed. The contract should deny them the right to go to the opposition with information developed in your employ; a penalty can be stated for infringement.

Contracts should have stated delivery times, indicate which principals of the firm will be available to the campaign for specific consultation, and for how long. There have been many lawsuits by candidates and organizations such as Senator Edward Kennedy and the Democratic National Committee against political consultants for non-delivery of services or for services that were not properly performed. Writing consultant contracts carefully can avoid some of the heartaches and expense of lawsuits.

6
Radio and Television Advertising

Nothing can be more annoying than to be obscurely hanged.

—Voltaire

This chapter deals with radio and television advertising in campaigns while the following chapter focuses on the various forms of print and mail advertising. Political advertising is a major component of any campaign, both in energies consumed and in monies spent. Press reports sometimes give the impression that this is a relatively new phenomenon, or that it is somehow undemocratic.* As a matter of fact, however, American political advertising has a long if not always noble history. Campaign broadsides from the eighteenth and nineteenth centuries and nineteenth-century campaign buttons can be found in many museums. Thomas Paine's *Common Sense,* which is now read in some literature courses, was a very effective political advertisement in its day.

What is new in political advertising is its potential for effective saturation in a short period of time. Broadsides were distributed to perhaps a few hundred people; a television commercial in a major city may reach millions of people simultaneously. Also, while political advertising broadsides generally took the form of ideas on paper that were aimed at the readers' minds, political advertising now makes use of many other stimuli: A candidate's television appearance or statesmanlike voice appeal to the emotions of voters at the same time that his (or her) ideas appeal to their minds.

Joe McGinness's best-selling book *The Selling of the President 1968* was one of the first to focus on the harshest characteristics of the process and made the sophisticated advertising techniques of Richard Nixon's 1968 campaign appear to represent a dramatic transformation in cam-

---

*What may be undemocratic is not the advertising but rather the "obscene" amounts of money that have to be raised to pay for it, obligating the candidate to individuals and special interests. Some politicians say such amounts will only guarantee "access," but access allows the options to be stated and makes "hardball" lobbying possible. Other positions, however worthwhile, may not be provided the same audience or "courtesies."

paigning. Actually, however, the change in the process (not to mention the expense) of political campaigning—particularly in campaigns involving larger districts with hundreds of thousands of voters—began in the mid-1950s, when television ownership became common. Television made a new, effective medium available to politicians and merchandisers alike. Its use by candidates simply made obvious the long-standing fact that campaigning depended partly on merchandising and that candidates were "sold" in much the same way as consumer products. McGinness's phrase, "the selling of the President," struck home to many as a recognized, shared truth.

Despite the technological revolution in political advertising, the time-honored techniques of newspaper advertisements, press releases, brochures, mailings, stickers, and giveaways remain a significant aspect of campaigning at all levels, and in fact are the only ones in use in the vast majority of elections for local offices, where television is usually neither desirable nor affordable.* This chapter reviews the use of the techniques made available by electronic technology.

THE IMPORTANCE OF CONSISTENCY IN ADVERTISING THEMES

Too many campaign managers or campaign committees waste money, and lots of it, by making expenditures based on the apparent assumption that one medium has nothing to do with another and that, without retaining what has been said in previous advertisements, the voter hears only one message at a time. For example, in his radio advertising one candidate emphasized that he could listen patiently to all groups in his state and work out solutions carefully; however, his billboard advertising featured his ability to get things done expeditiously. As a consequence, the two contradictory appeals probably canceled each other out and lost him at least as many votes as they gained. An overall media plan is required in every campaign to determine which themes to use when and to properly examine the impacts of alternative budgetary allocations.

---

*Despite the escalating amounts of money spent, informed judgments suggest much of the literature produced is uninspired and ineffective. A large part of cost increases for literature is the current fad that a seemingly endless barrage of direct mail by a candidate produces results; there is no hard evidence that this is actually the case. My judgment is that after 10 or 12 pieces there is little positive benefit possible.

The basic question in political advertising is what to say: this is the key judgment in every campaign, and it remains a creative judgment. No one knows with certainty the one best way to appeal to the voter. Whatever you do, if you use more than one medium, make sure that each one *reinforces* the other. If you have nothing new to say, don't waste your money saying it; you'll only irritate some voters, and you'll pay dearly for that privilege.

Whatever media you use, map out the basic structure of your advertising campaign as early as possible. If you are using radio and television, early planning is an absolute necessity, since you must buy the right spots well in advance, with careful choice of day and hour—for example, following certain popular shows.* To do this effectively, you will have to have some idea of the different ways in which you wish to utilize the various media in your theme development. You will therefore wish to lay out your basic themes as soon as possible. Be sure, however, to leave some degree of flexibility to enable you to take advantage of developing opportunities that cannot be anticipated and to be able to respond to your opponent's attacks.**

Basically, most campaign themes focus on two or three weaknesses of the opponent(s) while maximizing the candidate's own strengths. From the time that you and your campaign manager delineate the basic themes of your campaign, all advertising expenditures should be keyed to implementing them. All forms of advertising you use should reinforce each other by illustrating the same themes and appeals. Some voters become easily bored by campaigning; a candidate cannot hope that voters will remember and be interested in his/her stands on fifty issues. It is important to *select* and emphasize certain basic issues and themes early in the campaign and as much as possible stay with them. This does not mean not adding or modifying themes.

Different media are appropriate for different situations. In a small community you might rely on press coverage, street campaigning, mail-

---

*Radio and television time-buying is an expertise that should not be overlooked even in a local campaign doing radio only (see pp. 92-93, 173-174).

**Some campaigners (including Clifford White, a Republican campaign manager who has worked for Barry M. Goldwater and others) do not agree with this strategy. They believe that every campaign should be conducted positively and that response should not be made to opponents' attacks, since the candidate who responds to an opponent presumably no longer fully controls his or her own campaign. This theory sometimes underlies the strategy of refusing debates. In my judgment, no absolute of this sort is applicable to campaigning. Political campaigns involve many variables, and an inflexible response cannot always be right.

ings, and buttons and forget radio and television, since the costs would be excessive in relation to the number of people to be reached. In even smaller campaigns, you might rely entirely on personal canvassing and distribution of brochures. In certain communities, it may be possible to depend mainly on street campaigning, while in others, that could result in certain defeat. Each situation varies somewhat, and the response must be based on public-opinion research combined with experience in the area, political judgment, and an objective evaluation of your actual abilities. Some candidates, for example, are wonderful street campaigners, while others lose votes every time they conduct a walking tour. Some are inherently likable while some are perceived as somewhat slimy, and when some voters have these perceptions, word of mouth can exacerbate them quickly and relentlessly.

A campaign theme can consist of a phrase like Franklin Delano Roosevelt's "New Deal," Harry Truman's "Fair Deal," Adlai Stevenson's "Let's Talk Sense," Ronald Reagan's "Stay the Course," or Chicago Mayor Harold Washington's "Now It's Our Turn." It can be a phrase or a characteristic you want to emphasize—ability, experience, ideas, youth, honesty. A combination of research and intuition is necessary to provide a good theme. But regardless of its derivation, the theme must relate the the problems that are important in your district and the way the voters feel about them, and it should appear consistently in all your advertising. Sometimes a candidate with courage and confidence can perceive a policy issue that hasn't yet caught the public's attention and demonstrate its importance and relevance. This happens less and less: Caution is considerably more common than courage in the current political environment. The increasing costs of campaigning combined with the close review of candidates by PACs and organized self-interest groups have made many candidates mute. Too many politicians have stampeded to the center and to relative safety.

RADIO AND TELEVISION ADVERTISING IN SMALLER CAMPAIGNS

There are situations when it may be worthwhile to advertise on radio or television, even though for congressional and smaller campaigns you may be paying to reach many times the number of voters you really want to reach.* If your research shows you're still not getting full recognition after half the campaign is over, or if you feel you must answer an accusation that the press or public seems to be accepting, or if you wish to attack your opponent with something you believe will be conclusive, you might consider a radio or television saturation even though it is uneconomical. But usually, television advertising for smaller-area campaigns is not advisable, as it takes money from effective techniques such as mailings, brochures, newspaper ads, and telephone canvassing, which are more economical because they can be specifically targeted.

Radio advertising is cheaper than television and in the hands of creative technicians can be very effective. Sixty-second spots dramatizing a theme by simulated voter conversations, with some taste and humor, are more productive than the candidate's voice solemnly praising his own virtues. For obvious reasons, some media experts recommend scheduling these spots before or after evening news programs.

Radio spots are generally thirty or sixty seconds in length. Time is purchased for a set or mix of spots—so many during 8 to 12 A.M., so many 12 to 5 P.M., etc. (An illustration of a package buy in New York City is shown in Fig. 6-1.) You may want to emphasize customized appeals to voters who may be driving to work or to home, people at home doing chores, or people who work at night. Generally, radio advertising is effective when you don't exhort, but rather demonstrate reasons that make voting for you seem sensible and acceptable, by talking to listeners, not at them.

Some consultants find radio especially effective for negative material. In 1982, for example, there was a major upset in a race in the suburbs of New York City. The winner used a spot with an announcer's voiceover, an imaginative sound track with the text tying the opponent to the county leader, who was awaiting a jail sentence. It was regarded as a "heavy piece" that received a lot of criticism, but it proved effective.

Most often radio spots take one of the following approaches.

1. Limit each spot to one basic fact or idea, e.g., the opponent voted against a new high school in your area.

---

*This is so, for example, in New Jersey campaigns where congressional and senatorial candidates have to pay television prices based on reaching the Philadelphia and New York markets because there are no television stations physically located in New Jersey. Similarly, Jay Rockefeller, running for Governor of West Virginia, did a television saturation that included Washington, D.C., Maryland, and Virginia.

STATION A		
60 seconds		
No. of spots	*Time*	*Cost*
2	5 - 10 a.m.	$350
1	Sat. 6 - 10	175
2	M–F 10 - 3	130
3	M–S 8 p.m. - 12 p.m.	35
1	Sat. 10 a.m. - 8 p.m.	70
2	Sun. 6 a.m. - 8 p.m.	70
Total 13		$1590
4 weeks		$6360

Total four weeks buy

Number of spots	*Station*	*Total Costs*	*Adults (over 25 years old) Reached*
52	A	$6360	468,000
32	B	1240	468,000
6	D	780	42,600
51	D	1020	800,000
40	E	680	200,000
		$10,080	1,990,600 (estimated)

Fig. 6-1. Example of a four-week radio buy—New York City.

2. Incumbents usually say: I've done the job. I've kept taxes low.

3. Challengers focus on attendance records or allege that the incumbent didn't take care of the district: "He/she was traveling in Europe half the time."

4. Some consultants advise that the radio spots should be relatively varied as opposed to television, where spots can be repeated many times with effectiveness, since the audience is much larger and you reach new viewers while reinforcing viewers who have already seen them. It's a judgment call to determine when you've reached saturation, the point where voters have had enough. Again, campaigning consists of a strenuous succession of judgment calls; each campaign, to be effective and

economical, has to be customized to the campaigner's personality, issues, and appearance and to the specific chemistry of the candidate mix.

5. Endorsements are often critical components of a radio campaign. Some specialists advise using so-called "man in the street" endorsements while others prefer to use well-known politicians to read their endorsements.

6. Issue statements are now relatively unpopular in radio advertising although my experience suggests that these, if properly done on a good research base, can be very effective. They have to be credible and strike a responsive chord (in Tony Schwartz's apt phrase). The format is simply this: "I know you're worried about this problem. Here's what the candidate intends to do about it if elected."

7. Sometimes radio commercials have a familial endorsement. Considered by some mechanics an overly sentimental device, for some areas and circumstances it may be quite effective. Essentially, copy consists of a parent or spouse saying: "He's a good boy. He's worked hard. Please vote for him. I'm so proud of him."

8. When an incumbent is haunted by major mistakes that have been well-publicized by the media, the humble apologia made popular by David Garth in the second New York City Lindsay campaign (1965) is used. This goes: "I known I've made some mistakes but they were honest ones. But I've learned and I can do a lot better than the other guy who hasn't had the benefit of my experience."

9. In areas with sizable concentrations of ethnic groups, it has become common to use actors simulating (sometimes horribly caricaturing) these ethnic speech rhythms and accents, saying, in effect, "Did you hear about candidate A? He's really doing a job for us. Now he needs us. We have to stick together."

10. Very few political radio spots do humor effectively. If you can do it you have the advantage of your ads being different from most of the ads the voters hear; for that reason alone the ad will be talked about. Sometimes you can do it by simply mimicking your opponent's copy, which God knows often enough will be outrageous. For example, the M.C.I. business commercial advertising against the Bell system uses the very popular Bell slogan, "Reach out and touch someone," showing the same visuals as the Bell commercial but adding a tearful customer who is crying, explaining, "But do you know how much it costs!" I am convinced that the public appreciates a break in the heavy-handed, portentous, clearly self-serving partial truths that characterize most campaign commercials. Candor is so different as to guarantee favorable word of

mouth; candor, humor, and honest feeling would be a devastating combination.

An example of a radio script follows. It was prepared by the National Conservative Political Action Committee (NCPAC) for the 1982 Cutler-Evans congressional race.

MAN: I've heard that Lynn Cutler is the liberal candidate for Congress and is resorting to personal attacks and name calling. Is that true?

FEMALE: Yes, it is. Cutler made fun of President Reagan's speech, calling him very old, very tired. Then she called President and Mrs. Reagan the Emperor and Empress, and she falsely accused Mrs. Reagan of spending $994 a yard for silk for the White House. Cutler called conservative leaders "racists" and accused them of plotting to destroy Democracy and undermine our government. She accused President Reagan of spreading hatred. Recently, after her good friend Roxanne Conlan got into trouble over her taxes Cutler made fun of Congressman Evans because he paid a lot of taxes.

MAN: Gosh, no wonder people are getting turned off by the liberal Lynn Cutler. I'm going to vote to reelect our good Congressman Cooper Evans.

In 1980 the NCPAC had been extraordinarily successful in using saturation media to defeat leading liberal Democrats such as Senators Church and McGovern. The 1982 results of their campaigning were only minimally successful. There are fads in campaigning; it is not wise to copy one technique just because it worked for another candidate in another place and at another time. The voters are not that simplistic; they learn, are pleased or not, are outraged or not; they are not yet completely numbed by campaigning, but judging by the sharply declining proportion who actually vote, many are suffering considerable ennui with the campaigning process.

TELEVISION ADVERTISING IN LARGER CAMPAIGNS

Television campaigning has become almost a necessity in city-, state-, and nationwide campaigns. In many larger-scale campaigns, according to Walter Diamond, an experienced New York campaign manager, "the image coming out of the box controls almost everything." Most politicians acknowledge the importance of television in large-scale campaigns, and it commands a large proportion of the campaign funds of most candidates for major offices.* Nonetheless, spending the large sums of money that television requires is not by itself a guarantee of victory; the match-up between the candidates, their personality and drive, and the experience and judgment of their staffs still count for a lot.**

When you decide on expenditures for television, as well as for all other media, always try to determine your costs on the basis of cost per thousand voters reached. If you must choose among types of expenditures, make sure you're choosing among the net effective costs—that is, the cost per thousand voters actually reached. Viewing the situation in this way, it is easy to see, for example, that television in primaries has a very high net effective cost because you pay to reach the entire viewing public while only perhaps 10 percent of the viewing public at most are primary voters.*** (There may, of course, be other reasons—not the least of which may be your opponent's heavy use of television—that cause you to decide to use television in a primary despite its relatively high cost per voter.)

In planning your television budget, keep in mind the fact that if you buy television or radio time through an agency, the agency will receive

---

*In recent elections, many candidates use TV spots more and more to simulate news, since many voters seem to distrust outright political commercials, and their impact has appreciably diminished. That is one reason why news coverage is so valued by candidates.

**In their major 1970 campaigns, leading political television consultants had won-lost records on the order of 4-3, 3-3, and 5-4. After John V. Lindsay met disaster in his presidential bid in the spring of 1972, many commentators noted that the various television campaigns in the primaries had canceled each other out. David Garth, Lindsay's own media man, was quoted as saying that the role of television and media generally had always been exaggerated. In The New York Times of May 2, 1972, Warren Weaver, Jr., reported: "So far in the 1972 primary season, most of the Democratic candidates who made heavy investments in television and radio campaigning have failed, raising the question whether commercial use of the broadcast media still has a political impact on voters."

Such reports and explanations occur after every election. A decade later, in 1982, there were similar protestations that television could not do it all. For example, Tony Schwartz, in a lavishly financed campaign, lost with Governor Edward King (Massachusetts); David Sawyer, with a $10,000,000 campaign, lost in Chicago with Mayor Jane Byrne; while Roger Ailes lost with Louis Lehrman in New York, spending $14,000,000. These media men are experienced and reputable. But by itself television can't be controlling; the campaigning process contains too many dynamic variables. Nonetheless the consensus is that television remains the most powerful tool in campaigning. Also, many candidates seem to get considerable ego satisfaction from seeing their ads.

***That is why primary campaigns so frequently use the more focused mechanisms of direct mail and telephones, which can be designed to reach the primary voter and thereby minimize wastage. In primaries with fewer than 25,000 voters involved, I generally advise an emphasis on a telephone campaign, particularly in areas where unlimited local calling is permitted on a flat fee basis.

a 16 percent rebate from the station in addition to the fee you pay for the agency's or consultant's services. If you book your own radio and television time (which may be feasible in small areas), you yourself should be able to get the discount from the station.

TELEVISION ADVERTISING CONSULTANTS

General advice on choosing consultants will be found in Chapter I. It is wise also to remember that many consultants are extremely skilled salesmen, and sometimes these skills exceed those of their creative specialties. Candidates are often advised before retaining consultants to make certain that they feel comfortable with the specific staff assigned to their campaigns.

While this book is designed primarily for smaller campaigns, this section reviews television consultants in the unlikely event that you'll need one or be able to afford one. For example, a California State assembly race in 1982, usually a small-scale race, ended up costing $3.3 million, with both candidates using television and direct mail exceedingly liberally. One of the candidates was Tom Hayden, whose wife, Jane Fonda, is as able a fund-raiser as she is an actress and author.

There are many books describing television consultants and what they do in political campaigns, but the essence of the matter, in my judgment, is that there is not general agreement on the best approach for all political candidates.* Again, it depends on judgments as to the mood of the electorate, the issues and the solutions important to them, and to a degree what the whole ballot looks like. "You pay your money, and you take your choice," is what it comes down to.

Essentially, media consultants use polling data to discover which issues and aspects of personality and political record concern the voter, and with the candidate and his staff, plan and implement a television strategy that is orchestrated with the other media plans as to timing, emphasis, and targets. Some consultants will use focus group panels, some will travel with the candidate for a while, others will provide several themes to discuss; each has his own creative and production style. Generally, each will have a production crew with whom he or she works. The consultant

---

*See especially, Larry Sabato's *The Rise of Political Consultants* (New York: Basic Books, 1981) and Sid Blumenthal's *The Permanent Campaign* (Boston: Beacon Press, 1900) for descriptions and evaluations of the most famous and powerful of these consultants.

will generally produce the ads and do the time-buying as well. A consultant's work and judgments include:

1. Deciding when to do affirmative material and when negative. Some, for example, prefer to use television for affirmative spots exclusively, using radio to hit the opponent with negatives.

2. Deciding whether or not to respond to criticism. If yes, then deciding when, how, which media, and in what format and how often.

3. Advising the candidate on appearance: what his or her weight should be, his/her best colors, the type of ties and clothing that should be worn, the type of people with whom the candidate should be seen.

4. Rehearsing press conferences and public appearances with great care, particularly anticipating the questions the press will ask.

5. Deciding the most effective time-buying schedule; i.e., when to begin television (and radio), how many spots, which stations, how often, should they go for saturation, which groups to especially target, should the spots run every day or take off a week and hit with radio, etc. These buy decisions are again subject matter judgment calls and cumulatively can be as important as preparing the visual and auditory parts of the television spots.

6. Deciding how many themes to use and how best to present them. How many times in a campaign should themes be changed? How to stress accomplishments without sounding egotistical and grandiose? How to "negativise" the opponent without appearing sour and graceless? Use the candidate with "talking heads" or keep him/her off altogether and use surrogates? (In one campaign I was in recently, the candidate affected an English accent and contorted his face somewhat when being photographed and interviewed. His persona was absent from the campaign's television advertising.)

7. Deciding whether to use photographic stills or short clips or cinema verite, location or studios, actors or real people edited down.

8. Deciding whether to use the man in the street or celebrities.

9. Deciding on the use of professional, familial, military, business, or government backgrounds.

10. Determining whether the candidate should talk faster or slower, look directly at the camera, or always be shown talking to people.

11. Most basically, deciding how to surround the candidate with people, locale, words, music, and symbols that blocs of voters can emo-

tionally and intellectually relate to; how to make the candidate so credible or likable that the viewer will go out and vote for him or her.

Each campaign, big money or not, large area or not, contains a tremendous number of variables requiring thought and judgment; to complicate matters, the weights and shadings of each of these variables are always changing in the course of the campaign, depending on the personality mix, the issues that the voters select as important, the weight of the endorsements, the total party ticket, the economy, and the complications of multi-candidate races. It is important to remember that despite the amounts of money involved in television advertising, *it remains an art form whose effectiveness cannot be guaranteed.*

Each of the media consultants is best at certain aspects of the job. For example, David Garth is regarded by many as one of the shrewdest analysts of data and particularly good at presenting issues and accomplishments of incumbents. Others are best in their ability to dramatize a candidate with music, imagery, and quality hype. These are the Republican media advisor Robert Goodman's fortes according to many observers. Some consultants are especially skilled at defining the campaign with information crawls (the text writing that "crawls" along the bottom of the television screen). Despite their skills and high fees, most of the top consultants each election year in the big campaigns have records of 3-4, 3-3, 5-3, and the like. (I know one young consultant whose record as advisor in print and radio his first year was 2-11, yet his selling skills were so persuasive he was able to rationalize this record and go on to a successful practice.)

Preparing television ads has aspects of comedy at times. In one campaign in which I was recently involved, the problem was to dramatize the research findings that the opponent was liked and admired by many voters but they didn't think the office she sought was really suited to her skills and background. The campaign manager thought of the idea of having two small children playing trying to fit a square peg into a round hold, with the voiceover stating that the opponent and the office she sought were a poor fit. The ad agency refused to do the spot, saying that the connotations could be interpreted as too sexual! The manager, Walter Diamond, conferred with a hospital psychiatrist to check the validity of the agency's reaction. The psychiatrist suggested that the agency people might themselves need counseling. Diamond had the ad produced by someone else, and it proved effective.

In the Duryea-Carey campaign (1978) for Governor of New York State, in which over $10,000,000 was spent, mostly on television, Duryea's consultants felt the key ad would be the death penalty spot, since research showed that Carey's veto of a death penalty measure had bothered voters in both parties. They hammered away with this ad to the exclusion of almost anything else until a staff argument brought matters to a head. (Big campaigns have bureaucratic turf wars just as in government and with the same result—usually money and time are wasted in inordinate amounts.) Some thought that the ad had reached overkill and that no new conversions were likely. Duryea had had very negative press because he had decided not to make his tax returns public although his opponent had. Duryea and his advisors decided not to neutralize this criticism, and stayed with the same mix of ads. Carey came from over 15 points behind, hitting the tax matter and emphasizing his own record of achievements, and won in the last week of the campaign. The lesson is not to freeze ads but to retain some flexibility to be able to respond to emerging campaign developments; don't fall in love with any one spot.

Some consultants like to show their candidate working in different blue and white collar jobs. "He's really one of us, although he's a lot richer, and he knows our problems now" is the idea that the voters are to come away with. Robert Squier apparently initiated this approach years ago; it was recently adopted (1982) in a New Jersey Democratic primary for U.S. Senate. (Consultants borrow each other's ideas very freely.) Other consultants like to use family shots, the American flag, and a biography of personal achievements. "Will it play in Peoria?" is still the burning question. And the answer still is that no one can be sure.

Garth, regarded by many as one of the ablest media men, often controlling all aspects of a campaign, made his reputation with the second Lindsay for Mayor of New York Campaign in 1969. He produced a classic ad which became the basis for all subsequent "apologia" political advertising.

Since his first term as mayor had been filled with major problems, Lindsay was the underdog. Garth used two themes: (1) Being the mayor of New York City is the second toughest job in the United States; and (2) I've made mistakes, but now I have more experience and can do the job better.* In the judgment of many experienced political observers, the key television commercial, the "I've made mistakes" theme—one characterized by Lindsay's inner circle as the "Lindsay eats shit spot"— made the campaign because it was so credible and different.* This commercial, done in cooperation with the advertising firm Young & Rubicam, showed Lindsay saying:

> The school strike went too far—and we all made some mistakes; but I brought 225,000 new jobs to this town and that was no mistake; I fought for three years to put a fourth platoon [of police] on the streets and that was no mistake; and I reduced the deadliest gas in our air by 50 percent and I forced the landlords to roll back unfair rents, and we didn't have a Newark, a Detroit or a Watts in this city—and those were no mistakes. The things that go wrong are what make this the second toughest job in America. But the things that go right are what make me want it.**

For candidates who cannot afford the big name consultants, with upfront fees of $50,000 to $75,000 and more quite common, and still fell that they have to have a television presence for credibility if nothing else, I recommend Congressman Sam Gejdenson's approach. This consists of putting together one or two of your young, bright staff enthusiasts with young advertising people who are not yet well-established to produce your own spots. Sometimes, just sometimes, a few amateur touches in television can be effective—the voters will realize that you have money problems and can sympathize—but not in a statewide or big money race. In those cases an amateur's slip will be picked up and magnified by the opposition to your considerable detriment.

---

*The first theme was designed to make the voters think about Mario Procaccino, Lindsay's Democratic opponent, in the "second toughest job," and Procaccino didn't look the part. Appearance counts heavily in big campaigns, especially in those using television.

*Credibility has become an increasingly important theme in television advertising since continued exposure to political commercials appears to have made a significant number of voters skeptical. The *Wall Street Journal* pointed out, on January 28, 1972, that many candidates were attempting to give their commercials the appearance of straight news, apparently to counteract the "credibility gap" of political commercials.

**Quoted by Terry Galanoy in *Down the Tube, or Making Television Commercials is Such a Dog-Eat-Dog Business It's No Wonder They're Called Spots* (Chicago: Regnery, 1970, pp. 235-36). As Galanoy points out, the Lindsay commercials were based on a smart advertising principle which has also has been used to sell such products as bad-tasting mouthwashes: "If your product has a fault, don't try to hide it—try to make it an asset."

Some commentators have attacked the 30-second and 60-second spots, commonly pointing out that they are usually characterized by distortion and oversimplification, often mislead rather than inform, and fail to provide the voter with honest choices. (The distinguished consultant, Charles Guggenheim, is a leading exponent of this position in the trade.) Senator Adlai E. Stevenson, III of Illinois told the Senate some years ago, "These short spots are the ones offering the greatest potential for superficiality and demagoguery."*

Consultants have become as controversial as their clients. Their specialties and fees are reported as important campaign news. Many commentators have expressed misgivings about consultants' power, none more thoughtfully than Dr. Mark J. Wattier, who wrote, " . . . [campaigning methods] are depersonalizing. It has adverse consequences when it comes to governing . . . [and] takes away from the traditional political network [parties]. . . . It is fractionalizing and fragmenting the process. Consultants are a set of special interest groups. They are only interested in campaigning . . . [and] don't have a commitment to policy . . . [which] should be a cause of concern."**

NEGATIVE CAMPAIGNING

Years ago, when "consultants" in the political campaign world were the guys who ran errands for the county leaders, who said, "Yes, that's great" to any ideas of the bosses and "not that good" to anyone else's ideas, a dirty campaign was one where the opposition ripped down political posters and started rumors about a candidate's homosexuality or that a candidate wasn't really a practicing Catholic or a divorce was imminent.*** These days of innocence were only a generation ago.

---

*Writing in the *Wall Street Journal,* on March 9, 1972 (p. 12), Alan Otten observed: "Perhaps more influential with the politicians and practitioners than this moralistic type of criticism is evidence suggesting [that] spots may no longer be as effective as they once were, and perhaps [are] even counter-productive. Some of the slickest (and most expensive) recent campaigns didn't win. . . . The viewing public has gradually been raising its guard, more suspicious of politicians generally and particularly alerted by books and articles to the abuses of political commercials." Walter De Vries and Lance Tarrance, in *The Ticket Splitter* (Grand Rapids, Mich.: Eerdmans, 1971), actually rates paid TV ads 24th in influence on the critically important ticket-splitting group, voters well-informed on issues and highly distrustful of politicians." This year is seeing a trend towards . . . direct, issue-oriented spots," they write.

**Washington Post,* June 5, 1982, p. A6.

***Ripping down signs is still habitual in many even sophisticated campaigns. One New York campaign manager told me, "I know it's crazy. But it occupies the opponent's energies and shows our club people and workers visual evidence that we've got a campaign going on."

With highly paid consultants putting their creative minds to it, negative campaigning has become a necessary part of many campaigns. In part, saying nasty things about your opponent is perfectly natural in the heat of battle. When realizing that you may be losing, and that all your money and energy may be going down the drain, you panic. Modern tactics, however, are cold-blooded and quite deliberate. While I prefer to focus negative campaigning on issues, you must also be prepared for negative campaigning using personal matters and malicious distortions. If you don't answer these attacks, some part of the voting public will believe that the allegations, no matter how farfetched, are true.

Sometimes, negative advertising is simply taking advantage of something that the opponent has said or done and exaggerating it by focusing on it. For example, in a 1982 Virginia campaign, Robert Squier, a leading Democratic media consultant, featured a thirty-second tape recording of Paul Trible, his client's opponent, "stammering and groping for words as he attempts to answer a question about his proudest legislative achievement." A sympathetic legislator remarked, "Campaigns in the state seem to be degenerating. . . . It seems to be the influence of the political consultants who are the parasites of the political system." Squier's client, Lt. Governor Davis, pointed out that he was being attacked by last-minute lies and distortions. A National Rifle Association letter had been sent to 60,000 voters attacking Davis on gun control. A mailing by Rev. Jerry Falwell accused Davis "of having a bigoted opinion of the Bible believing people of the Old Dominion . . . and a campaign letter [had been distributed] saying Trible's defeat would be a victory for the pro-abortion forces."* It sometimes depends on your ideology as to what is negative advertising; unfortunately, there are not universal moral or taste standards for political advertising. Sometimes I think that such standards would be as important for the campaign process as putting an absolute lid on advertising expenditures.

Some campaigners will complain of mean and vicious tactics by their opponents when, as one politician pointed out, "he keeps picking up lit dynamite sticks and holding them in his hand," that is, the candidate himself provided his adversary with the ammunition to attack.

Negative campaigning can take non-media forms. In 1982, in Montgomery County, Maryland, a state senate primary was described as bizarre

---

*Washington Post, October 31, 1982, p. A8.

because it included these elements: "the incumbent's wife made anonymous telephone calls to the challenger, then taped the calls and played them at a press conference, the challenger claimed he narrowly avoided being seduced by a beautiful woman wearing skimpy designer running shorts and a tight T-shirt . . . and then an anonymous caller told his pregnant wife about their imaginary affair."*

California, always in the forefront of political campaigning fads, had many expensive negative media campaigns in 1982. In the Pete Wilson-Jerry Brown race for the U.S. Senate, the following television ad was so controversial that it was withdrawn. The ad was a 30-second spot showing show-business celebrities saying that they wanted to go on making music and go on acting; this was followed by a shot of a nuclear explosion and a child saying, "I want to go on living." Brown then appeared with a U.S. flag, saying " . . . Wilson opposes the nuclear arms freeze . . . Brown supports it. Vote for your life. Elect Jerry Brown for U.S. Senate."** (This was clearly an imitation of the Tony Schwartz TV ad in Lyndon Johnson's 1964 presidential campaign against Barry Goldwater—the famous "picking a daisy" spot).

A legendary and possibly apocryphal early negative campaign took place in a Florida Democratic senatorial primary between Claude Pepper and former Senator George A. Smathers was reported in Time Magazine, April 17, 1950. Smathers was supposed to have used the following in his campaign in rural areas: "Are you aware that Claude Pepper is known all over Washington as a shameless extrovert? Not only that, but this man is reliably reported to practice nepotism with his sister-in-law who was

---

*Washington Post, August 26, 1982, p. D1.

**Washington Post, October 17, 1982, p. A2. Ironically, Brown refused to debate Gore Vidal in the Democratic primary in 1982. Vidal based his campaign on nuclear disarmament in a very eloquent speech:

"One of the most ancient stories of our race is that of how Prometheus stormed the ramparts of heaven and stole the fire. In the 5,000 years since Prometheus we have laid constant siege to heaven. We've stolen the fire, we've yoked the atom, we've landed on the moon.

"But there is a somber side to our divinity. . . . In the name of tribal loyalty, sometimes called patriotism, the human race has permitted incredible atrocities against itself. . . We have shed oceans of blood, to no end at all. Now, there is a growing perception that what matters is the survival of the human race as a whole, and that this can only be done by tapping a new kind of loyalty . . . because the fire that we stole from heaven last time was nuclear fire, and nuclear fire can make this entire planet a perfect hell, while turning all of us into so much shining dust. . . . Let us now send to the military-industrial-political complex which governs this particular nation-state the unmistakable message . . . [that we want] peace, not only in our time, but for all time, as there is no alternative. We are for life and life must prevail." (Washington Post, May 25, 1982, p. A2.)

once a thespian in wicked New York. Worst of all, it is an established fact that Mr. Pepper, before his marriage, habitually practiced celibacy. . . . '' Pepper remembers the campaign less humorously. ''It was a campaign of vicious distortion, calling me red Pepper, calling me a communist. . . . ''*

Consultants and candidates have continued to use negative ads because they appeared to work in campaigns in 1978 and 1980, but in 1982 a significant number didn't work. Negative ads of the National Conservative Political Action Committee (NCPAC) worked in 1980, but by 1982 their record of success was very sharply diminished. Indeed, a number of candidates, such as Senator Paul Sarbanes (Maryland), attacked by the NCPAC, made the NCPAC ads a campaign issue and won by a substantial margin. Negative advertising was heavily used in the bitter Massachusetts congressional between Barney Frank and Margaret Heckler. One of Heckler's television ads showed a picture of Frank with the voiceover stating that he had voted to allow legalized prostitution and pornography in every town in the state. Across his face are the words ''prostitution and pornography.'' (In fact, Frank had supported a bill to keep prostitution and pornography confined by limiting adult entertainment operations to a single zone.) Frank's counter-ad showed his picture with the voiceover, ''Barney Frank knows that your image gets messed up at election time . . . '' and a hand pencils a mustache and goatee on him '' . . . but this is going too far.'' (His face is a mess of red magic marker.) ''There is a word for that kind of tactic . . . ''Then the screen is filled with the single word ''SMEAR.''** In Montana, the *Washington Post* reported that NCPAC used 1,000 commercials charging that ''Senator John Melcher is out of step with Montana.'' Melcher's counter-ad had ''two cows do the talking for him. The cows tell the voters that outsiders have been coming into the state to influence the race, but they have been stepping into what they have been trying to sell.''***

In New Mexico in 1982, Republican consultant Roger Ailes represented Senator Harrison H. Schmitt against Jeff Bingaman. One ad stated that Attorney General Bingaman had played a major role in freeing a convicted felon by recommending a pardon for a man who had been on the FBI's

---

New York Times, Feb. 24, 1983, p. A23.
***Washington Post*, October 30, 1982, p. A8.
****Ibid*.

most wanted list. Ailes did not include the fact that the U.S. Justice Department had requested that the man be released in its custody as a key witness in a murder trial. Ailes stated later that he had relied on an incorrect newspaper story.

The distinguished consultant Charles Guggenheim, who represented Senator John Danforth (Missouri), stated in the *Post* article, "I don't like negative ads and neither does the candidate. But we are beginning to get blips in our direction since [the negative ads] have been running. It's awful that you have to do this. . . . It's not a very good profession." Guggenheim is noted for his half-hour television ads that are beautifully done but lack zing according to some consultants. In this instance, I would agree with him about negative advertising. Many experienced mechanics look back fondly to shoe-leather campaigns and straight issue campaigns. Years ago, candidates didn't mention each other's names (GM ads would not, years ago, compare product lines to Ford). The concept was to make the opponent pay to get name identification.

It is difficult to see how the voters benefit from negative campaigns. They do nothing to solve local or national problems. Distortions, half truths, innuendo, an lies are bad campaign currency and, like Gresham's law, as soon as they are introduced, cheapen the whole process and drive honest campaigning out.

NEGATIVE CAMPAIGNING IN LOCAL RACES

Many political mechanics believe that the candidates themselves are inevitably the central and critical issues in any campaign. What they do, say, sound like, and look like all become more controlling determinants than ideology, party, or any single issue. They are the critical determinants because the questions most voters use to decide are: Which candidate is more likable, which is more credible, and which is more trustworthy? Anything a candidate does to dilute or diminish his or her opponent's overall credibility is as important as any promotion of his/her own programs and personality. For these reasons, negative campaigning has always been an important and natural part of the political process. In recent years, however, candidates in high-visibility races have reached rather far in attacking opponents; distortions, innuendo of the most vicious type, lies, and deliberate misstatements have never been as common as they have been in the last five years in American campaigning.

Candidates have to expect that the record of their private and public lives will be subjected to the closest, most hostile scrutiny. Exposing the more unfavorable and questionable aspects of an opponent's record is as much part of the process as extolling your own virtues. The issue is really not whether to do negative campaigning, but how to do it and how to respond to it.

In my judgment, negative campaigning to be effective should have factual content; if it does, it is reasonable to use it. Moreover, the voters will accept it despite all the outcries of the opposition. Harold Washington's problems with his income taxes were legitimate issues in the 1983 Chicago mayoralty; he won nonetheless. Unsubstantiated allegations can work against you in that you can lose more votes than you gain by the attack. For example, in the bitter race for mayor in New York city in 1977, some observers thought that Mario Cuomo might have won the election against Ed Koch if the slogan "Vote for Cuomo, not the Homo" had not "somehow" been put on the streets. The only basis for this slogan was that Mr. Koch was a bachelor. This is the type of mudslinging that much of the voting public does not appreciate.

It would not be surprising, unfortunately, if negative campaigning were to be more commonly used in local races because of the emphasis on it in major, very well-publicized races. If you're an incumbent you can expect the attack to take one of the following forms.

1. Your opponent selects one or two legislative votes and focuses exclusively on these. Generally, these could be a vote for a tax increase, a salary increase for officials, or a vote against a public facility for the community.

2. The other side challenges the motivations of the people and institutions that have given you large campaign contributions.

3. They assert that you don't really care about the community, but that you're simply interested in higher office or that you really reside outside the district much of the year.

4. The opposition declares that you encourage familial or political nepotism; that family members are employed by the government or that your staff members are not qualified and were politically referred to you by party leaders.

5. They seize on an emotional issue and make that the central focus of their campaign, e.g., social security, abortion, school bussing, etc.

6. They categorize you as liberal or conservative, making your purported ideology the focus.

There are a number of ways to respond to attacks, whether you are the incumbent or the challenger. You can simply ignore them, respond to the facts, or counterattack with your own negative attacks. The first course is seldom advisable. Too many voters will have seen or read the accusations or allegations, so that your lack of response will be taken as a sign of guilt or of weakness. You have to decide which form the response should take. If the negative attack is especially severe and seems credible to the public and to the press, you are probably well advised to call a news conference, respond to the facts, and attack the exaggerations. This is probably not the best forum to blast the opponent's record or personal life. If your opponent's attack is a lie or distortion extreme enough to bury your campaign, my judgment is that you should take out a large ad in the local newspaper and respond as forcefully and as factually as you can. You should also probably buy radio time using the same content. In addition, if the rules of campaign fair practices have been violated you should file formal charges with copies to all media. Should the attack be in the form of a political brochure, your reply should take the same form and use the same distribution.

When you attack, have a factual base, and present it in such a way that the voters will find it credible. If attacked, facts are an excellent answer, but they must be intelligently presented. If the facts are against you, then apologize and explain so that the voters might have a degree of sympathy and understanding.

It is very tempting when the opposition uses dirty tricks to do the same thing to them. There are always staff members for whom this type of a response is a delightful challenge. Generally, I would avoid this. Try to objectively measure the votes gained against the votes lost by this maneuver. The public certainly understands very well that people in public life are not above reproach, that it is unlikely that they all will have perfect private and public histories. (Somerset Maugham was said to have remarked that if everyone read in the *New York Times* a faithful record of their thoughts, feelings, and fantasies of the day before they would feel very much obliged to commit suicide.) Getting involved in gutter tactics and vicious rhetoric sours voters more than excites them. Voters are turned off when political mud-slinging starts to include excrement.

BUYING TIME AND SPACE

It would be prudent for you and your staff to make, as early as possible, a comprehensive evaluation of media impacts in your own area and decide on the basis of your study what percentage of your investments you wish to allocate among the various political advertising techniques, in the following fashion.

Type of Expenditure	1st Quarter	2nd Quarter	3rd Quarter	4th Quarter
Television	%	%	%	%
Radio	%	%	%	%
Newspaper ads	%	%	%	%
Brochures	%	%	%	%
Mailings	%	%	%	%
Telephone banks	%	%	%	%

It is also important to get some idea of the best phasing of these expenditures by analyzing past successful campaigns in your area and, if possible, discussing them with successful candidates and/or managers. If you are a new campaigner, you may decide to hit television hard in the beginning to get recognition and awareness and then rely on news breaks, discussion programs, etc., later on, while emphasizing direct mail in your own budget at that stage.

In one of the early humongous money races, the 1966 Nelson Rockefeller gubernatorial, the strategy was to run a quiet, low-keyed television campaign. It was reported that the campaign staff bought television and radio time months in advance, concentrating on day and late evening hours. His staff had decided which audience they wished to reach, found that it could best be reached at non-prime-time hours, and then bought the time well in advance when the spots they wanted were still available.

The point here is that if you are using radio or television you have to decide your schedule early, because you will have to compete with other commercial and political television and radio advertisers for the times and days you want. Other people also know which times are effective with which audiences, and time is sold on a first come, first served basis. Campaigners are now generally aware that the hour should be matched to the specific audiences; that buying time on the stations with the higher

Arbitron ratings is not enough. This is not to say, of course, that you should make all your radio and television commitments far in advance. Some leeway must remain in your plans to allow for modifications midway through the campaign.

Time buying is an art in itself. Most political television consultants have a staff or retain specialists whose job is to match the characteristics of the voters you want to reach as closely as possible with the characteristics of the listeners and viewers who are tuned in to a particular program at a particular time. Some politicians like radio time on serious music stations, assuming or knowing from research that listeners to those stations include proportionately more undecided voters, who tend to vote in higher proportions. (Similarly, some campaign managers prefer to place certain newspaper ads on the sports pages, where male voters are most apt to read them, and to use different copy on society or women's pages.) Other politicians emphasize television ads immediately before and/or after the 10- or 11-o'clock evening news. All these slots are popular and must therefore be reserved early. If you retain a specialist, you should go over these choices very thoroughly with him. If your staff is to perform this functions, your staff people should educate themselves in the options by talking to the advertising managers of the local radio, television, and newspaper offices and by examining the back files of the newspapers. They should definitely review the station's demographics (each station has survey data showing at least the age, sex, and income distributions of their viewers and listeners). In addition, you ought to ask your party's best campaigners and their managers about their experiences with the effectiveness of the local media.

COMPARISON OF MEDIA IMPACTS

In only a few campaigns, even when a great deal of money is involved, does anyone bother to investigate the relative impacts and effectiveness of the various media approaches being used.* One reason for this obvious

---

*There is not any absolutely accurate measure of exactly how much more effective one medium is than another. In commercial advertising, it is usual to test impacts of magazine advertising versus phone advertising or radio and television. Such a study is usually done by an independent research agency. But in political advertising time is very short and the variables—costs, criteria (unaided retention, recall, etc.), and continuity in motivation—are complex and constantly changing. Comprehensive, timely recommendations are, therefore, unlikely.

deficiency is that each medium is usually assigned a specialist, and co-ordination among the specialists is generally restricted to message content alone; there is hardly time to think of developing the most effective role for each. Each technician or consultant has a vested interest in encouraging investment or expenditures for his own medium. It is up to you and your campaign staff to do a comparative evaluation of the impacts of the various media and decide the emphasis to be given each one in timing and expense.

The campaign staff of Governor George Romney of Michigan was reported to have been among the first to develop some excellent evaluatory devices. James M. Perry notes that in 1966 the Romney staff, focusing on certain Michigan counties where vote-splitting was probable in the gubernatorial campaign, used a recorded telephone message campaign followed by market research evaluation of impact.* When they discovered the technique was successful, they went into a saturation campaign.** Evaluations cost money, but it makes considerable sense to spend several thousand dollars on research to make certain that it will be worth investing $50,000 on a particular campaign appeal. Evaluation techniques should also be applied when analyzing the impacts of direct mail versus tele-phoning or radio versus television, for example, in small campaigns as well as large ones. They involve marginal increment analysis and cost benefit analysis, techniques long in use in American business, and don't really require enormous technical expertise. Figures showing what it costs to reach a thousand people are generally available from the advertising directors of local radio and television stations and of newspapers and magazines. If you lack these figures, or wish to supplement them, there are other ways of evaluating relative effectiveness:

1. If you are doing public opinion research, a question on relative media effectiveness can be included in the survey questionnaire: Where did you hear of _____? Which political ads do you recall? Can you describe these ads? Which source did you find most helpful in deciding whom to vote for? This type of question is often asked, but my experience

---

*Some technicians think that recorded messages are effective, while others—including myself—regard them as having very limited impact. See De Vries and Tarrance *The Ticket Splitter* (Grand Rapids: Eerdmans, 1971).

**See James M. Perry, *The New Politics* (New York: Potter, 1968), for a good objective comparison of specific media in actual campaigns.

suggests that the answer to this isn't going to be too accurate because many voters don't really know exactly why they vote for a certain candidate.

2. Midway through the campaign, you can ask the same questions in a spot telephone check of 200 voters chosen at random (in primaries, only registrants of your party, of course), perhaps concentrating your survey in the swing areas or in the areas where the voters you're not sure of are concentrated, and keeping in mind that by this time up to 75 percent of the electorate have made up their minds. Your media allocations should then be revised to maximize cost effectiveness.

It is important to remember that personal likability and political credibility are the keys to most good campaigns. That is what you're always competing for. Weigh those objectives against the likely reactions of voters to negative campaigning that is more nasty than substantive. If funds allow, your research should include questions on voters' reactions to your opponent's probable attacks. If there is not sufficient time or money, the focus group panel technique described on p. 79 is a good way to get a good reading of probable reactions.

7
Print and Mail Advertising

The basic types of print and mail advertising used in campaigns include: brochures, handbills, palm cards, personal letters, "committee" letters, computer letters, mailgrams, newsletters, and newspapers. Secondary uses of print include shopping bags, buttons, bumper stickers, and lawn signs. (Print is used simply for the candidate's name or campaign logo in these forms of advertising). Other forms of advertising include the use of bullhorns, loudspeakers, and street campaigning.

POLITICAL BROCHURES

Preparing and distributing brochures accounts for a considerable portion of campaign activity. New candidates are often surprised at how much printing and mailing brochures can cost. In many campaigns that do not use television, this cost, including overhead (paid staff, rent, etc.), may account for 70 percent of all campaign expenses.

The largest investment is likely to be in mailings—which now run between 20 and 30 cents a letter, depending on whether you use first class postage. To justify the cost of printing (where unit cost decreases sharply with increases in quantity), mailings must be on the order of tens of thousands. Sending out a professional mailing requires: (1) an advertising agency or specialist to prepare copy and a camera-ready mechanical; (2) a printer; and (3) a group of volunteers or a computer for addressing and labeling.* (The use of a computer can result in a net saving over hand-addressing, since returned letters are entered into the computer file and the addresses, which include people no longer living at a given address, are removed from the computer file, saving on future mailing costs. The computer can also combine the same surnames at a single address, resulting in an additional saving on mailing costs.) Other necessary steps are bagging and delivery to the post office. All these cost money, and there is no way to substitute for them unless you risk a loss of quality by preparing the copy yourself.

---

*A large-scale computer can do 75,000 labels an hour.

Professionally managed campaigns normally do at least three mailings in addition to the sample ballot exemplified in Fig. 7-16: one introducing the candidate and his or her program, another attacking the opponent, and a final one, two or three days before the election, reinforcing the basic appeal. In many professional campaigns today, ten separate mailings may be used because each is targeted to a separate group. If money is a severe problem, the best way to save on costs here is to send mailings only to areas where your research shows "undecideds" living in considerable number and to the swing districts where voters are usually independent to a large degree.* Another economy comes from using pretested themes in these mailings, so that their appeal is maximized. Don't cram too much copy into these letters, and don't use too much "hard sell" in your appeal.

Some practical considerations can greatly increase reader receptivity to your campaign mailings. Voters nowadays receive so many mail appeals from political and other sources that they often do not even open the envelopes. Anything you can do to personalize your mail will increase the likelihood that they will at least go that far. If your funds permit, you may wish to consider sending your letters first class, with the stamps affixed by hand rather than stamped by a postage meter. This adds about 10 cents to the cost of each letter—assuming that volunteers do the stamping. Bulk-rate letters can also be stamped by hand, but a first-class letter is much less likely to remain unopened. For the same reason, hand-addressing is a good idea: People are much more likely to open a hand-addressed envelope than one with a duplicated label.** Hand-addressing is very tedious, however, and your volunteers may not stay around to finish the job. Professional office service firms will do hand-addressing (on envelopes with the return address printed on them) for about 6 cents an envelope.

---

*If you can afford to do so, by all means attempt to reach all the significant client groups. In most campaigns, however, this is a luxury, and a priority ordering for mailings becomes important so that limited funds can be used in the most effective way. A reasonable order of priority might be undecided, independents (general elections only), selected ethnic groups, and then the favorables. A few campaign professionals advise spending your time and money where your "sure" votes reside; see, for example, Stephen Shadegg, *How to Win an Election* (New York: Taplinger, 1964, p. 98), on using this approach in scheduling Barry M. Goldwater's appearances. I believe this is an inefficient use of resources.

**There were a number of press reports in late October 1972 that the Nixon campaign committee was launching the largest personally-addressed mailing in American political history: 12 million hand-addressed envelopes were to be sent to voters.

In my first state assembly campaign, after spending a full week working up a basic piece of campaign literature with a designer, we had the text printed on expensive paper, and we paid extremely careful attention to the typeface and the colors of the ink as well as to the description of the legislative program. But all this was so expensive that we had enough money to print only 10,000 pieces for a single mailing. In the last week, the opponent came out with several mailings through the district, and our single mailing was buried. You can't count, I've learned, on only one piece or theme; a vote on election day results from a cumulation of impressions in the voter's mind, and a single mail contact is not likely to win his vote by itself, without some reinforcement. As we have seen, mailings are expensive, and mistakes are both common and costly. If you make intelligent decisions and spend your money carefully so that your mailings reinforce your campaign themes, you can give yourself the best shot possible.

Selecting the right day to do your mailings can be critical. For example, many people subscribe to popular magazines such as *TV Guide, Time,* and so forth. In New York, most of these magazines arrive in mailboxes on Wednesdays and Thursdays. It is clearly not advisable to compete with these. Note which days of the week popular magazines arrive in your area, and try to time your mailings to arrive on a different day.

Similarly, all candidates commonly release a barrage of mail and literature two days before election day. If you hear that ten pieces are going out for competing candidates and candidates for other offices, I would recommend your sending your last piece a week before, if that is necessary to guarantee that yours is the only political piece of mail the voter receives that day.

In my judgment, the only piece that is mandatory two days before the election is the sample ballot displaying the slate you're running with and showing where your name appears on the ballot. A complicated ballot can destroy even the best campaign. In a recent New York election, the ballot was so complicated that people took ten minutes to vote even though the legal maximum was three; to accommodate all the voters the polls remained open in some precincts until 1:00 A.M. instead of closing at the scheduled hour of 10:30 P.M. Some ballots—including those in the New York election just mentioned—list so many candidates that they must contain multiple columns, so that the voter must read up and down as well as the normal left to right. In such cases, confusion often occurs, and candidates for lesser offices tend to lose votes owing to fatigue, as well as confusion, on the part of the voters. The best aid for a candidate in such a situation is a well-designed sample ballot such as that shown in Fig. 7-16. A palm card (see Fig. 7-17) usually spots the candidate's name, but a sample ballot shows the design of the entire ballot, with your position highlighted in color or by the use of a device that calls attention to it. In districts with particularly complicated ballots, a sample ballot can be the most critical piece in the campaign.

Another factor that is often overlooked is targeting the distribution of brochures. Mailing, of course, is the most important means of distribution, since it enables you to choose the recipients. Computer-assisted ways of working up a mailing list are discussed on pp. 220-229. But masses of literature are also distributed on the street, stuffed under doors and in mailboxes, and placed under windshield wipers of parked cars. In my experience, much of this is wasted effort and money, since many of the recipients may not be registered voters and, in a primary, a majority may not even be eligible to vote in your party's primary. Very little care is exercised in distributing handbills in most campaigns. One candidate I know took advantage of his opponent's laxity in this regard by simply sending his workers to the opponent's headquarters asking for literature to give out. The headquarters staff complied with the requests gladly. At 500 brochures per visit, the workers collected—and presumably destroyed—thousands of the opponent's brochures.

Even if care is taken in brochure distribution, few handbills are likely to be read or make an impact on the voters unless they contain extraordinary copy or they are printed on cardboard stock which voters tend not to discard so quickly as lighter paper which is easily wadded up and thrown away. Incidentally, if you do intend to have brochures distributed under doors, you might enlist your children for the job. Older children are likely to be happy to contribute their services, and adult backs frequently give out after bending over to stuff a hundred brochures under doors.

ETHNICATION OF LITERATURE

Targeting of telephone calls and direct mail were used in the money campaigns in the late 1960s. It is now common in almost all campaigns. The advisory literature of the Republican and Democratic National Committees both stress the need to target, to aim literature and design appeals toward the groups your research shows you must reach.

It is usual for literature to be developed in a big hurry in campaigns; a staff person or advisor liaison with a community group discovers that a piece does not exist to distribute to this group. This is often followed by a whirlwind of activity which usually doesn't produce an effective design or smooth copy. (Newcomers to campaigning sometimes think that the person or consultant they are talking to is actually the one who will be doing the work. This is seldom the case.) In preparing literature, the consultant or advertising person will set the theme and text of the copy; it then has to go to the design specialist who prepares the mechanicals, the camera-ready board that actually goes to the printer.

A common form of targeting is shown in the example of the 1982 flyer designed for street distribution by Mario Cuomo in his New York gubernatorial campaign (Fig. 7-1). While the Cuomo piece cannot be considered to be of the highest standards, it was probably designed to cover the need to distribute a piece in old age homes and in neighborhoods with concentrations of elderly people, who in many cities vote in large numbers. (In most cities perhaps 12-15 percent of the population are over 65, which implies that often 15-20 percent of the actual voters will be over 65). The key to the Cuomo piece was his defense of social security and medicare. Other designs might have keyed to those two lines and removed other copy. Note the endorsements by older adults whose names were not well-known. The piece is somewhat cluttered but probably got the message across.

In larger districts or city- or statewide elections, it is increasingly common to set one ethnic or racial group against the other. I think it is possible to campaign to get your natural support base without exacerbating the distrust and misunderstandings that exist between groups. With the budget crises that permeate every city, services are limited and bitterness is easy to feel. The Democratic cry in 1983 that Reagan and the Republicans weren't fair and were punishing the poor had some relevance, but it would have had more impact if at the same time it had been shown how fairness was to be objectively stated and monitored. In my judgment, positive, constructive appeals tend to be more powerful and longer lasting than purely negative attacks.

In a particularly bitter election in New York in 1982, which placed two popular assemblymen, one Italian and one Irish (Republican Guy

Older
New Yorkers
Need
MARIO
CUOMO

*"As Governor of New York, I will defend Social Security and Medicare
from those who would destroy it."*

Mario Cuomo will Protect the vital interests of all older New Yorkers.
HE SUPPORTS:

★ A criminal justice system which works, which *catches, convicts and jails* the criminal who preys on older people. Life sentences without parole for those convicted of heinous crimes.

★ A statewide, 24-hour half-fare transportation system for older New Yorkers.

★ The elimination of mandatory retirement policies in the public and private sector.

★ All efforts to increase the employment of older workers.

★ An annual increase in SSI benefits and in the personal care allowance for residents of nursing homes and adult homes.

★ Special attention to the special needs of the older woman, including the strengthening of Social Security and pension reforms.

★ Protection of elderly tenants and homeowners by:
● *vigorous opposition to federal cutbacks in vital housing programs,*
● *support of bills in the State Legislature to prevent automatic rent increases for tenants,*
● *working to increase the maximum income eligibility levels of the Senior Citizen Real Property Tax Exemption Program,*

● *supporting legislation to protect residents from eviction from buildings being converted to co-ops or condominiums (as already in effect in metropolitan New York).*

★ Keeping older New Yorkers in the community and out of institutions by:
● *expanding home health care programs across the state,*
● *establishing a statewide prescription drug insurance program for older persons,*
● *funding for the State Community Services for the Elderly Program continued and adjusted based on inflation rates,*
● *fighting to keep Senior Centers open*

As Governor, Mario Cuomo will use his powerful voice to protect the elderly. He will fight to protect Social Security, Medicare, Medicaid, Food Stamps, Senior Centers, Nutrition Programs for the Elderly and the Home Energy Assistance Program.

Vote for Mario Cuomo . . . He will work for you!!

LT. GOV. MARIO CUOMO ENDORSED BY OLDER ADULTS & OTHER ADVOCATES, Including:

Stella Allen	By Cohen	Lou Glasse	Eleanor Litwak	Pastor Michel	Janet Sainer
William Arnone	Thal Davis	Jane Gould	Vito Lopez	Jane Murgo	Matthew Schoenwald
Irma Badillo	Dante DiBiase	George Gromm	Jack Lustick	Fred Newdom	Frank Senior
Prof. Walter Beattie, Jr.	John Dillon	Mae Hall	K. Neil Lyons	Anthony Pietrovito	Jenny Silverman
Ida Benderson	Sulelka Cabrera Drinane	Joseph Harrison	Laora Magier	Robert Popper	Ethel Torgesen
Tema Bellinson	Ed Duggan	Samuel Hirsch	Robert Maier	Evan Pritchard	Linda Van Buskirk
Albert Blumberg	Judith Duhl	David Hoppenfeld	Max Manes	Caryn Resnick	Gertrude Van Kirk
John Boer	Patricia Easton	Brenda Hotaling	Dorothy Massara	Marjorie Riley	Andrew Virgillio
John Burns	Alpha Edmonson	Miriam Jackson	Joseph Massara	Stephanie Rogall	Earl H. Webber
Rena Button	John Foley	Theadora Jackson	Cornelius McGillicuddy	Homero Rosado	Charlotte Weinstein
Ed Carlson	Judge Morris Garber	Jean Janover	Lillian Meadows	Ricki Rubenstein	Sarah Werbel
Louise Chazin	Lillian Gartner	James Kyzmir	Loveria Melore	Vaughn Rudy	Judith Wineman

VOTE ON NOVEMBER 2nd
Polls Open 6 a.m. to 9 p.m.
OLDER NEW YORKERS FOR CUOMO COMMITTEE

Fig. 7-1. Example of a handbill targeted to senior citizens (New York, 1982).

Velella and Democrat John C. Dearie), against each other in a redistricted area, the ethnication device was used in what may be seen as almost a classic manner.

The following piece by Dearie's group (Fig. 7-2) was delivered to Irish families. (In actual use, such pieces present practical problems because many of the people delivering or "stuffing" the literature can't distinguish all the names precisely so that the wrong voters may be getting literature designed very specifically for other ethnic groups.) Other pieces went out to Jewish, Italian, and black voters. The Irish leaflet was a heavy piece; the line " . . . it is little wonder that the town that was our town, is our town no more," was picked up in the *New Yorker* magazine and the local newspapers. The endorsements of the Irish groups could have been important. The "Committee" was created for the purpose of the campaign, which is commonly done. In campaigning, all you need to form a committee is to design a letterhead; in most places there is no need to file any formal papers. Figure 7-3 shows another ethnic letter by an Italian committee for Dearie using the endorsements of Italian Democratic officials.

Figure 7-4 is another example of ethnication. The ostensible signers of this inflammatory document stated that it had been prepared by their opponents to create trouble. The piece attempted to fuel the anti-semitism that had been aroused by the then-current Beirut refugee camp massacre. Even in New York, where so-called dirty tactics are common in campaigns and some campaigners actually pride themselves on how clever and vile they have been, this piece was regarded as particularly vicious and outrageous. The "Concerned Citizens" who signed the piece constitute another example of a non-representative political committee created just for the purposes of one campaign.

When a campaign descends into the gutter, there are a number of things you can do. Some candidates, expecting a vicious hit, send out flyers saying that such and such is going to happen. During the Dearie-Velella campaign, a piece went out ostensibly to blacks stating that Dearie had done much to integrate the community, but it was delivered to the white areas of the district. Figure 7-5 is the piece sent out by Dearie in response.

Also shown is one page of Congressman Stephen Solarz's four-page brochure demonstrating to his Jewish constituency his achievements relating to Israel (Fig. 7-6). This used color and photographs liberally and was reportedly very effective in the district.

IRISH-AMERICAN COMMITTEE TO RE-ELECT ASSEMBLYMAN JOHN C. DEARIE

"...AND THE TOWN THAT WAS OUR TOWN AIN'T OUR TOWN NO MORE..."

DENIS O'GRADY
AILEEN RYAN
JOHN LOWE
MIKE BOYLE
JIM GLEESON
TOM McKENNA
MARTIN TIGHE
JACK McELLIGOTT
JIM HALPIN
JIM DORIAN
MAURICE CRIMMINS
PETER TARSNANE
MIKE EARLEY
MIKE O'CONNELL
ED KENNELLY
J.CE O'CONNOR
ELEANOR CASEY
FRAN MAHONEY
MIKE RYAN
SALLY GLEASON
MARGE GLINSMAN
JOHN O'NEILL
PHILIP PARKER, Esq
LORRETTA LOUGHIAN
JULIAN LEONARD
SALLY COLEMAN
HELENA SIMPSON
PATRICIA PARKER
ANN LYNCH
MARTIN KILLEEN
JOHN O'BRIEN
JIM MINNAUGH
MICKEY CARTON
DONALD ALBERT
DAVE SLATTERY
JIM HARRISON
JEANETTE McCORMACK
JACK DEVANY
JACI McGINTY
JOSEPH FEGAN
EVE CARROLL
GERALD B. RYAN
ANN MURPHY
KEVIN REILLY
JACK O'LEARY
MARY MOORE
JIM PURCELL
JOHN MULLIN
JOHN MURPHY
KENNETH McCLORY
MAE QUINN
FRANCIS X. RYAN
LAWRENCE BARLOW
BOB GREGORY
JIM SLEVIN
TOM HENDERSON
ED McCARTHY
DENNIS NAGLE
TOM O'BRIEN
ANN RYNN
DAN McLAUGLIN
CHIC DONOGHUE
JACK COOKE
MARGARET McARDLE
JOHN AHERN
JIM MURPHY
JIM McELLIGOTT
BILL LEE
ANN DARBY
KAY MALONE
PEG O'BYRNE
PAT FITZSIMMONS
TOM CULHANE
WILLIAM CARR
JOE CONLIN
PAUL GALLAGHER
JOHN LAVIN

Not long ago New York City was an Irish town. An Irish name on the ballot was tantamount to election. But time and suburbia changed that.

Today, a candidate with Irish roots is elected in New York City not because he is Irish, but because he appeals to the electorate in general. With fewer than 15% of the voters being Irish, it is little wonder that the town that was our town, is our town no more. Every so often however, a candidate does emerge who generates enthusiasm in his community.

On November 2, John Dearie is on the ballot for election as the Assemblyman for our neighborhood.

We know John as a respected member of the State Legislature, as a figher for homeowners, a proponent of stronger drug legislation, a friend of the elderly, and a supporter of strict punishment for criminals, including the death penalty, and an advocate of tuition tax credits for parochial school students.

We who are Irish are proud of John as a Hibernian and as champion of Justice for Ireland. He has denounced the illegal occupation of Northeast Ireland and worked for a free Ireland where equal rights and opportunities are guaranteed to all. That may sound easy, but we haven't found many politicians of Irish descent who speak so clearly, consistently and courageously as John Dearie.

As New Yorkers we support his election with enthusiam, knowing our vote can improve the way we live, work, travel and enjoy our town.

As Irish-Americans we urge his election with pride, aware that our community has a quality candidate and the opportunity to receive better representation than it has had in years.

Now it is up to you. Vote for John Dearie for Assemblyman in the General Election, Tuesday, November 2nd, and do your part in getting your family and friends to join you.

The Irish-American Vote Can Make A Difference

Endorsed by Patrolmen's Benevolent Association, Uniformed Firefighter's Association, Transport Workers Union, Phoenix Irish Action Caucus, Independent American Celtic Association, Mike Griffin's Parkside Social and Athletic Association.

Fig. 7-2. Example of a "Committee's" ethnicated (Irish) handbill (Bronx, N.Y., 1982).

ITALIAN—AMERICAN COMMITTEE FOR THE RE-ELECTION OF ASSEMBLYMAN JOHN C. DEARIE

MARIO CUOMO
AL DEL BELLO
MIKE DE MARCO
JERRY CRISPINO
FRANCES FRISCO
JAMES VACCA
FRED MONDELLO
CAROL PASCOCELLO
NICK MARINO
FRANK ROSETTI
BEN ARTINO
MIKE ERRA
AL SORRENTINO
DOM CAFARO
TOM BENEVENTO
GEORGE GAROFOLO
SUE CASERTA
JIM CERASOLI
PAT SALERNO
FRANK BIANCO
JOE MILONE
JUAN MILONE
ENRICO GALANTE
PETER TOSSI
PHIL CARUSO
NICK MANCUSO
JACK CARONA
MIKE BENEDETTO
WILLIAM ARNONE
EILEEN DI LISSIO
SAL NAPOLITANO
AL COLLETTI
ANTHONY FRANCAVIGILIA
JOE SCAVUZZO
KAREN ARGENTI
ROSE CATANIA
ARTIE FELICE
JOE CORNETTA
WALTER CARENA
GENE MELE
OLIVIA TOCCO
LUCY VERDICCHIO
PAUL VICTOR
FRED ROSETTI
TONY ROTA
AMELIA DI DONATO
JOHN MARINO SR.
JAMES MANDRAGONA
WALTER DONAT
JERRY MARINO
ANTHONY SEMINERIO
AUGIE PAESE
CHARLES CAROCETTO
SUSAN CASERTA
BEN ARTINO
RAY INDELICATO
PASQUALE ATTIANSE
MARY MENOTTI
JOE ALLESANDRO
SILVANA DEL BELLIS

Dear Friend,

We, the members of the Italians For Dearie Committee, are writing you this letter to bring you a special message: We need to re-elect a great Democrat, Assemblyman John C. Dearie.

We know John as a respected member of the legislature, as a fighter for homeowners and tenants, a proponent of stronger drug legislation, a friend of the elderly, a supporter of strict punishment for criminals — including the death penalty, and an advocate of tuition tax credits for the families of parochial school children.

John's record of community involvement is unsurpassed. His dedicated work has helped preserve our neighborhoods and our traditions and after all that's what an Assemblyman is for.

As our Councilman Michael DeMarco has said "John Dearie is a man Italian Americans can be proud of and when they've needed him he's always there."

As Italian-Americans we urge his re-election with pride. Aware that our community has a quality candidate and the opportunity to make sure that he is re-elected.

Now it's up to you. Vote for John Dearie for Assemblyman on Tuesday, November 2nd, and do your part to get your family and friends to join you.

VOTE THE DEMOCRATIC TEAM
CUOMO - BIAGGI
DEARIE - DE MARCO

Fig. 7-3. Example of a "Committee's" ethnicated (Italian) handbill (Bronx, N.Y., 1982).

CRISIS IN GREENPOINT

Dear Neighbor,

It has finally happened. The fate and destiny of Greenpoint
shall no longer be decided by those of us who live here.
Joe Lentol has made the deal with the Hassidic rabbis in Williams-
burg to insure his election to the Assembly.

Yes, people who live on the other side of Broadway shall decide
our politics and our childrens future.

The Hassidic community vote in a strange way. The head rabbi
says to vote for someone, and they all do so religiously and
obediently. They have decided that Lentol will be more useful
to them than Stefanizzi.

And they are right.

Nick Stefanizzi is a Greenpoint boy. And they know that. We
watched him grow up. play ball, get married, raised children. We've
seen him work for veterans and P.O.W.'s. We've marvelled at his
energy, his commitment. He has fought crime by setting up civilian
block patrols. He is one of us; a church man, a parent, a fighter,
and above all, a Greenpointer.

But, Joe Lentol thinks he will win. He thinks he has made the
right deal. The puny politicians that wrote Bartosiewicz out of
Greenpoint will prevail and Joey will forever be their pawn.

Look, to win we have to overcome 2,000 votes the Hassidic community will hand deliver to Lentol. But, our vote counts! Our
voice can still be heard. Let's not give up Greenpoint without a
fight! Sometimes honor is better than victory. And sometimes
honor brings victory.

Go for it!

                              Yours truly,

                              Patricia Tambakis

                              CONCERNED CITIZENS OF GREENPOINT
                              Co-Chairmen

                              Pat Tambakais

                              Joseph Stefanizzi

                              Joseph Stefanizzi

**Fig. 7-4. Example of ethnication with a vengeance by "concerned citizens"
(Brooklyn, N.Y., 1982).**

Dear Neighbor,

Ten years ago political dirty tricks disgraced our nation. **This weekend Guy Velella's dirty tricks have disgraced our community.**

He has betrayed every thing that an honest public official stands for. **He has lied, deceived, and worst of all he has insulted the dignity of the electoral process.**

Last Friday our mailboxes were stuffed with a piece of literature skillfully designed to confuse you into believing it was from my campaign. **It was in fact, sent for Guy Velella.**

The piece in question was designed to scare the members of your neighborhood and to stir up racial tension. This action harms the entire community and is a crime under federal law.

I am outraged, both personally and as an elected official that a political candidate would totally lose any sense of honesty and integrity, by deliberately trying to convey a false, inflamitory message in the last two days of the campaign.

It is insulting to the citizens of our area to think that such a degrading tactic would be successful. **Does Guy Velella think we are that foolish?**

When a politician resorts to this type of tactic it can mean only one thing. **Winning means more to him than anything, including telling the truth.**

Listen to your heart. Think of the man who has run on his record, and who has stayed to the issues. If you believe in fair-play, and the American electoral process you will show Guy Velella that his dirty tricks have no place in this community.

This Tuesday, vote your conscience.

Sincerely,

John C. Dearie

John C. Dearie

Fig. 7-5. Example of a warning (skull and crossbones) against dirty tactics (Bronx, N.Y., 1982).

No one has been a better fri
people than Congressman S

"A leading supporter of Israel. . . one of the most committed and hard working friends of Israel on Capitol Hill. . ."

THE JERUSALEM
POST

"His record is quite simply superb, combining uncommon legislative skill with profound compassion for vulnerable people around the world. For our country, for Israel and for the sake of victims everywhere, we need Steve Solarz in the Congress."
Elie Wiesel

Congressman Steve Solarz. He is Israel's best — and most effective — friend in Congress. He is successful because he is more than just a fighter for Israel and the Jewish people. He is a leader in the international fight for human dignity.

An expert on foreign policy, Solarz is Chairman of the U.S. House of Representatives Subcommittee on Asian Affairs. When he speaks, the White House, his colleagues and thoughtful people everywhere listen.

That's why, after the Israeli raid on the Iraqi nuclear reactor, when the White House wanted to sound out key members of Congress, Solarz was one of the first to be called. Solarz' influence is such because, according to the *Wall Street Journal*, "he has demonstrated that by combining legislative cunning and sheer determination, a lawmaker can leave his imprint on U.S. foreign policies."

Solarz' colleagues feel the same way. Here's what California Congressman Tom Lantos, a Holocaust survivor, says: "The leadership and wisdom of Congressman Solarz in international affairs have been of inestimable value to many of us in Congress. The people of New York — and indeed the entire nation — are fortunate to have an individual of Congressman Solarz' intelligence and integrity serving in Congress."

Solarz' voice is heard, and respected,

"Steve Solarz is more than just a staunch friend of Israel in the House. . .He is perhaps Israel's most effective advocate and supporter."
FORMER SENATOR Frank Church

when he speaks about Israel. But he does not simply articulate Israel's concerns for Israel's sake. Steve Solarz knows that there is a connection between the protection of human rights throughout the globe and the safety of the Jewish people. Establishing respect for democracies and defending human rights protects all nations and people . . . as well as the state of Israel and the Jewish people.

His voice has been heard and he has led the fight against human rights violations in El Salvador, Zimbabwe, South Korea and Cambodia, enabling him to be especially effective

Israel thanks Steve Solarz for his years

"Your efforts are wonde
deepest gratitude for al

Fig. 7-6. Example of an incumbent's ethnic appeal (Brooklyn, N.Y., 1982).

nd of Israel and the Jewish
ve Solarz.

"Solarz has made it his business to get involved and champion issues affecting Israel. But he has done so with a combination of intellect and flair which has won him admiration from all quarters."

JEWISH WEEK

"Steve Solarz is a prominent statesman, a young energetic leader who is, for us, the 'Zionist Congressman', with a reputation for honesty and integrity, committed to his people and dedicated to the Jewish state. . . ."

— Zvi Levin
Israeli Consulate General

in helping to protect Jewish communities in Syria, Russia, Iran and Cuba.

Solarz is in the forefront of the never ending battle to provide Israel with the resources it needs to survive, prosper and grow. He fights each year to increase aid to Israel and to liberalize aid requirements. In 1980 alone, his efforts resulted in a $400 million increase in U.S. aid. And in 1981, he got the U.S. to turn a $260 million loan into a grant.

He was the author and architect of the toughest legislation ever enacted to fight the infamous Arab Boycott and is responsible for the legislation that prohibits P.L.O. representatives from entering the United States.

Steve Solarz' record in international affairs and in the defense and protection of Israel is, as Elie Wiesel says, "quite simply superb."

The Solarz record on aiding Jewish life in the United States is equally outstanding.

"These are difficult times for those of us who are committed to Israel's survival. Steve Solarz' influence in Congress is critical if Israel's interests are to be protected."
SENATOR
Henry Jackson

As a man who understands that the phrase "never again" must always have meaning, Solarz sponsored legislation that created a Holocaust curriculum for use in public schools throughout the country. Knowing the need for the world to be reminded of the horrors of the Holocaust, he helped create and served as a member of the President's Commission on the Holocaust.

A Solarz-sponsored bill changed existing federal regulations to permit government employees to observe religious holidays without using vacation days. Employees are no longer

penalized for attending Synagogue on Jewish Holidays.

And Steve Solarz has worked successfully to get millions of dollars appropriated to help resettle Soviet Jewish emigrants in the United States. As a result of his efforts, thousands of resettled Soviet Jews are productive members of American society.

His work has earned him this praise from the United Jewish Appeal, "Your involvement has always reflected your deep concern for Jewish freedom. It is a great asset to have you in Congress."

Steve Solarz...an extraordinary man. Congressman Solarz...an extraordinary legislator. From Brooklyn to Washington and around the world, Steve Solarz is a fighter for his people, a fighter for the State of Israel and a fighter for human dignity. Steve Solarz is a friend we all can depend on.

service:
ful. Accept our
you've done."

Prime Minister
Menachem Begin

Fig. 7-6. (Continued)

EXAMPLES AND CRITIQUES OF CAMPAIGN LITERATURE

Campaign literature includes both mailings and brochures to be given out on the street or stuffed under doors or in mailboxes. Brochures are usually designed by a graphic specialist with text written by one of your staff or a consultant, and then the final "mechanical" is sent to the printer for production.

Campaign literature can include copies of newspaper endorsements, issue pieces, biographies and achievements, extracts from speeches, political leaders' endorsements, civic leaders' endorsements, negative pieces hitting your opponent on the issues and on background deficiencies, palm cards, sample ballots, reprints of newspaper articles, and anything that your imagination, experience, and creativity suggest would get the voters' favorable attention. They can be one page on one side of a single piece of paper, or they can be a ten-page tabloid-size newspaper. They can be postcard-size on cardboard stock or they can be outsized, tissue-thin, and have a complex eight-way fold.

Since so much of local area campaigning (and big money statewide campaigns as well; in the 1982 New York State gubernatorial race, Republican Louis Lehrman sent out three million pieces of mail in the last week alone) depends on campaign literature, the candidate is well advised to do a print plan relatively early in the campaign. It may be advisable also to do early mock-ups of each piece as well as the ideas start to jell.* This early start is important so that you can consider design and text options properly. This is a lot better than doing it on an "expedite" basis in the middle of the night, a situation very common in campaigning. (Samples of a print plan and a mock-up—rough layout—are shown in Figs. 7-7 and 7-8.)

To be effective, campaign literature should be creative and depend upon graphic design and text copy appropriate for the groups and geographic areas to which distribution is intended. Especially in lavishly financed campaigns there seems to be some tendency for ad agencies and consultants to overdesign—to make the pieces too slick, overproduced with luxuriant paper and the most exotic typefaces, often including retouched photos of the candidate and his or her family so that everyone

---

*This is like the composer's "short score": Just lay out the basic melody (or theme) and some ideas on orchestration, and then go back and do a full orchestration as you develop it.

PRINT PLAN–DEADLINES

NAME/CONCEPT PIECE	PERSON RESPONSIBLE (AND FINAL DATE)	WRITTEN AND REVIEWED (DATE)	GRAPHICS INCLUDING SET OF MOCK-UPS (DATE)	TYPESET (DATE)	PRINTER (DATE)	MAILHOUSE (DATE)	STREET, OR "STUFFED" SELECTED AREAS (DATE)
1. Constituent Questionnaire							
2. Newsletter to Constituents							
3. Major Negatives							
4. Crime Issue							
5. Economics/Unemployment Issue							
6. Basic Legislative Achievements							
7. Targets/Areas							
a. Senior Citizens							
b. Women							
c. Minorities							
d. Jews							
e. Italian							
f. North End							
8. Tabloid—Family, Army, Endorsements							
9. Letter from Civic Leaders							
10. Major Political and Newspaper Endorsements							
11. "Telegrams"							
a. Democratic Party							
b. Senior Citizens							
c. Jewish Appeal							
12. Appeal for Money Past Contributors List							

Fig. 7-7. Example of a print plan for a campaign.

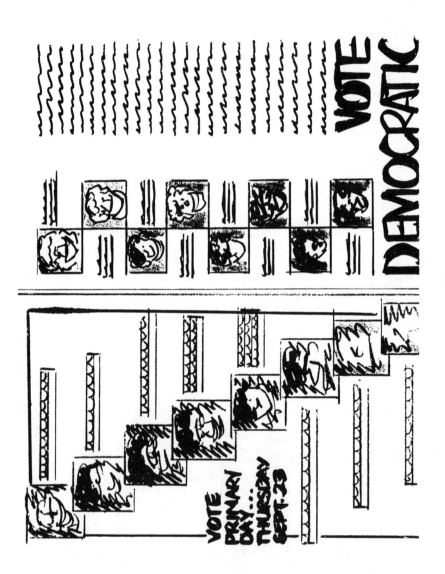

Fig. 7-8. Example of a mock-up for a handbill.

appears angelic, their faces without lines, like the soft focus television ads for cosmetics. One of the purposes of political literature is to develop a degree of empathy between the candidate and the voters; pieces that contain too obvious hype, with text too dramatic or too cute or too superficial and self-serving, don't often work. In my judgment, insane distortions and gross lies aren't going to be very effective either.

Effective literature usually has the following characteristics.

- Good, concise, well-written copy, stating and illustrating the key campaign themes, as simply put as is consistent with getting the points across, the fewer key points the better.
- Careful design, including reasonably good quality paper, attractive and easily legible typeface, and effective use of white space (and color if you can afford it); considering the most effective fold if a mailer, so that the basic message is on top, in case the voter doesn't open the brochure at all which happens more often than candidates like (sometimes for this reason it is appropriate to have a brief message printed on the envelope).
- Absence of conflicting or confusing themes or misplaced emphasis; voters are not a philharmonic of musicians that can be orchestrated to every nuance and complex shading at will by the campaign rhetoric; disharmonies and discords don't work any better in campaigns than they do in symphonies.
- Use of photographs, cartoons, and other interesting visual material. Even with black-and-white pieces, by far the most common color combinations in print because of the cost considerations, a good graphic designer can get very attractive effects by using white space, attractive typefaces, and captioning contrasts.
- Consistency in themes and always being conscious of who is to receive the literature and what their contexts for print might be; for example, sending pieces featuring the need for new elementary schools to a neighborhood with a concentration of retired people doesn't make a whole lot of sense. Perhaps such a piece should also use larger than average type faces.
- Literature that can be used in various ways: designing, printing, and distributing literature costs time and money—you can save both by designing a mailer, for example, that can also be used in door-to-door and street campaigning.

The style of literature used in a campaign tends to vary with many things—with the type of literature that people are used to, with what is perceived by campaign staff and consultants to have worked well before, what contributors, family, and friends like, and the degree of panic the candidate and his or her manager may feel. Also, the rhetoric, design, and distribution mechanisms are in part a function of what the opponent is doing or what they expect him or her to do. (It is common in thoughtful campaigns when developing the overall scenario to work out the probable outline of the opponent's strategy as well.)

It is usually well-advised to develop high print standards and to stay with them. The following examples of literature in recent campaigns are shown to suggest some criteria for these standards.

Figure 7-9 is an example of an effective mail piece, also distributed on the street, used a few years ago in the upper-income, relatively small commuting town of Westport, Connecticut. While Westport has an upscale population, its Democratic campaigns by current norms are traditionally underfinanced. This piece was developed for the race for First Selectman (Mayor) of the town. The Democratic incumbents had been heavily criticized and were way behind the Republicans on registrations. The independent voters, however, were significant in number. The party had never used polling before; I did a survey using volunteers and produced some findings that the manager and the candidates accepted and used in the literature and in newspaper advertising. (The latter was traditional, and the party workers expected to see these ads in their local papers.) The piece was succinct and dignified in keeping with the image and personalities of the candidates; the key was the section, "Fought to conserve Westport's unique character"—an issue that had come up very heavily in the survey. Notice the personalization on the return address— "Your Selectmen." This is the equivalent of closing a radio ad with, "This ad was brought to you by the friends of Candidate A who think you want to hear the facts." The mailer, using a three-way fold and black and white, was economical to produce and did the job it was intended to.

In the last decade, California has had an enormous number of "money campaigns," partly because the state is a favorite location for every new cause or movement in the nation with each seemingly able to develop both a constituency and a financial support base. Incumbents, by suing

THEIR ACCOMPLISHMENTS.

HENEAGE/DIAMOND
YOUR SELECTMEN
46 POST ROAD EAST
WESTPORT, CT. 06080
PH. 226-7501

BULK RATE
U. S. POSTAGE
PAID
Westport, Conn.
Permit #17

THE BEST REASONS TO RE-ELECT JACKIE HENEAGE AND TED DIAMOND OUR SELECTMEN ARE . . .

Fig. 7-9. Example of a basic mailer by incumbents (Westport, Connecticut, 1979).

Jackie and Ted
Kept our taxes down through sound management

- Held current tax increase to 3.8% despite general inflation rate of 6.9%.
- Instituted "Pay-As-You-Go" Plan — will save $300,000 on Town Garage.
- Maintained Westport's AAA bond rating — will save thousands in interest charges.
- Reinvested Employee Pension Funds — will double Westport's interest income.
- Obtained millions in State and Federal Grants — for policemen, roads, sewers, new Town Hall, open space.

"Watching the pennies isn't glamorous — but without it taxes would be out of sight."

Fought to conserve Westport's unique character

- Supported tough regulations to eliminate "floating zoning" and limit scale of commercial buildings.
- Pushed through major road reconstruction projects — like Whitney Street and Bayberry Lane.
- Established park land and open space — along Saugatuck, at Burying Hill Beach, and Greens Farms.
- Encouraged greening of the Post Road and Main Street.

"Talk never saved a tree — you plan to conserve beauty, and then execute the plan."

Improved quality of life for all

- Expanded recreation facilities — improvements at golf course, tennis and basketball courts, Doubleday Field.
- Planned renovation for Longshore Clubhouse.
- Provided tax relief for elderly — initiated elderly housing project.
- Conceived Youth Center.
- Supported Levitt Pavilion programs.

Westport works. In four years Jackie Heneage and Ted Diamond have built a remarkable record of accomplishment.

Re-elect Jackie Heneage and Ted Diamond
Vote the Top Row November 8.

Fig. 7-9. (Continued)

expensive media and direct mail saturations (used more liberally in California than in any other state) can make the ante an impossible one for many potential challengers to meet. (The California practice in direct mail is to subtarget much more than is usual elsewhere. For example, letters are sent to homeowners stating their actual real estate assessments and last year's exact taxes, with each letter in a mass mailing including the specific capital budget items of particular importance to that specific neighborhood.)

The mailer reproduced in Fig. 7-10 was used in San Mateo in 1982 in a supervisor's race. This is 8½ by 11 in dimension, easy to read and visually inviting without any appearance of hype. The design elements of layout, typeface, and pictorials are excellent. It folds once as a mailer and opens to four panels. The use of royal blue vividly brings the caption to life and was also used for ELECT JOAN STIFF. It is a simple and gracious piece, making good use of candid photos. Note that the candidate's photo has not been retouched. The lead panel states her professional credits and her background as a civic leader. My only criticism is that this panel includes an unidentified man with the candidate; the panel might have been more effective if the photo were with an endorser with a following among the voters. Indeed, the piece is somewhat unusual in not using any endorsements whatever.

The Leo T. McCarthy "Things I Gotta Do Today" mailer, (Fig. 7-11) was prepared for the California lieutenant governor's race in 1982. It was used as a mailer with a bulk rate envelope; the brochure contained eight panels, using black and white with green for accents. It was somewhat smaller than most mailers, 3½ by 8 folded. It is notable that the piece doesn't mention the party affiliation of the candidates and essentially tries to link the opponent to the unpopular Interior Secretary James Watt. The graphic design, in my judgment, is better than the rhetoric. For example, "Leo McCarthy's convictions have produced results . . . to conserve . . . the health of our planet. . . . [and] the laws he supported as state assemblyman helped preserve our precious resources: could be better stated. State assemblymen are not in any position to conserve the planet's health, and lieutenant governors have very little chance of doing it either. The voters are well aware of this. These campaign conceits are a needless bravado, and the voters don't buy it.

This mailer is also an interesting example of the developing trend of using negative material, emphasizing the opponent's name; the ancient political axiom was to make the opponent pay for his own name recognition. Like many political axioms, a little thought about them can result in major modifications.

An alternative design format might have keyed the endorsements of the Sierra Club and the League of Conservation Voters; this could have been done by replacing the caption: "Carol Hallet started on her agenda . . ." on the inside four panels with the endorsements. The theme, "Things I Gotta Do," could have included voting for McCarthy on election day.

Of course, these possible changes are easier to see in retrospect. I am trying to emphasize that the design of a good piece of literature has to take into account a number of creative and production variables. There are many ways of doing a piece, and at least a few alternatives should be considered before deciding. This mailer was produced on a very good quality paper stock and a good deal of thought obviously went into the design; it could have been more effective.

Campaigning deadlines usually don't allow the time to perfect each item. With so much money at stake, creative and careful attempts at good design should not be hampered by the compromises and revisions that the campaign bureaucracy, the candidate and his or her intimates often inflict on the graphic and text designers. Candidates should review the concept of each brochure; they are well-advised thereafter to let the technicians do their work.

There were several really bitter and expensive congressional campaigns in 1982, including Barney Frank vs. Margaret Heckler in Massachusetts, Richard Durbin vs. Paul Findley in Illinois, and Democrat Tom Lantos vs. Bill Royer in California. Two of these candidates spent over a million dollars in their races.* National PACs were heavily involved and the press gave each extensive coverage; each campaign was naturally overrun with consultants representing every possible form of political expertise.

A reproduction of a Lantos mailer is shown in Fig. 7-12. Measuring 4¼ by 10¾, it uses blue, black, and white in eight panels, using part of the address panel for a coupon for contributions and volunteers, a somewhat unusual format. Photographs, many featuring pictures of babies, are liberally used with little relevance to the platform summary which is the essence of the piece. Photos and art work should always be designed

---

*Frank spent $1,435,000, Lantos $1,164,373, Heckler $926,769, and Findley $772,594.

EXPERIENCE

in the things that really matter as a county supervisor

1976 to Present	— Elected Member of Woodside City Council
1979 – 1980	— Mayor of Woodside
1976 to Present	— Member and now Vice Chairman, San Mateo County Regional Planning Committee Chairman RPC Household Waste Committee RPC Parks, Recreation and Open Space Committee
1971 – 1976	— City Planning Commissioner of Woodside
1973 – 1974	— San Mateo County Watershed Task Force Member
1981 – 1982	— Association of Bay Area Governments (ABAG) Alternative Representative
1976 to Present	— Member and Past Chairman, Midpeninsula Cities Study Group
1960 to Present	— League of Women Voters Member
1954 to Present	— Active involvement in PTA, Church and Hospice
1953	— Graduate of Duke University, School of Nursing

Fig. 7-10. Example of well-designed brochure for a local race (San Mateo, California, 1982).

Joan Stiff — *Experienc*

Maintaining our precious heritage

A commitment to long-range planning and practical problem-solving will keep San Mateo County an ideal place to live and work. Many large issues loom as challenges for the 1980's — county parks, coastside/coastal plan, Devil's Slide/Highway 92, off-shore drilling, garbage and hazardous waste. As a council member, Joan dealt with consequences of the winter's monumental rainfall, working with professional staff to minimize damage and loss for citizens of her community.

Affordable housing must again be a reality

Joan Stiff believes that for housing to be truly affordable, it must be provided where the public facilities, safety and other support services already exist. While in San Mateo County these developed areas are mostly within the jurisdiction of incorporated cities, the Board of Supervisors can initiate cooperative approaches between various levels of government and developers. Business and labor unions must be welcomed into the process to provide the housing necessary for the San Mateo County people who will fill the 40,000 jobs which are forecast to be added over the next five years. All this must be accomplished in a system which ensures the air, land, water and historic qualities which our county enjoys.

Peninsula citizens have a right to expect optimum personal safety measures

Personal safety must be planned for as a high priority. Joan will act upon her convictons to ensure consistent law enforcement and crime protection programs. In addition, she will be alert to potential physical disaster threats, such as earthquake and the effects from intense rainfall as we had this winter.

Placing a priority on people

When it gets right down to it, an elected representative must be sensitive to the needs of the people. Joan Stiff's dedication to public service has demonstrated the essence of her commitment to people.

Fig. 7-10. (Continued)

e makes the difference

Balancing the budget remains the bottom line in serving the taxpayers well

Joan's experience as an elected nonpartisan town council member, mayor and businesswoman developed her skills in budgeting and tough decision making. There is less money available for services we have become accustomed to in San Mateo County. State and federal cutbacks in funding require the expertise and determination of elected officials willing to pay attention to needs. Operating on more modest budgets will require day-to-day management and accountability, as well as creative, cooperative solutions.

We must plan now for quality health care

San Mateo County's fastest growing population is its senior citizens. To ensure quality health care for them as well as other segments of our citizenry, long-range planning is essential. Joan, trained as a nursing professional, has demonstrated her concern for quality health care delivery and planning on both governmental and community levels.

Married to Robert Stiff, District Dean of Educational Services for the San Mateo County Community College District, Joan has four children and one grandson, all living in the Bay Area. As 27-year residents of San Mateo County, Joan and Bob Stiff raised their children here and have always been concerned and involved citizens of our county.

"In replacing Ed Bacciocco, who is not seeking re-election to the Board of Supervisors, I pledge responsible and practical representation for the citizens of San Mateo County. My years of work in local government and public service have equipped me with the kind of experience so necessary to meet the challenges of the 1980's. We must meet these challenges with innovative management and cooperative efforts to maximize the dollar spent for all citizens."

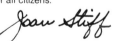

Fig. 7-10. (Continued)

Leo McCarthy's convictions have produced results in law to conserve our precious resources and the health of our planet.

A comparison with Carol Hallett's record makes her opposing convictions equally clear.

Air Quality

During Leo McCarthy's tenure as Speaker, California became a national leader in the fight for clean air. Because of James Watt's initiatives to dismantle federal air pollution standards, it is crucial that California have a leader willing to fight the polluters.

● In the last five years, Leo McCarthy has voted with the League of Conservation Voters 94 percent of the time on air quality; Carol Hallett voted for clean air 11 percent of the time.

● Hallett didn't cast one vote in favor of key air quality legislation in her first four years in office, while McCarthy supported every measure to control industrial pollutants, strengthen state standards, reduce smog levels from auto pollution, and toughen penalties for polluters.

Protection of Coast and Waterways

The California coastline is under attack again at the state and federal level. Water policy for the 1980's will be a top priority for the new state administration.

● In 1981, Carol Hallett supported an effort to repeal the California Coastal Act, while Leo McCarthy was an active leader in the fight against Watt's offshore drilling plans. McCarthy collected and delivered to Washington D.C., signatures of 100,000 Californians opposed to coastal lease sales.

● McCarthy worked for a passage of a California resolution opposing inclusion of environmentally sensitive areas in Lease Sale 68, while Hallett voted against the resolution.

● McCarthy authored the Clean Water Bond Act in 1981 — Hallett refused to vote for the bill.

● In 1979, Assembly Speaker McCarthy successfully guided an important water conservation law to enactment, against Assembly Minority Leader Hallett's opposition.

Wilderness and Wildlife

James Watt announced that he will sell up to 35 million acres of public land in the next five years. He's started in California with his plan to sell 107,000 acres of valuable national forest lands in Northern California to the

Carol Hallett started on her agenda

And now she'd like to be Lieutenant to carry out that agenda.

Fig. 7-11. Example of a smaller-sized mailer (California, 1982).

Louisianna Pacific Corporation. It will take a powerful California leader in conservation, like Leo McCarthy as Lieutenant Governor, to fight the special interests who are ready to move on the state's wilderness areas, wild rivers and wildlife sanctuaries.

● As Speaker, McCarthy pushed legislation through the Assembly to protect the Lake Tahoe Basin and preserve undeveloped land, measures opposed by Hallett.

● The California Wetlands Preservation Act was enacted under McCarthy's leadership, while Hallett voted to eliminate public access to and environmental protection for thousands of acres of wetlands and waterways.

● McCarthy and Hallett are on opposing sides on the issues of wildlife protection; McCarthy voted for the ban on recreational killing of mountain lions and the ban on product litter threatening wildlife, Hallett voted against these protections.

● Legislation ensuring protection of the South Fork of the American River was enacted with McCarthy's support and over Hallett's opposition; Hallett likewise opposed a broader measure, passed by the Assembly under McCarthy's leadership, to protect California's Wild and Scenic River Waterways.

Environmental Health and Safety

Laws to protect our environmental health and safety have a strong advocate in Leo McCarthy and a fierce opponent in Carol Hallett. Growing public awareness of this critical environmental issue must be translated into a powerful constituency, and we need a California leader to make sure the message gets across.

● Health hazards from pesticides can be deadly; exposure linked to cancer, birth defects, genetic mutations, nerve poisoning and sterility. Under McCarthy's Assembly Speakership, California gained national recognition for landmark efforts to regulate pesticide use, and he's fighting the chemical companies now in their battle at the state and federal level. Hallett has been a vocal advocate for the unrestricted use of pesticides, and led the fight against pesticide regulations in the legislature.

● Nuclear Power Plant Safety Siting laws of 1976 marked an historic accomplishment of Leo McCarthy's Speakership in the Assembly. Since then he's fought attempts to weaken the law, including the Sundesert plant exemption supported by Hallett.

● Hazardous waste transportation and disposal at California sites are now under strict regulation because of laws authored and fought for by Leo McCarthy. Hallett would not even vote for funding to clean up abandoned dumpsites and compensate victims of toxic chemicals.

before we'd even heard of James Watt.

Governor so she can have more power

Fig. 7-11. (Continued)

Election, 1982

Things I Gotta Vote On

Dear Californian,

No two candidates in California differ more sharply on environmental issues than Carol Hallett and Leo McCarthy, the candidates for Lieutenant Governor.

The League of Conservation Voters and the Sierra Club have formally endorsed Leo McCarthy for Lieutenant Governor because he has been a consistently strong advocate for environmental concerns. Under McCarthy's leadership as Speaker of the Assembly, the California Legislature became a national model for state action on cleaning up the air, controlling the use of pesticides, and regulating transportation and disposal of hazardous wastes.

His opponent, Carol Hallett, on the other hand, has been a strong advocate for the polluters. She has often ranked near the bottom of all legislators in her environmental voting record.

We urge your vote for Leo McCarthy for Lieutenant Governor on Tuesday, November 2, 1982. Conservationists must fight for Leo McCarthy's election, or we will be fighting against his opponent's agenda for the next four years.

Sincerely,

Carl Pope   *John Zierold*

Carl Pope,   John Zierold,
Executive Director   Legislative Advocate
League of   Sierra Club
Conservation Voters

Carol Hallett
California State Assembly

1. Support drilling in environmentally sensitive coastal areas	**Yes**
2. Repeal California Coastal Act	**Support**
3. Repeal air pollution standards	**Yes**
4. Weaken nuclear safeguards	**Yes**
5. Preserve Lake Tahoe	**No**
6. Preserve prime agricultural land	**No**
7. Protect California Wild and Scenic Rivers	**No**
8. Control water pollution	**No**
9. Regulate pesticides	**No**
10. Control hazardous wastes	**No**

VOTING RECORD
1977 - 1982
California Assembly Journals of Record

Fig. 7-11 (Continued)

No two Candidates in California differ more sharply on environmental issues than Leo McCarthy and Carol Hallett, the candidates for Lieutenant Governor.

Things I Gotta Do Today ☺

Leo T. McCarthy
California State Assembly

1. Support drilling in environmentally sensitive coastal areas **No**
2. Repeal California Coastal Act **Oppose**
3. Repeal air pollution standards **No**
4. Weaken nuclear safeguards **No**
5. Preserve Lake Tahoe **Yes**
6. Preserve prime agricultural land **Yes**
7. Protect California Wild and Scenic Rivers **Yes**
8. Control water pollution **Yes**
9. Regulate pesticides **Yes**
10. Control hazardous wastes **Yes**

LEGISLATIVE RECORD
1968 - 1982
California Assembly Journals of Record

James Watt
U.S. Secretary of Interior

1. Authorize offshore oil drilling **Yes**
2. Repeal coastal protections **Support**
3. Reduce air pollution standards **Yes**
4. Weaken nuclear safeguards **Yes**
5. Preserve Lake Tahoe **No**
6. Expand national parks **No**
7. Protect Wild and Scenic Rivers **No**
8. Control water pollution **No**
9. Regulate pesticides **No**
10. Control hazardous wastes **No**

AGENDA
1980 - 1982

Fig. 7-11. (Continued)

HE GETS THINGS DONE—FOR US

FIGHTING CRIME
Tom's tough and comprehensive bill to attack the related problems of violent crime and drug abuse has already been endorsed by almost half of the U.S. Senate. He vigorously supports mandatory penalties for the use of firearms in federal felonies.

DEFENDING SOCIAL SECURITY
Last year, Tom was one of the leaders in the successful fight by Democrats to protect our Social Security System. He is determined to continue the battle as the program faces new threats. A contract is a contract.

NO CONGRESSIONAL PAY RAISE
Tom was the first Member of Congress to author a bill calling for repeal of the back-door pay raise Congress voted itself late last year.

ADVANCING HUMAN RIGHTS
Tom's historic human rights legislation to help free Raoul Wallenberg from Soviet prison received national acclaim. His commitment to human rights ranges from preserving the Voting Rights Act, to providing the handicapped with an equal chance at life.

"TOM LANTOS IS A TOUGH NO-NONSENSE FIGHTER FOR THE PENINSULA - AND FOR THE NATION. HE DOESN'T JUST TALK ABOUT PROBLEMS - HE FINDS SOLUTIONS. HE'S A RARE KIND OF CONGRESSMAN."

— SENATOR ALAN CRANSTON

RE-ELECT OUR CONGRESSMAN **TOM LANTOS** Please Vote June 8th

Fig. 7-12. Example of a mailer used in a high-visibility congressional. (San Francisco suburbs, 1982).

OUR CONGRESSMAN TOM LANTOS...

BUILDING A STRONG ECONOMY

As a professional economist, Tom understands how to cut inflation, reduce interest rates and create more American jobs. He is an effective fighter against Administration policies that favor giant oil companies and huge corporations at the expense of the average American.

FEDERAL SPENDING

On the key votes involving civilian and military boondoggles, Tom voted to cut out the MX Missile, the B-1 Bomber, tobacco subsidies, and hundreds of millions of dollars in wasteful pork-barrel public works projects.

NUCLEAR FREEZE

Congressman Tom Lantos is one of the leaders in Congress working for a mutual and verifiable nuclear freeze as a first step toward the elimination of all nuclear weapons. As a key member of the Foreign Affairs Committee, Tom's number one priority is to preserve peace for our own and future generations.

 ## AT LAST!!

Tom secured federal funding for the 92/101 highway interchange, and construction of this life-saving project is now underway.

HELPING OUR NEIGHBORS

The first concern of Tom's office is to help individual citizens and groups in our communities with their special problems, ranging from relief for mudslide victims, to assistance for the elderly, and to cutting the red tape in Washington.

FOCUS ON EDUCATION

Good schools, from kindergarten to universities, are the cornerstones of our future. Tom is determined to keep the doors of opportunity open for all our children.

A BOOST FOR HOUSING

In order to combat soaring interest rates and high prices, Tom has authored innovative legislation to allow people to build a tax-free nest egg for the purchase of a home. He is working on ways to provide decent housing for Americans of all ages.

PROTECTING THE ENVIRONMENT

Tom is a nationally recognized leader in the effort to protect the environment. He led the successful fight to stop James Watt from drilling off the Northern California coastline. His ongoing efforts range from making Sweeney Ridge a national landmark to his full commitment to improve the quality of our air and water.

EQUAL RIGHTS FOR WOMEN

Tom has been in the forefront of the fight for women's rights in all facets of American life, and he is determined to eliminate discrimination and inequality aimed at women.

Fig. 7-12. (Continued)

to enhance copy, not to divert from its basic thrust. Senator Cranston's endorsement might be more convincing if his signature appeared. Another option could have been to have a replica of the actual endorsement letter more prominently featured in the design.

Lantos's primary and general election campaigns were both successful. The National Republican Congressional Committee (whose commissioned work is usually of the highest quality) was involved in the campaign against him. An example of their classic and highly professional mailer, used against Lantos, is shown in Fig. 7-13. Note the easy-to-read print and succinct text; it uses a four-way fold and measures 5½ by 8½.

Another tough congressional in 1982 was that of Nick Mavroules of Massachusetts.* An example of his literature is reproduced in part in Fig. 7-14. This was a four-page tabloid with large type and lots of white space. It emphasizes the critical issues of his district. The photographs are directly related to the copy or text while the programmatic ideas are clearly stated by individual supporters.

This is a mailer that I think most voters actually read and thought about. Any candidate is well-advised to remember that in campaigning season voters are inundated by political mail, including many solicitations for money, much of it thrown away unread. In a campaign, you're constantly competing for the voters' attention—even getting a few minutes to read a brief brochure can be very difficult. Your design should be clean and attractive, your copy crisp, emphasizing only a few ideas, and your captions should be perceived as relevant by the group of voters receiving the brochure.

Mavroules, a two-term Democratic incumbent in the Boston suburbs, beat a very tough challenger. His campaign also used a small street distribution piece, called *Nick on the Issues,* that is shown as Fig. 7-15. Using black, white, and green and an unpretentious family photograph, it undoubtedly was effective. Although most political handbills are thrown away within a block of the distribution point, this design should have been read by at least fifty percent of the people who got them. It was distinctive, attractive, brief, and straightforward. A very good grade of cardboard stock, 4 by 8½, was used. There was no time necessary to open it; all pertinent copy was contained on one side.

---

*This district was the site of the original gerrymander.

. . . FOR TOM LANTOS, THE AMBITIOUS, BIG-SPENDING POLITICIAN FROM HILLSBOROUGH.

1 In 1972, Thomas Lantos, a self-described international economist, was fired from a posh state job after Legislative hearings on his performance.

As Director of the International Studies Program for the California State College System, Lantos was accused of overcharging students $310,000, riding around Europe in a chauffer-driven Mercedes-Benz, hiring unauthorized "assistants" and entertaining friends at lavish cocktail and dinner parties. . . **at taxpayer's expense!**

Democratic Assemblyman Leo Ryan, Chairman of legislative subcommittee hearings, said, ". . .the way this has been run has been rotten." An investigator for the California State Department of Finance said, ". . .**you bet your * * * he was fired.**"

2 Insurance company kickbacks engineered by Thomas Lantos for the California Teachers Association in the 1970's led to Legislation by Democratic State Senator Arlen Gregorio, (now a San Mateo County Supervisor) to halt the practice.

As business manager and controller for the politically active teachers union, Lantos hit insurance companies for over $500,000 annually. The price was ultimately paid by taxpayers through higher insurance premiums paid by school districts across the state. Gregorio labeled Lantos' shenanigans "influence peddling."

Lantos' problems did not end there. He managed to run up a $1.7 million deficit in fiscal year '76-'77 for C.T.A! To clean up his mess, C.T.A. laid off 10% of its staff, cut programs and moved Thomas Lantos out the door!

3 Thomas Lantos, with other liberal big spenders, voted **against** a constitutional amendment to balance the federal budget.
(SJ Res. 58, October 1, 1982)

4 Thomas Lantos, voted **against** the 25% cut in our income taxes!
(HR 4242, Congressional Record vote #177)

5 The arrogant Thomas Lantos, after voting against a tax break for us, voted **for** a 29% tax break for himself. . . **$19,000 into his own pocket!**
(HR 5159, Roll Call #349)

Can we count on Thomas Lantos to protect our interests and to spend our tax money wisely? In a word. . . "NO"!

Fig. 7-13. Example of a National Republican Congressional Committee negative mailer (San Francisco suburbs, 1982).

Today's issues make the choice clear.

Nuclear Freeze

He was one of the first to publicly denounce the arms build up. He took the initiative in Congress for the nuclear weapons freeze. He sought to stop the MX missile because it was counterproductive and so expensive that its production would act as a detriment to improving our conventional forces.
He's a realist with regard to America's national security. He wants to see America maintain her strength without becoming 'trigger happy'.

Jean Knox Gibb
Cape Ann, Massachusetts

Small Business

High interest rates and cuts in small business aid programs are making it tough these days on businessmen like myself.
Nick Mavroules has made a good effort at bringing government contracts back home here to keep our small businesses going.
Quite frankly, it's a good thing we've got a guy like Nick around.

Ed Molin,
Berkshire Manufacturing,
Newburyport

Senior Citizens

Yes, I think Congressman Mavroules is doing a great job! He is really concerned about us elderly.

A.J. LeBlanc,
Salem

Fig. 7-14. Example of a tabloid (part) used in a congressional race (Boston suburbs, 1982).

Home Buying

My wife and I are paying 17½% on this house. We're considered lucky — at least we managed to buy a house.

Does 17½% sound lucky to you? And what about other couples? Our children?

I think Nick Mavroules is really trying to get interest rates down. For one thing, he's supporting a balanced budget.

Charles Carey,
Peabody

Education

Education has always been a step ladder to a better life — for my parents, my grandparents.

And I'd like to think I'm going to have the same chance.

Congressman Mavroules is working for public education.

Chris Tighe,
Salem State College

Jobs

It's important having a guy like Nick Mavroules on the armed services committee. It means jobs for us at Lynn's General Electric plant. And it means work for all the subcontractors in the area doing business with General Electric

Nick Mavroules went to the wall to save the FA18 jet fighter program, and the 3,000 jobs associated with the program here in the Lynn area. He told us he would fight for our jobs, and he's delivered.

Kevin Mahar
International Union of Electrical Workers
#201 — Lynn

Environment

When my farmland was threatened by the proposed SRS facility to be built next door, Nick Mavroules came right up here and said he was going to help us out.

Nick cared enough about what was happening to our land and water supply to help stop the construction of that waste facility.

Harold Rogers,
Haverhill

Nick Mavroules Democrat for Congress
There's only one choice on Nov. 2

Fig. 7-14. (Continued)

**RE-ELECT
NICK
MAVROULES
DEMOCRAT
FOR CONGRESS**

Nick on the issues

The Economy

■ Voted for a balanced budget.
■ Voted for a tax cut for working men and women and incentives for business aimed at increasing economic productivity.

Arms Control and Defense Spending

■ An early supporter of an immediate, mutual, and verifiable nuclear weapons freeze.
■ Led fight to kill wasteful defense programs like the $50 billion MX missile proposal.

Energy

■ Championed bill turning nation toward renewable energy, like solar power, and away from dependence on foreign oil.
■ Secured $2.7 million for a major solar energy project in Beverly.
■ Authored a law to develop a new, environmentally safe coal technology.

Paid for by the Mavroules for Congress Committee.
 19

Jobs

■ Led successful House floor fight to save FA 18 jet fighter, bringing 3,000 jobs to area, 6,000 state-wide, stopping the drain of defense contracts to other parts of the country.
■ Played major role in bringing hundreds of millions of dollars of federal contracts to the 6th district, creating numerous jobs.

Education

■ Opposed Republican cuts in educational assistance.

Older Americans

■ Opposed Republican cuts in Social Security.

Small Business

■ Authored legislation to attract federal contracts to small business.
■ Authored a law that cuts bureaucratic red-tape for small business seeking defense contracts.

**CONGRESSMAN
NICK
MAVROULES**

**DEMOCRAT
Election Day
Tuesday, Nov. 2**

Fig. 7-15. Example of a small-size street distribution piece (Boston suburbs, 1982).

A critical piece, the sample ballot, simply provides a facsimile of the ballot. The slate or candidate being promoted simply uses color, circles, or checkmarks to remind the voter where the names are to be found. Some mechanics suggest using the typeface of the actual ballot in designing this brochure. Almost all technicians recommend including the copy, "It is legal to take this sample ballot into the voting booth." An example is reproduced as Fig. 7-16.*

A final word of caution: With so many fancy flyers hitting the streets and mailboxes in campaign season, the candidate with limited funds and no ad agency or media consultant to support him is very naturally tempted to adapt, emulate, or simply copy someone else's brochure or handbill. In doing this, the candidate runs the risk of not being consistent with his or her own personality and the personality of the campaign —personal style is violated. A good piece of literature is usually custom designed to a specific candidate, that candidate's issues, personality, and campaign themes; it is unlikely that someone else's situation will be exactly comparable to yours. If, however, you have to copy, try for a style sympathetic and compatible with your own, whether natural or the image you have chosen to project. And, as in football, good execution often can make the difference.

REPRINTING LITERATURE FROM OTHER SOURCES

Not all your campaign literature need be original. You can—and should—reprint favorable newspaper publicity, letters and editorials endorsing you (see p. 215), and statements by local civic clubs, chapters of the League of Women Voters, or other prestigious organizations that may have a positive impact on the voters. (An example is shown in Fig. 7-17.) These should be duplicated soon after the endorsement and preferably delivered by volunteers or paid "stuffers" to the voters' residences. Preparing a mailing, in addition to being expensive, needs a certain lead time, and delay may take away some of the beneficial impacts of the endorsement.

Whatever you do, don't take extracts from an endorsement or newspaper article, as movie and other entertainment ads do when they carefully select complimentary words out of a basically unfavorable review. Use

---

*A variant of a sample ballot is a "palm card." This is a smaller version of a sample ballot and often highlights only one or two candidates instead of the entire party slate.

Vote September 14th. Make a difference for

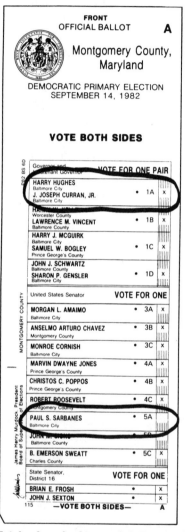

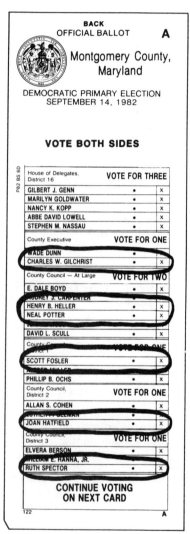

It is legal to take this sample ballot into the voting booth.

Polls open: 7am—8pm, Tuesday, September 14. PLEASE VOTE.

The Democratic State Central Committee of Maryland wants all Democrats to be aware of the candidates available to them in the coming primary election. This does not constitute an endorsement of a specific candidate or slate.

Fig. 7-16. Example of a sample ballot (Washington, D.C. suburbs, 1982).

What people are saying about Abbe Lowell:

"Abbe has worked for and with me on a number of federal, state and local issues. I could always depend on his excellent judgment and ability to get the job done. We need him in the Maryland House of Delegates."

Benjamin R. Civiletti, former U.S. Attorney General

"Abbe brought the DPT vaccine, child car restraints and school closing issues to the attention of my community so that we could make better decisions for our children. He has my support because he has shown he cares."

Sally LaLiberte, Bethesda mother and nurse

"From drafting our rules to stopping the pollution of our nearby stream, Abbe has been working hard for our civic association and has been one of its leaders. He has my vote because he is effective."

Jeffrey Wolpe, Chevy Chase attorney and civic association officer

"Because of his experience as assistant to the Attorney General, and his work with state and local law enforcement officials, Abbe Lowell is exceptionally well-qualified to deal effectively with the crime problems in Maryland."

Lenny C. Simpson, past president, Fraternal Order of Police, Montgomery County Lodge 35.

"The masterful legislative draftsmanship of Mr. Abbe Lowell provided the solution to most all of the difficulties which had doomed all previous efforts to protect the privacy of citizens' financial records."

Former Congressman John J. Cavanaugh

Fig. 7-17. Example of an endorsement brochure (part) (Washington, D.C. suburbs, 1982).

the whole text even if it contains a few negative or neutral statements. If you use the selectivity artifice, it may soon be found out and used effectively against you.

Negative editorial comment or unfavorable news articles about your opponent can be reproduced and distributed in the same way, in the style of the political broadsides of the eighteenth and nineteenth centuries.

Printed matter of this sort can be reproduced inexpensively by photo-offset. Design elements, paper quality, and the use of color and white space are basically the same as those applying to original literature. You may wish to superimpose the material to be reproduced on your letterhead or add a photograph or your campaign slogan at the top or bottom of the page.

THE RECOGNITION COMPULSION (OR THE NAME GAME)

Probably because candidates, like other human beings, have strong ego needs, billboard and poster advertising often gets an undeserved emphasis.* Many candidates enjoy seeing their names and pictures all over the district; they are gratifying, and they provide physical evidence of expenditures.

In some campaigns, billboard and poster activity becomes absolutely frenzied. For example, in a county campaign on the East Coast, the senior men of the campaign staffs wasted their time ripping each other's posters down. There were fistfights, and one group went to the extreme of carrying baseball bats as defense weapons. When the going became really rough, one team was accompanied by an armed off-duty policeman, the brother of one of the participants. Each evening they presented their candidate with trophies: stacks of the opponent's posters which they had torn down. These forays at night are conducted by so-called phantom squads. In one case, a young man was actually shot in a poster war. Some candidates use "cherry pickers" to mount posters late at night on telephone wires so that they can't be removed without considerable expense.

---

*In many areas, lawn signs in front of suburban homes are thought by candidates to be extremely effective. This idea depends on the assumption that if people see your name more often than your opponent's they'll vote for you. I don't subscribe to this. Advertising, to some degree, does depend on repetition for effectiveness. But repetition by itself is not controlling. There are just too many dynamic factors that affect voters' behavior. Lawn signs should be considered as helpful, but they should not be made the cornerstone of any campaign.

Despite the frequency of such occurrences, posters are very popular. They are tied on telephone poles and pasted on U.S. mailboxes, telephone booths, and anything else in sight. They literally disfigure areas and remain years later as shabby silent memorials to the campaign. Many candidates nowadays, realizing that permanently glued posters deface neighborhoods and may arouse negative reactions for that reason, put up posters with string or otherwise assure that they can be removed easily. At the bottom of each poster, it would be wise to print the line: "Not to be posted on telephone poles or public property."

There is controversy about the beneficial impacts of billboards and posters; there are reasons to believe that few voters determine their choice on the basis of this type of advertising.

Many members of political clubs insist that posters be used, since putting up posters is an activity they're used to and understand and a way for them to make a direct contribution. In any case, don't allow the poster-billboard mania to seize your staff. It isn't worth concentrated effort and can be destructive if it takes attention and money from more productive activities.

It is also common in campaigns to have large signs painted and placed in front of campaign headquarters. These are expensive to prepare and to have mounted and then removed, and they give almost no return in votes for an investment of about $1,000. If you face pressure from club members and other candidates to have such signs, you might consider using bunting or flags on which your name is stencilled in different colors: It is cheaper and pleasing to the eye, although it is no more likely to win voters to your side than is a conventional sign. A certain amount of hoopla is needed in a campaign.

Other devices to gain name recognition are bus and subway posters, car stickers, and car aerial pennants. Bus posters are usually purchased for placement in all the buses from one city garage. In larger cities this may be a problem, since the routes from a garage may not be coterminous with your district. Outside bus posters, although more expensive, may be a better value, since they are larger and can be seen by pedestrians as well as passengers.

NEWSPAPER ADVERTISEMENTS

Newspaper ads are to some small campaigns what television is to large ones: They are the means by which the candidate can reach a mass audience. Generally, each newspaper ad dramatizes one concept or one criticism of the opponent. Newspaper advertisements should be coordinated with other campaign publicity, and ads in series should reinforce each other. Sometimes, a series of ads appears on successive days in the same place in the newspaper, usually in a section, like the national news section or the radio-TV section, which is thought to be read by voters of all special interest groups. Series of this type are intended to be seen in sequence and to have a cumulative effect on the person who reads more than one of them. Some candidates prefer to run series of short, so-called bullet ads in different parts of the paper and direct them at different audiences—for example, placing an ad about food and drug legislation or about abortion reform on the woman's page. If you have a relationship with an advertising agency, the agency should help you to decide what space to buy to give your ad campaign the maximum effect. Otherwise, a trusted member of your staff who is involved in writing the ads will have to make these decisions.

It is traditional to include a photograph of the candidate in political ads; this is particularly useful if you plan to do any street campaigning and if your face is not already known to the voters. A candid photograph dramatizing the content of the ad—for example, one showing you conversing with an older person in an ad on medical benefits or social security, or hiking in a park or vising a recycling center in an ad on conservation of natural resources—is likely to be more effective than a formal one. Family photographs are much used and may appeal to some voters; whether you use them will depend on both your family and your constituency.

All your newspaper ads should include an address where volunteers may come and where you may be contacted if readers have further questions about your candidacy.

Pay attention to the appearance of the ad on the printed page. If it appears cluttered or if the type is too small, few people will read it. In a recent district leadership race, I spent a great deal of time working with the candidate, an experienced politician, to develop a series of newspaper advertisements that formed the basis of his campaign. The ads were carefully written to build upon each other in successive issues of the local weekly newspaper, which was widely read by the residents of the district. The first ad was relatively successful, and no change in format was contemplated for the rest of the series. The newspaper layout man, however, changed the typeface in the second ad without consulting the candidate or his staff, and used a small face that was difficult to read and that undoubtedly diluted the effectiveness of the ad. This small but serious fiasco illustrates a basic theme of this book: most campaign accidents can be avoided by proper detailing. When the copy for the third ad in the district leadership campaign was delivered to the printer, the typeface was specified explicitly.

Successful newspaper advertisements can be reproduced on good-quality paper and distributed throughout the district, either in conjunction with walking tours or street rallies, or by volunteers standing on street corners. Additional visual material—for example, a sample ballot showing the candidate's name in red type or boldface or the campaign slogan in large type—can be included with the ad on such a flyer.

Occasionally, candidates will prepare a simulated newspaper consisting of endorsements, activities, issues, etc. written in newspaper style. In some areas, this can be very effective. It is expensive and takes a great deal of time to develop, but voters do read them.

Personal Mailings

The use of computer letters as described on the following pages has become so common that a simple but effective approach is frequently overlooked. The device of having a candidate's friends send letters to their professional colleagues or fellow members of a fraternal order, school board, etc., making a personal appeal to vote for him, has considerable impact. The candidate supplies the prepared letters, stamps, and blank envelopes, and the friends supply their signatures (their personal credibility) and their personal mailing lists. To stay in keeping with the personal effect that makes them effective, these letters should be hand-addressed and hand-stamped.

Sometimes, a candidate can be embarrassed when a friend writes such a letter on the letterhead of an organization to which he or she belongs, thereby suggesting a nonexistent official endorsement from the organization. This usually offends many members and can cost you votes instead of increasing your support. Friends can also do you unwitting harm by supplying lists that are years old, without removing the names of colleagues or members who have died or have simply lost contact. Caution friends who offer you mailing lists about this problem and ask them to prune their lists so that letters are sent only to those whom they will not offend. Offer to provide staff assistance in this task if there is any way your staff can contribute to updating the lists.

USING COMPUTERS IN CAMPAIGN ADVERTISING

The use of computers in political campaigning is often referred to in a derogatory manner as the professional engineering of election campaigns, which permits candidates who can afford the technology to win elections regardless of their merit. This is simply untrue. Computer technology has merely given a new speed and efficiency to the old methods. (If you can afford a car, you don't ride a camel. Riding a camel is neither more nor less moral than riding in a car.) As far as I am concerned, it always makes sense to take advantage of whatever technology is available, if you can afford it and if the net results are more efficient or otherwise beneficial. This is certainly true in campaigning, where competition is tough and time is very short.

Over the last decade, I have frequently done voter profiling and analysis of a district's election returns by laborious hand-processing. These operations were arduous but not uncommon and did not appear "threatening" until computers, with their supposed depersonalization, were introduced. As a matter of fact, the computer has simply made it possible for me and others to do the same job with less effort and a greatly reduced margin of error. This applies equally to computers used in research and to those used in direct mail campaigns. As a practical matter, my experience leads me to predict that your main worry will be paying the bills for computer-related services rather than responding to adverse press and public reactions to your doing so. The remainder of this section summarizes the ways in which computers may be useful to you in the political advertising process.

Warren Weaver, Jr., described the use of computers to provide lists of voters who tend to swing back and forth between parties by a New Jersey statewide candidate who wished to direct recorded telephone messages to the "swing" voters identified by the computer.* According to Weaver, the firm of Bailey, Deardourff, and Brown used computers in the campaign as follows: (1) analyzed the last four elections for 5,000 election

---

*Warren Weaver, Jr., "Computers Counseling the Candidates," *New York Times,* October 30, 1970, p. 1.

districts to ascertain where liberal and moderate Republicans did well and why; (2) produced a list of 1,200 swing districts that were sometimes but not always carried by Republicans; and (3) isolated areas for special mailings and for the candidate's schedule of personal appearances. Jobs like this can be done by hand and are still done that way in smaller areas.

Weaver reported that Decision Making Information had a broad range of services for political candidates providing professional judgments based on computer-processed data. It offered a system of advising candidates how best to reach any one of 21 voter groups, each classed by degree of party affiliation and level of political interest. The service included advice on which media could best reach which voter group and whether ads would be more effective in the sports section or in the news section. Costs as of 1970 were based on a fee of $600 an hour for computer use; the comprehensive advice just described cost in the area of $2,000 to $3,000. By 1982, such services cost $10,000

William E. Roberts of Decision Making Information told Weaver that he didn't see anything particularly sinister in a candidate's scientifically determining the interest and opinions of the electorate; rather, he felt that "this enables the candidate to talk about issues which interest the public and not about those on which the public disagrees with him."*

Increasingly, the financial and political logic of a large-scale campaign forces such uses of the computer. The techniques are relatively elaborate and usually expensive. At a scale less than a congressional district, you may not need them, but you can put the same logic to work with less sophisticated instrumentation and obtain similarly good results.

COMPUTER-ASSISTED DIRECT MAIL ADVERTISING

Direct mail is perhaps the most important use of the computer in current campaigning on any large scale (over 50,000 voters). Lewis Lehrman's 1982 campaign for Governor of New York State involved millions of letters targeted with great success. Computers can also be used economically in small campaigns, but some computer firms will not accept smaller

---

*I believe this fairly common approach can backfire; many voters may disagree with a specific position of a candidate but so respect his integrity and courage that they will vote for him despite their disagreement on the issue. The best current example of this is of course President Ronald Reagan. Surveys show the majority of voters against him on many issues, but most still like him personally.

jobs since they involve fees of only several hundred dollars. Personal computers are available that could be put to excellent use in smaller campaigns for financial records, letters appealing for funds, letters appealing for support, statistical analyses, etc.

As a beginning, computers can save you considerable mailing expense by combining members of a single household (actually all voters with the same surname and the same address) onto a single card. There is an error margin of 5 to 8 percent on these combinations, since the computer will not combine the same surname at the same address if, for example, one card spells "Street" in full and one spells it "St.," or if apartment numbers don't match exactly. Such elimination ("suppression") of duplications alone can produce important savings, particularly in larger campaigns sending out several mailings, since otherwise the same household might receive two or three duplicate pieces, one for each registered voter. Some firms give political clients a choice among several options for suppressing duplications within a household and making other possible suppressions.

Computers can also economize on mailings after the first mailing by eliminating cards of voters whose first mailing was returned as undeliverable—usually deceased voters and those who have moved since the registration list was published. Such "nixies" can account for up to 20 percent of registration lists. But some companies will not do this since it costs them some of their business volume by reducing the number of labels, envelopes, and other items they provide a candidate.

Letters can be designed so that homeowners receive messages on property taxes while renters receive letters on crime on the city streets. Such letters can be constructed using one basic lead and closing into the computer and varying the second and third paragraphs depending on the issues of primary concern to the target group. This relatively simple device is regarded as one of the most powerful available in campaigning (see Fig. 7-18).

Computer letter shops, concentrated in major cities, serve the direct mail requirements of political campaigners. Such firms make available ethnication or ethnic-select lists which identify the religious and/or ethnic origin of voters and enables the client to direct focused appeals at the group or groups of his or her choice. Such files are made by selecting specific names and name endings known to be common among certain groups. For example, thousands of names can be stored in the computer's

KEVIN BRINKWORTH
645 ELLICOTT SQUARE BUILDING
BUFFALO, NEW YORK 14203

October

Mrs. Evelyn _____
675 _____ Ave 708
Buffalo, NY 14202

Dear Mrs. _____ :

When a candidate asks for your vote, his responsibility
should be to tell you how he sees the problems. He
should avoid political sniping. I am asking for the votes
of you and your family as 10th District Candidate for
our County Legislature. Why? I feel our major problems
are welfare, drug abuse and crime.

Welfare. Our system does not help people become
productive. The fault lies with State and Federal officials
playing politics with public dollars. For instance, my
opponent, as Assemblyman, voted against the one-year
residency requirement; a vote for spiraling welfare cost.

"Issue paragraphs can
vary by target group, be
sequenced differently,
or can vary as the
voters' concerns
change."

Drug Abuse. We must wipe this filth from our door,
now. I will fight for: One—legislation to hit hard drug
suppliers, to get at the source: Two—a new county-
wide program to teach our children about the horror of
drug abuse.

Crime. We fear to walk our streets or in our parks
at night. And now even our children are not safe walking home from school in daylight. Crime is increasing.

These problems demand new solutions. I intend to
deliver them.

As a Republican, I believe you feel as I do. We cannot afford the kind of indecision we saw on the Stadium
question. I ask your support for myself and for Ned Regan.

Sincerely,

Kevin Brinkworth

Fig. 7-18. Example of a computer letter.

memory bank as probably Jewish.* The charge for the process early in 1982 was about $25 per thousand names searched. Considerations of economy require pre-selecting the geographic areas to be searched (on the basis of census and historical data) rather than searching an entire large district. Lists of primary voters can be provided as well as two-Democrat or two-Republican voter households. Party registration lists are of course available. Some firms can match household by telephone number using computers.

A major service offered by these firms is the computer-generated personalized letter. Generally, this approach is most appropriate in fund raising. According to professionals in the field, the more personalized the letter in appearance, the higher the success ratio, measured in the percent return and the size of the average contribution.** In the last decade the great advance has been in the quality of the printing of these letters.

There are three ways to produce a letter in quantity: impact or contact printing, ink jet printing, and laser printing (IBM 6670 and Xerox 9700 lasers). Laser printing is regarded as a major breakthrough because the quality of printing is considerably enhanced while production is also dramatically increased. For example, the Xerox 9700 is rated at 6,000 pages an hour; the letters look personally typed to the untrained eye, and the margins often are not justified to enhance that impression.

Laser printing is not inexpensive; prices vary from $50 a thousand letters to well over $100 a thousand, depending on the quality of paper used, the number required, and the custom variations required. (These costs do not include charges for individualized envelopes.) For large mailings (over 10,000 pieces), offset or impact printing is still generally preferable for reasons of economy.

For personalized mail services, look in the Yellow Pages in large metropolitan areas under "Letter Shops." Costs seem to vary very considerably between houses as well as for the specific attributes of the letter

---

*No ethnic-select program of this type can be absolutely accurate, of course, since, for example, some Jewish people change their names, some Jewish women marry non-Jews and thereby acquire non-Jewish surnames, and some people with Jewish surnames have given names that indicate non-Jewish origin. (There are ways of matching common given names by ethnic group, but this increases the expense more than proportionately.) All told, however, the error margin is only on the order of 10 to 15 percent.

**I am indebted to Stockton, Inc., Automated Correspondence Systems, and Shabatt Mail House, all of Washington, D.C., for background for this section.

you may need. Besides fund raising, these relatively expensive letters may be suitable for very specific purposes such as making special political appeals to a trade association membership or members of a church on special issues.

Many mailing shops use Xerox's Cheshire machine, which cuts, then glues, computer-typed labels onto envelopes at a cost of $10-12 a thousand for self mailers plus perhaps $25 as an overall set-up charge. Insertion of a labeled piece costs an additional $3-4 a thousand. In calculating probable costs, add an amount for buying your mailing lists. The mail shop service includes bagging the envelopes for delivery to the post office. The Cheshire system makes it possible to produce carbon copies of labels—a considerable saving. This process is generally used for larger mailings.

Another process that is commonly used in smaller campaigns consists of putting on pressure sensitive-adhesive labels by hand—usually with volunteer labor—at a cost of about $6-10 per thousand, but no carbons are available for future mailings.* Some computer firms avoid the labeling problem altogether by inserting a computer-prepared card into an envelope with two cellophane windows side by side. In addition to eliminating labeling costs, this process is extremely useful for sending out attractive palm cards with the voting place marked in the first window and the voter's address in the second window. In this way, part of the message reaches the addressee even if the envelope remains unopened. Window envelopes can, of course, be utilized without using computers, but computer personalization (mentioned below) adds great appeal to the mailing.

Personalized letters reproduced by offset typography with the inside address and individualized lines produced by computer cost about $50 per thousand, including printing but not postage. These are typically produced using an IBM 370 type computer which prints the addresses on continuous-form envelopes—envelopes connected to each other that are "burst" or separated, after processing—at a rate of 2,200 lines a minute. There can be problems with computer-addressed continuous-form envelopes, in that a printer has to add the bulk rate stamp and return address. Some coordination is required between the printer and the computer house in selecting the right envelope—for example, flap in or flap

---

*Mail service houses charge about $25-30 to affix a thousand labels. This is in addition to the charge of $6-10 for a thousand labels.

out, size, etc.—to avoid foul-ups. Such coordination should not be assumed to be automatic. Most of these problems, however, can be avoided by allowing enough time and by careful planning—for example, the bulk rate stamp can be pre-printed.

A useful campaign device is the computer letter that looks like a personally typed letter, individually addressed and signed with a facsimile signature (see Fig. 7-17). (In smaller campaigns, the candidate should sign these letters by hand, and it is probably advantageous to have the letters addressed by hand as well; the voter is more likely to open such an envelope.) The costs for this run $150 to $275 per thousand, including bulk rate postage and stuffing and addressing envelopes.

Another effective computer piece is a mailer that resembles a telegram envelope with the machine-printed telegram form inside (see Fig. 7-19). It can be used in many ways and for many purposes. A study conducted in New Jersey found such a piece to be 9 percent more effective than any other computer letter, largely because voters opened it, thinking it might be a telegram. The envelope might bear a legend like "Special Election Information." Telegram-style pieces are generally partially done by photo-offset.

When great amounts of money are spent on something that has been used for some time, the press sometimes gets carried away and gives it the attention usually given only to startlingly new devices. For example, Lewis Lehrman's campaign sent out three million letters in the last week of his 1982 campaign. At that time it was reported that his opponent, Mario Cuomo, was 8-12 percentage points ahead in many polls. Cuomo won only by three points, and the *Washington Post* reported that Cuomo's manager said, "All things being equal those letters would have beaten us. . . . It was the most fearsome thing I've seen in politics."*

In the nation in 1982 it was estimated that 100 million dollars or 10 percent of all campaign spending was spent on direct mail. In the California gun control referendum, alone, ten million dollars were spent on direct mail. The *Post* reported that in New Mexico, political observers thought that a targeted mail effort, followed by at least three phone calls, helped the Democrats win the gubernatorial, a Senate seat and additional state offices.

Washington Post, November 17, 1982, p. A2.

ELECTION-GRAM ELECTION-GRAM

CAR-RT PRESORT **CR04

**VOTE TUESDAY
NOVEMBER 2nd**

THE BERMAN FAMILY
3022 FERNWOOD
SAN MATEO, CA. 94403

MY GOOD FRIEND BILL ROYER URGENTLY NEEDS YOUR VOTE AND THE
VOTE OF EVERYONE IN SAN MATEO TO HELP HIM WIN HIS RACE FOR
CONGRESS. THE INCUMBENT IN THIS CAMPAIGN IS SPENDING
NEARLY A MILLION DOLLARS IN A DESPERATE ATTEMPT TO STAY IN
CONGRESS. MOST OF THIS MONEY HAS COME FROM OUTSIDE THE
DISTRICT...INDEED FROM OUTSIDE CALIFORNIA...AND THE
INCUMBENT WILL BE REPRESENTING HIS FINANCIAL DONORS, NOT
THE CITIZENS OF SAN MATEO.

THE CHOICE FOR US IS VERY CLEAR. I DON'T THINK THAT SAN
MATEO WANTS A CONGRESSMAN WHO REPRESENTS THE OLD POLITICS
OF HUGE GIVEAWAYS, HIGHER TAXES AND MORE GOVERNMENT
REGULATION OF OUR LIVES. BILL BELIEVES AS YOU AND I DO IN
THE NEED TO TRIM THE WASTE IN GOVERNMENT, PROTECT OUR
ENVIRONMENT AND REDUCE INCOME TAXES FOR ALL.

I KNOW THAT BILL WILL DO AN OUTSTANDING JOB AS OUR NEW
CONGRESSMAN. HE'S A MAN OF INTEGRITY WHO WILL BE A HARD
WORKING, EFFECTIVE AND DEDICATED REPRESENTATIVE FOR THOSE
OF US WHO LIVE AND WORK ON THE PENINSULA. THE BERMAN
FAMILY'S VOTES ARE VERY IMPORTANT IN THIS ELECTION. PLEASE
USE THEM TO SEND BILL ROYER TO CONGRESS. THANK YOU.

CONGRESSMAN PETE MCCLOSKEY

Paid for by the Republican National Committee
and the National Republican Congressional Committee

Fig. 7-19. Example of "election-gram" (San Francisco suburbs, 1982).

In the 1982 California race for governor, a letter that had enormous impact was one sent with absentee ballots to Republican households; Republican candidate George Deukemejian did extremely well among absentee voters. While he lost San Francisco 2-1, it was reported that he won 3-2 among absentee voters.

Perhaps the most interesting of the reported uses of direct mail were letters used in 1982 by the Republican Stan Parris in his successful race to dislodge incumbent Congressman Herbert Harris (Virginia). Together Parris and Harris spent over one million dollars in a very high-visibility race in the suburbs of Washington, D.C. If you have enough money, the lesson is, you can target every major concern, bias, prejudice, special interest, and fear. Parris's direct mail campaign was extremely sophisticated in that special messages were targeted to 53 different groups of voters and sent to 50,500 homes in three neighborhoods. He carried these neighborhoods which he had lost against the same opponent three years earlier. In all, a reported 1.3 million letters went out: one to firemen, another to policemen, another to teachers. A letter targeted to Alexandria voters emphasized that Parris had been instrumental in getting money to repair a local bridge that was heavily used. A letter sent by the National Rifle Association called the candidate "a proven friend of the sportsman" and alleged that the opponent had compiled "one of the worst anti-gun, anti-hunter records in Congress."

The Parris staff thought two of the letters, the "sewer" letter and the "prison" letter, were the most critical. The race was regarded as a dead heat a week before the election. In the last week, the prison letter went to 50,000 households in an area where he had lost by 924 votes two years before; on election day he won this area by 1,101 votes. The sewer letter went out a week before the election to 500 homes that had been plagued by odors from a treatment plant' Parris claimed credit for getting a federal grant that had solved the problem. He had previously lost these election districts. This time he won by 48 votes. The Parris staff thought the two letters gave their candidate the one or two percent they needed to win.

In my view, the direct mail device may be overused in some campaigns. However, the usual approach is similar to the view of William Haddad, who stated, "[the public] had learned to take television ads with a grain of salt, but people still take letters seriously."* Television was overused

---

*Washington Post, November 17, 1982, p. A2.

in the 1970s; direct mail is now the obsession of the 1980s for candidates with ample amounts of money.

In larger campaigns, the ad agency or consultant buys the mailing lists. In a smaller community there may not be commercial lists to buy so you may have to develop your own. For example, you can obtain the membership lists of local senior citizens' clubs, ethnic or religious societies, union members, church and synagogue members, tenants' and homeowners' groups, etc. The voter registration books themselves provide a key listing, and sometimes the ethnic or racial concentrations are quite evident by reviewing the names and analyzing the neighborhoods. Finally, try the firms specializing in mailing lists; there may be some wastage because they don't specialize in your area, but it still might be worth it. These specialists develop their lists over a period of time based on responses to a series of mail solicitations. They also buy base lists such as the readership of business magazines, sports magazines, and upscale magazines such as *Town and Country*, and can usually predict whether a solicitation will have a 1 or 3 or 5 percent etc., success rate. An obvious example is to use the tape of subscribers to gun and hunting periodicals for a mailing for anti-gun control contributions.

OTHER USES OF COMPUTERS IN CAMPAIGN ADVERTISING.   In addition to producing advertising mailings, computers can also be used to keep records of which voters have received which mailings, which voters have received telephone calls and what responses they gave, and which voters have met the candidate personally, called headquarters for information, volunteered to help, *ad infinitum*. In this function the computer is used as a memory bank. It is very expensive to program such a memory bank, but the expense may be justified in a large, close race. Additional uses of computers in campaign publicity are limited only by available funds and by the ingenuity and creativity of campaign and computer-house staffs.

GIVEAWAYS

Almost every campaign features some type of giveaway largely because it has come to be expected and because it provides visibility. The most popular giveaways are of course buttons, which are produced by the thousands and hardly ever worn. William J. Pfeiffer, one of Nelson

Rockefeller's campaign managers, was quoted as saying, "Somewhere around this city [New York] there are two million Rockefeller buttons. Where are they? You can stand all day on the busiest street corner and not see one of them. On the other hand, if you didn't have them, you'd hear from every county chairman in the state that you weren't doing anything for them. Some day, somebody's going to have the guts to throw the buttons out."* Pfeiffer was right, yet most campaigns have buttons because that's the way it's always been done. Pfeiffer has also been quoted as saying that 25 percent of the money in any campaign is leaked right out the window. In my experience, the percentage is often higher than that, and buttons and other giveaways are responsible for a proportion of the waste. If you have fiscal constraints in a campaign, it's silly to spend funds for giveaways just because everyone else does, particularly if the potential return in changed votes is not great.

Joe Napolitan is among the big-name campaign consultants who doubt the utility of gimmick giveaways. Combs, bookmarks, ballpoint pens, rulers, rain bonnets, nail files, shopping bags, eyeglass cases, key chains, and balloons are expensive and rarely change a significant number of votes.**

Two giveaways, in my experience, do seem to be effective. One, used by Walter Diamond in congressional campaigns, consisted of a small ballpoint pen (with the candidate's name) enclosed with a thank-you card that was sent to every voter who had signed the nominating petitions. Purchasing the pens, handling, mailing, and printing the thank-you card all cost money, but it was a focused investment, a thoughtful gesture that pleased many people and could not offend anyone. Relatively inexpensive plastic shopping bags are in continued use and, unlike campaign buttons, are highly visible.*** Costs for good quality bags run from 25 cents to

---

*Robert MacNeil, *The People Machine: The Influence of Television on American Politics* (New York: Harper & Row, 1968, p. 233).

**In my home district, a local candidate offered people free car washes if they could show that they had voted; many voted but apparently for the other candidate, since the giveaway sponsor was defeated 4:1.

***Shopping bags have become an obsession. In the Bronx Democratic primaries of 1972, an estimated 2.5 million shopping bags were given out by congressional, judicial, and other candidates. There are only 150,000 Bronx Democratic primary voters. One Bronx voter told a candidate that he had collected twelve hundred political shopping bags; when he had five thousand shopping bags, he intended to have his name entered and run for office himself. Ten years later, the obsession remained just as compelling.

35 cents each including printing. The bags usually are ordered in lots of 10,000.

To provide maximum effectiveness for your money, shopping bags should be well-designed from both an artistic and a functional point of view. They should be attractive, with an uncluttered pattern and with clear colors that do not rub off, they should be convenient to carry, with handles that do not break or stretch out of shape, and they should be strong enough not to burst when they are full. They need not be the largest size available. Some New York department stores now provide relatively small (11 x 11 inches) plastic shopping bags, which are used over and over again judging from the frequency with which they are seen on the street. Whatever their size, the bags should be easily recognizable as yours and they should be convenient, attractive, and durable enough that people will carry them frequently.

In one senatorial campaign, a candidate had silk scarves and ties designed to be given to larger contributors as souvenirs. On a mass basis, however, scarves, balloons, rulers, or lighters are not really effective, in the judgment of most professionals. They are frequently used on the basis of "why not?—it's not that expensive," but taken together it *is* that expensive and the money could be better spent elsewhere.*

STREET CAMPAIGNING

In local campaigns, and to a lesser degree in national campaigning as well, meeting the voters on the streets remains an important part of campaign public relations. It is the most direct and often the best advertising technique. National candidates visit large factories or make lunch-hour speeches in areas where office workers are concentrated. In local campaigns, half of a candidate's energies may profitably go into street campaigning and personal door-to-door campaigning. This campaigning can be critical since voters meeting the candidate talk to their families and friends about their impressions; these impressions in local races can be more important than party or ideology.

Some basic rules do exist for street campaigning. If you're using telephones or direct mail in your campaign, use these media to give some

---

*In Milwaukee, for example, political candidates gave out blotters, despite the fact that most people now use ballpoint pens which do not require a blotter. In West Virginia, candidates provide liquor, since that is the custom. Now, *that's* sensible.

advance notice that you will be in a given public place at a given hour and day. You may wish to have workers with bullhorns advertise your presence int he neighborhood. Some candidates prefer to use cars equipped with loudspeakers that cruise the area indicating where you are and what your walking schedule will be. Other candidates prefer to be accompanied by a coterie to give out campaign literature or by members of their families to develop voter rapport. Stop and talk to groups of people if possible, but don't impose on them. Many voters will be cordial even if they have no intention of voting for you; do not make the mistake of thinking, as greater men have done before you, that a warm reception on the streets assures you a victory at the polls.

Obviously, street campaigning works out best in areas where there are clusters of voters. In major cities, campaigning at subway stops is popular. (In New York City, this is now automatic. I had something to do with initiating the custom in James H. Scheuer's congressional campaign in 1961.) Parks and shopping centers are also important. If you can find a place where voters are clustered and where other candidates are not campaigning, by all means use it. For example, one candidate running in a suburban New York district campaigned very successfully at the New York City terminal of the express bus line serving his area; soon his opponent, sensing a good idea, began doing the same thing.

In small campaigns—for assembly or district leader—the most effective campaigning is probably done door-to-door. Properly, you should start three to six months before election day, since you can cover only a few voters per evening. Meeting the voters in their homes is time-consuming and exhausting, but it is most effective not only in gaining votes immediately but also in setting up a base for direct mail, telephone calls, and newspaper ads if you can afford these reinforcements.

LOUDSPEAKERS

Many candidates send sound trucks through their districts blasting away with their endorsements and their qualifications. Some of these broadcast recorded cassettes, but usually the loudspeaker is manned by a campaign worker accompanying the driver. In some areas, this technique offends many voters and is not worth the investment. In my judgment, loudspeakers are seldom helpful except in special situations. In a recent four-way race for a judgeship, for example, *The New York Times* endorsed one candidate three days before the election. For the next three days, the endorsed candidate used loudspeakers to announce that he had been endorsed by the *Times* and selected as most qualified by a lawyers' screening committee. He won in a 4,000-2,000-1,000-1,000 break, despite the fact that he had not used direct mail, street campaigning, or telephones, while his opponents had put posters all over the district and put literature under multitudes of front doors. He won very handily and very economically as well.

Used purposefully—for example, manned by a celebrity or putting a last-minute endorsement before the largest possible audience—loudspeakers are a useful public-relations tool. Used indiscriminately, however, they are a blight to the ear, just as last year's campaign posters are blight to the eye, and they are likely to lose as many votes as they gain. Over the last decade, there seems to be less and less use of this device because voters seem to pay little attention or can't really hear the message distinctly from loudspeakers mounted on trucks or cars.

8
Press and Public Relations

The previous chapters on political advertising described a number of ways of getting the campaign message to the voters that all involved paying commercial rates for the privilege. These included the various forms of print, radio, and television advertising. In smaller-scale campaigns, coverage by newspapers, radio, and television stations affect voters' decisions to a great extent while requiring no direct payment. For this reason the details of press and public relations require the same degree of thoughtful planning and professional quality execution as paid media.

IMPACT OF NEWS COVERAGE

Newspaper, television, and radio news coverage are at least as important as direct advertising.* Most experienced political mechanics agree that newspaper and radio-TV news coverage alone can influence at least one-fourth of your vote. This estimate is based on the observation that undecided or independent voters often tend to make up their minds on the basis of news reportage. Some of these voters are also influenced by the editorial recommendations of their local newspaper, particularly in primaries and for secondary offices.

My experience indicates that the cumulative impact of television, radio, and newspaper coverage of the campaign will affect at least as many voters as will ideological, ethnic, racial, or religious ties. Because of this, getting television and newspaper coverage is a very serious consideration. In the larger cities and states, merely running for office will not assure you of receiving such coverage. Some county and township newspapers, on the other hand, find primary and general election fights very

---

*The dollar value of such free coverage has not gone unacknowledged by some candidates. There have been rumors in many campaigns that some newspaper reporters were on a candidate's personal payroll to guarantee coverage and a friendly interpretation of events. Such payoffs are not uncommon in American business, and it would not be surprising if they sometimes occurred in campaigning. Besides being immoral and possibly illegal, however, this tactic can backfire if it is discovered and made public by an opponent. I don't recommend trying it; the risks are greater than the rewards. But this doesn't mean you shouldn't be friendly with the journalists covering your campaign. It makes life easier and you'll learn as much as they will, even if your bar bill is likely to be greater.

interesting and often will go to the candidates for news. In larger states and cities, however, elections for Congress and local offices take place in districts, each of which represents only a small fraction of the newspaper readership or the radio and television audience. The mass media can't possibly give full coverage to all these races. There are so many primary fights in the New York metropolitan area, for example, that even *The New York Times,* which prides itself on being a newspaper of record, can give comprehensive coverage to only a fraction of the races in the metropolitan area that it serves. In such a situation, the candidate has the problem of making news, of being interesting without running naked through the streets—he can't assume that the press and television will come to him.*

Controversy creates news; emotional confrontations are interesting to the public; accusations and actions invite attention. One politician, seeking to dramatize the pollution crisis, made headlines and the six o'clock television news in New York by taking a brief swim in the Hudson River, whose filth is of legendary proportions. Issue papers hardly ever get press and television attention unless they include examples of corruption by the opponent or the opponent's party. Public service lawsuits—for example, a suit charging a public utility with polluting a river—are increasingly popular as a way of getting public attention, but they are expensive, and you run the risk of losing both the lawsuit and some credibility if you don't have a very strong case. If you plan on such a suit, your budget should include at least $10,000 for legal fees. The injustice must be a real one; to make it politically worthwhile, your cause should be one that already has significant public sympathy.

The basic device in campaigns to get media attention is the press release (see Fig. 8-1). They should be timely, succinct, and well-written. All facts and names should be checked for accuracy. There should be a number

---

*Stimson Bullitt, a two-time candidate for Congress in Seattle, advised: "Without sacrifice of the public interest, a compromise can be struck between saying nothing about anything and letting the chips fly. A man's duty demands candor, while his survival demands discretion. As much as possible, a politician must refrain from criticism of individuals and groups, except by inference; such talk is the main source of antagonisms . . . When asked about a pending issue, he has the duty to speak out clear and straight. But one may mitigate the rancor of those who feel the other way, phrasing one's declaration in terms which accommodate the audience. General answers of opinion are more likely to inflame than specific answers of fact. Arguing the merits of a specific solution to a problem is safer than asserting controversial principles, which may antagonize whether understood or misunderstood, and more useful than asserting principles on which everyone agrees." (*To Be A Politician,* New York: Doubleday, 1959, pp. 58-59.)

to call for additional information. They should be prepared and released only if there is real news content.

Television and press interviews may be an important source of free publicity in congressional, county, city, and statewide races; and Sunday discussion programs, innocuous as they usually are, cumulatively can be very significant in a campaign. Many technicians believe that a large proportion of undecided voters watch these programs and are influenced by them.

Managers often advise candidates not to say too much on specific issues on interview programs in order not to irritate too many client groups. If you're an incumbent, the advice generally is to emphasize your legislative achievements, particularly the construction of new facilities, as much as possible. If you're a challenger, regardless of which questions you're asked by a television interviewer, the most widespread advice seems to be to criticize your opponent's record. Candidates usually do not answer publicly asked questions in a straightforward manner. Their managers advise them to always present their own case; the questions are simply often ignored or answered ambiguously. Yet some politicians, such as New York's outspoken Mayor Ed Koch, have made reputations as sensational newsmakers by habitually speaking their minds.

COMPONENTS OF PRESS AND PUBLIC RELATIONS

The candidate's personal attention and concentration is required for developing speeches and preparing for debates, interviews and meetings with editorial boards. In large-scale campaigns there are usually specialists available who take care of these details—for example, speechwriters, schedulers, advance people, issue paper researchers, and press and media relations professionals, either on a full- or part-time basis. In a smaller-scale campaign it is unlikely that you will need all these specialists, even if you are lucky enough to be able to afford them. Generally, one person will take on these responsibilities, supplemented from time to time by volunteers helping on issue papers or on speechwriting, for example.

The logistics of press and public relations involve the following items.

- Press releases
- Issue statements (and their summaries)
- Texts of speeches

- Media Kits
- Preparation for public meetings
- Preparation for interviews by press and media reporters, and by editorial boards
- Preparation for press conferences
- Letters to newspapers and to community and/or neighborhood organizations
- Radio actualities (or "beepers").

PRESS RELEASES

A news release used by Congressman Nick Mavroules in his successful 1982 race is reproduced in Fig. 8-1. Note the brief paragraphing and simple sentence structure. The "lead" or first paragraph contains the essence of the platform. (Generally, the lead answers the questions: who, what, when, where, and, secondarily, why and how.) In preparing the press release it is helpful to write it so that it can be read aloud—the cadences and emphases should be natural and interesting to a radio listener as well as to a reader. The release shown was less than two pages long. The release date is stated. The number "30" at the end is simply the journalistic convention for the end. Note that the release is specific and concentrates on only one or two items. While not used here, it is common for the press release to contain on the top left of the first page the campaign press contact person and his or her phone number. Keep in mind that the sole object of a press release is to "get ink," to get space in a newspaper (or time on radio and television news programs). The release should be timely and newsworthy; otherwise, don't send it out. Should you send out what reporters regard as self-serving, gratuitous and ambiguous material, they'll simply stop taking you or your releases seriously.

Releases can be used for a number of purposes. Often, they are used to announce your campaign. Some candidates use their home or the steps of City Hall or a conveniently located hotel or motel suite to do this with their supporters, family, and friends providing a tumultuous backdrop that is good for radio and television coverage. In any case, the press release should say why you're running, what your issues are, your endorsements, and why you're better than your opponent. Press releases are used also to identify your key staff and consultants, to state your

Nick Mavroules
DEMOCRATIC CONGRESSMAN

FOR RELEASE AFTER:

6 PM, Tuesday, October 12, 1982

MAVROULES ENTERS HOME STRETCH IN RE-ELECTION BID

    Danvers - Democratic Congressman Nick Mavroules kicked off
his final drive to retain the Sixth District seat, listing as
national priorities jobs, a sound federal budget, and a nuclear
weapons freeze.

    Mavroules called the general elections, just three weeks
away, a "verdict" on the nation's future.

    Speaking before a packed house of well-wishers at the
King's Grant motel, the two-term congressman said that "We
must revive the American Dream of opportunity all Americans
can share -- the opportunity to have a good education, a job
and a home, and a secure future."

    "And the nuclear arms race must be stopped before we
reach the brink of economic ruin, or worse," added Mavroules,
a member of the House armed services committee.

    Mavroules' three point agenda for the nation would include:

    o A jobs program to put record numbers of Americans
back to work repairing and maintaining the nation's roads, bridges,
sewer and water systems, and other essential public facilities.

    o A Pay As You Go budget that would freeze spending at
1982 levels and require Washington to find the funding for each
new program it wants to authorize.

    o And immediate arms freeze between the United States and
the Soviet Union to remove the risk of nuclear confrontation and
to loosen up funds tied up in defense programs for social and
economic purposes.

    "This administration and my Republican opponent seem indifferent

Paid for & authorized by: Mavroules for Congress Committee, P.O. Box 3431, Peabody, Mass. 01960
A copy of our report is filed with the Federal Election Commission and is available for purchase from the Federal Election Commission. Washington. D.C

Mavroules - General Election Kick-off
October 12, 1982
Page 2

to the major concerns this agenda would address," Mavroules

charged.

    The two-term Democrat said it is the "job of a congressman"
to address the problems confronting the American people. "And
I believe that the voters of the Sixth District will return
me to Washington to do the job they expect their congressman
to do."

Fig. 8-1. Example of a campaign press release.

assets, income, and tax situation (increasingly necessary in campaigning because of the growing public awareness and distrust of public officials' venality), and to respond to attacks, criticisms and misstatements by opponents. In addition, they are used to state your stands on the issues and your reactions to local or statewide controversies and to legislative proposals of interest to your constituencies and to the press. Endorsements that you make or get are often newsworthy.

Your press liaison should be selected at the beginning of the campaign. It is good practice for this staff member to be the only one to deal with the press to assure consistency with news representatives of all media and to encourage timely and responsible follow-through; for example, he or she should make certain that press questions are answered and that reporters' phone calls are returned the same day. It is also a good idea to keep promises and appointments with press people; if you or your press person say you'll get a background piece over to the newspaper by 9:30 A.M., make sure that it's done. Your word should mean something; it helps develop decent personal and professional relationships with media people. Generally, most newspaper people regard themselves as fine writers; whatever you do, don't criticize their writing style. It is often counseled to treat each reporter in a straightforward manner; don't play favorites—don't give one reporter the best stories or a jump on the competition. It really doesn't pay and makes you and your campaign staff resented. Don't criticize reporters to their superiors unless their coverage was really outrageously biased and hurts your campaign. You can certainly discuss a published article with a reporter if you think the facts are wrong or that the information he or she got from the opponent failed to include some basic background, but try to avoid instructing a reporter how to write the story; *that* is really unforgivable to a professional journalist.

Your news person has to prepare literate, timely, and newsworthy releases. The effort is wasted if the distribution list is not complete. Also, the releases should get to everyone on the list at a time convenient for the press run or for the radio and television news at 6:00 P.M. and 11:00 P.M. They have to live by these deadlines, and you have to be sensitive to them as well.

It is generally a good idea for the press person early in the campaign to at least introduce him/herself on the phone to the city editor (of a newspaper) or the managers of the local radio and television news departments. It would be even better, if time allows, for your press liaison to visit the newspapers and station news people, delivering a set of brochures, slides, and photographs (often termed a media kit) that provides the basic campaign background material.

ISSUE STATEMENTS AND SPEECHES

Issue statements are essentially brief essays, usually written to be read and not spoken, that explicate your stands on the issues that are before the public as major policy proposals or critical decisions that have to be made. The choice of these issues very often has the effect of keying the campaign. Few voters read the full issue statements, yet when they are summarized and discussed by media, they become part of the vocabulary of the campaign.

It can be dangerous, then, to select inappropriate issues. By inappropriate I mean those that the public has not been prepared for or those they cannot perceive as containing any relevance to their family's day-to-day needs and concerns. Issues that are too far out or identified with super-radical or superconservative movements, which sometimes are quite legitimate expressions of public concern, can be made by your opponent to sound dangerously irresponsible. The selection of these issues, then, is not a casual matter. You should state the problem in terms that many voters can clearly recognize and identify with, indicating the basic alternatives (with cost, service, and related consequences), your position and why you've taken it, and, if at all possible, a comparison with your opponent's record and views. The press, and the public as well, are not likely to appreciate issue statements that are ambiguous, wordy, self-serving, and grandiose. For convenience, summaries of lengthy statements should be made available.

The same suggestions would apply to the preparation of major speeches. In smaller groups, extemporaneous sounding talks rather than ''speeches'' are much preferred and much more effective, in my experience. Copies and summaries of these speeches should also be made available to the press as well as to civic and community groups that may be affected. In writing the speech, you may want to block out portions that you can use for radio news or advertising.

MEDIA KITS

These are folders or envelopes putting together campaign material as a convenience for the reporters covering your campaign. Elaborate stationery isn't really required. The ''kit'' can include:

- The official biography
- Your personal professional/business/political background
- Your official photograph (a black-and-white glossy)
- Thirty-five-millimeter color slides and a matte finish black-and-white photo for use by television stations
- Your basic speech
- Important news releases
- A summary fact sheet
- The basic brochure that you're mailing.

It makes sense to inquire of political friends what they think is best for your area in the way of a media kit. It's also helpful to get some background on each reporter, how reliable and professional they can be expected to be, and which aspects of the campaign are likely to interest them. For example, one journalist may have an issues orientation, while another may be especially interested in the financial costs of campaigning.

PUBLIC MEETINGS

Important public meetings will usually get at least some press coverage. You should know something of the history of the group you are addressing and the names (and their proper pronunciation) of the key officials. You or your staff should have researched the issues and anticipated the questions they will ask. You or your community or civic group liaison perhaps should have lunch with the organization's leadership to discuss the issues most important to them. It is also essential that the advance function be take care of; people in the neighborhood should be advised of the meeting—by printed handbills or using the phone bank. Newspapermen have the habit of counting or estimating the number of people in an audience and correlating this, however wrongly, with the success of your campaigning. Allow yourself enough time for your presentation and for questions and answers. I have often seen candidates overbooked and rush from one meeting to the next abruptly. It leaves a bad impression with the audience and negates to a considerable extent the time and effort you've already put in.

DEMOCRATIC CONGRESSMAN

POSITION PAPER ON THE NUCLEAR ARMS FREEZE

"The accumulation of nuclear arms has
to be constrained if mankind is not
to destroy itself."

-Henry Kissinger
Former Secretary of State

Regarding the dangerous, ever-escalating nuclear arms race
between the United States and the Soviet Union, I favor the concept
of immediately imposing a mutual and verifiable freeze on testing,
deployment and production of nuclear weapons.

My position on this matter is clear, unequivocal and long-standing.
I first made public my support of the "freeze" as early as December
1981, before receiving petitions from over 10,000 concerned citizens
of the 6th Congressional District.

My support of the concept is based on the information presented
to me during deliberations I was privy to as a member of the House
Armed Services Committee.

No one is more concerned about the security of the United States
than Nick Mavroules. If I did not believe that a rough parity or an
acceptable equivalence of nuclear might presently existed between the
two super-powers, and if I thought for one moment there was a significant
imbalance that jeopardized our national security, I never would have
supported the freeze.

Because arms control agreements like the freeze affect the national
security of the United States, trust and good intentions are not enough.

-more-

Paid for & authorized by: Mavroules for Congress Committee, P.O. Box 3431, Peabody, Mass. 01960

A copy of our report is filed with the Federal Election Commission and is available for purchase from the Federal Election Commission. Washington. D.C.

Fig. 8-2. Example of press release. Boston suburbs, 1982.

page 2
THE NUCLEAR ARMS FREEZE

Rather, any arms control agreement must be based on the U.S. ability
to verify treaty compliance.

Among the most frequently expressed objections to the proposed
nuclear weapons freeze is the argument that a freeze on production
of nuclear weapons could not be verified.

Verification is both a technical and political process.

As former Secretary of Defense Harold Brown stated, adequate
verification capability does not mean "that we will be able to measure
every quanity on every test or every missile, bomber, cruise missile
or submarine." What adequate verification translates into, according
to Secretary Brown, is the assurance that the Soviet Union could not
"tilt the balance strategically by violating the treaty (SALT II) without our knowing it early enough to respond and prevent them from doing
so."

President Reagan's chief arms control negotiator, Paul Nitze, has
in the past testified that "verification capabilities should be tailored
to the security significance of any violation." A freeze would mean
to stop all activities in any weapons programs. The detection of even
one missile or bomber would be evidence of a violation, and force the
United States to respond appropriately.

Former Director of the Central Intelligence Agency, William E. Colby,
told the Senate Armed Services Committee, in expressing his belief that
arms control agreements are verifiable:

> We are responsible for our security. We must identify
> threats to our security before they become substantial,
> and that is the purpose of verification...All we need
> to do is identify a substantial danger to our country,
> and then we have the responsibility of reacting to pro-
> tect our security. That is what verification is all
> about.

page 3
THE NUCLEAR ARMS RACE

> The purpose of verification is to protect us, not to
> win legal points. The true standard then, is whether
> we can verify the agreement adequately to protect our-
> selves, a different question from whether we can detect
> every single action by the other side that might consti-
> tute less than the most precise compliance with the terms
> of an agreement.

Our nuclear arsenal is sufficient to deter, and if need be, ob-
literate our foe. In fact both the arsenals of the United States and
the Soviet Union are bursting at the seams.

Each new advance in weapons technology by one side compels the
other to counter with one of its own. That is one of the reasons why
I led the fight to stop production of the MX missile, a new "counter-
force" weapon that would act to destabilize the nuclear balance of power.

Because I believe there presently exists an acceptable equivalence
and because I fear time is running out on our ability to control the
nuclear arms race, I support the nuclear weapons freeze.

The time for a halt is now.

Fig. 8-2. (Continued)

PRESS AND MEDIA INTERVIEWS

These require the same careful preparation as described above. Often, the questions will be quite the same. But try not to sound bored and jaded. Try to vary the words, the expressions, the too-pat answers. If they're covering the campaign they've heard you say these things before. Try to answer to the point. (This is what lawyers tell their clients in court, preparing answers for the questions they know will be coming in the cross-examination; the idea is to impress the judge and the jury. It's much the same preparing for interviews by a journalist.)

You should sound assured, comfortable, and knowledgeable, but not egocentric, pompous, and overbearing. There's a big range in between these extremes. They don't expect you to be a Nobel prize winner. Don't condescend to press people; treat them as knowledgeable and somewhat cynical people. Don't go off the record unless you're absolutely certain the journalist is reliable. Journalists have an expression, "They'd give up their mother for a page one story," and some indeed will give up your confidence if the story is really extraordinary. If you allow personal interviews, all the journalists will expect handles for their stories different from their colleagues'; the only way to assure this is to schedule these individual interviews at intervals throughout the campaign.

Sometimes, in a close campaign, a newspaper editorial endorsement can make the difference. Some local papers take the matter lightly and endorse on the basis of ideology, party, or instruction from the publisher based on purely business reasons. But often, the editor or editorial board will invite you to a lengthy interview. (The *New York Times* usually interviews a local candidate for an hour; in many cases I am aware of, these interviews became decisive in determining the endorsement of this powerful, extraordinary newspaper.) This requires and is worth spending a good deal of time preparing for. The questions will be precise, the policy implications will be examined with care, and your relationships with other politicians and business interests will be questioned. Be candid, factually correct, and thoughtful as to the relationship of specific controversial decisions to one another; be sure of your numbers, particularly as to tax revenues, costs, deficits, levels of service, and numbers of aged, poor, sick, etc. Your personal presence will be very much part of this examination process. Dress well and comfortably. God help us, but appearance, as superficial a factor as exists, does help people make up their minds about us. Avoid the freshly blown-dry coiffures and manicured and buffed nails that many politicians seem to think is expected. Talk to other candidates who have been through the inquisition; get the names and backgrounds of the people who'll be torturing you. Avoid lobbying. One candidate I know had the editorial writer's tennis partner try to brainwash him and implored all their common social friends to "work" on the man. I really think this type of activity, more often than not, doesn't work and may achieve rather opposite results than those intended.

PRESS CONFERENCES

These require time to prepare, but much of that time will have already been invested in the other facets of press and public relations. There are a number of methods of organizing a press conference; the best is probably to give an advance news release to the journalists covering your race, followed by a personal invitation by telephone. If television coverage is expected, your staff will have to coordinate the logistics of lighting, power sources, wiring, etc. A copy of your comments or speech should be given out at the conference. Again, you should have anticipated the questions that will follow your presentation. The most important rule to remember is to be very certain that you're calling a conference to announce something that is "news" for the reporters, not something that you and your staff just think is news. These conferences should be limited to those subjects that will be interesting both to the journalists and to the voters.

A. Steinberg points out in his *Political Campaign Handbook* that common questions at news conferences are of the genre, "When did you stop beating your wife?" The correct response, he advised, is not, "I do not beat my wife," since the headline, "Candidate denies wifebeating charge," could result. The correct response would be, "I believe very strongly in the institution of marriage. Perhaps my happiness reflects the happiness my wife and I have shared for the last twenty-four years. . . . No marriage is perfect, but ours comes as close as anyone's."* This is good advice in avoiding troublesome yes or no questions in conferences; answer the question by stating your own views. While a calculated maliciousness

---

*Arnold Steinberg, *Politicial Campaign Handbook* (Lexington, Mass.: Lexington Books, exhibit 4-1).

DEMOCRATIC CONGRESSMAN

FACTS AT A GLANCE

United States Representative Nicholas Mavroules

DISTRICT: Sixth District, Massachusetts

PARTY: Democrat

COMMITTEES: <u>Principal</u>: Armed Services (Subcommittees on
               Procurement, Investigation). Small Business
               (Subcommittee on Energy, Environment, and
               Safety Issues).

               <u>Other</u>: Northeast-Midwest Congressional Coalition.
               The New England Congressional Caucus. The Demo-
               cratic Caucus Task Force on National Security.
               the Ad Hoc Committee on Irish Affairs.

HIGHLIGHTS: . Led floor fight to stop production of MX missile.
               . Endorsed mutual, immediate nuclear weapons freeze
                 movement, November, 1981.
               . Authored bill, approved by full House, that would
                 direct military to use renewable sources of energy.
               . Introduced legislation providing basis of new law
                 preventing excessive profits on defense contracts.
               . Led fight to save McDonnell FA-18 Navy jet and
                 3,000 area jobs.
               . Introduced legislation to encourage small business
                 contracting with federal government.

BIRTHDATE: November 1, 1929   PLACE: Peabody, Massachusetts

HOME: Peabody, Massachusetts

FAMILY: Married to Mary (Silva) Mavroules. Three daughters:
               Debbie, Gail, and Brenda

EDUCATION: Peabody School Systems

CAREERS: Peabody City Councilor, 1958-61, 1964-65
               Peabody Mayor, 1967-1978

Paid for & authorized by: Mavroules for Congress Committee, P.O. Box 3431, Peabody, Mass. 01960

A copy of our report is filed with the Federal Election Commission and is available for purchase from the Federal Election Commission, Washington, D C

Fig. 8-3. Example of fact sheet, Boston suburbs, 1982.

informs some journalists' questioning; most will question you on straight-forward matters in a direct way.

You should always be willing to talk about any legitimate issue. Try to be direct, interesting, and informed. Avoid ambiguities and trendy phrases.

LETTERS TO EDITORS

Sometimes this device is used to counter an error or genuine inadvertent misinterpretation that appeared in the news reportage. It's needed to clarify serious and unintentional misunderstandings. Letters, on specific issues and problems, to civic and community groups are also important for good public relations.

RADIO ACTUALITIES ("BEEPERS")

These are essentially spot news items that candidates make available to radio stations for news programs. Candidates cut tapes and make them available to the stations. Usually, the actualities consist of the most critical segments of a press release, read by the candidate, or news that is most effective released the same day (which only radio and television are capable of). The tape is usually 30 to 60 seconds in duration.

You can record the candidate making a speech (key segments), talking to voters at a civic group, stating positions on issues, etc. Generally, press releases make the information available to newspapers at the same time for publication the following day. The technical details of feeding the tapes to the radio stations should be worked out carefully, but it is a simpler matter than you might expect.

9
Using Telephones in a Political Campaign

In a campaign, effective phone calls are like a marksman's bullets; posters, signs, radio and television are like a sweeping barrage of artillery—maybe they'll hit some of the right voters, but the odds are they'll hit mostly the wrong ones. But at least an incompetent campaigner doesn't kill anybody.

—A Political Mechanic

In political telephone campaigns in the 1950s a simple canvass call was usual—for example, "Come out and vote on election day for Candidate A." Later, because many candidates were charmed by sophisticated technology, recorded messages had a period of popularity. Currently, professional campaigners use telephone calls to try to ascertain which voters are favorable, unfavorable, or undecided about their candidacy. In 1982, telephones were commonly used in large-scale campaigns to establish which issues concerned undecided voters, and a computer letter on the appropriate issue was then sent to each undecided voter. Despite all the possible approaches, however, the effectiveness of telephoning ultimately depends on the quality of the message and the individual caller's ability to gain rapport with the voter being called.*

An organized telephone effort is a feature of most larger-scale political campaigns. It may be directed by amateurs or by professionals and may range from the candidate's relatives and friends making random personal appeals, each different from the other, to campaigns such as the Bradley-Deukmejian gubernatorial contest in California in 1982, in which hundreds of professionally trained interviewers made over a million structured calls.

Telephone campaigns by paid or volunteer callers are useful if organized under experienced, professional direction and if the message content and method of delivery are supervised intelligently. Unplanned and un-

---

*In my view, quality includes a message that changes as campaign issues and emphases change; quality also depends on the ability to closely coordinate the telephone campaign with all media components.

supervised telephone campaigns can have negative effects. A voter insulted or annoyed by a telephone canvasser may tell friends and relatives about it, and several such occurrences can adversely affect a tight election. Word of mouth, the most powerful of all campaign determinants, in my judgment, can be both negative and positive.

A telephone campaign must be kept within the context of the overall campaign. Calls should present the same themes as other advertising media used in the campaign, but they should be primarily focused on groups that are minimally affected by the other media. They should be used when it is felt that conversation can make a more lasting and effective impact.

Telephoning should be regarded as a form of canvassing, for many of the same principles apply to both procedures. Whether contacting voters in person or by telephone, the caller is the candidate's personal representative and must be sufficiently well-acquainted with the candidate's stands on issues of particular concern to the voters to be able to answer reasonable questions immediately, courteously, and sensibly. A telephone call or personal visit in which the worker recites a memorized statement and is not prepared to answer questions is not likely to be effective. Asking voters who they expect to vote for doesn't convert voters, yet it is commonly done in massive and costly campaigns.* Engaging a voter in conversation and answering his or her questions in a forthright, friendly manner can have considerably greater impact.

BASIC REQUIREMENTS

Institute a comprehensive telephone campaign only if you or your campaign management team are convinced that significant benefits will accrue and not simply because your opponent is using telephones. The benefits may consist entirely of "firming up" friendly voters and proselytizing new voters, or they may also include research spin-offs, such as establishing just who the undecided voters are and how they may be reached through theme or issue development or through media.

To emphasize an important principle discussed at greater length in Chapter 3, the undecided are the 20 to 25 percent of the registered voters who do not make up their minds until late in the campaign. A few of

*This type of call is simply "I.D.," that is, to identify favorables to pull on election day.

them don't vote at all, but the group as a whole frequently casts the "swing" or determining vote in elections. Since the margin in most elections is usually under 10 percent of the total vote, they are critically important. Establishing their characteristics and number is worth money and time.

If the conversations are carefully structured, information gathered in your telephone canvass can provide a valuable supplement or "input" to your campaign research, as well as serving an advertising function.*

In some situations, calling every voter in a district—for example, in a district where research indicates that 90 percent of the vote is yours— is pointless and possibly harmful, since you may alienate voters who become annoyed at what they consider too many irritations in the course of a political campaign. You could probably spend the money more profitably in districts where you are not too popular. On primary or election day, however, brief calls usually should be made to remind "favorables" to vote.

Use telephones only when you can guarantee proper supervision to provide some control on message development, message delivery, and message follow-up. There are people whose telephone voice or manner is so bad—and even worse without direction—that, with all the good will in the world, they can cheerfully and energetically destroy your candidacy. Each voice on the telephone is the voice of the candidate for the 100 to 500 voters who hear it. In the judgment of many political professionals, a woman's voice and telephone presence are much more effective than a man's, particularly in areas where nuisance or obscene calls are common.

Use telephones when demographic and voting-pattern analysis and comprehensive, organized pre-testing indicate that worthwhile results are probable and that other techniques will not be more effective or less costly. Some areas have been so inundated by advertising and market research telephone campaigns that if you add your political calls, you can expect to arouse considerable irritation—and your money will have been wasted. In some areas, the local, state, and national parties and candidates all do telephone campaigning; in such a situation, your call,

---

*"Input," like "infra-structure" and "parameters," was a trendy word for politicians in 1982. Such words don't mean much—they are often used to avoid the necessity for original thinking—so they change almost every year.

one of many, tends to have minimum impact unless it is done with very experienced people, who tend to be quite expensive. Consider the impacts carefully, after pre-testing several hundred calls in various areas, before you launch a major telephone campaign.

Ideally, telephones should be used only in those areas where substantial numbers of voters live whom you wish to appeal to and whom your research shows to be at least 60 percent favorable or undecided. In selected cases, you may feel you have to call into areas where your opponent is strong to try to get some of his supporters to your side, but then you run the risk of reinforcing his or her vote rather than increasing your own. These are not simple decisions, and you should discuss the problems with experienced politicians and with other persons of mature judgment before deciding what to do.

Do not attempt to conduct a comprehensive telephone campaign (over 50,000 calls) unless professional supervision can be assured at each central location and some flexibility built into the calling procedures. In many campaigns where continuous professional monitoring and supervision are not used, the telephone message is frozen early and never changed, although issues and voter responses may change drastically during the campaign or may differ significantly in different areas.* Unless there is constant professional supervision of the operation to assure that the message reflects current developments, a great deal of money and motion will be wasted. If you can't retain a professional consultant but still wish to have a telephone campaign, give someone with mature judgment from your personal staff full-time responsibility for the telephone operation.

Calls should be made only from central locations. You can't provide supervision economically if you have numerous scattered locations or if calls are made from individual homes.

Use professionals as interviewers, if possible. Volunteers can't be properly supervised, and they don't always show up when scheduled. According to William J. Pfeiffer, Nelson Rockefeller's former campaign manager, one professional is usually worth five or ten volunteers.** I've

---

*Even professional phone consultants sometimes freeze the message quite early—some, because it reduces their costs considerably; some, because they have no understanding of the overall campaign. These consultants believe their function is simply to manufacture a given number of calls.

**James M. Perry, *The New Politics* (New York: Potter, 1968, p. 126).

seen campaigns that used both volunteers and professionals, and overall, I would advise employing professionals, who arrive on schedule and will accept direction. Even with volunteers, telephone campaigns involve expenditures for rent, furniture, telephone installation, food and refreshments, message development, and often miscellaneous items like transportation and babysitting. You can probably bring off a small-area campaign involving 5,000 to 10,000 calls with a few reliable volunteers, but in sizable telephone campaigns, volunteers tend to be inefficient and more costly than usually anticipated.

WHEN TO CALL

Telephone campaigns should start no sooner than four weeks before election day. If the time span is longer than that, the average voter tends to forget. Set-up work—looking up telephone numbers, obtaining computer printouts by election districts, developing the message (or messages) and the voters' probable questions and desired answers, and renting space, furniture, and other facilities—should start ten to twelve weeks before election day.

Calls should be made between 6 P.M. and 9:30 P.M. weekday evenings in order to get as many voters as possible at home. Don't call on public and religious holidays or weekends. Saturday calling between 11 A.M. and 3 P.M. can be effective unless local or religious custom prohibits it.

COSTS

A major telephone campaign runs to money. If it is done without relation to the central theme and without quality-control considerations, the net effective costs can be catastrophic, since the results from the investment will be substantially diminished.

Costs can range from $10,000 to $15,000 for a modest campaign in state assembly or city council races to hundreds of thousands of dollars for gubernatorial, senatorial, or presidential races. In many cases, a major campaign may be designed around the telephone component. That seemed to be the case when Congressman Joseph Resnick of New York State ran for U.S. senator in 1968. It was reported that his telephone campaign cost almost $500,000. Virtually every registered Democrat in the state was said to have been called to hear a recorded message from the candidate. Resnick lost badly, and in the judgment of many observers, the telephone campaign was of little help. Recorded messages, sometimes delivered with the help of computers, have been used in many campaigns, but their usefulness or lack of usefulness, as in the case of many other campaign techniques, has never been conclusively established. However, if everyone in a political party or in an area is called, a significant portion of the money necessarily goes down the drain.

In some campaigns, $1,000 spent on telephoning is too much, but in others, $100,000 can be too little. The proper amount can be determined only as a function of overall campaign strategy and from establishing which groups (and how many people) you can reach that you can't get to in any other way. A full saturation telephone campaign is never worth the cost.

Some advance thought and careful use of research can save you money by indicating which areas and client groups need not or should not be called. In one campaign in which I worked professionally as a telephone campaign consultant for a reform candidate, I recommended that the campaign staff provide me a list of election districts in the order of reform strength. (That was to be determined from past voting patterns, as described in Chapter 3.) Just developing the list eliminated the districts, amounting to one-third of the total, which were clearly strongholds of the opposing party faction from consideration for calling. Determining the sequence of election district priorities was particularly important since we were working with volunteers and there was therefore no way to guarantee that every productive district would be called. Clearly, if there is any significant possibility that all your calls will not be completed, the most productive areas (however you wish to define them on the basis of your research) should be called first.

As a rule of thumb, in campaigns of over 100,000 voters, telephone campaign costs should not exceed 20 to 25 percent of the total, particularly if a television emphasis has been decided upon. (Television can account for two-thirds of the entire campaign budget in larger campaigns). In smaller campaigns (city council, town supervisor, state assembly), telephone cost allocations can go as high as one-third, again with the caveat that well-trained, intelligent interviewers, with a reasonably prepared message, call the right people.

BUDGETING FOR A VOLUNTEER TELEPHONE CAMPAIGN

If you want to organize your own telephone campaign, your estimates of cost should take the following factors into account, adding 15 percent for contingencies.

SPACE RENTAL.   The space used for the telephone operation should not be located in or near your campaign headquarters. Usually a motel or hotel suite is fine, but cheaper space is frequently available in storefronts and office buildings. You must assume you'll need 50 to 60 square feet of space per caller (for furniture, telephone setup, aisle space, etc.). If you have ten women and one supervisor (to make 15,000 calls) you'll need 600 to 700 square feet, depending on how the room is laid out. If the climate is hot and humid, you may need to find a place with air conditioning. About ten dollars a foot, or $7,000 for 700 square feet, would be reasonable for a year's lease. Short-term leases are naturally more expensive on a pro-rated basis. For a six-week campaign, you'll need at least a two-month occupancy—it takes the telephone company about a week to set up, especially if new cable has to be installed. The rental charges for two months may thus amount to one-sixth of $7,000 plus a few percentage points for a short-term lease, amounting to about $1,500 for decent space.

MAINTENANCE OF SPACE.   Many landlords don't follow through on provisions of services for short-term tenants. If you make certain the place is clean, garbage is picked up, and coffee is prepared, your costs may amount to an additional $50 a week, or perhaps $300 for the campaign.

FURNITURE RENTAL.   Chairs and tables can be rented, shipped, and picked up at a cost of perhaps $350 to $400 for a month. Many furniture renters require a deposit to guarantee return of the equipment in good condition. Tables run about $30 each and chairs $100 a dozen, plus delivery charges.

TELEPHONE INSTALLATION.   Charges vary but average about $85 to $95 per telephone and about $200 for the "call director" (the instrument used by the supervisor to monitor the quality of the calls).* Installation for a

---

*In New York City in 1983, a touch-tone call director, with ten lines, was $219.65 installed plus $27.05 monthly. A touch-tone instrument was $95.71 installed plus $8.39 a month service charges.

ten-telephone operation with a call director will come to approximately $1,150. Touch-tone telephones are recommended; their extra cost is more than compensated for by the increased speed of dialing.

COST OF TELEPHONE CALLS.   In some areas, an unlimited number of calls may be made for a flat monthly fee, while in others the cost may be on the order of 9 to 12 cents per call, plus extra charges for calls over three minutes in length. If about 15,000 voters will be reached, we can assume that about 20,000 calls will actually be made. (First, about 20 percent of the persons listed in the telephone directory will have moved within a year, and some calls will be to the wrong person at an old number. Second, often a voter in a primary may have one party regis- tration, but the family member who answers the telephone may be of another party and you will have to call back. Finally, some interviewers will call home or their friends after a while to break the monotony of the calls.) The total cost of calls may run about $500 in communities with flat-rate telephone billing and about $1,750 in communities with message- and distance-rate telephone billing systems.

INSURANCE FOR PERSONAL INJURY.   It's a good idea to take out an insurance policy for injuries to cover people working in the campaign and visitors so that you're protected from lawsuits. Estimated cost: $500 to $700.

DEVELOPMENT OF MESSAGE AND PRE-TESTING CALLS.   One of your full-time paid staff or your advertising agency professionals will generally develop a message and arrange to pre-test it. You may not be charged directly, but eventually this will cost, either in your own payroll or in consultant's charges, about $500 for a small-scale test of various messages for different areas and voter constituencies in advance of the full-scale telephone campaign.

TRAINING EXPENSES.   For full-time staff, materials, cards, and refresh- ments, plan on spending about $200.

LOOKING UP TELEPHONE NUMBERS AND PREPARING CARDS.   This is the simplest step involved in the telephoning process, but even it can become complicated. Commercially, looking up numbers in large quantities costs about 9 to 10 cents per number. In some areas, the local telephone company may actually help you to do this for small jobs, but you can't count on their assistance.* At a minimum, you would have to have these things done:

- On 3 x 5 cards, list alphabetically, by street address, all voters to be reached.
- "Buy" (really rent, in most areas) the telephone company's reverse telephone book, which lists all numbers (except those unlisted) by street address, with all at a single street address listed alphabetically.
- Enter on the card the numbers of the assembly and election district, the name and address and telephone number of the voter.
- Scan the deck to combine family names at the same address. (This is also useful in saving on mailing expenses.)

If these chores will be done by volunteers, estimate that cards, reverse telephone book rental (over $100 for that alone), and space and refreshments for the volunteers doing this very time-consuming job will cost about $500.

If your local board of elections has a list of voters on computerized tape, you may be able to reduce the cost of preparing the 3 x 5 cards by having a computer transfer the basic information from the tape to 3 x 5 cards, leaving only the telephone numbers to be entered by volunteers.

PREPARATION OF MESSAGE-SUPPORTING STATEMENTS.   So that the callers can answer questions intelligently, the background of the candidate, issues statements, questions and answers have to be prepared, which require the use of campaign staff and possibly professional advertising people. This will cost, including typing and reproduction, perhaps $250 at a minimum.**

---

*In emergencies you may find it necessary to call Information. In many cities the operator will provide three numbers on one request. In a recent primary, there were twenty amateur and professional phone campaigns in one county. By the last week of the campaign, Information provided only one number at a time. Political computer firms can provide name-telephone number conversions; this service is not inexpensive, and the error rate is often over 15–20 percent.

**The best such issues book that I have seen was a printed pamphlet prepared for Senator Gary Hart's presidential campaign in 1983. A model of its kind, it was used for distribution to campaign staff and potential contributors, and as background for chairmen of volunteers. The preparation cost was very considerably in excess of $500.

REFRESHMENTS. Provide coffee, cold soda, cake, and other refreshments to give the telephoners a break each night from work that can become very tedious. If you budget $1.00 a person a night, the total cost for 30 nights of calling would approximately $330.

SUPERVISING EXPENSES. The supervisors, at least, should be paid. A minimum fee of $200 a week for 25 hours of work would amount, over a 4- to 6-week calling period, to between $800 and $1,200 each.

BABYSITTING AND OTHER EXPENSES. Some volunteers will need babysitters on certain nights. Anticipate a total of about $500 for this.

Adding up the items listed above produces a total cost of $8,000 (or more) for a campaign that comprises 20,000 calls attempted, including 15,000 completed calls—not that much less than a consultant would charge. Clearly, a telephone campaign requires a significant investment, even if you do it yourself. Since overhead and fixed costs, such as message development and insurance, are so expensive in telephone campaigns, the unit cost decreases significantly as the number of calls increases. In most cases it is uneconomical to do a small-scale telephone campaign unless the space and telephones are contributed.*

In areas with unlimited message units, where it is certainly sensible to emphasize telephone campaigns, costs may average 30 to 35 cents a call in volunteer-staffed campaigns of 20,000 calls and over. In other areas, where each call or message unit is separately charged, average costs may run between 35 and 40 cents a call.

MAKING A CONTRACT FOR A PROFESSIONAL TELEPHONE CAMPAIGN

Professional telephone firms charge approximately 50 to 55 cents a call for 50,000 calls or more.** Your staff and legal counsel must make certain that the contract stipulates which services you are to receive. If you have

---

*In larger cities, major unions often contribute telephone banks to candidates they support. On January 17, 1983, the *New York Times* reported that COPE had retained Peter Hart, a leading Democratic pollster, to train their locals in polling techniques as a prelude to direct mail and telephoning in political campaigns. (COPE is the AFL-CIO's Committee on Political Education.)

**Some telephone consultants, including myself, charge actual costs incurred plus a flat fee. For charges-per-call campaigns, I would recocmmend an independent validation to check that the calls are actually and properly made.

the telephone campaign done professionally, make sure that the contract states that you will pay the telephone bill directly. One campaign manager told me that a well-known political advertising man had charged him for 10,000 telephone calls he had never made. The candidate discovered this after the campaign was over, when the telephone company billed him instead of the advertising man, and he realized from the message unit count that the advertising man had charged him for 10,000 calls that could not have been made. In negotiating with a telephone consultant, ask for two prices—one in which the consultant performs all services and one based on your office's paying for the telephone installations and the message units. Some consultants may be available to provide advice on procedures and message development for a flat fee. Specify that the principal consultant should be available directly to your staff a certain number of hours.

Another useful service that should be in the contract (in large-scale campaigns) is the provision by the consultant of daily counts of telephone calls made by areas called, by numbers of favorables, unfavorables, and undecideds, and by developing issues in each area. If a campaign has a number of installations around a state, preparing such data and calling them in to headquarters can be very useful. If this type of service is not explicitly required in the contract, consultants are unlikely to volunteer it. You will be charged for this extra service, but it is well worth it.

Ask the consultant the percentage of unlisted numbers in the locality, which groups are receptive to phone appeals and which not, and how many completed calls he or she thinks likely. A reliable consultant will give you an estimate for nothing more than that is honestly possible. The prices are usually estimated on the total number of voters that you want to attempt to reach. If you have 50,000 unduplicated voter households that you want to contact, the probabilities are that only 35,000 to 38,000 can actually be reached.

Whom To Call And What To Say

In many professional telephone campaigns, with investments of several hundred thousand dollars, no research at all is done on the basics: Whom to call? What to say? In some campaigns, a junior staff member may make this determination and never bother to check it with the research or polling staff member. In the heat of campaigning, many basic decisions may get rushed through without your knowledge. For your telephone effort, no less than the rest of your campaign, *it is critical to do as much advance planning as possible before the actual campaigning begins.*

There is no simple, magical way to make these determinations. Research and thought are needed to protect your investment in the telephone operations. Either you should insist that your consultant demonstrate how he or she came to recommend a message, or you should have a mature staff member research the matter for you, concentrating on the three areas indicated below. In no case should you or your manager allow the message to be frozen before you (or your representative) examine the research and listen to recordings of calls made to pre-test the proposed message. In my own campaign work, messages are never completely frozen, because experienced interviewers are constantly finding new and better ways of presenting the candidate's advantages within the structured routine.

Whoever you make responsible for the telephone operation should:

- Analyze past elections by individual election districts to locate the favorables, unfavorables, and undecideds.
- Analyze client-group voting patterns
- Correlate these analyses with demographic analysis—the distribution of the voters by age, sex, income, race, and ethnic group.

After some preliminary hypotheses are made on the basis of this information, pre-test calls *with varying message contents* should be made to the client groups you want to reach. These calls should be made by experienced supervisors. The message starts to become finalized at this time. The campaign policy group should be involved here if in no other phase of the telephone campaign.

TRAINING TELEPHONERS

Several days in advance of the beginning of the telephone campaign, each telephoner should be provided with a copy of the candidate's biography and a list of questions and answers on his/her stands on issues that the staff anticipates will come up in the telephone conversation. (Examples of these materials will be found in Figs. 9-1 and 9-2.) By the time they arrive for the training session on the first night of telephoning, they should have read and mastered the information in the biography and

<u>Biography of Irwin Silbowitz</u>

Candidate for Civil Court Judge

Irwin Silbowitz is 38; he and his family (his wife, the former Eleanor Kaufman; daughter Donna, 13; and son Mitchell, 9) reside on the Grand Concourse in the Bronx. Since working his way through New York Law School he has had many years of legal experience in all phases of the law. At present he is a Senior Law Advisor to all the Justices of the New York State Supreme Court. His official title is Deputy Chief Law Assistant of the New York State Supreme Court--First Judicial District; he has worked in this section for ten years.

His experience includes:

1. Acting as Supreme Court Referee

2. Trial Counsel to the Appeals Court

3. Special Adviser to the Justices on matters of court procedure

4. Specialized legal adviser on all matters currently before the court

5. Participation in thousands of civil and criminal cases

6. Performance of legal research

7. Before his present post he was in private practice (Markewich, Rosenhaus & Beck) and was Law Clerk to Sidney H. Asch, presently a State Supreme Court Judge.

.   .   .   .   .   .

Mr. Silbowitz is the only candidate for Civil Court Judge who has developed a specific program for necessary court improvements and reforms. This program includes:

1. Neighborhood night courts to settle many disputes now clogging court calendars. These will also make it unnecessary for working people to lose a day's pay to get their day in court.

2. These courts would resolve landlord-tenant disputes.

3. These Neighborhood Night Courts would include small claims court; Mr. Silbowitz proposes to increase the limit on small claims cases from $500 to $1000 to help settle disputes quickly without the claimants having to lose a day's pay to settle their claims.

Fig. 9-1. Example of a candidate's biography for use as background information in a telephone canvass.

Questions and Answers -- Page 2

6. Why does he feel the present court system is mismanaged?

   The system is too centralized and filled with red tape creating
endless backlogs.   thinks that there should be more rotating
judges, and that some courts should be open weekends as well as nights
for the convenience of the working public.

7. Why is   running?

   He has a program that will work, and he can't make it work
unless he is elected. He has the experience and understanding to
be able to have insight into the community's needs.

8. Why would he be a better judge than his opponent?

   a) More experience in all phases of the court system

   b) Experienced as a trial referee, i.e. one who renders advisory
decisions for judges

   c) Experienced in legal research in all areas of the law

   d) Has written hundreds of decisions

   e) Experienced as trial counsel in Appellate Division of New
York State Supreme Court

9. He went to New York Law School. That's not a great school.

   He had to work his way through school and attend law school at
night. N.Y.U. and Columbia are both daytime schools. He had to work
days at the Post Office to support his family.

10. Why did the Liberal Party endorse him? They don't usually, do they?

   Both candidates were interviewed by an impartial panel, and
        was found more qualified.

Fig. 9-2. Example of "questions and answers" for use by telephone canvassers.

the questions and answers so that they will be able to refer to it comfortably and will not have to read it to respond to most questions which come up in the course of their work.

At the training session, the candidate should make a point of talking to the telephoners briefly and then answering any additional questions they may still have after having read the questions and answers. The supervisor or a member of the campaign staff should then pass out copies of the message and review it with them. Finally, the callers should be carefully instructed about the information that is to be registered on the card—usually an indication of whether the voter was favorable, unfavorable, or undecided, plus any special information gotten from the call such as "aged, needs help voting" or "has questions about grandson in jail."

If the campaign staff is prepared to follow through with it, it is a good idea to instruct the callers to answer all reasonable questions to the best of their ability based on the biography, the questions and answers, and any other materials provided by the candidate's staff, and to offer to have a member of the campaign staff call the voter back or send literature if the voter has a question that the caller cannot answer or that he or she feels is too sensitive to handle. This course should emphatically not be followed if the campaign staff is not prepared to follow through, since it is much worse not to follow through on such a promise than not to make it in the first place.

The following general advice should be included in the training session and repeated if necessary as the campaign progresses: (1) Never argue, and don't spend too much time on supporters of the opponent if there is little or no hope of bringing them over to your side. It is more productive to thank the person for his or her time as quickly as possible and go on to a voter who might be convinced. (2) Listen to the voter. Listening often has a more positive effect than talking. The call is too often treated as a recited message instead of a conversation.* Not only is the conversational approach more effective, it can yield research spin-offs that are usually helpful and sometimes critical for the campaign's success. (3) Don't spend too much time talking with favorable voters. Thank them and go on to another voter who might be brought into your camp. (4) Always maintain a friendly, interested tone (see Fig. 9-3.)

---

*The conversational approach was developed in 1968 and is now sometimes called the rap sheet technique.

PROFESSIONAL OR AMATEUR TELEPHONERS?

I would advise you to have your telephone campaign done professionally. As the California politician Jesse Unruh said, "You can't control what you don't pay for." When you work with amateurs in a campaign, you learn the true dimensions of anarchy. It can, and usually does, become community participation to the nth power, with each participant doing the job as he or she sees fit rather than as you want it done. This is true of telephone operations no less than of other campaign activities.

If you cannot afford to have a telephone campaign done professionally and think you need one, my recommendation is that your campaign policy committee sharply delineate the areas and groups to be called. Someone of maturity and judgment should be made responsible for the orderly development of research, message content, and training. Volunteers can be used to list voters' names, addresses, election districts, and assembly districts on cards; others should be assigned to look up telephone numbers and enter them on the cards. Pre-test calls may be made by carefully trained volunteers; questions and answers as well as a biography and issues position of the candidate should be prepared by the regular campaign staff. In no case, however, even in the smallest campaigns, should a telephone canvass be attempted unless you can afford to have at least ten telephones in a central location, with the telephones manned at given hours under some type of supervision. Since the operation is expensive, even with volunteers, considerations of economy of scale suggest the need for 10,000 calls as a minimum to make the effort worthwhile.

RESEARCH SPIN-OFFS

An advantage of a telephone campaign is that you can get major research findings at little or no extra cost. Keeping daily counts of results—favorable, unfavorable, and undecided—by district and by subpopulation group can be enormously informative about how the campaign is going and about how specific groups are responding to television, radio, and newspaper ads and to positions on issues.

In one recent campaign, the telephoners clearly established that the candidate's television saturation was starting to backfire in certain areas. But, as in many major campaigns, the channels of information and communication were blocked, and no one wanted to hear this finding, because it conflicted with the point of view of the policy committee. There was

[Example of telephone message designed for Italian voters.]

[Ask for the person specified. If not home, ask for any other adult at home.]

    HELLO. I'M _____ AND I'M CALLING FOR _____

    _____, WHO'S RUNNING FOR DISTRICT ATTORNEY IN THE

    DEMOCRATIC PRIMARY ON SEPTEMBER 10. HE'S ENDORSED BY

    CONGRESSMEN _____ AND _____. MAY I TAKE A MOMENT

    TO TELL YOU ABOUT MR. _____'S BACKGROUND?

(Yes)   Thank you.   (Continue)

(No)   Thank you. Could you tell me who you intend to vote for
        in the _____ - _____ race?

Continue

    MR. _____ IS A LAWYER WITH 12 YEARS OF EXPERIENCE AS

_____. HE'S

ALSO ENDORSED BY:

    - DISTRICT ATTORNEY _____

    - _____, PRESIDENT OF THE _____ UNION

    - _____, PRESIDENT OF THE _____ UNION.

    ARE THERE ANY QUESTIONS YOU HAVE ON MR. _____'S

EXPERIENCE OR PROGRAM?

[If yes, answer.] (If you don't know, indicate that someone from campaign headquarters will call them.)

[If no]   Thank you. Goodnight.

Fig. 9-3. Example of a telephone message script or "rap" sheet.

no coordination between policy strategy and data obtained from the telephone effort. Hence, the television campaign continued unabated, costing large sums of money and possibly actually losing votes. This not uncommon situation illustrates a principle of effective campaigning: To maximize his or her investment in the telephone operation, the candidate must assign a member of the immediate staff, with operational and policy discretion, as telephone liaison.

In a similar instance, the telephoners received complaints that the candidate was too sedate in televised debates with his opponents. The information was sent on to the headquarters staff, which in this instance passed it on to the candidate, who attempted to make some modifications in his speaking style. On another occasion, the telephoners picked up a complaint in a middle-class white district that Black Panther literature was being developed and mimeographed in one of the candidate's offices. The information proved to be true, and the potentially explosive situation, of which the candidate had been unaware, was quietly remedied.

ELECTION DAY TELEPHONE CANVASSING

Telephones can be used to advantage as a substitute for personal canvassing on election day. Most of the principles of election day canvassing apply equally well to telephone canvassing. If you have had a telephone campaign preceding election day, you should already have cards for the voters whom the telephone campaign identified as favorable to your candidacy. Ideally, these cards should be divided according to election districts. Your campaign staff can determine the order of priority in which the favorable voters are to be called; this order can be altered during the day, if your poll watchers report particularly light turnouts in areas that your research shows are largely favorable to you.

The message for election day telephone calls is brief—15 to 30 seconds. Your callers need only politely remind the voters that today is election day and that their vote is important to you and will be appreciated. However, if many candidates are making pull calls, you may be wise to cancel yours, to minimize voter irritation. It is advisable to offer specific information as to the location of the polling place or any unusual ballot problems.

10
Non-Political Elections

Don't run too slick a campaign. People will think you're just another politician.

—Nat Sorkin

Although the precise number of private organizations conducting elections each year in the nation is not available, the order of magnitude can reasonably be estimated. There are over 180,000 incorporated and unincorporated communities in the nation. Most of these communities have parent-teacher associations, men's and women's social clubs, and religious institutions; and many also have League of Women Voters chapters, businessmen's groups, economic development associations, alumni organizations, a Rotary club, a Masonic lodge, and other fraternal orders, labor unions, a chamber of commerce, bar associations, medical associations, a junior chamber of commerce, and various other organizations.

Most of these groups have boards of directors whose members are elected. An estimate of over a million private elections per year is probably conservative, even assuming that many organizations have only pro forma elections with a nominating committee or a major contributor controlling the outcome.

Many of these elections do not directly concern the public, although, cumulatively, civic groups do significantly influence the course of public affairs. Public policies are modified, and sometimes changed entirely, as a result of pressures brought to bear by these groups.* Yet, public drama resulting from these elections is likely to be minimal, owing to lack of interest on the part of the communications media; but for the people

---

*For example, the powerful consumer and ecology movements originated from such private groups, not from public officials. Such privately based groups have changed public priorities and policies, demonstrating that they have real political power. The political significance of these groups is only recently being accepted as part of the American political landscape; many have learned the rules of the game and provide money and workers to political parties and to individual candidates.

In 1983, the campaign against drunken driving started to achieve legislative success after years of effort by private groups of citizens; the nuclear freeze movement developed an enormous following in the early 1980s from a non-political base.

involved, and the communities and interests they serve, these elections are very important. This chapter suggests which political techniques may be appropriate in private-election campaigning and shows how they can be used.

The reasons people seek private office are not dissimilar from the motives of those who seek public office. The need for recognition, for ego gratification, for a sense of public purpose somewhat larger than the satisfactions of a job or of family life are major reasons motivating many people to run for office. Anger and frustration at complicated governmental bureaucratic response—when non-response or long delayed or inappropriate response become the anticipated responses—lead people to seek redress by working in community organizations. Some of the most effective local organizational campaigning has been done by housewives banding together to get a traffic light installed on a corner where a child has been killed by an automobile, or to picket a store having higher than usual prices, or to form an ecological interest group. People express their sense of impotence as individuals by joining together in community and civic groups which provide a vehicle for direct action and some accomplishment. If nothing else, they can at least be heard.

For varying reasons, many people find political clubs distasteful, so special-interest groups or general civic groups become attractive alternatives. Couples whose marriages are faltering may join civic clubs to develop new common interests; other people may join for purely social reasons. Retired people find civic clubs interesting and have leisure time to invest in their activities. Many business people (lawyers, insurance agents, and others) regard civic clubs as useful places to meet prospective clients or customers. Leadership potential originates from all these groups as people become knowledgeable, develop new ideas, and find that being president or chairman is a satisfying means to express and implement their ideas.

Semi-public groups serve many useful functions in a community. They dramatize local issues and develop alternatives, and they often provide training for people who later seek public office. Frequently, such clubs can be more candid on critical, controversial, and emotionally charged issues than can elected officials whose sensitivities and insecurities are naturally exacerbated by the necessity of running for reelection after relatively short terms of office, or whose friends, political allies, or contributors may be involved in activities that deserve critical attention.

With certain modifications, the political techniques described earlier can be applied to elections in these groups. Fortunately, the scale of these private elections is much reduced from that of elections for public office, and an individual interested member can more readily afford the costs both in time and in money.

The following steps should be taken:

1. Read and know the constitution or by-laws of your organization, including which offices are elective, when the elections are held, and how nominations are secured. In addition, learn the organization's procedural rules—often a modified form of Robert's Rules of Order.*

2. Know the history of the organization, its purposes, and its nonelected key cadre, the group that has provided organizational continuity. Has the organization taken stands on public issues? What were the results? Which issues are important to the membership now? Are there conflicts on matters of policy? How do members line up on these issues? Answering these questions usually involves reading the minutes of the meetings for the last few years and checking the voting pattern.

3. Learn which committees are called for by the constitution. How many members serve on a committee? Who appoints the committee chairmen? (This can be critical, because these offices provide a natural transition to running for organizational office.)

4. Find out who controls the way the organization operates. Who controls the membership and finance committee? Who provides most of the organization's funds if membership dues are not enough to make ends meet?

5. Learn which persons control the policy formation activities. What is the source of their power, and what type of following do they have?

6. Establish whether preventive defenses are necessary. For example, most organizations will not allow "stacking"—a candidate's paying for voting memberships for friends and family members—but you should make sure that this hasn't happened; if it has, get ready with a countertactic. Just before a club nominating vote, one idealistic, reform-minded

---

*Robert's Rules can be used for making meetings productive; they can also be used obstructively. See Pete Hamill's marvelous article in *New York* magazine, August 8, 1972, for a description of reform Democratic clubs and how these rules can bring everything to a standstill. Having been a member of such clubs, I can vouch for the accuracy of the article.

club president, anticipating what his less idealistic and more "practical" opponent would do, paid for 40 club memberships for personal friends. The presumably more practical opponent had never even considered such a course of action, and he lost. The reformer simply bought the nomination—an occurrence that is not uncommon in American organizational life.

7. Know the membership's voting background—information on the past voting behavior of the club membership is most important. How many people vote, and how is the vote usually divided?

After six months or so of active membership in a small club, you should have a pretty good idea of your potential, and you'll know the protocol—for example, whether there is a formal or informal line of succession in which the treasurer or some other officer automatically becomes the president.

In larger clubs, the basic political campaigning techniques described in earlier chapters are often appropriate, but they should be used with great care and selectivity.

An example of how so-called slick campaign techniques can backfire was described by Nat Sorkin, a leading New York printer of political brochures. Some years ago, he ran for vice president of his synagogue. Having learned in a generation of political work how brochures are used, he developed and mailed several brochures that included everything he had seen in political brochures he had printed for other candidates: pictures of his family, his dog, and his home, and explanations of his reasons for running. His opponent simply sent out one postcard that said, "I don't own a printing plant and can't afford to send you so many fancy brochures. I believe I've earned this position, and you all know how I feel about the things that concern us. Please vote for me." The opponent won a clear victory.

Sorkin's congregation probably had never experienced a professional-style election campaign, and many members may have resented the approach without regard to the possible real merits of his candidacy. Although precedent should not control your campaign, it should provide the basis for your deliberations on tactics and strategy.

Sometimes a simple, direct piece is much more effective than a number of professionally designed brochures, particularly in a community organization election. You must always keep in mind the voters to whom you wish to appeal. You can't do something completely out of context without taking risks.

In a recent hotly contested parent-teacher association campaign, for example, the candidate was not sure the membership would recognize from his name that he espoused the religion of most of the members. He wanted to have the secretary of his church call the congregants to remind them that he was running and to ask them and their friends to vote for him. He was counseled not to do this because of the probability of adverse reactions. Such a decision cannot be made on the basis of objective data; experience and judgment should control, supplementing any original research you can do on sensitive issues.

In larger organizations, you should consider having friends sponsor or host kaffeeklatches or teas for small groups of members, where you can explain your views on the future of the organization. These groups ideally should number 15 to 20; a larger number is an imposition on your hostess and also makes effective discussion almost impossible.

Professional research is generally unnecessary in these campaigns. However, you should make a practice of using discussion meetings and kaffeeklatches not only to get your ideas across to the members, but to listen to them and find out what they are thinking. Use these meetings to develop a program. You must give people a reason to vote for you besides geniality and access.

If your organization has 500 to 1,000 members or more, and attendance at meetings is light, you probably should prepare one simple mailing piece for those who have not attended, since the organization's hard core probably will make up their minds on other considerations. Any mailing that you do should be simply stated; avoid elaboration at all costs. Envelopes should be hand addressed: keep it constantly in mind that these are very personal campaigns. Computer letters should be ruled out completely, as they are more likely to offend than convince in non-political elections. "Nothing fancy" is probably the best strategy of all. Your letters should be signed by hand; the paper should be of good quality, but not extravagant. As in any social situation, always try to be tasteful and gracious. The return address for larger mailings should be printed, preferably in small type. These are in large measure social campaigns, and you must avoid the appearance of a high-powered political contest. This type of mailing can be supplemented, or substituted for, by a telephone call briefly asking people to vote for you and giving them a sensible reason for doing so.* These procedures require checking and transcribing membership lists against attendance lists. If attendance lists are not maintained, you may have to record attendance yourself. In developing ideas for your group, keep in mind that people tend to be uncomfortable with completely innovative concepts unless you prepare the ground very carefully.

In the early phase of campaigning, your appearance and a friendly manner will probably influence voters more than anything else. Try to listen to what's on their minds and react responsively and honestly to their sense of problems and priorities. If you criticize, do so constructively; don't relate criticism to the deficiencies, either real or imagined, of personalities. By midway through the campaign, you will have to supplement your charm with substance, being prepared to take intelligent stands on issues of interest to the membership. On election day, you can gently remind your friends and supporters how important the election is and ask them to vote.

---

*Sometimes you may be able to get the members' telephone numbers from the organization's secretary. But more often than not, you'll have to look the numbers up yourself.

11
Conclusion

If this system—this towering monument to man's capacity to live to-
gether in harmony, with tolerance, with justice, with freedom of thought,
spirit and deed—is to survive, those of us who have had the good fortune
to suffer, if you please, in the exposed position of public advocacy have
a great and abiding responsibility to talk sense, to tell the people what
the facts are, to give them the real alternatives and pose the real choices.
—Adlai E. Stevenson

Dubrovnik, on the Yugoslav coast, was a powerful, independent city-
state that survived and prospered despite repeated onslaughts over the
centuries by Romans, Turks, and pirates. Visitors to the city may see a
motto engraved in stone over the entrance to the old city hall proclaiming:
"All those who enter here must place their private passions in suspense,
for public needs shall be their only concern." In the same building are
exhibited dice that were used by the nobles of Dubrovnik in casting lots
to determine who would be governor each month.

Apparently the ruling class, for centuries, was composed of men of
such uniform distinction, ability, and integrity that the fate of the state
could be placed reliably in the hands of any one of them by a roll of the
dice, with absolute assurance that the interests of the state would not
suffer. I know of no parallel in history. I certainly know of no American
state or city legislature where a significant degree of risk would not follow
the determination of leadership and power focus in this manner, although
there may be many who believe that in certain situations, not only would
the quality of our government not be threatened by crap-shooting for
power, but possibly improvements in quality of leadership might result.

The point is simple: We need the best leadership we can get, yet the
methods and procedures attendant to our campaigning practices provide
no assurance either for the provision of able and responsible leadership
or for its continuity. This book was written partially in the hope of enabling
potential candidates, who may have much to contribute to society but
who presently avoid campaigning out of distaste and repugnance for a
"dirty business," to re-evaluate the techniques and requirements of cam-

paigning and perhaps see that no law of God or man dictates that it must be a dirty business or that only the wealthy, dishonest, or unscrupulous can win or can hold union cards.

Seeking public office can in fact be the most productive, meaningful role a citizen can take in our society, without necessarily compromising his honor, integrity, or family values. Working within our system—one of the best in the world, since it allows change to occur peacefully—so that deficiencies are corrected and the quality of life and living is improved is not a bad way to spend a career and a life.

Since Dubrovnik's method of deciding power is not likely to be widely embraced, the preceding chapters have concentrated on the skills you'll need to campaign effectively and economically and on some of the problems you'll probably come up against. The treatment of these matters was necessarily general, since each case has its own peculiarities and no amount of preparation can prevent some feelings of terror, panic, frustration, and futility; these are normal in campaigns, even for experienced politicians. But the first time is the hardest; the terrors and emotional exhaustion are usually somewhat muted in subsequent campaigns.

The book is intended primarily to be helpful to inexperienced campaigners, whatever their political persuasion. Taken together, these chapters are an attempt at an intellectual, economical, and emotional rationalization of the campaigning process. Implicit in all the book's recommendations is the assumption that all candidates will work within the system, whatever their personal values, whatever their party. Many books in the last decade have taken the view that the system isn't working and can't work, that society's priorities have become perverted, that the government doesn't reflect the popular will, and that the seniority committee system in our legislatures allows a handful of men, often from rural areas, to dominate public policy against the popular will.

This feeling is not unique to our generation. The great political commentator Walter Lippmann noted in 1925:

The private citizen today has come to feel rather like a deaf spectator in the back row, who ought to keep his mind on the mystery up there, but cannot quite manage to keep awake. He knows he is somehow affected by what is going on. Yet these public affairs are in no convincing way his affairs. They are for the most part invisible. They are managed, if they are managed at all, at distant centers, from behind the scenes by unnamed powers. As a private person he does not know for certain what is going on, or who i doing it, or where he is being carried. No newspaper reports his environment so that he can grasp it; no school has taught him how to imagine it, his ideals, often, do not fit with it; listening to speeches, altering opinions, and voting do not, he finds, enable him to govern it. He lives in a world which he cannot see, does not understand, and is unable to direct.*

I lived in New York City most of my life and have seen fear, hatred, and loathing take over in the last decade. Many describe the problem as emanating from racial passions that no authority or institution can successfully deal with, since the base is emotional rather than rational. I take the view that the fear of pain and death is eminently reasonable and is, in fact, human, not racial. I taught in a college located in a black ghetto, where my students described vividly the reign of terror brought by drug addiction and the cost of supporting the habit. Many were able to identify the pushers, yet the police did little and the conviction rate of dealers was quite low. The feeling of alienation that results from these and related experiences is not racial. Middle-income families of all races experience similar feelings, with the added irritation of paying additional taxes while the quality of public services deteriorates and merely getting to work becomes a traumatic, dangerous experience. It is known that heroin addiction in New York alone is a business involving billions of dollars, thousands of private individuals and people in government, as well as foreign governments whose permissiveness can hardly be accidental. The federal and state governments spend millions to combat this disease, which results in burglaries, muggings, and murders. Yet the spreading addiction provides a fulfillment that can only be transient and results in activities that are terminal not only for the addicts. Public authorities cannot even deal with the transit graffiti problem, which has become a public disgrace, let alone the drug problem, which is a national terror. In rural counties that I have visited in the course of my profession, I have heard reports of drugs being sold in schools and of burglaries and other crimes in areas where, until recently, the crime rate was so low that there was no full-time police officer. An obvious answer is to provide free drugs under supervised conditions, yet many regard this course as

---

*"The Phantom Public," quoted in Clinton Rossiter and James Lare (Eds.), *The Essential Lippmann* (New York: Random House, 1963, p. 35).

dangerous and a possible infringement of civil rights. Vast migrations, with attendant huge public costs because of wasted investments in public facilities, take place in the nation's major cities as people try to obtain some measure of neighborhood safety, decent schools, and a minimally agreeable ambience. Police officers see corrupt administrators every day, including overly amiable judges; attorneys and people in business participate in payoffs. After a while, many accept this pervasive corruption as a way of doing business that makes life more convenient. After all, the consumer or the government will pick up the tab, anyway. Shoplifting is estimated to account for 3 percent of the average annual gross of the nation's department stores. The stores naturally pass on to their paying customers this 3 percent, plus the costs of increased security. (Pinkerton and similar security firms have been major growth stocks in recent years.)

In 1972, many Democrats fell in love with the "New Politics" of George McGovern. "Fresh faces" and new groups were recognized and the party was to be revitalized with new ideas and a new energy. It didn't work; the party was instead weakened. It is difficult to develop a coherent, generally understandable policy when a multiplicity of special interests are curried to and when each effectively has a veto. In 1980, John B. Anderson's campaign for President was thought by many to be the beginning of a needed third major political party. Anderson chose not to take this route. As this is being written, the American labor movement has decided to endorse a Democratic presidential candidate in advance of the party convention. Should this nominee not win, the next logical move would be for the labor movement to start another political party. Judging by the "blank" votes on many ballots and the fact that almost one-half of eligible voters didn't vote in the 1980 presidential elections, many voters share the belief that as matters now stand it doesn't make much difference who's in national office. A third party offering real alternatives might persuade some of these voters that there were real differences to choose from.

Some believe that the public are getting what they deserve; they cheat, steal, compromise, lie on their taxes, concern themselves exclusively with the minutiae of making a living, don't vote, and don't participate. As Alexis de Tocqueville wrote of the United States in the nineteenth century:

> The first thing that strikes observation is an unaccountable number of men, all equal and alike, incessantly endeavoring to produce the paltry and petty

pleasures with which they glut their lives. Each of them, living apart, is a stranger to the fate of all the rest—his children and his private friends constitute to him the whole of mankind; as for the rest of his fellow citizens, he is close to them, but he sees them not; he touches them, but he feels them not; he exists but in himself and for himself alone; and if his kindred still remain to him, he may be said at any rate to have lost his country.

Others, whose view I share, hold that the public expect their leaders to be a little better than they themselves are and to provide a source of respected authority that can guide, consult, and lead (without looking back to see if something is gaining on them, in Satchel Paige's expression). However, too few politicians command continued respect because of their demonstrated integrity, intelligence, courage, and honesty. Even United States senators have business interests that must in some manner compromise their ability to serve the public interest. Men like Senator Estes Kefauver, who challenged major industrial forces to serve the public good, got chewed up in the process. Men like Ralph Nader have helped change the administrative concerns of government somewhat, but only by dedicating their entire lives to consumer advocacy and the pursuit of what I regard as a public equity. Men and institutions have devoted their energies to solving the nation's housing problems, but the nation still lacks 10 million units of decent housing, and in 1983, 2,000,000 Americans were homeless. Some rare public officials do try to do what needs to be done on major sensitive issues, but often they are unappreciated by the very public they serve and face bitter election challenges.

Nonetheless, the current sense of futility over the major frustrations in our society and the attendant warnings of doom may not be completely justified. We may not be on our way to a paradisiacal fulfillment, but we still have the capacity as a nation, if we have the will, to provide minimal income and environmental quality guarantees, to provide sufficient housing, parks, and mass transit to allow people to live in decent environments. The people, the various interest groups in this country do largely believe in fair play and the triumph of justice, but they don't think it happens more than once in a while right now.

In view of this widespread erosion of respect for the law, the average citizen, not surprisingly, seems to think that all politicians are in business for themselves, maximizing their private law practices and private investments while nominally being paid to protect and serve the public interest.

In twenty years of political work and 30 years in government service, I have seldom heard the public interest discussed by people in power as if it were a real, tangible thing. The political interest can be served only if our leadership discusses our needs and options openly and honestly. The credibility gap is real; politicians have not been held in lower repute in our modern history, according to recent Gallup polls. The Vietnam war occurred in part because the small, well-financed China lobby managed an effective campaign making the Chinese Communists our enemies at a time when decent, if not cordial, relations might have been possible. This took place despite the warnings of General Stilwell and other extremely able career soldiers and diplomats. Many citizens feel that, as a result of these tragic occurrences in postwar America, we as a nation are increasingly in the hands of lunatics, fools, and greedy incompetents—the whores and hustlers, the scandals of the Bobby Bakers and Sherman Adamses of each administration linger on in the public mind. More and more good, experienced legislators "retire" to private jobs. For example, Senator Howard Baker announced his retirement in 1983, saying in a *New York Times* interview that " . . . a lot of the pleasure of public service has dissipated. . . . I don't have to go through all this. . . . I don't have to disclose all these things and go through the innuendo and the accusations."

What has this to do with first-time campaigners? In my judgment, a very great deal. In your first campaign, even for relatively minor office, you will be shocked at the demands for favors friends and political allies will make. You'll be shocked at the number of accommodations on matters of public policy discretion you'll be asked to make as a matter of course before you serve one day in office.

If you go along with this, your political career will be set in very large measure; you will have been conditioned to accept all this garbage—for garbage it is, however frequently you'll encounter it, however often you're told: "That's the way it has to be." If you are a candidate who wants no more for yourself than to devote your life to the public service, you will find it truly tough going. And in many ways, your first campaign will control just what type of career you'll have and just what you will be able to accomplish. It is for this reason that I emphasize the necessity of being extremely cautious in your fund-raising activities.

Many good people walk away from the political life. It destroys families; thievery is common; betrayal by friends and allies is a monotonous fact; cut-throat corruption for favors and money is usual; and loyalty is sufficiently rare that campaign staffs of important legislators are hardly ever the same from election to election. People find political life callous, vicious, ungracious, shabby, and shoddy, and filled with greedy people. Those trying to do a decent job are in the minority in many localities and are often heartily detested by other politicians.

A number of things can be done to improve not only the procedures of campaigning but also those of governing—for the behavior of elected officials is necessarily influenced by the accommodations that campaigns seem always to require. I would offer the following proposals.

1. Campaign financing problems must be solved. The federal law allowing individual income tax deductions (up to $200 a couple) encourages more people to contribute and is a step in the right direction, as was earlier legislation requiring publication of the names of large contributors. Federal financing of presidential elections makes sense; it should be extended to congressionals and senatorials. Perhaps $200,000 of public money per qualifying candidate should be made available in general elections. A public indebtedness seems far better than a series of obligations to a few wealthy individuals and special interest groups. A few American radio and television stations now give free time to bonafide candidates. Many radio and television stations provide discounts to campaigners. The basic principle, even for local elections, should be that candidates bringing in a specified number of petition signatures should be granted some minimal funds out of public revenues so that each may be assured of the ability to communicate his or her program to the public.

2. Campaign fair practices acts, as they now stand, are largely words— no real muscle or penalties exist to back them up. Unscrupulous candidates send out outrageously false information and have their knuckles tapped lightly after having done considerable damage. Penalties under fair practices statutes should be imposed promptly and publicly.

3. Endorsements should be registered, as Congressman Mario Biaggi of New York proposed in 1972, since the practice of using phony endorsements of powerful political figures is widespread and, unfortunately, very effective with many voters.

4. Campaigns every two years are bound to detract from the public interest, since at least six months of each term of office may be devoted to the campaign for reelection. A six-year term for major offices has been

proposed frequently and has much merit. No term of office of city, state or federal elective positions should be less than four years.

5. Campaign polls should be checked for professionalism before publication of results is permitted in the press and other media. In New York State a bill was introduced in 1972 to register all pollsters to insure professionalism. In Canada, publication of poll results is not permitted although, of course, candidates are permitted to commission polls for their private use. In this way, polls of uncertain quality are prevented from influencing voters.

6. Candidates' credentials—their background and their explicit views on programs, taxes, and priorities—should be published by independent groups. This is now done in some localities but the check is too often pro forma only, and so general as to be valueless.

7. Legislation should require every candidate to make his financial situation, including his list of contributors, his personal and family assets, and seating lists at his political dinners, available to the public. Such controls exist for federal offices but seldom for local offices.

8. An elective office, except in small localities, should be a full-time job. Too many private business interests, so common in American political life, interfere with concern for the common good. Such a rule may have the effect of removing many attorneys from public office, but the system can survive the trauma, and may even be healthier for it, as a number of commentators have observed. According to Jimmy Breslin, "Our politics is rotten because it is almost exclusively made up of lawyers."* Mike Royko writes that "the undertaker-politicians and the saloon-keeper-politicians have given way to lawyer-politicians, who are no better, but they don't even buy you a drink or offer a prayer."**

9. Each candidate should be required to publish specific answers on what he would do on specific controversial capital items in his locality's budget, whom he would appoint to his staff if elected, and how he intended to solve the problems the public was concerned about. General answers should not be permitted.

10. Each board of elections should have an operating task force with power to bring legal charges for fraud, unfair campaign practices, etc.

---

*Quoted by Michael Gartner in his review of Joseph C. Goulden, *The Superlawyers* (New York: Weybright & Talley, 1972), in the *Wall Street Journal* (New York edition), August 9, 1972.
**Ibid.

Civil suits should follow immediately. If crimes of violence—for example, children beaten for stuffing brochures in mailboxes—take place, prompt investigations should follow and criminal charges should be brought. Most states do not now have a court apparatus that can handle this problem effectively and expeditiously.

11. Ballot design should be standardized by an independent committee so that the party in power does not exert influence, thus biasing the design.

12. Gerrymandering districts makes a sham of our democratic process. The rule for congressional districts now provides that the population size be similar in each district throughout the country. This allows the party in power to draw the lines any way they wish, without regard to neighborhoods, population characteristics, or other important variables that would assure equitable representation. If computers and technicians can't agree on what is a reasonable district, it should certainly be possible for the courts to do so.

13. Campaign challenges and other lawsuits should not be brought to lower courts (whose judges often are involved in local politics or who owe their jobs to leaders of one party or another) but should go directly to the state appellate division. Appellate courts tend to be less political but they judge matters of procedure, while the lower courts hear arguments on facts. What is needed is a specific hearing on facts. Current procedures should be changed to reflect political realities and to guarantee objectivity.

14. On patronage requests, a victorious candidate with discretion to fill jobs should have two options: He or she can (a) simply say, ''I'll take all referrals and pick the best,'' regardless of quotas or endorsements; or (b) take the county leader's referrals but with the proviso that if an appointee is incompetent, he or she will be replaced and that sponsor's future referrals will no longer be considered.

15. Political bank accounts of individual candidates and incumbents containing funds gained from fund-raising efforts should be public knowledge. Often these funds, ostensibly raised to support party activities, are kept for individual candidates.

16. There should be a monetary limit for each type of campaign. Congressionals should have a maximum of $500,000; Senate races, which averaged $1.7 million in 1982, should have limits based on the state's population—a range of $500,000 to $2,000,000 seems enough to get the message across. Races for governors should also be a function of the state's population—a limit of $750,000 to $2,500,000 seems appropriate.

17. There should be strict rules of appropriate conduct for campaigns, with candidates being held liable for slander and malicious distortions.

You will need luck and good health to be a good candidate and a good politician. A strong stomach and a thick skin wouldn't hurt. Your primary obligation conceptually is to serve the public as well as you are able, rather than to be re-elected. You must choose; the first campaign will force the choice, possibly without your being aware of it.

If you have any technical questions, or any comments on the book, I would be happy to hear from you.

12
Postscript: How It Feels To Campaign

So far as he is heard, seen, and understood, a candidate is a moral and intellectual teacher for better or worse. Like most means, a campaign is also in itself an end. It gives a chance to demonstrate virtue, to declare, defend, and illuminate the truth, and to do the statesman's duty to guide, to elevate and to instruct.

—*Stimson Bullitt,*
To Be A Politician

Often new candidates and students have asked me what political campaigning is really like. Many have been impressed by the glamour and the power that they read and hear about. When I describe some of the more prosaic and unpleasant aspects of campaigning, they are usually surprised and somewhat shocked. This postscript describes how it feels to campaign and what a candidate can reasonably expect.

Most American men who get drafted into the armed forces have definite anticipations, based on stories told by brothers, fathers, and friends, and visual images originating from war movies and television dramas. It is hard for them to imagine that the absence of toilet paper could ever become critical or that they could hate their sergeants more than any enemy. When women start to prepare for their wedding, even in today's liberated environment, that great day of days, they are so thoroughly briefed and rehearsed that they often think there can be no surprises. In both situations there are usually considerable differences between the anticipations and the actual event.

Entering politics is like getting drafted in that, at any level of office, many people will take delight in telling you what to do and what not to do and often without the slightest idea of what they are talking about. It's like getting married because there are fulfillments but also many frustrations, conflicts, and misunderstandings. David Garth, a leading political consultant, says, "There's nothing like campaigning. It's your ass out there. You're on your own and anyone can take pot shots. There's no experience like it."*

---

*Professor Susan Tolchin's tapes, Seminar on Women in Politics, George Washington University, 1977.

In campaigning and political life, few great people dedicate their lives and fortunes to public service, despite what television series, movies, and political hyperbole would have you believe. Such people are uncommon, and when they appear are often resented, distrusted, and feared by other politicians and misunderstood by the public. Every day you spend in political life won't be exciting, and everyone you meet won't be glamorous, intelligent, and decent. Much of the American public has a deserved distrust and distaste for politicians; after the scandals involving Presidents, Vice-Presidents, congressmen, and governors in the last generation, it is not surprising that many Americans ask who in authority we have reason to look up to.

By and large you'll find that most of the people you meet are enjoying the power game and trying to make a living; lawyers who want a judgeship or who are hoping to build up their practice by meeting the "right" people, real estate professionals, political groupies, special interest people, lobbyists, and others who use politics to get an economic or social competitive edge. Idealists are very much in the minority and regarded as kooks by party professionals. "Better" government movements too often on inspection turn out to reflect expressions of narrowly defined self-interests, regardless of ideology.

But you will also encounter politicians and individuals struggling to find and do the right thing and having one hell of a time coming up with workable solutions to social and economic problems that voters will understand and accept, and that will get by the unofficial veto power of special interest groups and PACs. "Muddling through" (Professor Charles Lindblom's theory) seems to be the major activity both in campaigns and in government.*

If you win, you'll learn that holding public office is a job that can be more satisfying than any other—if you have the taste, patience, energy, and guts for it. To survive whole, you'll have to become at least partially a "political animal"—one whose instincts are quick and accurate and for whom the political context of any decision is always paramount. To be re-elected is perceived by most politicians as the first necessity; no other priority is normally allowed to interfere.

This postscript is intended to give the new candidate a realistic idea of what campaigning is like and perhaps to provide other readers with a

---

*The theory states that real innovative change in government isn't possible; all we can hope for are small increments of improvement as we deal with immediate short-range problems.

more sympathetic understanding of candidates and the pressures of political campaigns.

CAMPAIGNERS' IMPRESSIONS

The following are common impressions of first-time campaigners: There are constant and urgent demands on your time, money, patience, and emotions. You will have to learn to suffer both fools and insults gladly. You'll spend hours with people with whom you would not be found under any circumstances except for the needs of campaigning. You'll start to distrust certain friends and staff members and wonder whether they're really loyal to you; you'll discover that a certain amount of paranoia is normal in a campaign and often is justified. All of your volunteers and contributors will feel that they own a piece of you and will act accordingly, whether or not their contributions are really significant. Incompetents tend to be as greedy and demanding as competent campaigners, if not more so.

Perhaps most unnerving, your family may have to make appointments to see you. You will have to listen to seemingly endless boring speeches, while eating indifferently prepared food, and applaud and congratulate dutifully. Your past will come under careful, hostile scrutiny. Your finances, sexual predilections, and business arrangements are constantly reviewed by journalists, civic groups, and actual and potential opponents seeking and sometimes creating the worst possible interpretation. The Mike Wallace *Sixty Minutes* inquisition will seem kind in comparison. You will have to shake countless hands and make idle conversation with people whose faces become blurs, and whose discourses and conversation are not as interesting or as important as they seem invariably to think they are. You will have to watch your every public word and public gesture at times when few of your words and gestures are not public.

Often, in a quiet moment, you will wonder why you got involved in the first place and whether it is really worth it. This question is much better asked before the campaign begins than after you get seriously involved. I always ask first-time candidates who are potential clients to think this through carefully at the very beginning. It is an exercise well worth the time. *If you have any doubts at all, you should not campaign for public office.* The physical, emotional, and financial costs are too high to entertain any reservations. Many experienced politicians are hardened to a degree by the constant round of trade-offs, accommodations, deals, and counterdeals; the need for important decisions on little data and less time, and the pressures from lobbyists and constituents whose needs are selfish and often without real relevance to long-term public concerns. Their sensitivities necessarily become reduced in order to survive.

In campaigning, speaking your mind candidly and fully will also be a luxury. Speaking out for the public interest is usually the hard way to go. A 19th-century European Jewish thinker, Achad Ha'am ("One of the People") wrote:

> I live for the perpetuation and happiness of the community of which I am a member; I die to make room for new individuals who will mold the community afresh and not allow it to stagnate and remain forever in one position. When the individual thus values the community as his own life and strives after its happiness as though it were his individual well being, he finds satisfaction and no longer feels so keenly the bitterness of his individual existence, because he sees the end for which he lives and suffers.*

Not many political leaders now appear to feel that it is politically feasible to act that way. The tremendous power of the PAC has made speaking plainly very difficult for candidates and politicians.** Public service needs often conflict with private ambition and the pervasive practical needs of government (working with other politicians, getting along with the leadership and your peers, representing conflicting client groups, etc.) under tremendous time and emotional pressures.

EXPENSE

J. Pierpont Morgan was reputed to have replied to the question, "How wealthy do you have to be to afford a yacht?" by saying: "If you have

---

*Quoted in Stimson Bullitt, *To Be A Politician* (Garden City, New York: Doubleday, 1959, p. 41).

**Many observers feel that politicians on the national scale, statewide, and in large cities measure all policy recommendations in campaigns and in office as to the likely effect on the larger PACs (political action committees representing special interest groups) to a larger extent than ever before seen in American politics. Many political science specialists believe that the problems government in America has to deal with are more massive than ever before and with a declining resource base; the existence of aggressive, well-funded PACs may have the effect of making many of the problems completely insoluble since the system allows only a small part of the problem, deferred by each special interest, to be dealt with, and always in the short term.

Presidential candidates Gary Hart and Walter Mondale in March 1983 indicated that they would not take PAC funds; congressmen were saying in early 1983 that public financing of congressional campaigns was desperately required. There are 11,000 registered lobbyists in Washington, D.C.

to ask, you can't afford it." To a certain extent, the same principle holds true for politics. Campaigning is expensive.* Once you decide to run for office, one of the first things you will note is the amount of money that must be spent and the bewildering variety of goods and services on which to spend it. In 1982, over one billion dollars was spent in the United States on political campaigns; almost all of it was raised privately.**

The novelist Gore Vidal, considering a U.S. Senate primary race in California in 1982, thought it obscene that $2,000,000 was required in order to be thought a credible candidate. Campaigns are costly and by their nature tend often to exclude potential candidates of only moderate means. If, after carefully listing your probable expenses and potential sources of funds, you have any doubts about whether you can afford to campaign for public office, you probably ought to forget it.*** This is not to say that only the very rich can run for office; but certainly, without reasonably generous access to other people's money, poor people cannot.

Governor Nelson A. Rockefeller shocked many political observers by spending $5,000,000 on his 1970 New York campaign for re-election. But by 1978, candidates Perry Duryea and Hugh Carey, who did not have Rockefeller's vast personal resources, each exceeded that amount in campaigning for the same office in New York. In 1982, the New York Republican Louis Lehrman spent $14,000,000, largely his own money, in his unsuccessful race for Governor. Jay Rockefeller spent $11,000,000 running for governor in West Virginia. Senatorial campaigns cost from $1,000,000 to $4,000,000 or more, for primary and general elections each in 1982. Senator Daniel Patrick Moynihan (New York) spent $3,000,000 in a general election against an unknown opponent without

---

*Although there have been many studies on the costs of elections—the most notable being Herbert E. Alexander's *Financing the 1968 Election* (Lexington, Mass.: Heath, 1971) and Alexander Heard's *The Costs of Democracy* (Chapel Hill: University of North Carolina Press, 1960)—"[no] rigorous examination has been made of the bearing on the size of campaign funds on the outcome of popular elections." V. O. Key, Jr., *Politics, Parties and Pressure Groups* (5th Edition: New York: Crowell, 1965, p. 617). The *New Yorker's* Washington correspondent Elizabeth Drew published a brilliant two-part examination of the influence of money on politics. (*New Yorker*, December 6 and 13, 1982.) She concludes that the influence of contributors on the political and legislative process has grown at an alarming rate.

**It is widely believed that there is an exponential mark-up on this; I would not be surprised if the ratio is 50:1 that is, for every dollar of private contributions 50 dollars of public monies is committed to the wrong purpose (disturbed public priorities) or to the wrong contractors.

***I have always found it advisable to add 35 percent to even carefully developed preliminary budget estimates of campaign costs. But economical campaigns, if well thought out and intelligently executed, do win, even against vastly superior financial resources.

significant funds. Congressionals in 1982 averaged $400,000 to $600,000. Congressmen Tom Lantos (California) and Barney Frank (Massachusetts) each spent over $1,000,000 in their 1982 congressional campaigns.

Candidates Mark Green and William Green, competing in 1980 for a Manhattan congressional seat, in an unusual act of statesmanship agreed to what they thought a very modest limit of $367,000. Such an agreement is very rare in campaigns, although it makes a great deal of sense.

State Assembly campaigns, featuring bitter primaries, are also becoming expensive, according to several accounts. Andrew Stein spent more than $200,000 in his campaign to represent Manhattan in the State Assembly in 1968. (Usually Assembly races cost from $35,000 to $65,000.)* By 1977, Andrew Stein was running for borough president and spending over $1,000,000 in his successful race.

These are exceptionally costly campaigns. However, even in 1984, most smaller campaigns should run $25,000 to $50,000. There are over 500,000 local elective offices in the U.S. and over 13,000 offices chosen in statewide campaigns. The great majority of these local races are probably under $35,000 in campaign costs.

Exogenous events also can control, despite money, to a large degree; e.g., top-of-the-ticket weakness (Carter in 1980), three- and four-candidate races, disgust and fear of inflation and unemployment, a scandal breaking, the wrong publicity (in 1977, a federal agency announced two weeks before the New York mayoral primary that the city's fiscal problems were largely the incumbent Mayor Beame's fault). In a four-week congressional campaign to replace Congressman Ben Rosenthal (Queens, New York), who died, Doug Schoen, 29, a leading political pollster, spent over $350,000 using TV, radio, phones (100,000 calls), and the state of the art in political technology. He ran as an independent and lost to the Democratic candidate; only 28,000 people voted and the line (party) controlled. Schoen came in third.

TIME CONSUMED

Running for election takes a lot of time, and while campaigning you can't expect to have a normal professional and family life. In some states, a

---

*Campaign cost figures are best thought of as approximations. Most experienced observers do not believed published estimates of campaign costs because there are too many ways of getting around disclosure regulations; cash contributions and cash payments are commonly used although they are illegal.

candidate entering a primary must prepare physically and emotionally for a six-month siege. Many consultants ask their candidates to lose weight, and not just for telegenic reasons. A candidate needs to be in good shape for a grueling, physically and emotionally demanding schedule. The length of time involved in campaigning has been criticized as impossible and unnecessary, but thus far there have not been any significantly successful attempts to reduce it.*

Since some offices involve elections every two years, many public officials may be campaigning and away from important public business for as much as one-fourth of their time in office. The actual public campaign may take as little as two or three months, but preparations usually begin about six months before election day. Jimmy Carter apparently started a precedent by running for the presidency a full two years before the election. Reagan and his Republican primary colleagues also started years before the actual election. For the 1984 presidential primaries, campaigning by Democrats got seriously underway in mid-1982.

In reality, legislators are often forced to choose between the demands of governmental business and the requirements of winning re-election. Almost all legislators take the view that re-election is the first priority, so there is in effect a consensual sacrifice of the public interest for a certain period of time every two years. Political parties do not criticize each other for taking the time away from public work to campaign despite other pressing legislative duties, since the structure of the system really forces this course for all members of both parties. This is one reason why a number of political scientists have suggested that the democratic process would be improved if each legislator—and even the President—were allowed only a single, six-year term of office. President Carter urged this course for the office he held.**

CAMPAIGNING FRUSTRATIONS

Every campaign has its frustrations, and you can expect your full share. Even very good, experienced campaigners go through agony in each

---

*Basically, the recommendations are to use the English system, which limits campaigns to two months; recently critics have also recommended banning television advertising, which would cut costs in half for large area campaigns, and in my judgment, save an awful lot of public money in the sweetheart arrangements (political contracts) that often follow a successful campaign.
**New York Times, March 19, 1981, p. 20.

campaign. Raising funds is usually difficult; dealing with the press and with radio and television reporters is always demanding. Misinterpretations of views are common; even sympathetic and knowledgeable reporters tend to focus only on the dramatic, sometimes distorting and sometimes clouding the differences between candidates. Politicians with serious views to impart often have difficulty getting their views publicized. Media people don't think it's news; it's not interesting. Issues that are complex are often distorted by the press and TV news in the effort to be punchy and interesting, making the voters' choices more black and white than they ever were or could be. Professionally, each campaign is a life-or-death affair, no matter how distinguished the candidate's past record. A loss can finish a candidate's political career. Because of this, many candidates feel constrained from speaking their minds freely. Professional politicians become very guarded in their public statements.

ROLE OF THE PRESS

Many campaigners find the role of the press in political contests particularly distressing. In a very real sense the press provides the issues and the choices by defining for the public the parameters of the campaign. Often newsmen can completely miss the point, a fact which works in favor of some candidates and against others. Until relatively late in his second term of office, Mayor John V. Lindsay led an almost completely charmed life with the New York (and national) press. *The New York Post* adored him and long refrained from criticizing him in its columns. (The publisher's son-in-law, Werner Kramarsky, was for some years one of Lindsay's chief executive assistants.) *The New York Times* for years congratulated Lindsay for his progressivism and began to express doubts about his performance only halfway into his second term office. Not until 1970 did the newspapers discuss Lindsay's massive consultants' costs, regarded by many as a modern form of patronage.* The additional 60,000 persons added to the city's payroll, the breakdown of services, the mounting taxes all somehow were not regarded as worthy of newspaper attention until very late. Lindsay ran for a second term in 1969 *against* his record in his first term, with only minor criticism from the major local news-

---

*Martin Tolchin of the *New York Times*, in a series of articles in 1971, indicated that New York City spent $75 million in 1970 in consulting contracts completely controlled by the mayor's office.

papers. Any politician running against Lindsay would have felt frustrated by the press treatment of his opponent.

In 1981, Mayor Koch running for re-election in New York also seemed to be living a charmed political life. Although he had inherited a very troubled City Administration, he was receiving very high approval ratings in all published polls despite declines in all major public services, a rapidly deteriorating subway system, increasing crime, lack of adequate housing, a low quality yet very expensive public education system. Luck is important for politicians. Sharply inflationary trends had increased sales, personal income, and business tax receipts so that the City's fiscal situation had notably improved.* And, probably as importantly, the press corps liked him—he made good copy. He clearly enjoyed being Mayor and always had good one-liners available. His luck turned in his campaign against Mario Cuomo for governor; his candor in a *Playboy* interview hurt him badly in upstate New York.

Most candidates cannot expect to be so fortunate as Lindsay and Koch, who are attractive to newspapermen and their editors as well. Lindsay and Koch also exemplify another trend in campaigning: Personality has become as important as ideology, performance, or party labels. A little arithmetic may clarify this point.

In the average primary election, perhaps 30 to 35 percent of a party's enrolled voters come out. Of this number perhaps two thirds have made up their minds from the very beginning. Consequently, the "undecided"—the key group in all campaigns—amounts to perhaps only 10 percent of the party's total enrollment.

In a general election, perhaps 60 percent of enrolled voters actually vote, and studies show that party labels mean less and less; a third of the voters in the United States are now independents. Most polls suggest that a substantial proportion of voters make up their minds soon after the candidates announce, but that a full 15 to 20 percent of all voters still haven't made up their minds even a few days before the election. Many experienced professionals believe that at least 10 percent of all voters actually decide in the voting booth. The odds are that many of the decisions are made on the basis of primal "gut" reactions to the candidate's personality that emerges from press reportage and TV coverage as much as on ideological considerations—political philosophy, a view of nec-

---

Wall Street Journal, March 20, 1981, p. 1.

essary public policy, or a judgment of which candidate can best provide the leadership to implement preferred public policies. Also, many voters decide, not out of love of a particular candidate but because of their distrust and sometimes distaste for the candidate's opponent. The 1980 presidential campaign between Reagan and Carter illustrates this very well. Reagan seemed a nice guy who wouldn't bomb Russia and end life on this planet. His ideas were those of Goldwater, who badly lost to Johnson, but his communicator skills were better. Many voters simply didn't like Carter.

THE "WHOLE SHMEER" SYNDROME

There are pressures on candidates to buy every possible device in campaigning. Consultants and salesmen will be all over campaign headquarters if they sense a "serious money" campaign. Because of the constant pressures, and because campaigning is not an exact science, some candidates tend to rely on buying the "whole shmeer."* Many campaigners believe that if they use literally (and liberally) everything— TV, radio, newspaper and magazine ads, billboards, posters, telephone campaigns, computerized mailings, professional TV and public relations people, advertising technicians, market research people, sampling survey people, and giveaways—they guarantee a victory. In my judgment, all that candidates guarantee by using this smorgasbord of techniques is that they will spend a hell of a lot of money and that much of it will be wasted.** The German proverb, "less is more," which the great architect Mies van der Rohe made famous, is appropriate in guiding campaign investments. Selectivity, thought, creativity, and targeting are the keys to good campaign tactics; money can never be a surrogate for good judgment, although many politicians and consultants act as if it could be.

CANDIDATES AND CAMPAIGN MANAGERS AS ADMINISTRATORS

Many first-time campaigners, and even some experienced campaigners, make the mistake of believing they can simultaneously campaign (make

---

*"Shmeer," a word which has come into English from Yiddish, is defined by Leo Rosten in *The Joys of Yiddish* (New York: Pocket Books, 1979, p. 358) as "the whole package," "the entire deal." Among its other meanings, interesting enough, are "a bribe" and "to spend," and "to smear."

**Many politicians and consultants say at least 50 percent of campaign costs are a waste; the problem is to determine which half.

appearances and give public addresses, for example) and manage or direct the campaign. It's a very natural temptation. As Walter Diamond, an experienced New York campaign manager, remarked, "The only way you can really keep a candidate out of managing a campaign is to have his signed resignation in the safe." But as much as possible, after the campaign strategy has been mapped out, the candidate should stay out of day-to-day direction of campaign details.*

Some candidates feel that their administrative interests will be best served by hiring the most expensive campaign manager available, on the theory that high costs assure high quality. That is not always a guarantee, of course. In such situations, the candidate simply tells the manager, "Take care of everything. Don't bother me with details." Other candidates lay out policies carefully with staff consultation, indicating how much is available for what and giving the manager discretion within those agreed upon limits. This course, in my view, is preferable.

From my insider's view, a number of campaigns that the press thought creative and professional could more accurately be characterized as creative chaos. In some measure, this can't be avoided. Decisions are not always enforceable, since in many instances the people involved, particularly contributors and personal friends, take it as their natural right to appeal back to the candidate or the candidate's spouse or family. Often campaign decisions are made as if prior experience didn't exist. Talk knowledgeably and—*poof*—you are an expert. In some cases, the last man to see the candidate tends to control a decision and even a major policy.

In one congressional campaign in which I was involved, I learned afterward that the candidate checked each decision, no matter how trivial, with seven advisors, none of whom were ever seen in campaign headquarters, and none of whom were in communication with one another. Like show business people, whose insecurities are legendary, politicians tend to be doubting and unsure in campaigns while on the surface very decisive. In the course of a campaign no one is ever certain whether he has a hit or a flop, no matter how great the star, no matter how lavish the expenditure.

---

*A. Steinberg, in his *Political Campaign Management*, analyzes campaigning using business management theory. This assumes rationality: I have never seen or heard of a major campaign that was conducted rationally in all particulars using business management techniques. The way a candidate's campaign is managed tells a lot about the type of public official he will be if elected.

Partly because of these very natural insecurities, and partly because of the growing complexity and expense of major campaigns, candidates have increasingly relied on professional managers. After successful campaigns, these managers often take an important role in government affairs. For example, President Carter made his campaign manager, Hamilton Jordan, the second most powerful man in the federal government. President Reagan did the same with Richard Meese 3rd. Having been a campaign manager perhaps may be adequate experience for running a huge, complex bureaucracy, but it doesn't seem that likely. Professional campaign managers of experience and talent come high. Salaries of $2,000 to $5,000 a week have been reported in large city- and statewide campaigns.

WHY DO THEY DO IT?

Psychoanalytic critiques of the lives of politicians and statesmen suggest that a neurotic compulsion is often at the root of the desire for public office. Sometimes revenge against parents is cited; sometimes the subliminal defeat of the candidate's father or brother or sister. Whatever the validity of theories such as these, it does seem clear that the personal lives of many leading politicians cannot be normal; when their insecurities and defense systems are threatened, they need different types of ego reassurances than do people whose lives are less pressure-packed. For many candidates, of course, the public actually seems to become a sort of family.

Considering the emotional and financial drains involved in campaigning, and keeping in mind that most office seekers make very good livings in law, business, or other professions, ''Why do they do it?'' still is a difficult question to answer.

Years ago, in *Psychopathology and Politics,** Harold D. Lasswell stated that Freudian insights could explain much of political behavior. More recently, practitioners of psychiatry who perceive history in personal emotional terms made news when they attempted to apply their methodology to explain the behavior of President Nixon.

In my experience, simpler explanations, like the enjoyment of the excitement and the love of power, may explain the motivations of many politicians. Mayor Robert F. Wagner used to say that he sometimes woke

---

*Chicago: University of Chicago Press, 1930.

up depressed by New York City's problems but that he would be cheered by the prospect of naming some judges that day—he had the power to decide whether to make or unmake a man's fortune overnight. Some politicians sincerely wish to serve the public, and have established in their own experience what has to be done. They want the power to implement their views.* Many hope that public office will give a meaning to their lives that their personal fortunes do not provide. For a certain number of men, the enticement of the available and attractive women one frequently meets in political life is a significant factor. People look up to elected officials, and this in part motivates many candidates to aspire to become a governor or senator. This may even result in aspirations for the presidency. There is a sense of money and power and excitement about political life, and for many candidates this is reason enough to sustain the ordeals of campaigning.

However, a sobering perception seems to be developing among mayors, congressmen, and senators. Overwhelmed by constant tensions and frustrations, by what they report is the inability to govern without sufficient resources at their disposal, many are retiring early. Congressmen and senators have given up their seats in significant numbers in recent years; the job has become too much of a strain, too much of a financial and emotional sacrifice.

If you have any doubts whatever, avoid political life. If, however, after considering all the disadvantages, you still wish to run for public office, I believe this book will show you how to organize the most effective possible campaign with the resources available to you.

---

*Once people with such hopes are elected to office, they are often surprised to discover how little power they actually have. Implementing even a proposal which has been commonly agreed to usually turns out to involve a multiplicity of obstacles, participants, and compromises. Nothing seems to go in a straight line in the government process—there are usually erratic ups and down in any major decision or policy. The absence of an understandably valid long-term view as a context for decision making in large part causes this enormous waste of time and public monies.

Appendices

Major Cost Items

The following listing is included to help you determine the cost of a campaign. Almost every item has been discussed in the book. I hesitated including this listing because the sheer number of cost items in a campaign can frighten a lot of new candidates. Don't let it. Many of the items can be managed quite reasonably if you think things through and make careful plans. To each item, add consulting charges if you don't intend to or can't do it yourself.

1. Logistics
   a. Headquarters
      1. Rent
      2. Gas, electricity, oil, water, cleaning and maintenance, insurance
      3. Office furniture
      4. Telephone—installation and message units
      5. Typewriters
      6. Supplies—paper, pens, ribbons, etc.
      7. Copy machine
      8. Refrigerator—cold drinks, coffee, etc.
   b. Salaries—paid staff, social security, etc.
   c. Logistic support—volunteers
   d. Legal expenses
   e. Bookkeeping expenses
   f. Staff travel, advance costs, renting hotel suites, restaurant meals
2. Research
   a. Survey research
      1. Benchmark or comprehensive survey
      2. Tracking surveys
      3. Flash surveys
      4. Focus groups
      5. Computer tabulation charges
   b. Negative research
      1. Personal and professional record
      2. Legislative record, including attendance
      3. Newspaper subscriptions
   c. Issue research
      1. Reference books
      2. Travel to library and state capital, if needed

3. Media
   a. Radio—production, cost of time and time buying service; consultants fees, if required
   b. Television—same as (a)
   c. Brochures, handbills, mailers, etc.—design, mechanicals, printing, bagging and delivery, consultants' expenses, if used
   d. Other—design and printing of stationery, buttons, stickers, logo design, billboards, yard signs, bus-subway signs, etc.; consulting fees, if used
   e. Direct mail—preparation of copy, buying and/or developing target lists; getting postal permits, postage, folding and stuffing costs, labels, design (this is used for fund-raising, converting voters, and getting-out-the-vote mailers)
4. Telephone banks
   a. Buy registration lists
   b. Convert to telephone numbers
   c. Install telephones (plus message charges and a huge deposit in most states)
   d. Rent and supporting costs—utilities, etc.
   e. Supervisor's salary
   f. Callers' salaries if no volunteers available

Outline Timetable For A June Primary

This book has described and analyzed the functional requirements of a campaign. This appendix puts these requirements in outline form in a time frame—that is to say, in a logical continuity. Although dates of state primary elections vary, this model traces the steps in a typical period from the decision to run to primary day, assuming a June primary. (If you win the primary, you would, of course, repeat the cycle in the general election.)

In thinking about costs, you ought to assign an amount to each function in the outline, depending on whether you intend to use amateurs or professionals, and then add up all the items. After you recover from the shock, go through the list again and subtract from those you think are less effective. Keep examining each cost against possible combinations of strategy with the advice of experienced people, until you get your basic budget total. Remember that the "first cut" tends to decide the other expenditures—if you favor direct mail, for example, there will be less for radio and television. If you can raise the amount of money that you have projected as a total, then go ahead. If not, that's a good reason not to run. Also, you may win the primary, so you ought to calculate the campaign costs of the general election as well, and judge whether you'll be able to meet these costs, making the reasonable assumption that your fund-raising capability in that case will be increased appreciably.

Time	Decision or Process Requirement	Things that Have to be Done	Cost Range
January or February or earlier	Precampaign phase: decide on whether or not to run; examine financial requirements.	Check for party and political club potential support; family, friends, business associates' reaction; recognition survey (usually shows you are less well-known than incumbent but also gives idea of opponents' weakness); check with party on potential funds from other candidates, etc. If you run, can you develop a personal staff? What will happen to your business and family? How much will it cost? How many people? Can you afford consultants? Set up bookkeeping system.	Cost for recognition survey—$3,000 (not absolutely required); time taken from work in this phase—may forego normal income. Survey results may help in getting contributions.
January– February	Pull together background data.	Talk to politicians in your party and to political reporters on local newspapers; buy enrollment books and election maps of district from board of elections; examine census data and past voting patterns of area carefully. Establish your base and target groups.	Income foregone; entertainment and book expenses—approximately $150, election maps— $35–$75.
March	Decide whether or not to make race—if no, you're still a free man; if yes, you'll have your hands full from now on. Find campaign manager and secretary and set up skeleton headquarters with their assistance	Find small headquarters, for perhaps five or six people, with some expandability. Need fifty to sixty square feet/person; usually space has to be designed—cubbyholes or bullpens, etc. Locational factors include prestige, costs, convenience, safety, accessibility. Campaign manager should talk to real estate people—hotels, motels, offices, storefronts, and homes have all been used successfully. Keep in mind the uses of headquarters and make your choice early.	Overhead: rent, staff salaries, furniture rental, etc.

Time	Decision or Process Requirement	Things that Have to be Done	Cost Range
March–April*	Full campaign staff (people in charge of volunteers; media; research; logistics; political liaison).	Decide who's responsible for what. Do print and media plan.	Continuing overhead costs.
	Start petitioning and canvassing.	Get experienced person to train canvassers. (Note: To make certain that petitions are legally correct, get legal advice on format, filing form, etc. Also you must usually have a committee on vacancies in case you become ill, apart from normal political wear.) Determine who is in charge of volunteers. Determine how many "good" signatures are desired and where to get them.	Care and feeding of volunteers.
	Get full campaign activities underway.	Pick printer after reviewing samples from each one considered; check out reliability—does he meet deadlines? Prepare literature to be distributed by canvassers. (This is often overlooked.) Set up required financial filings.	Designing and printing.
	Do sample survey to ascertain priority requirements on issues, relative standing, areas, and client groups.	Hire research consultant or start training volunteers rapidly; arrange for sample design, interviews, coding, editing, and analysis. Results should be due fifteen days after first survey (March 20). This research is absolutely critical. It will be the basis for your major time and expenditure decisions and will provide the context for the issues you want to emphasize.	Varies greatly—figure $6,000–$8,000.

Time	Decision or Process Requirement	Things that Have to be Done	Cost Range
March–April	Development of campaign theme.	Hire advertising agency or media consultant, or appoint one staff member to act exclusively in this area. This phase has to be completed before the others, since for canvassing and literature distribution copy must be written and billboards, mailings, etc., coordinated. Publicity should be designed to dramatize issues and points of view and to attack opponent in carefully chosen areas where he or she is potentially weak. Finalize print and media plan. Decide on direct mail for contributions.	Media costs are higher than you will think reasonable. Estimates depend on target groups, number of first class mail pieces, etc.
	Full headquarters complement should be at work.	Hire additional staff or recruit volunteers. Candidates and campaign manager should interview for key support staff spots—e.g., liaison to client groups as need is indicated by research.	Continuing overhead; maybe additional salaries.
	Publicity campaign is active.	Retain direct-mail consultant if direct mail will be used; retain telephone consultant if telephone campaign is planned (actual telephoning begins in May). Based on research, settle on client groups to be emphasized. Decide on giveaways (if any); pick supplier. If doing own mailings, make sure to have bulk rate postage data and necessary Post Office permit. Arrange for any necessary rentals of cars, trucks, or loudspeakers; buy bullhorns.	Depends on options chosen and volume desired—calls, direct mail, brochures, etc. Count on more, not less, than you expect.

Time	Decision or Process Requirement	Things that Have to be Done	Cost Range
March–April		Media emphases must be decided by end of March. Television and radio time must be purchased *early*.	Expensive. What can you afford? What will help? Which groups must you reach? What do you have to do to be credible?
		Do your scheduling. Make it consistent with research findings; forget your intuition! Prepare key speech but try to vary it; try to speak extemporaneously as much as possible. Professional speech-writers are expensive but worth it in large-scale races.	Continuing overhead; possibly fees for writers.
		Check press and research reactions to your issues. By the end of March, you should pick the basic issue you want to hit and stay with it.	
		Fact sheet should be made for each area in your district including names of local politicians and civic leaders. (Best to include these, but if you miss one name, miss them all: the one will hate you eternally; all will forgive.)	Continuing overhead; printing or duplicating.
		Direct mail: decide how many pieces, exactly where and what, and which day of the week. First mailing announcing your candidacy should go out in mid-April. (Brochure should be suitable for street distribution as well.)	Varies. See pp.

Time	Decision or Process Requirement	Things that Have to be Done	Cost Range
March–April		Telephones: see pre-test results, approve message; prepare questions and answers on issues; settle on location; get phones installed.	See 248-265
		Endorsements: check research to see whose endorsement will help, and pursue it.	
		Prepare for opponent's attacks, using staff rough questioning routine, especially before press conference or tough appearance. Plan special strategies for debates and joint appearances with opponents. Do your negative research.	Continuing overhead.
	By end of April, total budget should be set.	Analyze commitments of funds, other anticipated expenses, and resources. Once budget is settled, stay within it, despite panic.	
May	Second opinion poll to check media impact; develop issues and priority of issues; walking tour areas; area emphasis for direct mail, client-group emphasis.	Second poll results should be due early in May. Spend half a day with research person or consultant analyzing results; then decide how you want to hit opponent(s).	More than you thought, but by this time exhaustion deadens the shock.
	Review relationship with the press.	Try to get some "action" with each campaign publication or proposal. Tie community deficiencies to opponent if some reasonable relation exists. Press is more likely to pick up short, action-oriented issue papers than longer conceptual ones.	

Time	Decision or Process Requirement	Things that Have to be Done	Cost Range
May	Publicity	Send out second mailing—why they should vote for you rather than opponent; key targets.	
		Design and print street literature, including palm cards and piece attacking opponent.	
		Telephone set-ups begin early in May; calling begins at end of May.	
	Review coordination of scheduling and research.	Make certain that telephone campaign is coordinated with speaking engagements in areas being telephoned, etc.	Continuing overhead.
June	By this time, the key issue should be staring you in the face.	Identify the key issue on the basis of your research and your sense of the way the campaign is going, and meet it straight on—but, for God's sake, pick the right one.	
Election Day	The time for decisions is past!	Maintain contact with poll watchers, and have canvassers get out the vote in "favorable" areas.	
		Prepare something for radio and television for either outcome. Say what you really want to; you've been holding it in, and now you're entitled—within reason.	
		Try to relax; you've done all anyone could.	
	The election day tabulations that some candidates pay for are a waste of money: In an important election, the press will do them anyway, and in any case, you'll learn the results soon enough.		
	Renting ballrooms is a stupendous waste of money. Have a quiet victory party a week later—and if you lose, why spend more money?		

*All these March–April activities go on simultaneously. Unfortunately, usually there is not enough time for sequencing, no matter how well you plan.

Bibliography

If you're going to campaign for the first time, you may not realize that campaign memos and the daily newspapers are the only reading you will have time for in the course of the campaign. The time to do background reading is at least one year before you start officially or unofficially to campaign.

There are hundreds of books that you might look at, but most are academic discussions of the influence of campaigning on the voter or anecdotal discussions of what a certain candidate said to his campaign manager (and author of the subsequent book). I have tried here to sort out the books that might be directly helpful to you for the specific requirements of a campaign.

Since the dynamics and the money available vary from one campaign to another, and since campaigning is an art and not a science (despite the mass of magazine and newspaper discussions of computers, political technology, etc.), I believe that, although the books listed and discussed here may help you, more often they will show you that a specific emergency response can't be made from any book. You can only try to prepare yourself as thoroughly as possible. In reading these books, bear this in mind, for in the final analysis it is *you* who must provide the unique style, the synthesis of emotion, intellect, energy, and response to issues that every campaign is and in the last analysis must be.

If you're a first-time candidate, some of these books may give you the sense of what your options are. If you're a student in a political science course, some will convey the essence and significance of campaigning and its place in the political system. Books that I would especially recommend for both groups are starred.

GENERAL BACKGROUND

Alexander, Herbert E. *Financing the 1960 Elections.* Lexington, Mass.: Heath, 1962.
_____. *Financing the 1964 Elections.* Lexington, Mass.: Heath, 1966.
_____. *Financing the 1968 Elections.* Lexington, Mass.: Heath, 1971. A leading authority on the financing of election campaigns explains why campaign costs have gone up so rapidly, who the contributors are, and how funds are used.
Alinsky, Saul D. *Rules for Radicals: A Radical Primer for Realistic Radicals.* New York: Random House, 1971. Alinsky was a successful organizer of groups for political action. The book points out that much effort is required to accomplish what often should be regarded as minimal public performance standards.
Beyle, Thad L. (ed.). *Planning and Politics.* New York: Odyssey, 1970. Public housing locations and other planning issues are by now almost completely political. Candidates

should familiarize themselves with the issues and the options that are open to elected and appointed officials. This book can be a start in that direction.

Blumenthal, Sid. *The Permanent Campaign*. Boston: Beacon Press, 1980. Interesting description of the leading media and polling consultants.

Boorstin, Daniel. *The Image, or What Happened to the American Dream*. New York: Atheneum, 1962. An interesting discussion of politics and "pseudo-events."

*Bullitt, Stimson. *To Be a Politician*. Garden City, N.Y.: Doubleday, 1959. A strikingly thoughtful, well written account of what it's like to campaign for public office, by a man who ran twice, unsuccessfully, for Congress.

Cantril, Albert H., and Roll, Charles W., Jr. *Hopes and Fears of the American People*. New York: Universe, 1971 (also available in paperback). A statistical analysis, broken down by demographic details and based on surveys of what concerns Americans, provides a context for congressional, city, and state campaigns but is of limited utility for local campaigns.

Committee for Economic Development. *Financing a Better Election System*. New York: Committee for Economic Development, 1968. Proposals to diminish the inequities that give the edge to monied candidates.

Congressional Quarterly *Weekly Report*. Available by subscription from Congressional Quarterly, 1925 K Street, N.W., Washington, D.C. 20006. A useful source for background on issues that are important in local as well as congressional races.

Curtis, Michael (ed.). *The Nature of Politics*. New York: Avon (paperback), 1963. A wide-ranging selection of essays on politics.

Facts on File. A well-indexed summary of political events, available by subscription from Facts on File, Inc., 119 West 57th Street, New York, N.Y. 10022.

Factual Campaign Information. Washington, D.C.: U.S. Government Printing Office, 1972. A basic reference work containing tables of past election data and federal statutes that control election procedures.

Farley, James A. *Behind the Ballots: The Personal History of a Politician*. New York: Harcourt, Brace, 1938.

Flynn, Edward J. *You're the Boss*. New York: Viking, 1947. Candid picture of how the "regular organization" operated in Bronx County, N.Y. Although the once-pervasive role of the organization in big-city politics is diminishing, Flynn's description is still largely accurate.

Heard, Alexander. *The Costs of Democracy*. Chapel Hill, N.C.: University of North Carolina Press, 1960 (also available in abridged form as a Doubleday-Anchor paperback). Thorough analysis of the impacts of campaign costs on the democratic process, based on data from the 1952 and 1956 elections and still the best work on the subject. By the board chairman of the Ford Foundation.

Heckscher, August. *The Public Happiness*. New York: Atheneum, 1962. A discussion of the large public issues by a man who became one of Mayor Lindsay's commissioners.

Hofstadter, Richard. *The Paranoid Style in American Politics and Other Essays*. New York: Knopf, 1965. A lucid, balanced analysis of right-wing American politics.

Kelley, Stanley. *Political Campaigning: Problems in Creating an Informed Electorate*. Washington, D.C.: Brookings Institution, 1960. An intelligent discussion by one of the first academics to write realistically about modern American politics.

Lane, Robert E. *Political Life: Why People Get Involved in Politics.* Glencoe, Ill.: Free Press, 1959. A summary of American political behavior.

Lasswell, Harold D. *Politics: Who Gets What, When, How (With Postscript—1958).* New York: Meridian, 1958 (paperback). An excellent discussion of what politics is all about, originally published in 1936 but still worth reading.

_____. *Psychopathology and Politics.* Chicago: University of Chicago Press, 1930. A work of originality, developing the theory of neurosis and political behavior.

Lippmann, Walter. *Essays in the Public Philosophy.* Boston: Little, Brown, 1955. Brilliant insights by a man who has always tried to see what was there, not what was supposed to be there.

_____. *Public Opinion.* New York: Macmillan, 1922. A discussion of the larger issues.

Lubell, Samuel. *The Future of American Politics.* New York: Harper $ Row, 1965. Worth reading for general background, even if you don't agree with all his theses.

MacNeil, Robert. *The People Machine: The Influence of Television on American Politics.* New York: Harper & Row, 1968. A comprehensive discussion of television in politics by an able newspaperman. The chapter entitled "Campaigning by Commercial" will be particularly useful to new campaigners.

Mazlish, Bruce. *In Search of Nixon: A Psychohistorical Inquiry.* New York: Basic Books, 1972. One of a number of interesting recent books that examine the psychological bases of politicians' activities. (Don't start asking yourself if you're neurotic because you want to run for office. Your motivation isn't as important as your political performance.)

McCarthy, Richard D. *Elections for Sale.* Boston: Houghton Mifflin, 1972. The high costs of campaigning and the constraints lack of money places on a candidate.

Mendelsohn, Harold, and Crespi, Irving. *Polls, Television, and the New Politics.* Scranton, Pa.: Chandler, 1970. The impact of television and political surveys on political campaigning. Useful descriptions of the importance of sampling accuracy and the interpretation of research data.

Moos, Malcolm. *Politics, Presidents, and Coattails.* Baltimore, Md.: Johns Hopkins Press, 1952. An amusing controversial story of national voting patterns in the first half of the twentieth century.

New York State College of Agriculture. *Your Road to Better Meetings.* Ithaca, N.Y.: New York State College of Agriculture, 1964. (Cornell Extension Bulletin 1134.) An excellent brief guide to organizing meetings properly and with maximum impact.

The New York Times Guide to Federal Aid for Cities and Towns. New York: Quadrangle, 1972. A helpful list of what funds are available and for what. (A federal manual, available from the Office of the President, Washington, D.C., describes the types of monetary assistance available.)

O.M. Collective. *The Organizer's Manual.* New York: Bantam, 1971. Details on the structuring of social change. Not intended primarily for political campaigns, but useful for ideas on fund-raising, organizing meetings, etc. Shows why some youth movements have been so successful: they're intelligent and they work hard.

Politeia: The Quarterly of the American Association of Political Consultants. Available from the Association, 1028 Connecticut Ave., N.W., Washington, D.C. 20036. A journal aimed primarily at political professionals rather than candidates. Interesting although not particularly helpful in planning campaign details.

Polsby, Nelson W.; Dentler, Robert A.; and Smith, Paul A. *Politics and Social Life: An Introduction to Political Behavior*. Boston: Houghton Mifflin, 1963. An excellent academic presentation.

Rosenbloom, David L. *The Election Men*. New York: Quadrangle, 1973. Description of consultants and their activities. (There is more published on this than on the details and options in campaign methods.)

Rosi, Richard. *Influencing Voters: A Study of Campaign Rationality*. New York: St. Martin's Press, 1967.

Royko, Mike. *Boss: Richard J. Daley of Chicago*. New York: Dutton, 1971 (also available as a Signet paperback). The Chicago Democratic machine and how it works.

Ruchelman, Leonard I. (ed.). *Big City Mayors: The Crisis in Urban Politics*. Bloomington, Ind.: Indiana University Press, 1970. Selected articles for reading by undergraduate students in political science.

Safire, William. *The New Language of Politics: An Anecdotal Dictionary of Catchwords, Slogans, and Political Usage*. New York: Random House, 1971. An amusing, instructive review, by a former member of the Nixon staff now with *The New York Times*.

Schlesinger, Arthur M., Jr. *The Crisis of Confidence: Ideas, Power, and Violence in America*. Boston: Houghton Mifflin, 1969. Contains an essay on the New Politics.

Scott, Andrew M. *Competition in American Politics: An Economic Model*. New York: Holt, Rinehart & Winston, 1979.

Scott, Hugh D., Jr. *How to Go into Politics*. New York: John Day, 1949. Revised as *How to Run for Public Office and Win*. Washington, D.C.: National Press, 1968. A rather general introduction by a U.S. senator from Pennsylvania.

Schwartz, Tony. *The Responsive Chord*. New York: Doubleday, 1973; and *Media: The Second God*. New York: Random House, 1982. This is the radio and television media consultant who candidates travel to see in his W. 56th Street house in Manhattan since he won't go to see them. These books are not on specifics but on the concepts of media. He has provided the conceptual vocabulary for much of what is done in media campaigns.

Sharkowsky, Ira. *The Routines of Politics*. New York: Van Nostrand Reinhold, 1970. A description of political conditioning processes, by a University of Wisconsin professor. Not an exposition of the mechanics or details of campaigning, but rather a discussion of what is customary in a larger, governmental sense.

Spero, Robert. *The Duping of the American Voter*. New York: Lippincott and Crowell, 1980. Specific campaigns and how the voter may get misleading information.

Tolchin, Martin, and Tolchin, Susan. *To the Victor: Political Patronage from the Clubhouse to the White House*. New York: Random House, 1971. The former City Hall bureau chief of the *New York Times* and his wife, a professor of political science, describe how political patronage motivates individuals and can affect even the most major public policies.

Ujifusa, Grant, Matthews, Douglas, and Barone, Michael. *The Almanac of American Politics*. New York: E. P. Dutton, 1980. A reference book providing brief political profiles of all 50 states and 435 congressional districts, with social and economic background and incisive commentary on each. Barone is now on the *Washington Post* editorial staff.

Voters Time: Report of the Twentieth Century Fund Commission on Campaign Costs in the Electronic Era. New York: Twentieth Century Fund, 1969. The impact of television on campaigning in general rather than in terms of the needs of individual campaigns.

Voting Rights and Residency: The Young Voter's Guide. Washington, D.C.: Youth Citizenship Fund, 1971. An examination of state laws.

Watts, William, and Free, Lloyd A. (eds.). *State of the Nation.* New York: Universe Books, 1973 (also available in paperback). A detailed survey and analysis of the public mood that provided a remarkably accurate guide as to the way voters intended to vote in November 1972.

Whale, John *The Half-Shut Eye: Television and Politics in Britain and America.* London: Macmillan; New York: St. Martin's Press, 1969. Not quite as good as MacNeil, but humorous and easy to read.

Wilson, James Q. *The Amateur Democrat: Club Politics in Three Cities.* Chicago: University of Chicago Press, 1962. A discussion of reform politics that may help those new to political clubs.

Wolfe, Alan, and McCoy, Charles. *Political Analysis: An Unorthodox Approach.* New York: Crowell, 1972.

GENERAL CAMPAIGN METHODS

Agranoff, Robert. *The New Style in Election Campaigns.* Boston: Holbrook Press, 1972. Also, *The Management of Election Campaigns,* 1976. Both are worth reading.

Allyn, Paul, and Green, Joseph. *See How They Run.* Philadelphia: Chilton, 1964. A practical but somewhat simplistic manual on campaign organization.

Atkins, Chester. *Getting Elected.* Boston: Houghton Mifflin, 1973.

Banati, Robert (ed.). *Winning Campaigns in the New Politics.* New York: Popular Library, 1972.

Baus, Herbert M., and Ross, William B. *Politics Battle Plan.* New York: Macmillan, 1968. More a historical study than a handbook of practical advice.

*Cannon, James M. (ed.). *Politics U.S.A.: A Practical Guide to the Winning of Public Office.* Garden City, N.Y.: Doubleday, 1960. Essays by John F. Kennedy, Adlai E. Stevenson, Richard M. Nixon, Louis Harris, and others, describing fund-raising techniques, polling, and campaign strategy. Although the details are sketchy, this useful book is interesting for the views of important political figures, including "Boss" Crump on fund-raising, Murray Chotiner's prescriptions for the campaigns of California candidates (including Richard M. Nixon in a senatorial race), and California Governor Edmund "Pat" Brown's views on the limits of research.

Cass, Don. *How to Win Votes and Influence Elections.* Chicago: Public Administration Press, 1962.

COPE (Committee on Political Education), AFL-CIO. *How to Win.* Washington, D.C.: COPE (815 16th St., N.W.), 1972. A practical booklet on campaigning, written especially for unions but useful for candidates as well.

Costikyan, Edward N. *Behind Closed Doors: Politics in the Public Interest.* New York: Harcourt Brace & World, 1966. Sketchy descriptions, by the former Democratic county leader (i.e., Tammany Hall chief) of Manhattan, of the use of political brochures, fund-raising, and canvassing. Helpful background about the role of district and county leaders and political party administrative problems.

Cutter, Cornelius. *Practical Politics in the U.S.* Boston: Allyn & Bacon, 1969.

Democratic National Committee, Office of Campaigns and Party Organization. *Campaign '72: Voter Registration Manual.* Washington, D.C.: Democratic National Committee, 1972. Good practical suggestions for registering voters.

Democratic National Committee, Washington, D.C. Workplace: Candidate activity; fund-raising; getting out the vote; media; budget and management; targeting. Separate brochures that should be useful to candidates of any party.

Edwards, Lee, and Edwards, Anne. *You Can Make the Difference.* New Rochelle, N.Y.: Arlington House, 1968. A practical book for concerned conservative Republican activists.

Emmet, Grenville T. III, and Emmet, Patricia B. *What the Pros Know: The Anatomy of Winning Politics.* New York: Information, Inc., 1968 (paperback). Amateurish and incomplete but nevertheless contains useful reminders.

Ertel, James. *How to Run for Office.* New York: Sterling, 1960. Useful, though dated.

Evry, Hal. *The Selling of a Candidate, 1971.* Los Angeles: Western Opinion Research Center, 1971. A sketchy book prepared by the president of a California firm that manages candidates. Very little detail, but useful for the presentation of a point of view in campaigning.

Felknor, Bruce L. *Dirty Politics.* New York: Norton, 1966. An analysis of several particularly dirty campaigns going back to the nineteenth century. In my experience, every campaign has some "dirty" aspects, but those described here are dramatically so.

Gaby, Daniel M. *Election Campaign Handbook.* Englewood Cliffs, N.J.: Prentice-Hall, 1976. Very lucid and worthwhile presentation, and at the time of publication it had the distinction of being the most expensive handbook published in the last ten years.

Hershey, Marjorie R. *The Making of Campaign Strategy.* Lexington: Lexington Books, 1974.

Hiebert, Ray E., et al. (eds.). *The Political Image Merchants: Strategies in the New Politics.* Washington, D.C.: Acropolis, 1971. Interesting brief papers, but of limited help for campaign specifics.

Howe, Quincy, and Schlesinger, Arthur M., Jr. *Guide to Politics, 1954.* New York: Dial, 1954. Essays on campaigning prepared for the Americans for Democratic Action. Dated but interesting reading.

*Huckshorn, Robert J., and Spencer, Robert C. *The Politics of Defeat: Campaigning for Congress.* Amherst, Mass.: University of Massachusetts Press, 1971. Careful analysis of congressional races and why certain candidates lost. The chapter on campaign organization and management is particularly useful, as is "Auxiliary Candidate Services," describing research, polling, and other campaign activities.

Johnson, Jerry. *How to Be Successful in Politics Without Really Being Competent.* New York: Vantage, 1968.

Kelley, Stanley. *Professional Public Relations and Political Power.* Baltimore, Md.: Johns Hopkins Press, 1956. A fine discussion of the first important professional campaign management firm, Whitaker-Baxter, which started the trend in California almost two decades ago. Examines the "selling of a candidate"—the use of public relations men and marketing techniques in campaigns. Now useful mostly for background.

Kirwan, Michael J. (as told to Jack Redding). *How to Succeed in Politics.* New York: McFadden-Bartell, 1964. A former congressman's reminiscences of Chicago politics and Democratic organization procedures, not intended as a focused guide to strategy and tactics.

*Levin, Murray B. *The Alienated Voter: Politics in Boston.* New York: Holt, Rinehart & Winston, 1960. A good discussion of the undecided voter and campaign techniques.

Lyford, Joseph P. *Candidate.* New York: Holt, 1959. What it's like to campaign for Congress.

Murphy, William T. *Vote Power.* Garden City, N.Y.: Anchor Press, 1974.

*Nimmo, Dan. *The Political Persuaders: The Techniques of Modern Election Campaigns.* Englewood Cliffs, N.J.: Prentice Hall, 1970. An excellent summary of campaign techniques, written by an academic. Also, *Political Attitudes and Public Opinion.* New York: David McKay, 1972.

Nimmo, Dan. *Candidates and their Images.* Pacific Palisades, Calif.: Goodyear Publishing, 1976. Interesting and worthwhile reading by a prolific writer on campaigning.

Parkinson, Hank. *Winning Your Campaign: A Nuts and Bolts Guide to Political Victory.* Englewood Cliffs, N.J.: Prentice-Hall, 1970. Written by an advertising man, this book touches all the bases but is very sketchy.

Patterson, Thomas. *Political Advertising: Voters Reactions to Televised Political Commercials.*

*Perry, James M. *The New Politics: The Expanding Technology of Political Manipulation.* New York: Potter, 1968. A newspaperman's analyses of Milton Shapp's Pennsylvania gubernatorial campaign in 1966 (directed by Joseph Napolitan) and the campaigning methods of Governors Nelson Rockefeller of New York, Winthrop Rockefeller of Arkansas, and George Romney of Michigan. Accurate descriptions of the new technology and the detailed "routines" of political campaigning. If you read only one book for background, this is the one to read.

Pohl, Frederik. *Practical Politics.* New York: Ballantine, 1971 (paperback). The author, a well-known science-fiction writer, entered politics as a volunteer in the McCarthy presidential campaign of 1968. His book contains many useful suggestions.

Polsby, Nelson W., and Wildavsky, Aaron B. *Presidential Elections: Strategies of American Electoral Politics.* New York: Scribner, 1964. An excellent analysis of national elections by two academics. Not particularly appropriate for local candidates, but succinctly written and among the best in the field—the section on research and surveys is worthwhile. Wildavsky's books on public administration and program budgeting are well worth reading if you attain public office.

Republic National Committee, Washington, D.C. has a set of beautifully produced and succinctly written booklets on public relations, fund-raising, etc.

Republican National Committee, Washington, D.C. *The Art of Winning Elections,* 1968. Well worth reading but hard to find in most area libraries. it consists of very perceptive articles by mechanics of quality.

Ribicoff, Abraham, and Newman, Jon O. *Politics: The American Way.* Boston: Allyn & Bacon, 1967. A good, quick review of campaigning intended primarily for high school and college readers.

Rose, Richard. *Influencing Voters.* New York: St. Martin's Press, 1967.

Rosenbloom, David L. (ed.). *The Political Market-Place.* New York: Quadrangle, 1972. Lists of elected and party officials and of campaign professionals and consultants whose services are available to candidates, with a bibliography and advertisements from professionals that might prove useful to some campaigners.

*Sabato, Larry. *The Rise of Political Consultants.* New York: Basic Books, 1981. A best-selling description by a University of Virginia professor. Describes media and polling beautifully; has critical comments on the consulting corps. Not designed as a manual on campaigning but very well worth reading because of the backgrounds supplied and because of the perceptive insights.

Shadegg, Stephen. *How to Win an Election: The Art of Political Victory.* New York: Taplinger, 1964. Revised as *The New How to Win an Election,* 1972. Probably won't be very helpful to new campaigners who need specific advice, but it is easy, interesting reading. Shadegg, the former state chairman of the Arizona Republican Party, was an adviser to Senator Barry M. Goldwater.

Simpson, Dick. *Winning Elections: A Handbook in Participatory Politics.* Chicago: Swallow, 1982 (also available in paperback). Excellent for the mechanics of petitioning, kaffeeklatches, and other such details, but not designed to help with overall campaign strategy. Simpson is an academic who ran for public office.

*Steinberg, Arnold. *Political Campaign Handbook* and *Political Campaign Management.* Lexington: Lexington Books, 1976. This handbook should be read by any serious student of campaigning.

Swing, Meyer D. *The Winning Candidate: How to Defeat Your Political Opponent.* New York: Heinman, 1966. One of the better books, with focus on preparing press releases, managing meetings, etc.

Tufts University, The Lincoln Filene Center for Citizenship and Public Affairs. *Practical Political Action: A Guide for Citizens.* Boston: Houghton Mifflin, 1970 (paperback). An introductory book for high school students; possibly useful for new candidates.

Van Riper, Paul P. *Handbook of Practical Politics.* 3d ed. New York: Harper & Row, 1967. Somewhat dated, but nevertheless useful.

SPECIFIC CAMPAIGNS

Bruno, Jerry and Greenfield, Jeff. *The Advance Man.* New York: Morrow, 1971. Interesting description of the work of Jerry Bruno, who was active in the Robert F. Kennedy, Goldberg, and Lindsay campaigns. Greenfield is a political speech writer who has worked for Lindsay and David Garth.

Buckley, William F., Jr. *The Unmaking of a Mayor.* New York: Viking, 1966. A chronicle of the 1965 New York mayoralty campaign, which gained John V. Lindsay his first term, written with humor and considerable style by Lindsay's Conservative opponent.

Chester, Lewis; Hodgson, Godfrey; and Page, Bruce. *An American Melodrama: The Presidential Campaign of 1968.* New York: Viking, 1969. A fine description by British journalists. The section "See How They Run" is excellent for campaign dynamics and for showing how research was used in developing and handling issues.

Flaherty, Joe. *Managing Mailer.* New York: Coward McCann, 1970 (also available as a Berkeley Medallion paperback). Norman Mailer and Jimmy Breslin ran for mayor and comptroller in the New York City Democratic primary of 1969, on the theme "Make New York City the 51st State." This book, by their campaign manager, describes the not-so-uncommon anarchy of even experienced campaigners and the constant squabbling that is typical of many campaigns.

Lebedoff, David. *The Sixth Ward.* New York: Scribner, 1972. A description of the activities of a local political club.

Leuthold, David A. *Electioneering in a Democracy: Campaigns for Congress.* New York: Wiley, 1968. An analysis, by an academic, of congressional elections in the San Francisco Bay Area in 1962. A useful analysis of campaign methodology based on the author's detailed survey.

*Levin, Murray B. *Kennedy Campaigning: The System and the Style as Practiced by Senator Edward Kennedy.* Boston: Beacon, 1966. A well-documented book on Edward M. Kennedy's first senatorial campaign, 1964, describing the formulation of strategy and the dynamics of campaigning as seen by campaign participants. Very explicit about the impact of big money properly used in a sophisticated "New Politics" campaign and how an effective TV campaign was directed.

*Levin, Murray B. and Blackwood, George. *The Compleat Politician: Political Strategy in Massachusetts.* Indianapolis, Ind.: Bobbs-Merrill, 1962. One of the best books on an individual campaign, describing the dynamics of Endicott ("Chub") Peabody's race for governor of Massachusetts, and how decisions get made and unmade in the course of a campaign. See especially pp. 179-225 on polling and pp. 271-309 on the decision-making process.

McGinniss, Joe. *The Selling of the President, 1968.* New York: Trident, 1969 (also available as a Pocket Books paperback). The use of television in Richard M. Nixon's 1968 presidential campaign.

Napolitan, Joseph. *The Political Game (and How to Win It).* New York: Doubleday, 1972. Anecdotes, reflections, and reminiscences, as well as campaign memoranda from the 1968 presidential contest, by a former newspaperman who was associated with the original Kennedy group and is now a well-known campaign professional.

Shadegg, Stephen. *What Happened to Goldwater: The Inside Story of the 1964 Republican Campaign.* New York: Holt, Rinehart & Winston, 1965. A criticism of Goldwater's campaign staff and speech writers and of the press.

Sorenson, Theodore. *Kennedy.* New York: Harper & Row, 1965. Useful discussion of primaries, convention strategies, and campaign dynamics.

———. *The Kennedy Legacy.* New York: Macmillan, 1969. More intellectual than practical, but helpful in describing how John F. Kennedy responded to issues and how he developed what came to be known as "the Kennedy style."

White, Theodore H. *The Making of the President, 1960.* New York: Atheneum, 1961 (also available as a New American Library paperback).

———. *The Making of the President, 1964.* New York: Atheneum, 1965 (also available as a New American Library paperback).

————. *The Making of the President, 1968.* New York: Atheneum, 1969. The best overall accounts of the politicians and issues involved in these three presidential campaigns, but not particularly oriented toward the specific details of winning elections that might be useful in local campaigns.

RESEARCH AND SURVEYS

Abrams, Charles. *The Language of Cities: A Glossary of Terms.* New York: Viking, 1971. An excellent survey of nomenclature and the bureaucratic processes involved in housing and other urban programs.

American Society of Planning Officials. *Advisory Reports,* issued by the Society, 1313 East 60th Street, Chicago, Ill. 60637. Periodic reports on zoning and housing legislation, matters that often involve local controversies and thus may be important in campaigning.

Backstrom, Charles H., and Hursh, Gerald D. *Survey Research.* Evanston, Ill.: Northwestern University Press, 1972 (paperback). A brilliant book that avoids mathematical statistics but describes the mechanics very well. The authors "will attribute any errors to each other." There aren't many.

Bean, Louis. *How to Predict Elections.* New York: Knopf, 1948. Bean, a well-regarded statistician, correctly predicted the Truman victory in 1948, and his book still has utility.

————. *How to Predict the 1972 Election.* New York: Quadrangle, 1972. Historical and statistical background for sorting out available data to predict the outcome of the 1972 presidential election.

Cantril, Albert H., and Roll, Charles W. *Polls: Their Use and Misuse in Politics.* New York: Basic Books, 1972. An informative book well worth reading for background before you decide what type of poll to commission.

Fenton, John M. *In Your Opinion: The Managing Editor of the Gallup Poll Looks at Polls, Politics, and the People from 1945 to 1960.* Boston: Little, Brown, 1960. A description of how Americans felt and thought about political questions.

Fitch, Lyle C., and Walsh, Annamarie Hauck (eds.). *Agenda for a City: Issues Confronting New York.* Beverly Hills, Calif.: Sage, 1970. Essays by specialists in housing, transportation, economic development, and other fields containing useful ideas and background for any campaign staff preparing position papers in larger cities.

Frankel, Martin R. *Inference from Survey Samples: An Empirical Investigation.* Ann Arbor, Mich.: University of Michigan Institute for Social Research, 1971. A technical discussion of problems in statistical sampling, useful for someone with professional statistical experience.

Hansen, Morris H.; Hurewitz, William N.; and Madow, William G. *Sample Survey Methods and Theory.* 2 vols. New York: Wiley, 1953. One of the best texts in the field. Vol. 1, *Methods and Applications,* will be most useful to campaign staffs.

Holleb, Dorothy. *Social and Economic Information in Urban Planning.* 2 vols. Chicago: University of Chicago Press, 1970. Particularly useful discussion of survey techniques; lists detailed sources for published data valuable to candidates for issue and demographic analysis.

Journal of the American Institute of Planners, 917 15th Street, N.W., Washington, D.C. 20005. A quarterly technical publication that may be valuable in local campaigns in researching local housing, taxation, transportation, and zoning issues.

Kaplan, Abraham. *The Conduct of Inquiry: Methodology for Behavioral Science.* Scranton, Pa.: Chandler, 1964. A fine text; not easy to read, but worth the effort for any serious student.

Konrad, Evelyn, and Erickson, Rod. *Marketing Research: A Management Overview.* New York: American Management Association, 1966. Articles by professionals in market research include "Television Audience Research Basics," "Measuring Advertising's Sales Effectiveness: The Problem and the Prognosis," "Advertising Readership Studies," "Pretesting Television Commercials," "Motivational Research," and "The Art of Using Marketing Research."

Lansing, John B., and Morgan, James N. *Economic Survey Methods.* Ann Arbor, Mich.: University of Michigan Institute for Social Research, 1971. A lucid, thorough discussion of sampling, survey design, and procedures. Useful for candidates intending to do their own polling.

Lansing, John B.; Withey, Stephen B.; and Wolfe, Arthur C. *Working Papers on Survey Research in Poverty Areas.* Ann Arbor, Mich.: University of Michigan Institute for Social Research, 1971. Methods of doing sample survey research in inner-city poverty areas.

Municipal Yearbook, issued by the International City Managers Association, 1313 East 60th Street, Chicago, Ill. 60637. An excellent source book of statistics, with particular emphasis on trends in legislation.

*National Municipal League. *The Citizen Association: How to Win Civic Campaigns.* New York: National Municipal League (47 East 58th Street, 10021), 1963 (paperback). Especially interesting for civic groups. The League issues the *National Civic Review* and many other publications of interest to local and state-wide candidates.

*Payne, Stanley L. *The Art of Asking Questions.* Princeton, N.J.: Princeton University Press, 1951. The importance of questionnaire design in research; not intended particularly for political surveys but worthwhile for its insights on the components of a quality survey.

Public Opinion Quarterly, Room 510, Journalism Building, Columbia University, New York, N.Y. 10027. Contains many interesting items on polling techniques and sample design.

The RAND Corporation, 1700 Main Street, Santa Monica, Calif. 90401, a well-known research organization, issues technical reports of value for issue and background papers in larger campaigns. A complete listing of hundreds of available reports is obtainable free of charge from the corporation.

Robinson, John P.; Rusk, Jerrold G.; and Head, Kendra B. *Measures of Political Attitudes.* Ann Arbor, Mich.: University of Michigan Institute of Social Research, 1968. A historical study of ways of measuring political attitudes, with many practical applications useful to campaigners.

Selected Scientific and Technical Reports. Springfield, Va.: Clearinghouse for Federal Scientific and Technical Information. This U.S. Government service provides scientific papers at reasonable costs on housing, taxation, pollution, urban transportation, economic analysis, and other subjects, which may be useful in preparting position papers.

Shryock, Henry S., and Siegel, Jacob S. *The Methods and Materials of Demography.* 2 vols. Washington, D.C.: U.S. Bureau of the Census, 1972. A comprehensive, painstaking work intended for technicians but of value to the research staff of any professional campaign.

Stephan, Frederick J., and McCarthy, Philip. *Sampling Opinions.* New York: Wiley, 1960. A competent book for use as background in doing attitudinal surveys.

Survey Research Center, Field Office, Institute of Social Research, University of Michigan. *Interviewer's Manual.* Ann Arbor, Mich.: Survey Research Center, 1969. A training manual explaining how to record and edit and other sampling procedures; brief and to the point. Valuable for setting up your own research.

Tallmer, Jerry. Six articles in the *New York Post,* October 30, 1972-November 4, 1972. This is the best newspaper analysis of polling processes and problems I have seen.

U.S. Department of Commerce. *County City Data Book.* Washington, D.C.: U.S. Government Printing Office. Published several times a decade, this standard reference work provides data on all counties and cities. Topics include land areas, budgets, employment, farm production, race, and income. The best single overall summary available.

U.S. Department of Commerce, Bureau of the Census. *Atlantida: A Case Study in Household Sample Surveys,* prepared for the Alliance for Progress. 14 vols. Washington, D.C., U.S. Government Printing Office, 1966. This work, the most thorough one I know of, covers all aspects of planning a household sample survey program.

————. *Congressional District Computer Profiles for the . . . Congress.* Washington, D.C.: U.S. Government Printing Office. Statistical tabulations, issued every two years, for the congressional districts as districted for the November election, including data on population, employment, and housing as well as scale maps showing the boundaries of each district.

————. *Congressional District Data.* Washington, D.C.: U.S. Government Printing Office. Biennial summaries of census data conveniently arranged in one booklet per state, providing district maps, population, housing, and voting data for each congressional district.

————. *Current Population Survey.* Washington, D.C.: U.S. Government Printing Office. This periodic survey of 50,000 American families provides information throughout the year on the demographic characteristics of the population, including age, labor force, income, and other characteristics such as school enrollment trends and the number of 18-to-20-year-old voters. A serious candidate should familiarize himself with these data and with the methods used.

————. *Decennial Census.* Washington, D.C.: U.S. Government Printing Office. These data, the most complete set available, unfortunately become dated rapidly, so that by 1974, for example, the 1970 figures will have lost their value for local analysis, while by 1978 they will be almost entirely worthless. Campaign staff will have to use local sources—even rough estimates from local health departments and planning boards—and/or other Bureau of the Census publication to update.

_____. *Directory of Federal Statistics for Local Areas.* Washington, D.C.: U.S. Government Printing Office, 1966.

_____. *Directory of Federal Statistics for States.* Washington, D.C.: U.S. Government Printing Office, 1967.

_____. *Directory of Non-Federal Statistics for States and Local Areas.* Washington, D.C.: U.S. Government Printing Office, 1969. These three inexpensive, thorough publications can be invaluable in helping campaign staffs wade through the abundance of government data. Data for small communities is extremely difficult to track down without these guides.

_____. *Introduction to Small-Area Geographic Subdivisions for Which the U.S. Bureau of the Census Collects and Tabulates Data.* An excellent brief description of the various types of local areas for which U.S. Census data are available. Obtainable without charge from the Data Access and Use Laboratory, Social and Economic Statistics Administration, Bureau of the Census, U.S. Department of Commerce, Washington, D.C. 20233.

_____. *Metropolitan Area Statistics.* Washington, D.C.: U.S. Government Printing Office. A convenient reprint (costing only 35¢) of a section of the annual *Statistical Abstract* offering a survey of data for 155 metropolitan areas, including population change, employment, voting patterns, business patterns, and housing.

_____. *The 1970 Census—and You: A General Introduction to Census Data.* Washington, D.C.: U.S. Government Printing Office, 1971. A basic ten-page guide to census data and their practical applications, for the layman.

_____. *Sampling Lectures.* 2 vols. Washington, D.C.: U.S. Government Printing Office, 1968. A fine exposition of basic sampling theory; quite brief compared to the monumental, extremely detailed *Atlantida* study cited above. Worth studying if you intend to do your own sample surveys of political opinion.

_____. *Statistical Abstract of the United States.* Washington, D.C.: U.S. government Printing Office. All the important statistics in one annual volume, but not down to the level of small communities.

_____. *Supplemental Courses for Case Studies in Surveys and Censuses.* (Demography Lectures, ISP Supplemental Course Series, No. 25.) Washington, D.C.: U.S. Government Printing Office, 1969. Very useful if you're doing your own surveys.

_____. Social and Economic Statistics Administration. *County Business Patterns.* Washington, D.C.: U.S. Government Printing Office. These annual reports providing employment trends by industry and by county are excellent for use in economic issue development. They are appropriate for use by laymen as well as by the economists for whom they are designed.

*U.S. Executive Office of the President, Bureau of the Budget. *Household Survey Manual.* Washington, D.C.: U.S. Government Printing Office, 1969. The best single publication describing the methodology of professional surveys, very useful for the candidate doing his own opinion surveys.

U.S. Executive Office of the President, Office of Management and Budget. *Catalog of Federal Domestic Assistance Programs.* Washington, D.C.: U.S. Government Printing Office. An annual listing of the federal financial aid programs available to states, cities, and communities.

In addition to the foregoing, regional offices of the U.S. Bureau of Labor Statistics provide current analyses of trends in wages, unemployment, prices, and manpower.

VOTING PATTERNS

Bailey, Harry A., Jr., and Katz, Ellis (eds.). *Ethnic Group Politics.* Columbus, Ohio: Merrill, 1969. A general reader.

Burdick, Eugene, and Brodbeck, Arthur J. (eds.). *American Voting Behavior.* Glencoe, Ill.: Free Press, 1959. Excellent essays, especially Brodbeck's comparison of electioneering with the techniques of psychotherapy. Somewhat dry reading overall, but interesting for the serious student.

Campbell, Angus, et al. *The American Voter.* New York: Wiley, 1960. Probably the definitive statistical analysis.

DeVries, Walter, and Tarrance, Lance. *The Ticket Splitter: A New Force in American Politics.* Grand Rapids, Mich.: Eerdmans, 1971. A study of the independent voter in Michigan, which has increasing application throughout the United States.

Friedheim, Jerry. *Where Are the Voters?* Washington, D.C.: National Press, 1968. Interesting for breakdowns by client groups.

Fuchs, Laurence H. (ed.). *American Ethnic Politics.* New York: Harper & Row, 1968. Good essays by Daniel Patrick Moynihan on the Irish voter, James Q. Wilson on the Negro voter, and others.

Hawkins, Brett W., and Lorinskas, Robert A. (eds.). *The Ethnic Factor in American Politics.* Columbus, Ohio: Merrill, 1970. An academic presentation of ethnication as a critical factor in American political life.

Kent, Frank R. *The Great Game of Politics: An Effort to Present the Elementary Human Facts about Politics, Politicians, and Political Machines, Candidates and Their Ways, for the Benefit of the Average Citizen.* Garden City, N.Y.: Doubleday, 1923. The subtitle says it all. Still worth reading for background and for pleasure, even though it won't change any campaign decisions.

————. *Political Behavior: The Heretofore Unwritten laws, Customs, and Principles of Politics as Practiced in the United States.* New York: Morrow, 1928. Like its predecessor, one of the first books that tried to tell it straight. Out of date, but good for comparing how politicians viewed the voters then and how they do now. Charmingly written, with a high level of candor.

Key, V. O., Jr. *Politics, Parties and Pressure Groups.* 5th ed. New York: Crowell, 1964. A widely used text that contains useful information on the national campaigning process.

————. *Public Opinion and American Democracy.* New York: Knopf, 1961.

Lazarsfeld, Paul F.; Berelson, Bernard; and Gaudet, Hazel. *The People's Choice: How the Voter Makes up his Mind in a Presidential Campaign.* 3d ed. New York: Columbia University Press, 1968 (paperback). A standard work.

McPhee, William N., and Glaser, William A. (eds.). *Public Opinion and Congressional Elections.* Glencoe, Ill.: Free Press, 1962. Thirteen essays on voting behavior.

Murphy, Reg, and Gulliver, Hal. *The Southern Strategy.* New York: Scribner, 1971. An interesting analysis, by two journalists, of Southern voting strategy.

Novak, Michael. *The Rise of the Unmeltable Ethnics: Politics and Culture in the Seventies.* New York: Macmillan, 1972. A provocative description of American Greeks, Italians, Slavs, and other ethnic groups in American life.

Phillips, Kevin P. *The Emerging Republic Majority.* New Rochelle, N.Y.: Arlington, 1969 (also available as an Anchor paperback). How the Republicans can unite client groups to develop a continuing dominance in national politics. Widely quoted and allegedly used in the Nixon presidential reelection strategy.

Pool, Ithiel de Sola; Abelson, Robert; and Popkin, Samuel. *Candidates, Issues and Strategies: A Computer Simulation of the 1960 and 1964 Presidential Elections.* Cambridge, Mass.: M.I.T.Press, 1964. Academically oriented, but useful in providing a context for evaluating campaigns.

Scammon, Richard M. (ed.). *America at the Polls: A Handbook of American Presidential Election Statistics, 1920–1964,* Pittsburgh: University of Pittsburgh Press, 1965. Statistical analysis of presidential elections by the former director of the U.S. Bureau of the Census.

_____. *America Votes.* 8 vols. Originally published (1956) by Macmillan, New York; more recently by Congressional Quarterly, Washington, D.C. A handbook of contemporary election statistics.

Scammon, Richard M., and Wattenberg, Ben J. *The Real Majority: How the Silent Center of the American Electorate Chooses its President.* New York: Coward McCann, 1970. A widely read and discussed book, worth looking at even if you don't agree with the authors' thesis.

POLITICAL ADVERTISING

American Association of Advertising Agencies. *Political Campaign Advertising and Advertising Agencies.* Available on request from the association, 200 Park Avenue, New york, N.Y. 10017.

American Newspaper Publishers Association, Bureau of Advertising. *23 Winning Ideas for Political Advertisers.* Available from the association, 750 Third Avenue, New York, N.Y. 10017.

Broadcasting Yearbook, 1735 De Sales Street,N.W., Washington, D.C. 20036. A compendium listing bassic data and personnel of television and AM and FM radio stations throughout the nation as well as marketing information and other data for interest to political advertisers.

Direct Mail Advertising Association. *How to Win Your Election with Direct Mail.* Available from the association, 230 Park Avenue, New York, N.Y. 10017. Brief, simple information about the use of direct mail in politics; can help candidates by telling them where to find direct-mail agencies and how to pick the right one.

McCaffrey, Maurice. *Advertising Wins Elections.* Minneapolis: Dillon, 1962.

Seehafer, Gene F., and Laemmar, Jack W. *Successful Television and Radio Advertising.* New York: McGraw-Hill, 1959. A useful text despite its age, with helpful chapters on writing TV and radio commercials, testing programs and commercials, measuring sales effectiveness, time buying,spot TV and radio advertising, and a glossary, which may facilitate communication between candidates and media representatives.

Votes Unlimited. *Campaign Specialties*. Retail catalog available on request from Votes Unlimited, Ferndale, N.Y. 12734. A priced commercial shopping list for buttons, shopping bags, and other giveaway items.

Index